Alister E. McGrath and Evangelical Theology

A Dynamic Engagement

PATERNOSTER PRESS

Alister E. McGrath and Evangelical Theology

A Dynamic Engagement

Edited by
Sung Wook Chung

09 08 07 06 05 04 03   7 6 5 4 3 2 1

Paternoster Press is an imprint of Authentic Media,
P.O. Box 300, Carlisle, Cumbria, CA3 0QS, UK
www.paternoster-publishing.com

Baker Academic is an imprint of Baker Book House Company,
PO Box 6287, Grand Rapids, MI 49516-6287
www.bakeracademic.com

British Library Cataloguing in Publication Data
A catalogue record for this book is available from the British Library

ISBN 1-84227-202-0

Library of Congress Cataloguing-in-Publication Data
Alister E. McGrath and evangelical theology : a dynamic engagement / edited by Sung
Wook Chung
   p. cm
   Includes bibliographicalreferences and index.
   ISBN 0-8010-2639-3 (pbk.)
   1. Evangecalism. 2. Theology, Doctrinal. 3. McGrath, Alister E., 1953- I. Chung,
Sung Wook, 1966-

BR1640.A55 2003
230'.04624—dc21

2003052200

Cover Design by FourNineZero
Typeset by WestKey Ltd, Falmouth, Cornwall
Printed in Great Britain by Bell & Bain Ltd, Glasgow

Contents

Preface – Sung Wook Chung   vii
Contributors   ix
Foreword – James I. Packer   xiii

Part I: The Theology of Alister E. McGrath

1. Alister E. McGrath on the Cross of Jesus Christ   3
   Graham Tomlin
2. Alister E. McGrath and Justification   24
   Gerald L. Bray
3. The Scientific Theology Project of Alister E. McGrath   33
   John J. Roche
4. The Uneasy Evangelical: Alister E. McGrath on Postliberalism   90
   Dennis L. Okholm

Part II: Dynamics and Vitality of Evangelical Theology

5. Machen's Warrior Children   113
   John M. Frame
6. Evangelical Theology of Divine Openness   147
   Clark H. Pinnock
7. Toward a Trinitarian Evangelical Wesleyan Theology   165
   Elmer M. Colyer
8. Karl Barth's Evangelical Principles: Reformation Legacy
   in his Theology   195
   Sung Wook Chung
9. An Evangelical Narrative Christology for a Religiously
   Plural World   213
   Gabriel Fackre
10. *Semper Reformanda* in a Changing World: Calvin, Usury
    and Evangelical Moral Theology   235
    Andrew Goddard

11. Revelation and Natural Theology   264
     William J. Abraham
12. Postmodern Evangelical Theology: A Nonfoundationalist
     Approach to the Christian Faith   280
     John R. Franke
13. Postmodern Evangelical Apologetics?   310
     David K. Clark
14. Contributors: An Appreciation and Response   333
     Alister E. McGrath

Preface

Sung Wook Chung

Alister E. McGrath, Professor of Historical Theology at the University of Oxford and Principal of Wycliffe Hall, Oxford, has had a tremendous impact on the renaissance of evangelical theology over the last twenty years. He has written and edited over forty books and one hundred scholarly articles. Most of his books became best-sellers and his articles have attracted much scholarly interest and debate. Due to his prolific and creative scholarship, he is now regarded by many scholars, within and without the evangelical camp, as one of the most influential and significant theologians in world Christianity. His theological work has made a great contribution to the enhancement of the vitality and dynamics of evangelical theology.

In addition to his scholarly work, Alister E. McGrath has been energetically involved in consolidating Wycliffe Hall, Oxford as one of the foremost educational centres of evangelical theology in Europe and beyond. He has been working at Wycliffe Hall for more than twenty years as a teacher and administrator and has been its principal since 1995. His teaching and administrating ministry has made an indelible impact upon a new generation of evangelical church leaders both in the Anglican Church and in the church worldwide.

Alister E. McGrath is fifty years old in 2003. In celebration of his fiftieth birthday, this book aims to provide an opportunity for evangelical theologians from various backgrounds to demonstrate the appeal and attraction of evangelical theology through discussing its maturity, vitality and dynamics. The contributors will focus on the essence, character, identity, methodology, task, strengths, weaknesses and future of evangelical theology. Evangelical theology is no more a theological movement within a ghetto and in isolation. It is increasingly maturing through its dialogical engagement with other theological camps, including postliberal theology and religious pluralism. However, the maturing of evangelical theology could have a negative implication if it does not continue to stimulate a vital and dynamic discussion and ongoing revision and reformulation in accordance with the Word of God, witnessed to in Scripture.

I hope that this collection of groundbreaking essays will give an excellent opportunity for all evangelical theologians to think over our legacy, resources, task and responsibility for a more successful and productive future. I would like to express my gratitude to Dr Errol G. Rohr, my colleague at King College, for his encouragement. Special thanks go to my wife, In-Kyung, who helped me with the editing of this book.

Contributors

William J. Abraham is the Albert Cook Outler Professor of Wesley Studies at Perkins School of Theology, Southern Methodist University, Dallas, Texas, USA. A native of Northern Ireland, he has a DPhil in the philosophy of religion from the University of Oxford. He is the author of numerous books and professional articles. His most recent book is *Canon and Criterion: From the Fathers to Feminism* (Oxford: Clarendon Press, 1998). He is currently pursuing research on the renewal of the church and on the epistemology of divine revelation.

Gerald Bray is Anglican Professor of Divinity at Beeson Divinity School, Samford University, Birmingham, Alabama, USA. He received a doctorate in classical literature from the University of Paris (Sorbonne). He is the author and editor of many professional books and articles. Among his major publications are *The Doctrine of God* (Downers Grove, Illinois: InterVarsity Press, 1993), *Biblical Interpretation: Past & Present* (Downers Grove, Illinois: InterVarsity Press, 1996) and *The Personal God* (Carlisle: Paternoster, 1998).

Sung Wook Chung is Assistant Professor of Theology at the Peeke School of Christian Mission, King College, Bristol, Tennessee, USA. A native of South Korea, he received his MDiv from Harvard University and DPhil from the University of Oxford and is an ordained minister in the Presbyterian Church (USA). Chung is the author of *Admiration and Challenge: Karl Barth's Theological Relationship with John Calvin* (New York: Peter Lang, 2002) and many other professional articles. He also serves on the task force for the Doctrine of the Trinity in the Presbyterian Church (USA).

David K. Clark is Professor of Theology at Bethel Seminary in St Paul, Minnesota, USA. He previously taught at Toccoa Falls College, Toccoa, Georgia, USA. He earned his MA at Trinity Evangelical Divinity School and his PhD from Northwestern University. In addition to many articles, he has written or edited seven books. He is known for *Dialogical Apologetics: A Person-Centered Approach to Christian Defense* (Grand Rapids, Michigan: Baker, 1993), and has completed work on a major work on theological method, entitled *To Know and Love God: The Soul of Evangelical Theology* (Wheaton, Illinois: Crossway, forthcoming).

Elmer M. Colyer is Professor of Historical Theology and Stanley Professor of Wesley Studies at the University of Dubuque Theological Seminary, Iowa, USA. He received his PhD from Boston College, is an ordained minister in the United Methodist Church, and is President of Christian Theological Research Fellowship. Colyer is the author of *How to Read T.F. Torrance: Understanding His Trinitarian and Scientific Theology* (Downers Grove, Illinois: InterVarsity Press, 2001) and *The Nature of Doctrine in T.F. Torrance's Theology* (Eugene, Oregon: Wipf & Stock, 2001). He edited *The Promise of Trinitarian Theology: Theologians in Dialogue with T.F. Torrance* (Lanham, Maryland: Rowman & Littlefield, 2001) and *Evangelical Theology in Transition: Theologians in Dialogue with Donald Bloesch* (Downers Grove, Illinois: InterVarsity Press, 1999).

Gabriel Fackre is Abbot Professor of Christian Theology Emeritus at Andover Newton Theological School, Massachusetts, USA. He received his PhD from the University of Chicago and is an ordained minister in the United Church of Christ. He is past President of the American Theological Society and the author of numerous books and professional articles. Among his major publications are *The Doctrine of Revelation: A Narrative Interpretation* (Edinburgh/Grand Rapids, Michigan: Edinburgh University Press/Eerdmans, 1997), *The Christian Story* (Grand Rapids, Michigan: Eerdmans, vol. 1, 1996³; vol. 2, 1987) and *Restoring the Center: Essays Evangelical & Ecumenical* (Downers Grove, Illinois: InterVarsity Press, 1998).

John M. Frame is Professor of Systematic Theology and Philosophy at Reformed Theological Seminary, Orlando, Florida, USA. He received his BA in philosophy from Princeton University, his BD from Westminster Theological Seminary, and his MPhil in religious studies from Yale University. He served for twelve years on the faculty of Westminster Seminary in Philadelphia, and for twenty years at Westminster in California. He has published ten books and numerous articles in the areas of epistemology, apologetics, ethics, systematic theology and worship, most recently *No Other God: A Response to Open Theism* (Phillipsburg, New Jersey:

Presbyterian & Refomed, 2001) and *Doctrine of God* (Phillipsburg, New Jersey: Presbyterian & Reformed, 2002).

John R. Franke is Associate Professor of Theology at Biblical Theological Seminary, Hatfield, Pennsylvania, USA. He received his DPhil from the University of Oxford. In addition to a number of articles and reviews, he is the co-author (with Stanley J. Grenz) of *Beyond Foundationalism: Shaping Theology in a Postmodern Context* (Louisville, Kentucky: Westminster John Knox, 2001) and the editor of *Joshua – 2 Samuel* in the Ancient Christian Commentary on Scripture series (Downers Grove, Illinois: InterVarsity Press, forthcoming). He is also a fellow of Emergent and currently serves as the Chair of the Evangelical Theology and Postmodernity study group of the Evangelical Theological Society.

Andrew Goddard is Tutor in Ethics at Wycliffe Hall, Oxford, UK and a tutor for the Certificate in Politics and Theology at Sarum College. He studied Philosophy, Politics and Economics at the University of Oxford before completing a theology doctorate on the life and work of Jacques Ellul, now published as *Living the Word, Resisting the World* (Carlisle: Paternoster, 2002). He has written Grove booklets on the European Union, homosexuality and the just war and published articles in ethics and New Testament journals. He is also the author, with Bishop James Jones, of *The Moral Leader: For the Church and the World* (Leicester: InterVarsity Press, 2002).

Dennis L. Okholm is Professor of Theology at Wheaton College, Wheaton, Illinois, USA. He received his PhD in Systematic Theology from Princeton Theological Seminary. He previously taught at Western Kentucky University and Jamestown College in North Dakota. He is ordained in the Presbyterian Church (USA). Among his several books and many articles, his most recent publications include, with Timothy R. Phillips, *A Family of Faith: An Introduction to Evangelical Christianity* (Grand Rapids, Michigan: Baker, 2001) and, co-edited with Timothy R. Phillips, *The Nature of Confession: Evangelicals and Postliberals in Conversation* (Downers Grove, Illinois: InterVarsity Press, 1996).

Clark H. Pinnock is Professor of Theology at McMaster Divinity College, Hamilton, Ontario, Canada. He received his PhD in New Testament studies, under F.F. Bruce, from the University of Manchester. His major publications include *A Wideness in God's Mercy: The Finality of Jesus Christ in a World of Religions* (Grand Rapids, Michigan: Zondervan, 1992), *Flame of Love: A Theology of the Holy Spirit*

(Downers Grove, Illinois: InterVarsity Press, 1996) and *Most Moved Mover: A Theology of God's Openness* (Grand Rapids, Michigan/ Carlisle: Baker/Paternoster, 2001).

John Roche teaches courses in the history of physics at Linacre College, Oxford, and courses in applied mathematics at Oxford Brookes University. For the past five years he has been Co-director, with Alister McGrath, of the John Templeton Oxford Seminars on Science and Christianity. His chief research interest lies in using history and forensic analysis in an attempt to clarify some of the more difficult concepts in classical physics. He is the author of *The Mathematics of Measurement: A Critical History* (London: Athlone Press and Springer, 1998) and of several professional articles.

Graham Tomlin is Vice Principal and Tutor in Historical Theology and Evangelism at Wycliffe Hall, Oxford, UK. He studied English literature and theology at Oxford University, and completed his PhD in theology through Exeter University. He is a member of the Theology Faculty of Oxford University, where he teaches on the Reformation in general and Martin Luther in particular. He is the author of *The Power of the Cross: Theology and the Death of Christ in Paul, Luther and Pascal* (Carlisle: Paternoster, 1999), with Peter Walker, *Walking in His Steps: A Guide to Exploring the Land of the Bible* (London: HarperCollins, 2001), *The Provocative Church* (London: SPCK, 2002) and *Luther and his World* (Oxford: Lion, 2002).

Foreword

James I. Packer

It is a privilege and a pleasure to commend this set of weighty and wise essays that is being published to mark Professor Alister McGrath's fiftieth birthday.

Contemplating the material from the perspective of a fairly long life in the same trade as his, a life that he himself chronicled as far as 1996,[1] I find three lines of thought breaking surface in my mind, as follows.

First, how different today is the academic study of theology from what it was when I began.

It is more than fifty years since, as a convert of five years' standing and a graduate in Greats (classics and philosophy), I enrolled for an Oxford theology degree. At that time, theology was in the doldrums. Liberal revisionism was stifling it. The halfway rationalisms of 'critical orthodoxy', 'biblical theology', 'liberal evangelicalism' and, among Anglicans, 'liberal catholicism' were riding high. None of the great themes of Christian faith was being explored in depth, nor were the problems of theological method being faced. Noises made by Karl Barth in Basel and Thomas Torrance in Edinburgh were not understood in England, nor even heard in Oxford. The only Continental theologian who was at all widely read was Emil Brunner, and the only American was Reinhold Niebuhr. Liberal crypto-unitarianism went unnoticed, the architectonic significance of the Trinity for theological construction was unsuspected, Chalcedon was thought barren, and the Holy Spirit was called, justly, the displaced person of the Trinity and the Cinderella of theology. Systematic theology was under a cloud and said to have no future; ecumenical melding of ecclesiastical traditions on a lowest-common-denominator basis was the order of the day. How good it is that all this has changed.

Secondly, how different today is the state and status of evangelical theology from what it was when I started.

---

[1] Alister E. McGrath, *To Know and Serve God* (London: Hodder & Stoughton, 1997); US edition *J.I. Packer: A Biography* (Grand Rapids: Baker, 1997).

When I was a student, evangelicals meant by theology an inherited belief system, usually Calvinist or Arminian in origin, passed down from the Bible-believing days when it was formed and now needing to be protected against erosion. Academic study of theology, as of philosophy, was frowned on, as likely to have an eroding effect. Scriptural exposition, resourced by nineteenth-century commentaries and the notes of the Scofield Bible, was seen as all that anyone needs. Apart from the far-off faculties of Westminster and Calvin seminaries, evangelicalism as I knew it had no living theology or theologians, certainly not in Oxford. No wonder then that we were thought crude, obscurantist, and marginal to the church's life. To my knowledge, I was the only evangelical taking the Oxford theology degree at that time, and a tutor told me I was the first evangelical with a positive attitude to philosophy and theology that he had ever met. How good it is that all this, too, has changed.

Thirdly, how remarkable has been Dr McGrath's achievement in evangelical theology during the past twenty years.

The person from whom I first heard his name said he was 'very big potatoes'. So he is. In what evangelicals once saw as shark-infested waters he swims happily, and his track record is spectacular. Moving into systematic theology via historical theology, and writing books and articles the way the rest of us write lectures (two books and four journal articles on average annually), he has given us soundings in Reformation life and thought and a full-scale history, the first in English, of the doctrine of justification; several widely used textbooks; intellectual biographies of Thomas Torrance and myself; several books arguing that reinvigorated evangelicalism is the true path for tomorrow's church; two-thirds of a three-volume exploration of the science and theology interface – and, as advertising flyers put it, much, much more. Evangelicalism was already establishing itself afresh in the mainstream of Christian thought before he had arrived, but he has imparted vast impetus to that process. His energy seems endless, and the thought of what he may do if God gives him twenty more years is a concept to conjure with.

So God be with you, Alister, as on you go. In a somewhat different sense from that of the old-time gladiators, I and many more of my generation say: *nos morituri te salutamus*. May your range and your acumen not diminish, your clarity not be clouded, and your vision of evangelicalism as the true wisdom, the true catholicity, and indeed the true Christianity never blur. Hold high the torch that has been passed to you – and keep the books coming. We need them.

J.I. Packer

Part I

The Theology of Alister E. McGrath

1

Alister E. McGrath on the Cross of Jesus Christ

Graham Tomlin

As a theology student in Oxford in the late 1980s, I was not known as an avid attendee of lectures. I reasoned, with some bitter experience to back me up, that great scholars are not always great teachers. So, given the option of listening to a rather dry presentation of someone's notes from years ago, or spending an hour in the library curled up with a stimulating book that I could read at my own pace, I would normally choose the latter. However, there was one lecturer who bucked this trend. I recall turning up for a lecture series by a new young tutor at Wycliffe Hall on 'The Theology of the Reformation: Luther' one Thursday morning in the college's neo-medieval lecture room and instantly realizing that here was something different. The sense that, despite his comparative youth, we were in the hands of a master was conveyed by the confident tone of the lecture handout:

> There are very few good books in the English language on Luther, and the enormous progress in Luther studies since 1970 has meant that much earlier literature is now seriously outdated. Any student who has German and would like guidance as to what to read should consult the lecturer. The lectures will deal with some of the more important translation mistakes in the American edition, in case you miss them.

Unusually, I stayed fascinated, turning up each week until the end of the lecture series eight weeks later. The lecturer was, of course, Alister McGrath, who has since become a much-valued colleague and friend. It was the last lecture in particular that caught my attention and those of many of my fellow students, on an idea few of us had encountered before: Luther's theology of the cross. Unknown to us, this lecture touched on a topic that explains much of McGrath's own theological development up to that point and subsequently.

From very early in his theological work, Alister McGrath was concerned to grapple with the centrality of the cross to Christian faith. Having completed his undergraduate and research degrees in the natural sciences, he began serious study of theology with, first, an undergraduate degree at Oxford, followed by further study on the patristic and medieval understanding of the doctrine of justification. This work, which eventually grew into his (originally) two-volume work on the history of justification,[1] spawned an interest in Martin Luther's early theological ideas. This led on in turn to a fascination with Luther's theology of the cross, the topic of the final lecture in the course, and the role it played within the Reformer's early theological development. In fact, McGrath's first major published work was not his history of justification (which finally appeared in 1986), but his book on Luther, entitled *Luther's Theology of the Cross*,[2] which appeared a year earlier, just before McGrath left a curacy in Nottingham to take up a position teaching doctrine at Wycliffe Hall, Oxford.

From this initial starting point, a number of other works emerged that developed and explored the contours of the meaning of the cross of Christ, including the more popular but still fairly weighty *The Enigma of the Cross*,[3] several articles on the subject, and the more popular still *Making Sense of the Cross*.[4]

In subsequent years, McGrath's theological interests moved away from their origins in late medieval and Reformation thought, and moved into areas dealt with elsewhere in this volume, such as the identity and history of evangelicalism, Christian apologetics, spirituality and, more recently, the interface between science and theology. However, as this chapter will hope to demonstrate, this early work on the centrality of the cross of Christ remains a key component of McGrath's own theological vision, and still shapes his thought, even though the more immediate focus of concentration has passed elsewhere.

---

[1] Alister E. McGrath, *Iustitia Dei: A History of the Christian Doctrine of Justification* (Cambridge: Cambridge University Press, 1998[2]).

[2] Alister E. McGrath, *Luther's Theology of the Cross: Martin Luther's Theological Breakthrough* (Oxford: Basil Blackwell, 1985).

[3] Alister E. McGrath, *The Enigma of the Cross* (London: Hodder & Stoughton, 1987).

[4] Alister E. McGrath, *Making Sense of the Cross* (Leicester: InterVarsity Press, 1992).

1. McGrath on Luther

McGrath's work on Luther's *theologia crucis* was soon deservedly acclaimed as a major contribution to Luther scholarship. It took the form of a detailed study of the late medieval intellectual and theological background from which Luther's theology emerged[5] and of some key texts from Luther's work over the period 1514–19. It introduced many new English-speaking readers to an ongoing discussion, much of which had been conducted in German up to that point, and helped place Luther's theology of the cross on to the centre stage in discussion of the emergence of his Reformation theology. Luther's thought in this vital area had remained largely unnoticed before the publication of the great Weimar edition of his works, beginning in 1883, and in particular before some key documents of Luther's early career had been rediscovered around the same time. After the Second World War, fed by the rediscovery of this theme in Luther's thought and the experience (especially among those on the losing side) of devastation left behind by this European catastrophe, the theology of the cross began to emerge as a seminal theme in theological attempts to make sense of the horrors of Auschwitz and the rise of what became known as 'protest atheism'. In the 1970s, Jürgen Moltmann's *The Crucified God*[6] explored the theme in creative depth, and Eberhard Jüngel's *Gott als Geheimnis der Welt* (1977) was soon translated into English in 1983.[7] While these were more general theological works on the theme of the theology of the cross and its implications for contemporary theology, McGrath's book on Luther was the first since Walther von Loewenich's 1976 study[8] to focus specifically on Luther's contribution.[9]

---

[5] A task widened and continued in Alister E. McGrath, *The Intellectual Origins of the European Reformation* (Blackwell: Oxford, 1987).

[6] Jürgen Moltmann, *The Crucified God*, R.A. Wilson and J. Bowden (trs) (London: SCM, 1974).

[7] Eberhard Jüngel, *God as the Mystery of the World: On the Foundations of the Theology of the Crucified One in the Dispute between Theism and Atheism* (Edinburgh: T. & T. Clark, 1983).

[8] W. von Loewenich, *Luther's Theology of the Cross* (Belfast: Christian Journals, 1976).

[9] Although McGrath's and von Loewenich's books have the same title, they are quite different in focus. Von Loewenich offers an exposition of Luther's *theologia crucis* by looking at a wide range of his writings, arguing for its place as a central theme in Luther's entire theological life, rather than just in his early stage. McGrath's book focuses upon the years 1513–21 and seeks to relate the *theologia crucis* to Luther's Reformation breakthrough.

McGrath insisted, along with Reformation scholars such as Heiko Oberman, that the right way to read Luther was not by looking for traces of the later, mature Reformer in his early works, but instead to read him in the light of the various currents of late medieval theology present in northern European universities such as Erfurt and Wittenberg at the start of the sixteenth century. As such, this work helped in the general reorientation of the study of Reformation theology, towards locating it firmly in its late medieval background rather than in some teleologically inevitable march towards a fully orbed Reformation world of thought.

Despite its title, the bulk of McGrath's book is taken up by a close analysis of Luther's early theological development, especially in the Psalms lectures of 1513–15, with a particular eye to the emergence of a Reformation theology. Only the last chapter turns in detail to the meaning and content of the theology of the cross proper. McGrath's textual analysis displays his characteristic grasp of an impressively wide range of late medieval theological literature. If it can be criticized at any point, it might be that the book misses the significance of the widespread fascination with the cross of Christ as the focus for devotion in late medieval piety. Luther clearly develops his theology of the cross out of this cross-centred spirituality. This perspective qualifies the extent to which Luther broke from late medieval Catholicism. To see Luther's breakthrough in solely theological terms, as McGrath's book tends to, is to stress the ways in which he broke from the standard paths of late medieval theology. However, when we consider the important themes he picked up from late medieval piety, not to mention the vital role played by the cross-centred spiritual theology of medieval spiritual theologians such as Bernard of Clairvaux, Luther's breakthrough can be seen as continuous, in some important respects, with aspects of late medieval Christianity – Luther was more of a Catholic than he is often given credit for.[10] However, this historical point does not detract from the significance of McGrath's work, not just for Reformation scholarship, but also for his own theological development.

In a semi-autobiographical chapter published in 1993 entitled 'Why Doctrine? The Confession of a Disillusioned Liberal'[11] McGrath writes

---

[10] I have argued this point in greater length in Graham Tomlin, *The Power of the Cross: Theology and the Death of Christ in Paul, Luther and Pascal* (Carlisle: Paternoster, 1999), pp. 111–13, 144–7.

[11] Gordon Kuhrt (ed.), *Doctrine Matters* (London: Hodder & Stoughton, 1993), pp. 1–18.

about the period in which the research for his book was conducted. After initial conversion in evangelical circles, he describes his theological position in the late 1970s:

> I realized that I had become a liberal – someone who looked to human reason and secular culture, instead of scripture, for religious guidance and inspiration ... I kept thinking throughout my period at Cambridge, and on into my first curacy at a suburban parish in Nottingham. And I found myself plagued by doubts. It seemed increasingly to me that liberal Anglicanism often amounted to little more than a conglomerate of transient theological responses to events in the academic world. It seemed as if there was no theological or spiritual core. As I struggled with the issues thrown up by preaching and pastoral work, I found myself continually wondering whether liberalism actually had anything to say to the world, other than uncritically endorsing its latest trends.[12]

McGrath's work on Luther coincided with his theological migration from a generally liberal catholic style to a more clearly delineated adherence to evangelicalism, and it seems that many of the themes that emerge in his study of Luther's theology of the cross can be seen as largely responsible for this shift.

McGrath points out the way in which Luther's emerging *theologia crucis* took the form of a strong critique of the role of Aristotle in late medieval scholasticism. Aristotelian ethics had smuggled into scholastic theology the notion that God rewarded people according to their deserts, thus leading to the very theology of human merit that Luther's doctrine of justification by faith did so much to undermine. This was a crucial aspect of Luther's rejection of the validity of human reason (closely allied in Luther's own mind with Aristotelian philosophy) as a guide to a true knowledge of God. Reason could not make sense of God's unmerited, freely given grace, insisting instead on strict justice by which sinners could only inevitably (in Luther's view) be condemned. Grace is not what we would expect, and because it is not what we would expect, those very expectations come in for radical questioning. Thus reason betrayed itself as an unreliable guide. Instead, it is only the self-revelation or Word of God that can be trusted as a sure guide to knowledge of God and his will. The critique of Aristotle developed in Luther's own mind into a determination not to seek the sources of theology anywhere else than in the Scriptures.

---

[12] Ibid., p. 3.

These insights, demonstrated in McGrath's work of the time,[13] have their parallels with his own theological movement. His move from adherence to theological liberalism, which he increasingly saw as lacking a 'theological and spiritual core', can be seen as a response to Luther's own growing insistence on the essential independence of Christian theology as a discourse that must be understood on its own terms, not those borrowed from elsewhere, whether from medieval versions of Aristotelian philosophy or twentieth-century liberal humanism. The significance of this move, and more particularly the role played by this theology of the cross is reflected in some comments in the preface of McGrath's book on Luther:

> *Crux probat omnia.* For Luther, Christian thinking about God comes to an abrupt halt at the foot of the cross. The Christian is forced, by the very existence of the crucified Christ, to make a momentous decision. Either he will seek God elsewhere, or he will make the cross itself the foundation and criterion of his thought about God. The 'crucified God' – to use Luther's daring phrase – is not merely the foundation of the Christian faith, but is also the key to a proper understanding of the nature of God. The Christian can only speak about the glory, the wisdom, the righteousness and the strength of God as they are revealed in the crucified Christ.[14]

This 'momentous decision' is one that McGrath himself faced over this period. His work on Luther had, it seems, entailed a decisive shift in his own theological horizons. The cross, understood as a revelation of God, confounds all human expectation. It is the last place we would expect to find a revelation of God. We would normally choose to look at a fine sunset, the highest achievements of rational human thought or the insights of mystics straining to glimpse the divine nature for wisdom on the big 'question of God'. Instead, we are directed to a man, hanging limp and in agony upon a Roman place of torture, as the central point of God's self-revelation. Only by allowing our attention to be turned towards the place where God has indicated that he can be found – the crucified Christ – can true knowledge of God begin. And in that very move, human attempts to understand God on our own terms are shown

---

[13] Bernhard Lohse, *Martin Luther's Theology: Its Historical and Systematic Development* (Minneapolis: Fortress Press, 1999); McGrath, *Luther's Theology of the Cross*; Alister E. McGrath, ' "Mira et nova diffinitio iustitiae": Luther and Scholastic Doctrines of Justification', *Archiv für Reformationsgeschichte* 74 (1983).

[14] McGrath, *Luther's Theology of the Cross*, p. 1.

up as futile and mistaken. If this is the last place we would look for God, a scene that to all human wisdom looks like the very opposite – the place where God seems most absent – then so much the worse for human wisdom. It is his encounter with this dramatic and radical Lutheran theology that explains much of McGrath's turn away from a vague theological liberalism towards a convinced form of evangelicalism. At this point, the implications of this move are not so conspicuously explained, yet they become clearer in a further work that explored the contemporary significance of the theology of the cross, *The Enigma of the Cross*, published two years later in 1987.

2. The Centrality of the Cross

In this work, McGrath extends his reflections on the significance of the theology of the cross to an extensive critique of the Enlightenment and the liberal theology to which it gave birth. Only a theology that starts at the cross can be dignified with the name of truly *Christian* theology. The book resounds with the sense that theologians are not at liberty to choose where they will look for God. They are, rather, *told* where to look for him. Supposedly 'disinterested' academic scholarship is unmasked as often resting on unconscious and unexamined philosophical assumptions, by no means as neutral as they are supposed to be. Every system of thought needs its own starting point, its own distinctive basis, and the only valid foundation for Christian theology must be God's self-revelation, focused in the cross of Christ. Liberal Protestantism is attacked for its inversion of values: 'whereas the early church had suggested that the cross ought to be the basis by which culture was judged, Liberal Protestantism effectively inverted this order'.[15] Liberalism allowed 'external criteria' to stand in judgement upon Christian theology, which, in the light of his study of Luther, McGrath had by now come to see as determined by its own internal norms, focused in the cross of Christ.

His early work on the theology of the cross is therefore central to McGrath's theological move towards evangelicalism, both in providing a growing distrust of the whole liberal approach, and also in leading towards a distinctive view of Scripture. Luther's, and increasingly McGrath's, theology entailed a robust rejection of any kind of 'natural theology'. Liberalism was compromised by its tendency to smuggle in

---

[15] McGrath, *The Enigma of the Cross*, p. 67.

passing cultural fads from outside the Christian faith to act as unquestioned criteria by which the essentials of Christian doctrine can be either accepted or rejected. The rejection of any kind of external criterion by which Christian theology must be judged led to a consideration of the internal criteria and sources for authentically Christian theology, and McGrath did not have to look too far. Just as Luther had turned to the Word of God in the Scriptures as both norm and source of Christian theology, McGrath also increasingly moved towards a view of Scripture as the place where this cross-shaped theological centre was found, and thus towards a view of Scripture as the authoritative bedrock of Christian theology.

This theological move went on to influence the distinctive shape of McGrath's evangelicalism. In a 1996 work, *A Passion for Truth: The Intellectual Coherence of Evangelicalism*,[16] he describes and evaluates the nature and impact of evangelical theology. The shape of the book betrays the particular way in which he conceives of evangelical theology. Before three lengthy chapters given over to evangelicalism's response to different contemporary theological and cultural trends (postliberalism, postmodernism and religious pluralism) are two chapters that focus on the twin themes that mark out for McGrath the contours of evangelical distinctiveness. They concern the 'uniqueness of Christ' and the 'authority of Scripture'. These are the twin pillars upon which McGrath's evangelicalism is built. It is not that these are the only important factors in evangelical thought; rather they stand out as the two distinctive features that give evangelicalism its identity and mission.

The centrality of Christ and the 'particularity of his cross and resurrection'[17] in evangelical theology stands as the mark of the true church, true to itself and refusing to be determined by external pressures and norms. Christ himself becomes the internal determinative criterion for truly Christian theology, which in turn is responsible finally to him. Christ is presented for us in Scripture, and therefore there is a vital and intimate theological relationship between Christ and Scripture, so that 'an appeal to Christ is simultaneously an appeal to Scripture, just as an appeal to Scripture is an appeal to Christ'.[18] Because a primary loyalty to Christ and Scripture offer an alternative to meek adherence to every passing social and academic fashion, the authority of Scripture becomes for McGrath a truly energizing doctrine:

---

[16] Alister E. McGrath, *A Passion for Truth: The Intellectual Coherence of Evangelicalism* (Leicester: Apollos, 1996).

[17] Ibid., p. 50.

[18] Ibid., p. 51.

Acknowledging the authority of Scripture is thus something profoundly liberating. It frees us from the slavish demand that we follow each and every cultural trend, and offers us a framework whereby we may *judge* them, as the Confessing Church chose to judge Hitler, rather than follow him – despite the enormous cultural pressure placed upon them to conform to the prevailing cultural climate. Reclaiming the Bible allows us to imitate Christ, rather than the latest whim of a fragmented and confused culture.[19]

This language, reminiscent of Luther's language of discovery and liberation, reflects the link between McGrath's early research into the theology of the cross and his theological development. If the cross stands at the centre of Christian theology, questioning any attempt to begin anywhere else in seeking God, then attention is directed to a commitment to the uniqueness of Christ and the authority of Scripture (the place where the meaning and significance of that cross is authoritatively described) as the places to start. And with these commitments in place, only evangelicalism seemed to offer a clear vantage point from which culture could be critiqued, rather than uncritically absorbed into Christian theology.

As we have noticed above, in subsequent years McGrath's work moved on to other areas of interest. However, this early work on the centrality of the cross for Christian life and theology continued to exert a significant influence on his theological development. That development can be traced by following his thought on the cross of Christ into two subsequent areas of thought: apologetics and pastoral theology.

3. The Cross and Apologetics

In *The Enigma of the Cross* McGrath considers the relevance of the cross in a secular age that finds it difficult to make sense of language about God. Those who find themselves unable to imagine God, or to conceive of him, are invited to consider the cross and resurrection of Jesus Christ. They are invited to stop guessing or imagining, and instead consider the question of the relationship between the scene of the cross

---

[19] Ibid., p. 62. Lamin Sanneh makes a similar point from the missionary context when he writes that nineteenth-century missionaries, by translating the Bible into the ethnic languages of the people they came to evangelize, 'gave local people a standard by which to question claims of Western cultural superiority'. Lamin Sanneh, *Encountering the West* (London: Marshall Pickering, 1993), p. 17.

and the empty tomb: ' "God" is whoever or whatever turned Good Friday into Easter Day.'[20] This insight, as McGrath points out, turns the mind away from metaphysical speculation, and instead roots Christian theology in a very earthy, earthly, historical event. The cross thus serves as the distinctive connection between Christianity and a sceptical world.

Taking these thoughts further, McGrath sees in the *theologia crucis* a mandate for the proclamation of the cross as the church's most characteristic and perennial task. True, the church is called to social comment and criticism. However, the proclamation of the basis from which that criticism is made must take logical and theological priority. By implication, these ideas lead in the direction of an emphasis on evangelism and apologetics, or in other words the command to address any given culture with the word of the gospel. The primary calling of the church is not to bolster a failing world with acts of kindness, nor to stand apart from culture in an attitude of aloof distance, but to address that culture with the distinctive message of cross and resurrection.

These concerns are characteristic of McGrath's later work. In subsequent years, he turned extensively to the study of apologetics, with a number of works exploring Christian approaches to the task.[21] In this subsequent work, McGrath turns, perhaps surprisingly given the emphases noted above, to the doctrines of creation and redemption as 'starting points' in the task of building bridges to a sceptical world.[22] Despite his insistence on the independence of Christian theology from any external criterion or foundation, McGrath does not choose a more Barthian path that would reject the value of apologetics altogether. Nor does he adopt the neo-Reformed presuppositionalist apologetics of such as Cornelius Van Til.[23] Nor, of course, does he seek to construct a natural theology that can lead to a true, if only partial, knowledge of God. By using the language of 'points of contact', he locates a position between these two. And by identifying the starting point of apologetics as the doctrines of creation *and* redemption, he retains a continuity (yet a developed continuity) with his earlier radical cross-centred theology.

In the created order we can discern glimpses of God, a 'latent memory' (Augustine) of intimacy with our Creator. However, much as this might

---

[20] McGrath, *The Enigma of the Cross*, p. 115.

[21] Alister E. McGrath, *Bridge-Building: Effective Christian Apologetics* (Leicester: Inter-Varsity Press, 1992); Alister E. McGrath, *Explaining Your Faith* (Leicester: Inter-Varsity Press, 1988).

[22] McGrath, *Bridge-Building*, pp. 15–25.

[23] For example, as expounded in Cornelius Van Til, *The Defense of the Faith* (Nutley, New Jersey: Presbyterian & Reformed, 1955).

act as a provocation to ask questions and to search for God, these hunches do not serve as the basis for a true knowledge of God. Instead, the focus on redemption as well as creation (and hence on the fallen-ness of that creation) emphasizes the way in which such perceptions of God need to be 'taken up and transfigured by the Christian revelation'[24] before God can truly be known. At this point, McGrath's debt is to Calvin rather than to Luther, as he develops this idea explicitly from Calvin's reflections on the knowledge of God in the early sections of the *Institutes*.[25] Barth's radical rejection of any value in a 'natural knowledge of God' is noted, but rejected as 'rhetorical exaggeration'. Here we see a development in McGrath's thought. His earlier more sweeping state-ments on the impossibility of starting anywhere else than the crucified Christ are modified into a position where a 'natural knowledge of God' can provide a provisional 'point of contact' for those outside Christian faith, if not a theological foundation. It is, however, a tactical rather than a fundamental theological shift. In the change of focus of his historical work from Luther to Calvin, McGrath found a way of connecting to a sceptical world without falling into the trap of foundationalism – the adoption of external criteria that serve as foundations for thought and theology from which Christianity may be judged and evaluated – the trap into which he felt liberalism had unwittingly stumbled.

4. The Cross and Pastoral Theology

The Enigma of the Cross not only outlined the challenge of a *theologia crucis* to liberal theology, it also explored some further implications for Christian pastoral theology. The cross serves as a sign of the necessity, yet also the unreliability of experience as a guide to theological truth. Again, in line with Luther's dictum 'it is living, or rather dying and being damned that makes a theologian, not understanding, reading or speculating',[26] McGrath also shares a deep sense that experience is the true test of theology: 'Perhaps the most difficult and most important test which any ideology (whether religious or secular) can face is how it copes with the negative side of life – with despair, with hopelessness, with the growing awareness of the process of dying and the event of

---

[24] McGrath, *Bridge-Building*, p. 23.

[25] Ibid., pp. 31–6. This borrowing from Calvin reflects the work McGrath had done on Calvin in preparation for his *A Life of John Calvin* (Oxford: Blackwell, 1990), published two years before *Bridge-Building*.

[26] From Luther's *Operationes in Psalmos* of 1519–21: AWA 2.296:8–11.

death.'[27] The point, however, is paradoxical. The experience of anguish or despair is the true test that distinguishes weak, unstable theology from that which is durable and deep-rooted. In this sense, experience is vital to theology. On the other hand, the same point shows up the 'sheer unreliability of experience as a guide to the presence and activity of God'.[28] Human experience would tell us that God was absent on Calvary. The resurrection showed that perception to be entirely false. McGrath carries through this same insight into a more general and powerful pastoral observation – that in those experiences where God appears to be most absent, whether grief, hopelessness or doubt, faith may still cling on to the hidden presence of God in these things, in the same way that he was present in hidden form on the cross.

In a number of more popular theological/pastoral works in the following years, McGrath continued to engage with questions of doubt and suffering from a similar perspective.[29] In particular, a book jointly written with his wife, Joanna, in 1992 explored the significance of the theology of the cross for the notion of self-esteem.[30] Here, the focus shifts from the cross as the basis of Christian theology (the *theologia crucis*) to the cross as the basis of true self-worth. In particular, the cross is now seen in its soteriological, as opposed to its theological, sense.

The cross offers a verdict on human life that is at the same time honest and liberating. Unlike some modern psychoanalytical theories, the cross takes the reality of human sin seriously, showing in Anselmian terms the vast cost to God of dealing with human sin. On the other hand, it offers a new standing before God, a restored relationship not on the basis of pretending or achieving any personal or psychological wholeness, but instead on Christ's work on the cross.[31] It offers a way between the Scylla of self-loathing and the Charybdis of arrogant pride. The cross tells us that we are sinners who are embroiled in compromise, lust, selfishness and envy, yet it also tells us that we are none the less acceptable before God 'on account of Christ, through faith'.[32] We are, in Luther's memorable phrase, 'at the same time righteous and sinful'.

---

[27] McGrath, *The Enigma of the Cross*, p. 159.

[28] Ibid.

[29] Alister E. McGrath, *Doubt: Handling it Honestly* (Leicester: InterVarsity Press, 1990); Alister E. McGrath, *A Journey through Suffering* (London: Hodder & Stoughton, 1996[2]); Alister E. McGrath, *Suffering* (London: Hodder & Stoughton, 1992).

[30] Joanna McGrath and Alister E. McGrath, *The Dilemma of Self-Esteem: The Cross and Christian Confidence* (Wheaton/Cambridge: Crossway, 1992).

[31] Ibid., pp. 85–101.

[32] Ibid., p. 97.

5. The Cross and Atonement

There is in all this, however, an unspoken question about the centrality of the cross for McGrath's theology, and, in turn, the identity and shape of evangelicalism. In this analysis of self-esteem, McGrath explores the pastoral implications of the cross as the means of reconciliation with God. Up to this point, unusually for an evangelical theologian, his writings on the cross have usually taken the form of reflection upon its significance for theology in general, rather than for the doctrine of the atonement. Understanding the route McGrath took into evangelicalism, as we have tried to do above, explains something of why the atonement does not take as large a place as we might expect in his writings. Again, *The Enigma of the Cross* gives us a reason why this might be the case. Towards the end of the book, McGrath protests against the tendency to relegate attention to the cross of Christ merely to sections of systematic theology dealing with the atonement.[33] Instead, the cross must be seen as normative for *all* Christian life and theology. In order to stress this point, this book, and indeed the earlier book on Luther, largely avoids discussion of the significance of the cross for atonement.

However, McGrath's subsequent reflections on this theme do display a characteristic approach, which defends the centrality of an objective, sin-bearing atonement to Christian theology, while not being too prescriptive about its precise meaning. On the one hand, his writings explain a strong belief in the inadequacy of exemplarist theories of the atonement. Taking the nineteenth-century theologian Hastings Rashdall as a conversation partner, a 1985 article mounts a vigorous critique of the supposedly Abelardian 'moral theory of the atonement', whereby Christ's death, as a demonstration of God's love, moves the sinner to a response that tries to imitate Christ's compassion – thus ruling out any objective transaction or change in the sinner's relationship to God.[34] Not only did Abelard fail to teach such a theory, Immanuel Kant is called as a witness to the necessity of divine grace and pardon. The *theologia crucis*, with its emphasis on the depth of human sin, is cited, along with the experience of two world wars, as one of the factors prompting a shift in twentieth-century theological thinking away from such naïve moralism towards a sense that human evil goes much deeper, and therefore needs a much more radical solution than mere example.[35] The 'moral theory' is

---

[33] McGrath, *The Enigma of the Cross*, p. 187.

[34] Alister E. McGrath, 'The Moral Theory of the Atonement: An Historical and Theological Critique', *Scottish Journal of Theology* 38 (1985).

[35] Ibid., p. 218.

little more than disguised salvation by merit, takes an unrealistic view of human capacity to overcome evil, and fails to deal with the sense of *bondage* to powers greater than ourselves, which is an integral part of the human experience.

On the other hand, despite his strong defence of an objective understanding of the atonement, McGrath refuses to be tied down to one particular theory of it. Conscious of the inability of human language to capture God and the resistance of the cross to interpretation, his understanding of atonement typically takes the form of outlining a number of pictures that help make sense of the way in which the cross transforms our standing before God. So, for example, he will often use images from a battlefield (Christ winning the victory over sin and death), a court of law (the legal acquittal of guilty sinners, effected by Christ's death on their behalf), a relationship (Paul's idea of reconciliation of sinners estranged from God to their Creator), a prison (Christ's death bringing freedom from oppressive, dominating powers), and a hospital (healing brought about by the transformation in the human situation achieved by the cross).[36] The biblical idea that Christ died 'for our sins' (1 Cor. 15:3) is firmly in place, yet McGrath does not commit himself to any one way of defining and describing the way in which the cross effects salvation, finding instead in the New Testament a multiplicity of images seeking to convey the underlying reality.[37] For example, he places the idea of 'substitution' alongside 'representation' and 'participation' as authentic biblical categories for understanding the way in which the cross effects human salvation.[38] He clearly believes in 'substitutionary atonement', but does not think that this category exhausts the meaning of the cross. It is not that these are *competing* categories for understanding the meaning of the cross, but McGrath argues that they are *complementary*, even overlapping, ways of making sense of the cross of Christ.

To understand this position, we need to turn again to McGrath's study of Calvin, and in particular his view of revelation. In *The Enigma of the Cross* he writes:

---

[36] McGrath, *Making Sense of the Cross*, pp. 49–85. See also the summary of Christian teaching on the cross in Alister E. McGrath, *Christian Theology: An Introduction* (Oxford: Blackwell, 1994), pp. 341–60; and McGrath and McGrath, *The Dilemma of Self-Esteem*, pp. 89–101.

[37] For example, in the passages 2 Corinthians 5:14 – 6:2 and Romans 3:24–26, as cited in Alister E. McGrath, 'Theology of the Cross' in Gerald F. Hawthorne, Ralph P. Martin and Daniel G. Reid (eds), *Dictionary of Paul and his Letters* (Downers Grove: InterVarsity Press, 1993), p. 195ff.

[38] McGrath, *Making Sense of the Cross*, pp. 58–9.

the cross has always maintained a resistance against reductive interpretation. We cannot distil the meaning of the cross into a simple single proposition on the basis of which we can deduce further propositions. As Luther pointed out: 'the wisdom of the cross is hidden in a deep mystery'. In the end, the cross, itself mysterious, points to an even greater mystery which lies behind it – the living God.[39]

Constant throughout McGrath's theology, alongside his confidence in the Bible as the norm and foundation for Christian theology, is a profound sense of the mystery of God, the importance of wonder, and therefore the provisionality of theology and its inability to do full justice to the nature and character of God.[40] This deep-rooted approach to theology finds an echo in, and to some extent derives from, Calvin's understanding of revelation. Calvin poses the question of how mere human language can do justice to God, a question that incidentally comes with even greater force with contemporary postmodern distrust of the capacity of language to convey truth in any ultimate sense. The answer comes in Calvin's doctrine of 'accommodation', where the Reformer understands God's revelation in Scripture not as somehow capturing or defining the essence of God, but rather a self-accommodation to human understanding, describing himself in terms we can understand. It is not that God *is* a shepherd, father, teacher or judge in some anthropomorphic sense – it is just that these are offered to us as concepts we can understand, but which convey in a dependable and trustworthy way the nature of God and his relationship to us.

Like any good orator, God adjusts his speech to his audience, and speaks of himself in Scripture in terms that make sense to us. These then become authoritative images, human language in which we are authorized to speak of God, and which are reliable guides to his nature, yet we are aware all the time that these concepts do not define or capture God, but that he remains beyond and unconfined by them.[41] McGrath's

---

[39] McGrath, *The Enigma of the Cross*, p. 88.

[40] This aspect of his thought comes to the fore in McGrath's various popular works on spirituality. For example, Alister E. McGrath, *The Journey: A Pilgrim in the Lands of the Spirit* (London: Hodder & Stoughton, 1999).

[41] This touches on a controversial and sometimes misunderstood aspect of Calvin's theology. Calvin's doctrine of accommodation does not intend to imply that there is more to God that is unknown to us, beyond his revelation of himself. Although the notion of the '*extra calvinisticum*' has sometimes been taken to imply this, more correctly it is Calvin's way of underlining the belief that it was truly God himself who become incarnate in Christ, and that

reading of Calvin makes a good deal of this very point, as providing a way of acknowledging the frailty of human language as a vehicle for speaking of the living God, at the same time as preserving the authority and validity of specifically *scriptural* language for this task.[42] Human language and concepts are indeed inadequate to do justice to God. And it is precisely for this reason that God *gives* us a language with which to speak of him – in fact, it is only the language of Scripture that enables us to speak meaningfully of God, and we must learn that language if we are to do so.

These ideas lie close to the heart of McGrath's own understanding of revelation and determine his approach to the relationship between theology and experience. For him, experience of and encounter with God in Christ have priority over doctrinal statements about him. Doctrinal statements serve as a framework by which that same experience may be understood, interpreted and conveyed to future generations, ensuring it is the same Christ we are dealing with, ensuring continuity within the Christian community from age to age.[43] Naturally, this leads to a certain (surprising?) reticence about theology, particularly more dogmatic formulations of it. When it comes to the doctrine of the atonement, we find, on the one hand, a sense that the cross brings about an objective transformation in the sinner's standing before God, a transformation that cannot entirely be tied down in words to one particular theory, but instead must employ a range of metaphors to capture its full richness. On the other hand, given the fact that God has provided us with language to make sense of his action in the cross and the importance of guarding and conveying this experience of reconciliation to God accurately to future generations, we find also the necessity of speaking of it and using language that interprets it. This is no apophatic theology that refuses to speak of God or gives up entirely with human language as doomed to failure. It is instead a theological humility that

---

[41] *(continued)* while fully incarnate God was not confined or restricted by the human body of Christ. See John Calvin, *Institutes of the Christian Religion*, Ford Lewis Battles (tr.), John T. McNeill (ed.) (Philadelphia: Westminster, 1960), II.xiii.4; David E. Willis, *Calvin's Catholic Christology* (Leiden: Brill, 1966).

[42] See McGrath, *A Life of John Calvin*, pp. 130–2, 255–7; F.L. Battles, 'God was Accommodating himself to Human Capacity', *Interpretation* 31 (1977). Also e.g., Calvin's *Institutes of the Christian Religion*, I.xiii.1; II.vi.4; II.xi.13–14; IV.i.1; IV.xvii.1.

[43] E.g., Alister E. McGrath, *Justification by Faith: What it Means for us Today* (Basingstoke: Marshall Pickering, 1988), pp. 129–31.

tries to do justice to the range of language used in Scripture to describe atonement, yet stops short of claiming to define the meaning in any final way.

The kind of approach that McGrath adopts has drawn some criticism from within evangelical ranks. On the one hand, his refusal to make penal substitution the central and final understanding of atonement has come in for some criticism.[44] On the other, his notion of experience as prior to theology has also been questioned in some quarters.[45] The two points are linked – McGrath's tendency to opt for a range of models or metaphors of the atonement derives from his sense that experience precedes theological formulations, that 'underlying the Christian faith is first and foremost an experience, rather than the acceptance of a set of doctrines'.[46] The cross of Christ effects an indispensable objective transformation in relationship to God for those who trust in it. It radically alters the human situation (in contrast to the Abelardian view, which essentially leaves the relationship unchanged). This transformation, however, can be expressed in a number of complementary ways.

6. The Cross, Experience and Theology

What, then does McGrath mean by his belief in the theological priority of experience over theology? One interpretation would be that he is taking up a position close to Schleiermacher's celebrated insistence on religious feeling (*das Gefühl*) as opposed to revealed doctrine as the central object of theological study. Is this what he means? If so, then he is not surprisingly taken to task by some evangelical theologians for a drift back towards the kind of liberalism from which he had earlier escaped.

An answer to this question, and a deeper understanding of what McGrath means by this, can be explored through an article written in 1986 about Christology and soteriology.[47] In this piece, McGrath

---

[44] For example, Melvin Tinker (ed.), *The Anglican Evangelical Identity Crisis: A Radical Agenda for a Bible-Based Church* (Fearn: Christian Focus, 1995). For an exposition of the central place of penal substitution as an understanding of the atonement, see David Peterson, *Where Wrath and Mercy Meet* (Carlisle: Paternoster, 2001).

[45] Tinker, *The Anglican Evangelical Identity Crisis*, pp. 47–50.

[46] McGrath, *Justification by Faith*, p. 129.

[47] Alister E. McGrath, 'Christology and Soteriology. A Response to Wolfhart Pannenberg's Critique of the Soteriological Approach to Christology', *Theologische Zeitschrift* 42 (1986).

mounts a strong defence of the primacy of soteriology over history in discerning Christological meaning. Taking Wolfhart Pannenberg to task for insisting that the historical facts about the life of Jesus must provide the basis for Christology, McGrath counters that soteriology comes first. Pannenberg's approach requires a level of historical knowledge that is simply unavailable to us – we do not have the 'raw data' of history to construct a Christology for ourselves. The main sources for our knowledge of Christ (the gospels) are themselves an interpretation of the significance of his life for those he encountered in the flesh. They already contain an implicit or explicit soteriology, so cannot be used as the kind of material Pannenberg needs to construct Christology from history rather than soteriology.

The problem McGrath identifies in Pannenberg is a desire to possess an objective knowledge of Christ that is independent of a personal apprehension of him. It is the desire to know Christ 'after the flesh' (2 Cor. 5:16), to have a kind of documentary knowledge of him prior to a transforming experience of encounter with him. Even if this were to be historically possible, it is theologically improper. Or at least it is to the strand of theology that comes to us from the Reformation. Melanchthon's famous dictum, 'to know Christ is to know his benefits', denies the possibility of a true knowledge of Christ that is objective in the sense of leaving the observer, or knower, untouched by that knowledge. Theologically speaking, such knowledge is just about useless. Calvin also makes a similar point:

> Now the knowledge of God, as I understand it, is that by which we not only conceive that there is a God, but also grasp what befits us and is proper to his glory, in fine, what is to our advantage to know him. Indeed we shall not say that, properly speaking, God is known where there is no religion or piety … What is God? Men who pose this question are merely toying with idle specu-lations. It is more important for us to know what sort he is, and what is consistent with his nature … what help is it, in short, to know a God with whom we have nothing to do?[48]

The point is that it is impossible to have an objective knowledge of God independent of experience of him, or at least that such knowledge is not worth very much. Knowledge of God is in itself transforming, and Pannenberg's attempt to delve behind the New Testament *kerygma*, which offers us the record of the way in which Christ impacted the lives

---

[48] Calvin, *Institutes of the Christian Religion*, I.ii.1, 2.

of those he encountered and already contains an implicit soteriology, is fundamentally flawed. As McGrath puts it, the question 'Who is Christ' presupposes a deeper and more important question: 'Who is Christ for me?[49] It is this concern, to safeguard the priority of a knowledge of Christ as he is *pro nobis*, as personally encountered, rather than objectively assessed, that drives McGrath's sense of the priority of experience over formulation, the encounter with God over precise descriptions of what that encounter means.

McGrath's concern appears to be that theologies that seek to place certain verbal constructions or statements of faith as prior to an encounter with the living Christ fall into the same trap as Pannenberg. They try to posit a kind of objective knowledge of Christ that is independent of actually knowing him. It is possible to 'know' the doctrine of the atonement backwards, having studied it and written essays on it as an academic topic in an undergraduate theology class. However, this is not true knowledge of God, or, as Calvin would put it, 'saving knowledge' of him. True knowledge of God comes about when there is a transforming encounter with the living God, which kindles faith. As Augustine, Luther and Calvin all knew, our fallen minds are not capable of apprehending God unless God first touches our hearts. As Pascal puts it: 'It is the heart that perceives God and not the reason. That is what faith is: God perceived by the heart, not by the reason.'[50] This may come about through the study and understanding of theological concepts, but is not necessarily confined to it. At the heart of the New Testament witness to Jesus Christ is the impact he made on those he met. At the heart of the Christian church today is a personal encounter with this same, now risen and ascended, Jesus Christ, through the Holy Spirit. An encounter with the risen Christ requires words to express its meaning and to communicate it effectively to others, and, as Calvin reminds us, we are given words by God with which to speak of these things. Yet such a living encounter cannot be reduced to or replaced by words, and while inseparable from doctrine and theology, it must remain logically and theologically prior to them.

This is different from Schleiermacher's approach for at least two reasons. First, Schleiermacher does not maintain the priority of scriptural language as the language in which we are authorized to speak of God. Instead, in Schleiermacher's system, scriptural or subsequent doctrinal

---

[49] McGrath, 'Christology and Soteriology', p. 232.
[50] Blaise Pascal, *Pensées*, Alban J. Krailsheimer (tr.) (Harmondsworth: Penguin, 1966) L424, p. 154.

concepts such as the Trinity are judged as to their value by the external criterion of their usefulness in describing religious experience. Secondly, McGrath is not suggesting that the religious experience of the Christian community today is the raw material of theological reflection. Scripture retains that role of foundation and norm, yet Scripture itself reveals God by recounting the impact made upon people by the presence and intervention of God in history and supremely in Christ. Scripture is not understood primarily in terms of a set of objective propositions about the nature of God to be analysed and assessed – it is the authoritative story of God's dealings with humankind, which can only be properly understood within a transforming relationship with him.

McGrath is keen to stress the absolute centrality of a personal, transforming encounter with God. And because this lies at the heart of Christian faith, he maintains a certain reserve when it comes to human theological formulations. This is not, of course, to say that theology becomes unimportant. As we have seen above, he is keenly aware of the unreliability of experience on its own as a guide to the nature or will of God. Experience always needs interpretation – an encounter with God, especially the shocking and disturbing encounter with the God who hangs on a cross, needs words to make sense of it. But theology does become in a certain sense secondary to this encounter with the living God. Again, we are back with McGrath's initial engagement with Luther's *theologia crucis*. Human reason (and liberal theology) is brought up with a jolt not by an argument, but by a picture and an encounter – the picture of the crucified God, which confounds all expectations, and makes the would-be theologian think again. Moving from the theological significance of the cross to its soteriological meaning, the same underlying principle applies. Underlying all verbal formulations of the atonement lies an encounter with the God who reconciles, rescues and heals. McGrath prefers to offer a range of different and complementary images that help explain its meaning (as long as those images are present in Scripture itself) rather than being tied down to one definitive and fixed theory. This, for him, preserves the sense that the cross itself, as the place where a holy God and sinful humanity meet, will always remain, at least on this side of heaven, a mystery beyond our understanding. It contains, as C.S. Lewis put it, a 'deeper magic'.

The debate between McGrath and his critics points to a tension within evangelical theology that has lain at the heart of the movement since the nineteenth century, and is not always successfully resolved. One very prominent emphasis within evangelicalism has been the insistence on the importance of a personal knowledge of God. Deriving from the pietistic movements of the seventeenth and eighteenth centuries in continental Europe,[51] Wesley, Whitefield and the evangelical revival in Britain,[52] and on into the charismatic movement of more recent times, this strand has placed the emphasis upon a personal encounter with God as the centre of evangelical religion. On the other hand, especially since the nineteenth century, evangelicalism has felt itself compelled to articulate and defend classical Christian theology against modernist or liberal critics. This factor has led in some circles to a contrasting emphasis upon correct doctrine as the heart of evangelical identity. These two tendencies are, of course, not altogether incompatible, and evangelicals have usually tried to hold them together, not always successfully. Here, the contrast is perhaps too starkly drawn, but the two emphases do and have sometimes come into conflict. McGrath's sympathies certainly lie on the more pietistic side of this debate, concerned to preserve the priority of the personal knowledge of God over doctrinal formulations. Others within evangelicalism want to argue for the priority of doctrine over experience. The debate will no doubt continue, yet evangelicals would do well to be aware of the potential for conflict here, and continue to work at clarifying the precise relationship between orthodoxy of doctrine and a living, transforming faith in Christ.

Alister McGrath's theological work places the cross of Christ squarely at the heart of Christian faith and theology. It occupies a place at the very centre not just of Christian understandings of salvation, but of the whole of Christian theology. It raises important issues about the relationship between faith and doctrine. But most importantly, it invites its readers into an encounter with the God who is present in the crucified Christ. And for that, however we view McGrath's own theological reflections on the significance of the cross, we must remain profoundly grateful.

---

[51] See W.R. Ward, *The Protestant Evangelical Awakening* (Cambridge: Cambridge University Press, 1992).

[52] See David W. Bebbington, *Evangelicalism in Modern Britain: A History from the 1730s to the 1980s* (London: Unwin Hyman, 1989).

2

Alister E. McGrath and Justification

Gerald L. Bray

When Alister McGrath first published *Iustitia Dei* he noted in the preface that there had not been a similarly comprehensive treatment of the subject of justification since Albrecht Ritschl's *Lehre von der Rechtfertigung*, which had appeared as long ago as 1870.[1] For more than a century afterwards, neither in Germany nor in the English-speaking world, had theological writing on the subject been at the forefront of academic concerns. To be sure, there had been a good deal of work done on the atonement, particularly in the first half of the twentieth century, but most of this had been slanted in a different direction, being primarily concerned with the question of the suffering of the incarnate Son of God, not with justification in the traditional sense. Liberal Protestantism, with its universalistic tendencies, found the doctrine uncongenial, and Karl Barth's development of it formed part of his more general neo-orthodox reaction against liberalism. The rise of ecumenism improved matters somewhat, but this was mainly because Roman Catholic scholars were increasingly inclined to return to sixteenth-century theological controversies in an effort to come to terms with the Protestant Reformation. It is indicative of the general state of contemporary Protestant theology that the most significant work on the subject was the magisterial thesis of Hans Küng, which sought to show that, if Karl Barth's opinion was at all representative, then there was no fundamental difference between Rome and the Protestant churches on this doctrine.[2] That claim inevitably sparked a good deal of

---

[1] Alister E. McGrath, *Iustitia Dei* (Cambridge: Cambridge University Press, 2 vols, 1986), vol. 1, p. xi.

[2] H. Küng, *Rechtfertigung: Die Lehre Karl Barths und eine katholische Besinnung* (Einsiedeln, 1957). English translation: *Justification: The Doctrine of Karl Barth and a Catholic Reflection*, Thomas Collins, David Grandskou and Edmund E. Tolk (trs) (London: Burns & Oates, 1964).

discussion, much of which revealed just how ignorant most theologians then were of the details of the sixteenth-century controversy to which the enduring schism caused by the Protestant Reformation has usually been attributed.

Dr McGrath's intention, and ultimately his achievement, was to fill the gap in scholarly understanding and in the process to bring justification back to the centre of theological discussion, from which it had been inexcusably (if not entirely unaccountably) displaced. Almost two decades have passed since then, and justification is once more a major theological topic, both within and beyond ecumenical circles. Dr McGrath's *Iustitia Dei* is now in a second edition.[3] In terms of his own career, it remains his most substantial work, and the one by which he continues to be most widely known. An occasion like this one gives us an opportunity to assess its significance in the wider picture of academic scholarship and to suggest where we might go from here.

First of all, there can be no doubt that Dr McGrath has performed a great service in making the doctrine of justification and its history accessible to a wide range of theologians and church historians. He has navigated not merely the treacherous waters of the Reformation, but also the muddy streams which lead back from it to St Augustine, and which have been too little explored in the past. Given that Protestants have traditionally wanted to regard Martin Luther as a great pioneer who rediscovered a long-lost belief, and that Roman Catholics have usually been more interested in other things, it is hardly surprising that neither side has found it congenial to examine the later Middle Ages to see what it might turn up on the subject of justification by faith. Dr McGrath has not only overcome these prejudices and done this, but he has also built his research into a wider framework designed to show the perennial interconnectedness of theological thought, regardless of the fashions of the moment. Even those who might disagree with some (or all) of his conclusions must be grateful for this, and acknowledge that Dr McGrath has set new parameters and new standards for all students of the subject.

Dr McGrath begins his study with a ringing reaffirmation of the classical Reformation statement that justification is the article of a standing or a falling church. He quotes Luther in the original Latin, but then goes on to expound the thesis in his own words, showing not only that,

---

[3] Alister E. McGrath, *Iustitia Dei: A History of the Christian Doctrine of Justification* (Cambridge: Cambridge University Press, 1998²). The second edition has appeared in a single volume with an updated bibliography and two additional sections at the end of the original work.

but also why, justification is the real centre of the theological system of the Christian church.[4] At the heart of the doctrine, claims Dr McGrath, is nothing less than the transition of the believer from a state of sin to a state of righteousness, from the status of *homo peccator* inherited from Adam to that of *homo iustus* redeemed by Jesus Christ. Without this doctrine there can be no Christian church, and history shows that when justification has been forgotten or obscured, as it was in the century after 1870, the church has suffered and been weakened as a result.

Of course, Dr McGrath recognizes, as he must, that justification as a doctrine has been developed only in the Western church, and that Eastern Christianity has followed its own, rather different, historical development. That fact, coupled with the survival of Eastern Christianity over the centuries, might call Luther's famous dictum into question, but Dr McGrath compensates for this to some extent by pointing out that there was a *concept* of justification that preceded the developed *doctrine*. That concept is the common inheritance of both Jews and Christians, and in some form or other, it will be found in every theological system derived from the Bible. In fact, the biblical and most of the patristic witness to justification belongs under the 'concept' heading, since the doctrine as we know it cannot really be traced back before the time of St Augustine. Even then, it may be too much to speak of 'doctrine' in any systematic sense. Dr McGrath shows that it was not until the late twelfth century that real analysis of the concept began, and not until Thomas Aquinas (1226–74) and his successors got to grips with it that a true 'doctrine' comes into view. Moreover, as Dr McGrath demonstrates, it was only then that serious debate on the subject began to emerge within the church, leading eventually to the great crisis of the Reformation era.

Dr McGrath weaves his way through the complexities of late medieval thought and concludes his first volume with a schematic presentation of the four main schools that had worked out a doctrine of justification – the Dominican, the early Franciscan, the later Franciscan and the 'modern' or 'nominalist'. He demonstrates that however different these schools were from each other, they were all agreed in maintaining that justification meant being made righteous, and for that reason included what we would now distinguish as the separate doctrines of 'sanctification' and 'regeneration' as well. From the standpoint of the Reformation, Dr McGrath concludes:

---

[4] McGrath, *Iustitia Dei*, vol. 1, pp. 1–2. Unless otherwise indicated, all references are to the original 1986 edition.

The significance of the Protestant distinction between *iustificatio* and *regeneratio* is that a fundamental discontinuity has been introduced into the western theological tradition *where none had existed before*. Despite the astonishing theological diversity of the late medieval period, a consensus relating to the *nature* of justification was maintained throughout. The Protestant understanding of the *nature* of justification represents a theological *novum*, whereas its understanding of its *mode* does not. It is therefore of considerable importance to appreciate that the *criterion employed in the sixteenth century* to determine whether a particular doctrine of justification was Protestant or otherwise was *whether justification was understood forensically.*[5]

Dr McGrath goes on to admit that there is no *practical* difference between justification and regeneration, since one cannot occur without the other, but he insists that the Reformers established a *conceptual* difference between them. In the end, this proved to be of such importance that, if it cannot be said to have provoked the Reformation, it nevertheless came with hindsight to be seen as the single most important theological factor that split the Western church down the middle.

The most controversial aspect of this treatment of the pre-Reformation history of the doctrine of justification is undoubtedly Dr McGrath's revisionist attitude towards Martin Luther. He acknowledges that Luther was preoccupied with the true meaning of justification by faith, but downplays the significance of this for the Reformation itself. Instead, he prefers to see Luther as a transitional figure whose thought was deeply rooted in certain strands of late medieval theology, but whose own spiritual concerns paved the way for his disciples, and especially for Philipp Melanchthon, to develop what was to become the classical, forensic model for understanding the doctrine.

The second part of *Iustitia Dei*[6] is devoted to Martin Luther and all that followed him. Dr McGrath traces the post-Reformation development of the doctrine of justification by dividing it into three distinct stages. The first of these is represented by Luther himself. According to Dr McGrath, Luther borrowed a good deal from different medieval sources, but he created a new mix. In particular, he taught that God, not humankind, is the author of sin, that the slavery of humankind's will is the result of creation, not the fall, and that there is a double predestination – to eternal damnation, as well as to eternal life. The second stage,

---

[5] Ibid., vol. 1, p. 184.
[6] Originally published as a second volume; pp. 188–395 in the second (1998) edition.

represented by both Melanchthon and Calvin, abandoned or radically modified these notions and reconstructed the doctrine along more tradi-tional lines, though they both insisted that justification was a forensic term which had to be understood in that context. Calvin made it a subset of his Christology and therefore interpreted predestination as dependent on the doctrine of salvation. In the third stage, Calvin's disciples, and especially Theodore Beza, objectified the doctrine by taking it out of the sphere of Christology and making it part of the eternal divine decrees. As a consequence, they also developed a doctrine of limited atonement and put predestination before, not after, salvation.

Reactions to this process were many and varied. The Roman Catholic Church resisted it and canonized an understanding of justification in which theories of merit continued to play an essential part. The Church of England officially adopted a form of Melanchthon's teaching, while the Puritans within it went all the way with Beza and the later Calvinists. Confessional Lutherans maintained Melanchthon's position in principle, but in practice they moved more towards an emphasis on the experiential dimension of justification, largely because of the challenge posed by the emergence of pietism.

Subsequent developments began with the Enlightenment and contin-ued through various reworkings of that, associated mainly with the writings of Schleiermacher, Ritschl and Barth in Germany, and with John Henry Newman in England. Dr McGrath has little difficulty in polishing off Newman, who completely misrepresented the Protestant doctrine(s) of justification, of which he had only a superficial know-ledge. More daringly, he also claims that, despite their own protests to the contrary, each generation of German 'revisionists' has in fact done little more than repristinate the Enlightenment understanding of justifi-cation, with its strong emphasis on moralism, and has therefore failed to understand the theological seriousness of the doctrine within the framework of traditional orthodoxy.

The first edition of *Iustitia Dei* ended at this point, although Dr McGrath made it clear in his concluding remarks that he was aware of a new debate on the subject that had started to emerge. By the time the second edition appeared, that debate had advanced too far to be passed over, though because it was still in full flow and there could be no telling where it would eventually end up, treating it with any kind of authority was extremely difficult. Reviewers of the first edition had commented on the almost complete absence of any discussion of the Apostle Paul, a charge Dr McGrath countered by saying that every generation of theo-logians felt that it was reacting directly to Paul and therefore under-standing his 'true' meaning differently. To have tackled Paul directly would therefore have been to add another chapter to the history of the doctrine rather than to help us understand the historical evolution of the interpretation of Pauline thought.

This was a somewhat lame excuse, however, and with controversy raging over the work of E.P. Sanders, Dr McGrath could hardly avoid tackling Paul, or at least current New Testament scholarship on Paul, directly. He also felt that it was necessary to add a chapter on recent ecumenical discussions, which he believes have been deeply influenced by the work of Hans Küng, whose controversial conclusions we have already mentioned. Other than that, the second edition contains no new material apart from an updated bibliography, and we must assume that Dr McGrath has not changed his basic outlook in any significant respect since 1986.

As it happens, Dr McGrath's attempt to tackle recent debates on justification by adding two short chapters to an already completed work reveals both the strengths and the weaknesses of his overall approach. On the one hand, his book is meant to be a survey of the main currents of thought throughout Christian history, and to have devoted more space to the current discussion would have compromised that intention. Too many books tend to give a relatively brief summary of the historic positions on whatever subject they are discussing, before launching into a detailed examination of the latest trends, which may soon turn out to be ephemeral. For that reason, Dr McGrath could not afford to distort his overall presentation by giving too much space to the most recent controversies, which may not be significant in the longer term and which therefore have to be kept in some kind of perspective. At the same time, the modern reader is all too aware that to reduce discussion of the latest trends to the work of only three major theologians – E.P. Sanders, Ernst Käsemann and Hans Küng – creates another kind of distortion. These men were not engaged in direct dialogue with one another and without providing a great deal more background material it is hard to see why there should be a lively debate going on at the moment. The contemporary scene is extremely varied, and there is no guarantee that the 'big names' mentioned above will carry the day in the end. To go no further, it seems as if Sanders is likely to be superseded by a much less radical approach to the question of Palestinian Judaism, and Küng's place in ecumenical dialogue is controversial at best, since he is no longer recognized as a Roman Catholic theologian.

What these chapters show is that Dr McGrath's technique is to go for a few major characters whose thought he then distills into easily learned points of reference. For the non-specialist in any given area, this is a godsend, because it enables him or her to get a handle on what is going on without having to plough through large and dusty tomes written in an obscure and difficult language. However, it also carries the danger of oversimplification, and makes whatever errors in perception there may be extremely difficult to track down and correct. Most readers today will realize that the additional chapters are inadequate and will look elsewhere for an analysis of the current theological scene, but how many will do the same for the Middle Ages, or for the age of Protestant orthodoxy? When dealing with the distant or largely forgotten past, the 'big names' approach is understandable and likely to be widely accepted, since it is usually only the big names who have left any lasting impression. The thought of lesser figures may be more significant in terms of theological debate at the time, and in many cases the statements of the major characters may derive from contemporaries who are now little-known, but the effort to document this is such that only another specialist of Dr McGrath's degree of competence and erudition could even begin to make the effort.

Dr McGrath's work is therefore likely to be the first and last port of call for most non-specialists in the field, and it is clear from looking at the footnotes of more recent publications on the subject that *Iustitia Dei* is frequently quoted as *the* source for whatever view of justification is under discussion. This, of course, is a great tribute to Dr McGrath, and there can be no denying the breadth of his learning, which extends even to such arcane matters (for the average theologian) as Gothic philology. Few readers are likely to have that kind of information or know where to get it, and, thanks to Dr McGrath, everyone who works through *Iustitia Dei* will come away with a good idea of how much is involved in any serious treatment of the doctrine of justification.

At the same time, questions are bound to be raised about the way in which certain individuals and periods are treated. Anyone with a knowledge of current New Testament scholarship will be dissatisfied with the opening chapters, as Dr McGrath has himself acknowledged in the preface to his second edition. More significantly, and within the parameters Dr McGrath laid down for his original study, his revisionist interpretation of Luther and his followers is bound to raise eyebrows. Is it really possible to argue that, although Luther was preoccupied with the significance of justification, it was not a major factor in his theological protest against the medieval church? Can it really be the case that Melanchthon and Calvin (albeit in their somewhat different ways) rejected Luther's main theses on justification while at the same time claiming to be his authentic followers on that very subject? It is difficult to avoid the suspicion that these matters have been simplified, even to the point of distortion, and specialists in the field are likely to chip away at Dr McGrath's analysis, using it as a target rather than as a resource for ongoing scholarly discussion.[7]

In one sense, of course, that is probably inevitable, and no fault of Dr McGrath's. It is the fate of great works to be picked apart by succeeding generations, who love to point out that on innumerable points of detail there is a good deal more that needs to be said. In the present case, there is no doubt that *Iustitia Dei* will still be read long after most of these critiques have been forgotten, and the clear way in which Dr McGrath presents his material will make the book an invaluable teaching aid for at least a generation, and perhaps longer. But what if this ends up producing a generation of theologians whose view of justification is as one-sided in its way as that of Albrecht Ritschl?

The truth of the matter is that *Iustitia Dei* is a young man's book, which holds out the promise of greater things to come. It shows that Dr McGrath has a broad sweep of knowledge that he can draw on to construct a pattern of thought capable of making sense of the doctrine of justification, particularly as that has developed over the course of centuries. Some of this erudition is superfluous, of course, and occasionally it gets in the way of the argument. To give but one obvious example, there is a great deal of untranslated Latin, which for most modern readers is nothing but an insurmountable obstacle. Doctoral students, such as Dr McGrath was when he started writing, usually have to lower their sights considerably when they start teaching, and a future edition of *Iustitia Dei* could certainly benefit from this process.

But much more serious is the question of in-depth study of the particular areas Dr McGrath merely touches on. Now that he is securely established and in mid career, it is time for him to work through the byways of his great book, filling in the gaps and deepening his own – and then our – understanding of the subject. The need to rework the biblical material is too obvious to need repetition, but the patristic section also requires serious revision, particularly in the light of recent developments in our understanding of the biblical interpretation of the church fathers. This was an obscure subject back in 1986, but in the past few years there has been an outpouring of books and articles dealing with commentaries on the Apostle Paul, for example, which are of direct relevance to Dr McGrath's thesis. He mentions them in passing, but that is no longer enough – they now need to be studied in

---

[7] In this respect it is noticeable – and alarming – that the footnotes have not been updated in the second edition. It must also be said that they reveal an over-dependence on secondary literature, whose accuracy is sometimes questionable.

detail, and the extent of their influence on later theological discussion has to be brought out in a clear and unambiguous manner.

Similarly, there is now much more material available on late medieval theology, and that too needs to be worked into the discussion. Dr McGrath is right to sense that this is *the* key period for our understanding of Luther, and so it needs to be examined with much greater care than is usual in theological studies that purport to explain the Reformation. Luther's own role needs to be rethought, and the post-Reformation period can and should be worked on to a much greater depth. This applies as much to the age of Protestant orthodoxy as it does to the current scene, where some of the most interesting work is being done by theological conservatives – a largely invisible minority in Dr McGrath's treatment. To go no further, we would say that a careful engagement with Mark Seifrid's growing body of publications in this field might well lead Dr McGrath to revise his whole outlook; at the very least, it would challenge his thinking in substantial ways and stimulate him to delve more deeply into the subject.[8]

Perhaps when Dr McGrath started to write *Iustitia Dei* he had no desire to end up as the leading contemporary authority on justification, but in the preface to the second edition he acknowledges that this honour has been conferred on him whether he wanted it or not. Such a status confers obligations as well as privileges, the greatest of which is the duty to produce a truly definitive study of his chosen subject. As we congratulate him on his achievements so far, we should not forget that he still has many years before him in which he can (and will be expected to) make such a definitive contribution as the crowning monument to his life's work. Let us hope that he will take heart from his successes so far, and be encouraged to embark on the next phase of what we can only hope will be a long and productive career.

---

[8] The revised bibliography in the 1998 edition contains a reference to Dr Seifrid's *Justification by Faith: The Origin and Development of a Central Pauline Theme* (Leiden: Brill, 1992) but there is no discussion of his thesis in the main body of the text.

3

The Scientific Theology Project of Alister E. McGrath

John J. Roche

I have approached Alister McGrath's programme of publications in science and religion in the only way I can, as a physicist and historian of physics with some background in the philosophy of science and in the history of philosophy, and as someone who is deeply interested in the field of science and religion. My knowledge of theology, especially of the traditions deriving from Luther and Calvin, is limited, and I have not attempted to assess McGrath's critiques of the theological positions of others, or to examine the theological implications of his own methodology. I have concentrated, rather, on an analysis of the manner in which he deploys science as a methodological tool for theology.

In preparation for this article I have studied five works by McGrath: *The Foundations of Dialogue in Science and Religion*; *Science and Religion: An Introduction*; *Thomas F. Torrance: An Intellectual Biography*; *A Scientific Theology Volume 1: Nature*; and *A Scientific Theology Volume 2: Reality*.[1] This represents five books published in as many years.

Those of us who have struggled to produce a book per decade may be tempted to justify this on the grounds that scholarship takes a great deal of time, and one does well to complete a work of substance in ten years. Surely no one can produce five truly scholarly books in as many years. I

---

[1] Alister E. McGrath, *The Foundations of Dialogue in Science and Religion* (Oxford: Blackwell, 1998); Alister E. McGrath, *Science and Religion: An Introduction* (Oxford: Blackwell, 1999); Alister E. McGrath, *Thomas F. Torrance: An Intellectual Biography* (Edinburgh: T. & T. Clark, 1999); Alister E. McGrath, *A Scientific Theology Volume 1: Nature* (Edinburgh: T. & T. Clark, 2001); Alister E. McGrath, *A Scientific Theology Volume 2: Reality* (Edinburgh: T. & T. Clark, 2002).

can say that I have discovered signs of haste in at least one of them. Another year's labour over some of these texts would have allowed a better ordering of materials. Also, McGrath's indexes are generally sparse and do not adequately reflect the wealth of material in the text. Some of these books seem to have been written almost with a sense of controlled urgency. Undoubtedly, his pressing responsibilities as Principal of Wycliffe Hall severely limit the time he has available for editorial polishing. Nevertheless, these are petty criticisms. The weight and originality of McGrath's analysis in so many issues show that his publications in the field of science and religion represent the outcome of many years of preparatory study and deepening analysis.

McGrath is a highly sophisticated thinker, aware of the nuances and current status of an impressive variety of issues. His style is crisp. With a deceptive ease he seems able to identify clearly the key points in the dense arguments of others. He is a minimalist, always favouring short sentences. He is economical with technical terminology, whether in science or theology. He does not labour issues: he makes a point quickly and just as quickly moves on. These aspects of his style are best reflected in his summing ups, which are superb, and always deepen and generalize the understanding of the issues that have just been examined. All of this allows McGrath to cover a great amount of material in a brief compass, while making his books refreshingly easy and attractive to read. He has admitted to me that he has been much influenced in his style by the pressures exerted upon him by scientific journals to edit down. But I believe that an even stronger motivation is his wish to make an impact. An author who cannot easily be understood, or who labours his points, has a limited appeal and influence.

As I read book after book, my reaction became one of increasing respect: McGrath has engaged on a reading programme of massive proportions. He has read everything of relevance in the history of science, in contemporary science, in the history of philosophy and in the history of the philosophy of science, in historical and in current theology, in the history of science and religion, and also in the current field. And in each of these fields he brings a professional competence to bear. This is rare indeed. On top of that, he reads Latin, German and French. Samuel Johnson's quip that Irish scholars are not thorough[2] certainly does not apply to Alister McGrath.

Perhaps McGrath, therefore, is an encyclopaedist with a good writing style. However, the vision that unfolds in these works of the relationship

---

[2] *Boswell's Life of Johnson*, George Birbeck Hill and L.F. Powell (eds) (Oxford: Clarendon Press, 1964), vol. 2, p. 132.

between science and religion, and the quality, range and developing architecture of his analysis, made the reading of these texts a highly satisfying intellectual adventure for me, indeed exhilarating at times.

McGrath has a very ambitious view of what he wishes to accomplish in the field of science and religion, and a very demanding conception of the knowledge and skills required to accomplish it. His dramatic vision is that scientific method can function as a powerful auxiliary tool for theology today, as Platonism did in the patristic period and as Aristotle did for Aquinas in the Middle Ages. This courageously turns the conflict notion of science and religion precisely on its head. This vision may alienate some of those who are persuaded that philosophy is the natural auxiliary of theology, but it will surely inspire others, as it did me.

McGrath's writings represent a succession of refreshing new insights, which are often built upon, but always go beyond, the labours of others. He is concerned to establish a series of simple but powerful points clearly and persuasively, all targeted on his ultimate goal. His approach is to read everything of relevance, both historical and current, on each topic he considers, to examine it from a variety of perspectives, to unravel ambiguities, to clarify and to move on to a fuller elucidation of issues, and thereby to produce a refined analysis that aims for high standards of historical, scientific and theological rigour and accessibility.

A partial explanation of the maturity and originality of these writings is that, as he informs us, his work in science and religion has been the long-term goal of his scholarly life. He has been reflecting on these issues since his undergraduate days, and preparing for the present task for about twenty-five years. As well as pursuing the historical and theological studies that he felt were required, he has deliberately built up an arsenal of additional skills that are necessary and adequate for such a grand task.

It is possible to identify various broad methodological commitments and orientations in his writings in this field. Perhaps the most obvious feature is his deeply historical approach: he attacks every problem in the first instance historically. This is not an amateur dipping into history; this is the history of a professional who has honed his art through years of historical work on the Reformation.[3] More important still, this is the history of ideas, arguably the most difficult form of historiography. To do it well, the history of ideas requires a series of additional skills, including a strong grasp of conceptual analysis, an ability to see significance

---

[3] Alister E. McGrath, *The Intellectual Origins of the European Reformation* (Oxford: Blackwell, 1987); Alister E. McGrath, *A Life of John Calvin: A Study in the Shaping of Western Culture* (1990).

overlooked by others, a recognition of how a larger setting, personal history and authentic originality all co-operate in shaping thought, and, of course, a clarity of style.

The historical approach allows him to gather in and reflect upon the various viewpoints that have been expressed on particular issues, sometimes over a period of centuries. This leads him to articulate an interpretation or even a solution that takes all of these into account. An analysis of issues that have arisen within the historical process, but which are not informed by a detailed study of the history of that process, often lack interpretative maturity and authority because they can fail to notice inner structures and ambiguities that may lie hidden below the surface of the modern concept.

Good history also requires a sympathy and tolerance for all sources. I have found this to be almost always present in these writings, but occasionally there is a hint of impatience with theologians, philosophers and scientists who make assertions that are historically inaccurate.[4] As a competent scientist – with an Oxford first – McGrath is also irritated by erroneous or naïve science.[5] He barely conceals his impatience, also, with those who are intolerant and polemical.[6] Occasionally, even, he judges movements of thought, such as process theology, to be transitory episodes within the orthodox Christian tradition.[7] Such remarks, always restrained, spice his writings wonderfully. His polite but frank criticisms of the positions or particular concepts of luminaries in the field such as Ian Barbour and Wolfhart Pannenberg guarantee a lively response.[8] My only reservation here is that, although McGrath's criticisms are always well founded, the tone of his criticism of some of the more heterodox Christian thinkers can be quite stern.[9]

Another feature of his method is the manner in which he distances himself as an author from his own strong commitment to Christian orthodoxy. We never hear the voice of the apologist, or of devotional literature, or of the pulpit. These books can be read profitably by someone committed to Islam or to Buddhism, or without a commitment to any religion, or even to any spiritual belief, who will discover an examination of the internal coherence of arguments, or the consequences of granting certain Christian and other principles. As McGrath's writings

---

[4] McGrath, *The Foundations of Dialogue in Science and Religion* pp. 14–17.
[5] Ibid.
[6] McGrath, *Science and Religion*, pp. 191–2.
[7] Ibid., pp. 105–9; McGrath, *A Scientific Theology Volume 1*, pp. 38–41.
[8] McGrath, *A Scientific Theology Volume 1*, pp. 39–40, 135–8.
[9] Ibid., pp. 38–41.

develop, his own nuanced positions on a great variety of issues unfold, but the principles on which they are based are clearly posited for scholarly inspection, without any demand or expectation that the reader will accept them.

Those who might argue that one cannot expect objectivity in the field of science and Christianity from a Christian clergyman might well consider whether one can expect objectivity in the study of evolution from a biologist, or objectivity in the study of history from a Marxist. For studies to be scholarly, one needs to declare openly as much as one can recognize of one's own assumptions and spectacles, one needs to be critical of them, to keep them at a certain distance and justify them by some rational method. One must also respect one's readers by assuming that they need to be persuaded by honest arguments, and by not taking it for granted that they agree with you. A reader will find all of this in McGrath's project.

An interesting feature of McGrath's science is not simply that it is authoritative, as one would expect from someone with a doctorate and research experience in biochemistry. Far more interesting is the freshness and clarity of his accounts of scientific topics. He has also studied the most recent historical scholarship illuminating the scientific fields he introduces. He has gone beyond the usual conventional explanations of modern physics and biology and avoided clichés and terms meaningless to the layman and to many scientists (such as 'space-time curvature'), which are, nevertheless, frequently paraded in public by popularizers, and even by professional scientists, as if they had an obvious meaning. McGrath has carried out a deeper analysis and found ways of explaining the scientific concepts he is interested in which are both rigorous and accessible.

McGrath openly acknowledges his debt to the Scottish Barthian theologian Thomas F. Torrance.[10] Torrance's commitment to the importance of the relationship between science and religion had made him very appealing to McGrath. Although McGrath never even hints at this, Torrance does not have a formal scientific training, and McGrath's model in this field is a fully professional competence both in science and in theology. More important for McGrath, perhaps, is Torrance's emphasis on the possibility of a new or refreshed natural theology anchored within a larger Christian theological framework, which sees nature as God's creation, man as made in the image of God, and which stresses that our primary access to God is through Christ.[11] A second

---

[10] McGrath, *The Foundations of Dialogue in Science and Religion*, pp. 34–5.
[11] See McGrath, *Thomas F. Torrance*, part II.

figure to whom McGrath acknowledges a considerable debt is the philosopher of science Roy Bhaskar,[12] for his articulation of a satisfying critical realism that takes into full account the importance of the social setting of science.

The major theme that runs through these books is McGrath's examination of the structures of scientific reasoning and their comparison with the structures of theological reasoning. He considers again and again how theology has influenced the foundational assumptions and content of science in the past, and vice versa. Another constant theme is the recognition of diversity and a suspicion of essentialism. For McGrath, there is no such thing as scientific method, but only scientific *methods*, finely adapted to their subject matter. The same applies also to theological method.

He considers a wide range of methodological points of comparison and diversity, such as the criteria for justification of basic principles both in science and theology, how theories are tested in each discipline, whether any part of positive science may safely be considered authoritative for theology, the role of theoretical entities and conjecture both in science and theology, and whether and in which respects theological theories can consider themselves provisional, as many theories in physics do. He is not afraid to face any issue with the same analytical and critical apparatus, however difficult it may have been historically for theology or science. Perhaps his most striking methodological achievement is to show the enormous range of parallels, despite marked differences, that exist between scientific and religious or theological thinking.[13] This should put an end among reflective thinkers, once and for all, to simplistic assessments of the relations between the methods of science and theology.

The same dislike of essentialism is noticeable in his reluctance to take sides on an old dispute: How have science and religion been related in the past? How ought they to be related today? It is clear that McGrath believes they have been related in an enormous variety of ways in the past, and in particular since the late nineteenth century in some circles in terms of a warfare metaphor. McGrath clearly expects that this variety of relationships will continue into the future, and that it is futile to try, in any simplistic way, to identify what this relationship *ought* to be, or has been. Indeed, he adopts a studied indifference on this issue. He is clearly concerned, nevertheless, that it ought *not* to be one of

---

[12] McGrath, *A Scientific Theology Volume 2*, p. xv.
[13] These will be discussed throughout this chapter.

warfare, that dialogue should be established, and that the tone of discussions should be one of mutual respect.[14]

A slightly puzzling feature of his rhetorical strategy is that from time to time he makes vigorous statements apparently defending 'the fall of classical foundationalism'[15] or social constructivism or postmodernism. It soon turns out, however, that his positions are more modest. In his frequent attacks on 'foundationalism', he is criticizing a narrow view of acceptable foundations for theology, or overconfidence in the possibility of deducing theology from a set of axioms in a complete logical sequence. Similarly, he is no social constructionist, but he does defend a balanced view of the importance of social influence and tradition on theological thinking.[16]

An interest in postmodernism runs through McGrath's texts, a movement that he interprets as a cultural sensibility without absolutes or fixed certainties or foundations.[17] Undoubtedly, this has made him more aware of diversity in all fields of thought, and responsive to the cultural influences that shape thought. But McGrath is no postmodernist. He thanks the postmodernists for their insights, but pursues a course of investigation with an attitude to the furniture of nature, and to our knowledge of it, that belongs to the central traditions of Western science, theology, historiography and law. The concern of almost all scientists to discover truths about nature, and the enormous success of the sciences, again and again in his writings feature for him as a very strong reason to take their claims about the facts and contents of nature seriously.[18]

An important argument, therefore, running through all of these texts is the possibility of access to genuine knowledge, whether in science or in religion. For example, McGrath carries out an extended examination and critique of the Kantian position that all regularity in nature is a construct of the mind, and of the more recent position that all thinking is socially determined.[19] In the end, he settles into a position which accepts that we can sometimes project our own constructs on to nature, and which emphasizes the social location of all theorizing, both in science

---

[14] McGrath, *The Foundations of Dialogue in Science and Religion*, pp. 20–8, 33.

[15] McGrath, *A Scientific Theology Volume 2*, p. vii.

[16] See especially ibid., ch. 10.

[17] McGrath, *The Foundations of Dialogue in Science and Religion*, p. 9.

[18] McGrath, *A Scientific Theology Volume 2*, pp. 178–80.

[19] McGrath, *The Foundations of Dialogue in Science and Religion*, pp. 37–8; McGrath, *A Scientific Theology Volume 1*, pp. 223–5; McGrath, *A Scientific Theology Volume 2*, pp. 180–91.

and theology. However, he views all of this as perfectly compatible with the 'critical realism' he adopts and which is a pervasive feature of his texts. McGrath the theologian is clearly influenced here by the attitudes towards knowledge embedded in the praxis of science by McGrath the scientist.

I have noticed strong developments in these books, and they are best examined in chronological sequence. I will select those themes that I have found of special interest, or that I feel are of particular importance for the field of science and religion.

1. The Foundations of Dialogue in Science and Religion

This book attempts to establish the foundations for dialogue between science and Christianity by studying and comparing methods used in each field – how knowledge is gained and tested, how evidence is assimilated, and how an understanding of the world of nature, or of Christianity, is constructed and represented. McGrath is concerned to respect the enormous diversity among religions, and also among the sciences, and to avoid simplistic generalizations. He focuses on Christianity, which, uniquely perhaps, has grown up in a close and even intimate relationship with natural philosophy. He also focuses on the 'grand tradition' in Christian theology,[20] understanding theology as intellectual reflection on the content of the Christian faith. He stresses the complexity of relationships. Physics and cosmology, for example, stand in a very different relationship to religious thought than biology or psychology, with different deep-level assumptions and commitments, as well as different methodologies, styles of theorizing and terminologies. These differences need to be respected in any dialogue.

He accepts, of course, that science today is committed to searching for natural rather than supernatural or divine explanations of nature. He interprets this commitment as a working assumption defining the natural sphere of science, which can be shared by believer and unbeliever alike. A variety of recent changes in the intellectual interests of scholars, and in global circumstances, have opened up new possibilities of dialogue between science and religion. The abandonment of a 'whiggish' approach to history – which, with certain historians of science, had focused interest only on those features that led to present theories – has led to the recognition of religious belief as a major factor in the history of scientists and of science. Another attitude common in

---

[20] McGrath, *The Foundations of Dialogue in Science and Religion*, p. 32.

the mid twentieth century was the belief that religion was in permanent decline, and that the number of believing scientists would gradually dwindle to insignificance. However, polls have shown that as many as 40 per cent of scientists have some form of personal religious belief today, and that this percentage has remained fairly stable throughout the twentieth century. Today, no scientific body can assume that it speaks for the overwhelming majority of its members if it adopts a hostile attitude to religion. Furthermore, there is now a greater respect for minorities within every profession.

Again, the resurgence of religion worldwide, in particular of fundamentalist Islam and Christianity, have forced the recognition that it needs to be taken seriously, even if in terms of political prudence only. It is also recognized that any militant hostility or triumphalism of science towards religion, or vice versa, can only damage the common good. The present climate is best served, therefore, by mutual respect and dialogue. Indeed, even as recently as the 1980s, science often seemed quite hostile to religion, and theologians seemed little interested in science. All of this seems to be changing rapidly today.

McGrath is concerned, as many historians of science and religion are, to rebut the myth that, historically, science and religion have always been locked in mortal combat. Science has, indeed, often fulfilled the role of rebellion against an oppressive prevailing ideology, whether it be secular or religious. However, conflict may have many dimensions, and can rarely be reduced simply to a conflict between science and religion. It can represent a struggle within Christianity itself – between different groups of equally committed Christians. It may also represent a power struggle between different elites. Indeed, Christianity has often become associated with a particular clerical or other power elite, thereby provoking hostility from scientists and others. The polar opposite, the view noticeable within certain religious circles today, that science is its enemy, appears to have emerged within the context of twentieth-century North American fundamentalism.[21]

For McGrath, a major revision of the state of the relationships between religion and the natural sciences is now required. A combination of a more accurate and tolerant historiography, with a recognition of the importance of social and cultural influences in shaping both scientific and religious thought, should assist in making this possible.

For McGrath, influenced by Torrance, the sciences and theologies are distinct chiefly in terms of their subject matters, their methodologies and their historical developments. Nevertheless, each of these features of

---

[21] Ibid., pp. 20–8.

both fields overlap, and it is inappropriate to try to force them into isolated compartments. This overlap undoubtedly creates difficulties, but it also means that they can mutually stimulate and illuminate each other at various points.[22]

Three major methodological concerns common to both fields are found by McGrath to be the explicability of the world, how to deal with the extra-systemic reality that controls interpretation and theorizing, and how this external reality is to be represented.[23] Science and religion also share deep-level commitments to the intelligibility of the world, for example, and to the search for an order underlying the complexity of being.

1.1. Order and law and beauty[24]

One of the most significant parallels between the natural sciences and religion is the fundamental conviction that the world is characterized by order and intelligibility. This commitment, originally derived from Greek concepts of order and intelligibility, was enhanced and reinterpreted by the Christian doctrine of creation, and by the doctrine that humankind is made in the 'image and likeness of God'. Developing this theme, McGrath discusses the emergence of the doctrine of *creatio ex nihilo* towards the end of the second century, partly as a response to Gnosticism, partly from a more sophisticated reading of the Old Testament.[25] This was also accompanied by a reaffirmation of the Old Testament declaration of the fundamental orderliness and goodness of the natural world, a concept that was of foundational importance for the encouragement both of science and of ethics. This eliminated a radical dualism between God and creation, and the natural order was seen as reflecting the truth, beauty and goodness of God in a stable manner, all enabling and encouraging conditions for the emergence of science.

The doctrine of creation, seen as the creation of an order and coherence that reflects God and points to God, justifies the study of nature. Even more important historically for science, perhaps, is that the doctrine of creation, and of the concomitant doctrine of the continual and consistent exercise of God's sustaining will, underpins a belief in the uniformity of nature, and in the existence and persistence of the 'laws

---

[22] Ibid., p. 34.
[23] Ibid., pp. 34–5.
[24] Ibid., ch. 2.
[25] Ibid., pp. 43–4.

of nature'. The latter term – which began to be used widely in the eighteenth century – was not simply a description of discovered regularity, but also carried with it the connotation of a divine law-giver.[26] For Carl Linnaeus (1707–78), the great Swedish taxonomist, the order within the plant and animal kingdoms rests upon and somehow reflects the divine creation of the world.[27]

The association of the concept of a law of nature with a divine law-giver, or even the notion that there is a 'law-giver', has been largely lost with the Western secularization of scientific concepts and foundations. Nevertheless, these remain private beliefs for many scientists and for others. Of course, a confidence in the orderliness of nature is now supported by much evidence about nature and by the success of the rational enterprise of science itself.

However, the notion of laws of nature has been ambivalent for the relationship between science and Christianity.[28] McGrath discusses the peculiarly British tradition, largely deriving from Isaac Newton (1642–1727), that science is the ally of religion, and in particular of natural theology. In the case of Newton's cosmology, the very mathematically expressed order that he found in the cosmos became self-sufficient for the eighteenth-century deists, leading gradually to a view of the irrelevance of God to the world of nature. Nature as clockwork could, indeed, be seen as implying a great clockmaker, but others saw it in terms of nature's self-sufficiency. Of course, once God is fully removed, the old problem of justifying a belief in the uniformity of nature over space and time returns.

The more recent development of what is somewhat misleadingly known as 'chaos' theory essentially shows that in many exercises of the quantitative laws of nature outcomes are so sensitive to initial and trajectory conditions that they are unpredictable and highly contingent. 'Chaos' theory does not mean that nature is always chaotic in the outcomes of its laws, and, indeed, a kind of order does generally emerge even from the more 'chaotic' processes. The full implications of this theory for a theology of nature have yet to be worked out.[29]

McGrath pursues further the analysis of the concept of a 'law of nature' with respect to its bearing on theories of divine action in the world. Here it becomes a concept of enormous importance and even

---

[26] Ibid., p. 59.
[27] Ibid., pp. 65–7.
[28] Ibid., pp. 57–8, 67–9.
[29] Ibid., pp. 58–9.

tension in the science and religion dialogue. He summarizes the views of one modern scientist, Paul Davies,[30] according to whom the laws of nature are *universal*, *absolute* (in the sense that they do not depend on the state of mind of the observer), *eternal* (and perhaps not just coeval with the age of the universe, because they somehow reflect eternal mathematical relations) and *omnipotent*, in that there are no exceptions. Most if not all of these claimed features of scientific laws can, of course, be challenged in specific instances even by scientists, and seem to apply to physics much more than they do to biology or psychology. However, it is perhaps a not-uncommon expression of the views of many natural scientists about scientific laws.

One apparent implication of assuming these characteristics of laws of nature is that God cannot be omnipotent, since even God cannot violate a law of nature.[31] McGrath points out that this issue has been accommodated since the Middle Ages by the distinction made by William of Occam (*c.* 1285–1349) between God's 'absolute' power and his 'ordained' power. The latter represents the manner in which God respects the integrity of the creation he has established, deciding to restrict his own exercise of power. Of course, even within the self-imposed restrictions of his ordained power, God is still able to interact with the world. In this view, therefore, there is no tension between God and the laws of nature. One recent attempt to explain how God can act in nature, without violating the laws he has committed himself to observe, is through the many choices of outcome offered by the true randomness of quantum events. Such solutions are, of course, highly speculative.

Turning to philosophers,[32] McGrath summarizes as follows some of the views they have adopted of the laws of nature: an ordering imposed by the mind; a regular association of phenomena without any underlying causal nexus; and a realist interpretation which interprets the laws as reflecting a true casual nexus. McGrath points out that within the practice of science itself, which is as much the focus of his investigations as is philosophy, laws of nature are seen as an intrinsic feature of the world.

McGrath also explores the theological implications of the enormous interest today in symmetry in modern physics According to Pierre Curie (1859–1906), the symmetry of the cause is transmitted to the effect, but

---

[30] Ibid., p. 60.
[31] Ibid., p. 61.
[32] Ibid., pp. 63–5.

it can be equal or less there, not greater.[33] Similarly, in the tradition of Thomas Aquinas (1225–74) the 'perfection' of God is somehow reflected in his creation, although it will be present there to a lesser degree. He points out that perfection has long been associated with symmetry in Christian thinking. By analogy with Aquinas' 'Fifth Way' of inferring God's existence from nature, symmetries in the fundamental laws of nature can be argued to reflect the perfection and beauty of God, giving a new lease of life, perhaps, to the Fifth Way.

In the twentieth century a growing emphasis has been noticeable among scientists on the beauty of physical and mathematical theories as a mark of their truth. Some even argue that the search for a beautiful theory has led to scientific discoveries. McGrath feels that beauty in nature is an important implication of the doctrine of creation[34] – despite the postmodernist claim that what is beautiful is so defined by a power elite to establish their hegemony. The 'beauty of God' is an enduring theme in Christian thinking. It is particularly emphasized by the eighteenth-century American theologian Jonathan Edwards (1703–58) and by the twentieth-century Roman Catholic theologian Hans Urs von Balthasar (1905–1988) that the beauty of God is to be found in the creation. It can be argued, therefore, that a strong doctrine of creation leads to the expectation of beauty and symmetry in nature as a reflection of God. There are problems with this, of course, since some mathematicians view mathematics as uncreated, simply existing timelessly and everlastingly, waiting to be 'discovered'.

McGrath does not wish to draw the conclusion that these correlations between science and a theology of creation constitute a proof of God's existence. He is concerned, rather, to draw attention to the convergence and complementarity or consonance in these matters, between science and religion. Although no longer significant for the academy, privately these consonances continue to influence the views of many scientists and others.[35]

---

[33] John Roche, 'A Critical Study of Symmetry in Physics from Galileo to Newton' in M. Doncel, A. Hermann, L. Michel and A. Pais (eds), *Symmetries in Physics 1600–1980* (Barcelona: Bellaterra, 1987), pp. 19–24; McGrath, *The Foundations of Dialogue in Science and Religion*, pp. 69–73.

[34] McGrath, *The Foundations of Dialogue in Science and Religion*, pp. 73–9.

[35] Ibid., p. 80.

1.2. *Comparing modes of investigation*[36]

McGrath next looks at the investigation of the world, accepting that there is a considerable divergence here between the disciplines of science and of theology. Experimentation and revelation seem to be the chief distinguishing features of the primary access of science and religion, respectively, to their proper subject matters.

Increasingly, however, modern science relies on experiment and observation to justify inferences to entities that are not themselves directly observable – such as the spin of the electron. In other cases, the testing of theories by experiment has to be delayed indefinitely, or is even impossible – as in the many worlds hypothesis in cosmology, or in the historical sciences such as geology and evolution. However, granting the enormous complexity and ambivalence of the relations between theory, observation and experiment in science, there is general consensus among scientists that, ultimately, theories stand or fall at the court of exact observation or experiment. Is religion and theology very different from this?

According to McGrath, in the consensual classical Christian understanding of revelation,[37] God discloses his nature experientially to humanity through the life of Jesus Christ, especially through the Christian experience of his death and resurrection. This, however, is interpreted as God seeking humans, and not as humans taking the initiative in seeking out God. This is a very different conception, of course, from the active exploration of nature under human initiative that commonly occurs in science. However, although science and Christianity are based on experiences of a very different kind, there are resemblances in the impact of those experiences. Just as certain critical scientific discoveries have forced a revaluation of scientific theories, the death and resurrection of Christ, for example, forced a revision among Christians of the later Roman Empire of the received 'Classic' Greek concept of God. Could God be said to suffer, for example? This revaluation led to radically new concepts about God, such as that of the Trinity. The religious experiences of Christians throughout history have led again and again to doctrinal revaluations and transformations, most notably in the High Middle Ages and also during the Reformation. Reflection on revelation and the reactions of individuals and religious communities to fresh interpretations are, therefore, routes by which Christianity revaluates and develops its doctrines.

---

[36] Ibid., ch. 3.
[37] Ibid., pp. 84–7.

McGrath also discusses whether experience can falsify Christian doctrines: for example, whether the existence of evil constitutes a compelling refutation of the belief in a good omnipotent God.[38] McGrath points out that this can be interpreted as an observation confronting a theory. Such situations arise frequently in science. If we follow the scientific method, must the theory of a good omnipotent God be abandoned? McGrath shows that, in science, such confrontations do imply a conflict between observation and the theory as a whole, but it can be very difficult to identify precisely where the conflict lies, whether in the interpretation of the evidence or in some as yet unidentified aspect of the theory. In the case of the problem of evil, our own cognitive limits may also be responsible for the conflict – does it represent a complexity in nature perhaps, or in the reasons behind divine behaviour, which are beyond our grasp? Alternatively, is there a greater good at work here, which we are at present unable to understand? Correspondingly, although it troubled him, Charles Darwin (1809–82) did not abandon his theory when Lord Kelvin (1824–1907) argued that the sun was much younger than required for his theory. Darwin hoped that subsequent research would resolve this difficulty, as it did. Similarly, a sophisticated knowledge of scientific theory-change in the face of evidence suggests that arguments against the classical concept of God on the basis of evil, though real difficulties, must not be naïvely interpreted as immediate refutations.

Both the scientific and theological communities can be thought of as wrestling with the ambiguities of experience, of very different kinds and in very different ways, of course, but in ways that are not totally different.[39] Both disciplines generate theories that are highly complex and often counter-intuitive, and both view these theories as consistent with, even demanded by, the 'phenomena'. Science is by no means raw experiment: it is interpretation, it is theorizing and it involves theory-change. Its concepts are moderated by experiment, but in ways that leave considerable room for exploratory theorizing. Furthermore, it is not true that science only believes what is empirically given. Unobserved entities – such as evolutionary missing links or the virtual photon – are frequently postulated as the best explanation of a known body of data. Very similar features can be identified in theology: God, for example, could reasonably be inferred as the best explanation of the way the world is. These structural parallels – although by no means complete – are not surprising, since both scientific and theological theorizing are the products of minds that have been schooled in a richly connected cultural milieu for 2000 years.

---

[38] Ibid., pp. 94–8.
[39] Ibid., pp. 87–8.

1.3. Natural theology[40]

McGrath raises the issue of whether, in the many-faceted dialogue between science and theology, there may be areas where they can meet and create a true interdisciplinary subject. He asks whether natural theology might be one such subject. McGrath is not concerned here to develop a natural theology that is a kind of extension of natural science. His interest is to explore the kind of natural theology that emerges from within the framework of a Christ-centred Christian doctrine of creation. He is concerned to answer the question, if the world is God's creation, how might this creation bear the hallmark of God's handiwork – perhaps as an artist's distinctive style is revealed in his or her handiwork? Is it to be looked for in human reason as an image of God, or in the ordering of the world, or in the fertility of mathematics in describing the world, or in the beauty of the world? McGrath sees each of these as pointers to the greater reality of God's self-revelation.

He draws attention to strong theological traditions, especially the two-book tradition (Scripture and the 'book of nature'), which in different periods have explored each of these aspects of God's self-revelation in the world. Of course, these traditions stress that the epistemic distance between God and creation is vast, and that we can arrive only at intimations of the nature of God from creation. A natural theology, pursued in this manner, while beginning with and guided by a belief in God, can find further reinforcement of that belief in nature. This kind of virtuous circle is often very evident within science itself: guided by a commitment to a theory, further insight and confirmation is often found for that theory.

Theologians have criticized natural theology in its historical manifestations – most severely, perhaps, by Karl Barth (1886–1968).[41] Natural theology can seem to offer knowledge of God arrived at under human initiative and by human efforts alone, unaided by divine revelation, thereby undervaluing the importance of revelation. It makes God an inference from natural evidence rather than a basic belief; it pretentiously claims to grasp the ineffable nature of God; it has led to Deism, to a view of God as a clockmaker otherwise uninvolved with the world, and has thereby functioned in the past as a halfway house to atheism. It can even seem to set itself up as a 'natural' religion, independent of any existing religious tradition. In more recent versions – as in some interpretations of the intelligent design movement – it can even seem to make God directly responsible for creating horrors in nature, such as the Aids virus.

---

[40] Ibid., pp. 98–118.
[41] Ibid., pp. 103–11.

Over the past two millennia Christian theology has gradually developed an enormous sensitivity to the theological implications of a great raft of intellectual positions. Its criticism of an autonomous natural theology cannot be seen as a kind of theoretical imperialism that wishes to bend everything new to its own established framework. There are real problems with forms of natural theology whose theological implications for Christianity have not been fully thought through.

Following Torrance, McGrath's concern here is to rehabilitate natural theology among theologians in the face of such severe criticisms. My own view is that many natural theologies are being promoted today, not all of which merit these criticisms, even though they may be neutral with respect to a specifically Christian setting. In some of these the existence of God is held to be 'consonant' with science, rather than a demonstrative proof from natural evidence. The cosmic Big Bang and the anthropic principle – the fine-tuning of the forces in nature – and even the remarkable fact of our own existence, all of which seem to be highly contingent phenomena, are examples of 'consonance' or 'consistency' with the concept of a non-contingent Creator God. Such a natural theology seems to be immune from some, at least, of the criticisms mentioned above. It does not pretend to infer any account of the nature of God from nature itself, beyond declaring a consonance with the view that God created nature. Indeed, this approach often borrows the Christian concept of God to give content to the term 'God' itself. Of course, it must be made clear that theology in this sense is not anchored in, or part of, the central theological tradition of Christianity, and must not pretend to belong to that tradition. Nevertheless, this approach is more likely to be influential on those who do not already believe in Christianity, or even in God. Indeed, for many, anthropic fine-tuning functions as a powerful intuitive argument for God.

1.4. Biblical interpretation[42]

Another important and enduring theme pursued by McGrath, in the context of relationships between scientific and religious thinking, is biblical interpretation.

During the patristic period Augustine of Hippo (354–430) stressed the importance of respecting the conclusions of the sciences in relation to biblical exegesis when interpreting passages open to diverse interpretations. Science can assist in finding the most appropriate interpretation. McGrath argues that this helped to ensure that Christian theology

---

[42] Ibid., pp. 118–29.

never became trapped in a pre-scientific worldview. Nevertheless, he points out that a problem with this approach was that by deferring to scientific beliefs, such as that of Aristotelian cosmology, they became so firmly rooted in the thought of the church that they became an obstacle to later revisions by science itself, and by the church, of these beliefs – most notably in the Galileo affair. Augustine himself imported current psychological theories into his doctrine of the Trinity.[43] The insistence of the Council of Trent (1545–63) that the consensus of previous generations in interpreting Scripture should remain normative trapped early modern Roman Catholic theologians in the scientific worldview of late Antiquity.[44] The problem here lies in drawing a distinction between the permanent factual discoveries of science and the more transitory components of scientific theories, a distinction that is by no means easy to draw even by scientists themselves, and not simply by theologians.

McGrath pays most attention to the history of that biblical interpretative tradition which views the language of the Bible as accommodated to the people for whom it was written.[45] This view was particularly developed by medieval theologians, as well as by sixteenth-century Protestant theologians such as John Calvin (1509–64). McGrath stresses that the real issue with the church in the whole Galileo affair concerned the correct interpretation of the Bible, although a series of other issues and events related to authority, patronage and politics made matters much worse. Galileo and his supporters applied an accommodationist approach to the Bible in justifying heliocentrism, an interpretive approach that was not itself controversial. The controversy lay in directing this approach to passages of the Bible for which there was no precedent, an application recently forbidden by the Council of Trent.

McGrath also draws attention to a major trend within historical evangelicalism, which has sought to reconcile traditional biblical accounts of creation with established insights of the natural sciences.[46] He lists instances where this tradition has used accommodationism to find ways of reconciling God's action in the world with the theory of evolution.

---

[43] Ibid., p. 120.
[44] Ibid., pp. 120–1.
[45] Ibid., pp. 122–9.
[46] Ibid., pp. 129–30.

1.5. Explanation[47]

By interpreting much scientific theorizing as 'inference to the best explanation', McGrath asks whether religion carries out similar explanatory inferences. For McGrath, although an explanation of the way things are is not the primary purpose of religion, religions do offer some explanations.[48] The philosopher Richard Swinburne, for example, points to the explanatory power of theism in relation to the existence and ordering of the universe.

Granting the extraordinary variety of meanings of the term 'explanation', McGrath attempts no systematic survey of this topic, and instead takes as a case history Darwin's appeal to the best explanation of problems that arose from his fieldwork in the study of organisms.[49] These included how to explain adaptation; how to explain the disappearance of some species; the uneven distribution of geographical life forms throughout the earth; and vestigial structures, such as male mammalian nipples. This search led Darwin, of course, to the doctrine of 'natural selection', and he argues powerfully that it possesses greater explanatory power than its older rival, the doctrine of fixity of species. Darwin, although he recognized serious anomalies and loose ends in his theory, nevertheless felt it was valid. Even today, loose ends remain, yet the theory is enormously authoritative and there is a confident hope among biologists that anomalies and unanswered questions will gradually be cleared up.

Precisely the same explanatory issues arise in any religious system.[50] Anomalies exist that are similarly tolerated on warranted grounds. Both science and religion accept that they confront present mysteries. The Christian understanding of the world offers to its supporters a coherent and plausible explanation, yet it does not explain everything with equal plausibility – most obviously the problem of evil and suffering. These difficulties can give rise to intellectual, institutional and existential tensions. Is this a difficulty that will eventually be resolved, or a fatal flaw that will eventually overthrow the theory? There are, of course, many puzzles and anomalies both in science and religion that are man-made – or mind-made – rather than reflecting true (ontological) features of reality. Logic and history suggest that, as with science, we cannot now tell what the eventual outcome will be, but it does not prevent those

---

[47] Ibid., pp. 131–8.
[48] See also McGrath, *A Scientific Theology Volume 2*, p. 294.
[49] McGrath, *The Foundations of Dialogue in Science and Religion*, pp. 132–4.
[50] Ibid., p. 135.

committed to either system from remaining committed to it. There is 'credal commitment' to theories both in science and in religion.

McGrath then discusses eschatology – the doctrine of the last things – one of the most speculative areas of the relationship between science and theology.[51] In particular, he is interested in eschatological 'verification'. The eschatological approach argues that present problems will be resolved at the end of time. Issues such as the apparent incompatibility between a loving and all-powerful God and suffering are viewed as too complex at present for our limited understanding to resolve, but that these issues will be resolved when we die. McGrath points out that there is a secularized version of this view to be seen in many scientific theories which suppose that anomalies will be resolved in the fullness of time.

A related point is that there is a deep intuition within science that the forbidding complexity of some scientific theories are more likely to reflect our feeble attempts at theorizing rather than nature herself. It is widely believed in science that nature, when properly understood in the fullness of time, will be found to be simple.

It is clear that science and theology share to a remarkable degree a common rationality and have cross-fertilized each other in innumerable ways since Antiquity.

1.6. Critical realism[52]

McGrath then goes on to address philosophers and theologians more than scientists on the issue of the relationships between our interpretation and theories, on the one hand, and the reality of the world on the other. The extraordinary predictive success of the exact sciences, and of the technologies deriving from them, have deeply persuaded scientists of the physical reality of most of the laws and theoretical entities that have been discovered. The laws of hydrodynamics, for example, have shaped the design of aeroplanes and also explain why aeroplanes fly. Natural scientists tend to be realists, at least with respect to significant portions of their theories. Even unobserved entities, such as the bound electric field, or seemingly inaccessible entities, such as the first group of homo sapiens, are interpreted by science as candidates for physical reality, which admittedly have not yet achieved that status. Nevertheless, they tend to be granted it in an honourary way. Scientists also generally regard objective nature as the ultimate goal, norm and court of appeal of

---

[51] Ibid., pp. 135–8.
[52] Ibid., ch. 4.

their researches. For most scientists there are truths of nature 'out there', even if we do not now know what they are or cannot test or verify them. How does this attitude in science to nature, and to our knowledge of it, relate to the central tradition in theology, which also is realist?

Various philosophers, such as Immanuel Kant (1724–1804) and Ernst Mach (1838–1916), and more recently Michael Dummett and Bas von Fraassen, have postulated such a restricted view of reality as effectively to reject the claim that much of science describes facts independent of the human mind.[53] McGrath critiques a narrow verificationism,[54] which would write off most historical statements, and even the statement that the far side of the moon existed before we observed it. Furthermore, what began as theories or theoretical entities, such as the roundness of the earth, or atoms, have often been brought into the scope of observation through the microscope or telescope, or by some other advance in the technology of science, to the satisfaction of scientists. What is now unobservable may not always be so. Scientists often have reason to be confident that an entity exists and of its identity (an ability to distinguish it sharply from other objects) even if knowledge of its properties is limited or if that knowledge changes with time. The evolution of the concept of the electron, from an entity arising from experimental work on electrified gases in the late nineteenth century to the present extraordinarily complex concept, is a case in point. The grounds for the assertion of the existence of an entity are not to be confused with the grounds for asserting exactly what its nature is, and may be compatible with a great variety of views of the latter. From this perspective, McGrath, following Rom Harré,[55] distinguished three types of theory: theories that concern observables; theories that infer from observables to the presently unobserved (which may later become observables); and theories (often of an abstract mathematical type) that represent entities that are unobservable in principle, such as quantum states.

In applying these reflections to theological theorizing[56] McGrath notes that the classical theological tradition is analogous to science in that it holds that God exists independently of our recognition or otherwise of this fact. Indeed, although God cannot now be known directly, and knowledge of God is by analogy or by accommodation, this does not imply for religion (as it would not imply in science) that God is

---

53 Ibid., pp. 141–8.
54 Ibid., pp. 148–50.
55 Ibid., p. 148.
56 Ibid., pp. 151–5.

purely a construct of our minds or of our culture. Christianity also maintains that, although the Godhead is unobservable by present human means, he will ultimately be observed directly in the beatific vision.

Scientists, such as Albert Einstein (1879–1955), view nature as scientifically intelligible and see scientific explanations of nature as grounded in and controlled by an objective nature itself. Similarly, theology attempts to give a faithful account of an intelligible and objective reality that requires description. McGrath points out, however, that the parallel with science is not exact. The doctrine of the incarnation, for example, affirms the interaction of God with human history. This makes inevitable, much more than in the natural sciences, the intermingling of historically and culturally conditioned elements in the way in which God and the Christian life are conceived and expressed.[57] Nevertheless, a critically realist theology would wish to affirm the reality of all of these elements independently of our attempts to describe them, and that these rich realities control our descriptions. Although there have been anti-realist theological traditions within Western Christianity, there is noticeably a growing commitment today to realism within theology. This is paralleled, interestingly, by a similar growth of realism within the philosophy of science. McGrath also argues that a rejection of overconfidence in the powers of deductive reason and an acceptance of the historical and cultural location of all theologizing[58] is quite compatible with a form of critical realism in theology.

1.7. To what does religious language refer?

Is the language and conceptualities of Christian discourse an arbitrary construction reflecting the whims of historical accident, or is it somehow controlled by external, extra-cultural and extra-historical constraints? McGrath speaks of a long tradition of theological enquiry that asks how affirmations about God are derived and how they relate to affirmations about the world of the senses.[59] Christian theology, of course, asserts that God exists independently of our knowledge, and also somehow transcends our possibilities of knowledge. Here there is a tension between a recognition of the ineffable nature of God and attempts to express that nature. Even those who pursue 'apophatic' or 'negative' theology – God is infinitely beyond all human understanding – nevertheless do generally assert that he exists independently of us. McGrath

---

[57] Ibid., p. 158.
[58] Ibid., pp. 160–4.
[59] Ibid., pp. 151–4.

detects both a tradition of naïve realism and of critical realism in talk about God in Christian history. He pays particular attention to the postliberal 'Yale School' of divinity and other thinkers who insist that religious and ethical conceptions and theories are mediated through the historical faith communities in which believers and theologians live.[60]

An important point that might be developed further here is that, even if we do see objects through the lenses of our cultural and historical locations, this does not necessarily mean that we are unable to distinguish between the object and the lens. Indeed, the very fact that we can make such distinctions demonstrates that they have been recognized in the past. It takes considerable effort to do so, of course, but much can be done, especially if we engage with a community of critical scholars who are attempting to identify just such frameworks. Similar considerations apply to science, which itself, of course, has emerged within certain communities, and is coloured and shaped by them in various ways. This is well known intuitively within science, and non-scientists such as Thomas Kuhn (1922–96) have explored it in some detail. Once we know what these influences are we can usually distinguish between content and context.

Social factors are also important in determining the positive reception or otherwise of scientific theories and of theological innovations. In religion and theology ideas that are mooted may either receive a warm reception and eventually become 'doctrine' or even 'dogma', or a consensus of the religious community may eventually emerge which views these innovations simply as theological 'opinion', or more negatively. Cultural and other circumstances, not simply religious, may influence this reception. This element of the community response to the acceptance or otherwise to theories is, therefore, at least as important in religion as it is in science. McGrath here makes the reflexive point that dialogue between science and religion itself takes place within a community, and it is important to ensure that the community values the dialogue.[61] For social effectiveness it must be linked to the development of research programmes, institutions and societies within the community.

1.8. Models, analogies and metaphors[62]

McGrath then goes on to study ways in which the world is represented in science, and in religion. One of the most significant functions of models,

---

[60] Ibid., pp. 153–4; McGrath, *A Scientific Theology Volume 2*, pp. 38–43.
[61] McGrath, *The Foundations of Dialogue in Science and Religion*, pp. 163–4.
[62] Ibid., ch. 5.

analogies and metaphors in both science and religion is to offer a visual image of something that may lie beyond our natural or even assisted powers of sensory experience. These simplified models can allow some features, a least, of enormously complex systems to be studied and understood.

The manner in which analogies are generated, validated and applied provides one of the most interesting parallels between science and Christianity. Newton maintained a doctrine of 'the analogy of nature': that nature in her myriad operations somehow maintains close analogies with herself.[63] There remains in today's science a deep-seated belief that analogies and metaphors can give us telling insights into the real properties of the 'term' of the analogy. Some authors have seen this 'analogy of nature' as imprinted in nature by the Creator. Metaphors, in particular, can, of course, become 'dead', having fulfilled their role of bridging the new with the old, and can take on the new meaning intended without ambiguity – as in the case of the concept of the electric 'field', or of the electric 'current', for example. Nevertheless, especially with models and analogies, there are dangers of various sorts, and the natural sciences have gone to considerable lengths, while recognizing the heuristic value of analogies and models, to regulate their use.

As a case in point, McGrath examines in some detail Darwin's concept of 'natural selection' created by analogy with the 'artificial' selection long practised by plant and animal breeders.[64] This analogy can imply a conscious process of selection in nature. For Darwin, this was not implied, and he feels it is natural for the metaphor to be modified in the light of the character of its new field of application. Nevertheless, McGrath detects hidden anthropomorphisms in some modern reasonings about evolution using this analogy. Can a skilfully constructed and deployed analogy 'conjure away' a serious issue in molecular biology by systematically minimizing the difficulties in understanding its origins and development?[65] Analogies possess an extraordinary propensity to mislead.

The Christian Bible and creeds make much use of models, analogies and metaphors.[66] In religion, the critical issue is that of accommodation: that access to God is not denied to those who lack knowledge or intellectual ability. The use of imagery – such as Jesus as 'the Son of God' – has often been debated within the Christian tradition. Christian theology has been forced to address the process of transition from imagery to

---

[63] Ibid., p. 169.

[64] Ibid., pp. 170–3.

[65] Ibid., p. 175.

[66] Ibid., pp. 179–80.

valid theology. Aquinas, for example, stresses that it is not appropriate to say that God is like some created object, but rather that the creature is like God in a certain analogous manner, although falling far short of the Deity.[67] Nevertheless, the analogy is not arbitrary for Aquinas, but is grounded in creation itself. There have, indeed, been inappropriate analogies introduced to Christianity, such as the 'mousetrap' theory of the atonement, in which the Devil unwittingly crucified Christ.[68] The community of believers, however, eventually rejects these.

Sometimes analogies that later prove to be false nevertheless turn out to be extremely useful in science, such as nineteenth-century analogy between sound waves in air and light waves in a supposed luminiferous ether. McGrath feels it is doubtful whether there is any exact parallel to this in Christian theology. Furthermore, he points out that the key themes of formulation, validation and possible ultimate rejection of models and analogies in science have no exact parallel in Christianity, since they are often quantitatively predictive, and subject to experimental testing and measurement.[69] Furthermore, the scientific community is not committed to any one model, and is prepared to abandon any if they fail experimental testing. In revelation, however, multiple models of God – as 'shepherd' and as 'father', for example – are used, which have considerable authority and would not be abandoned under any circumstances. They have assumed the status of 'root metaphors'. They may, indeed, require reinterpretation, but the model itself remains fundamental. Theology, of course, argues that the majesty and ineffable character of God means that any metaphor or analogy can only be partial, and that it is altogether appropriate that many are used, each capturing an intimation of some aspect of the Divinity.

1.9. Complementarity in science and religion[70]

A closer relationship between models in science and theology may be seen in relation to the concept of complementarity. Within science, early quantum theory experienced considerable difficulties of visualization, leading Niels Bohr (1885–1962) to the recognition that two complementary yet mutually exclusive models (the particle and the wave model) were both needed to represent the quantum phenomenon adequately and to describe it in an accessible manner. For Einstein and others, this was

---

[67] Ibid., p. 181.
[68] Ibid., p. 182.
[69] Ibid., pp. 184–5.
[70] Ibid., pp. 186–205.

incompatible with their belief in the underlying coherence and unity of natural entities, such as the electron. Indeed, quantum theory eventually found an abstract but unitary mathematical (and non-intuitive) language to describe quantum entities (the state vectors), which cannot be represented in classical language.

McGrath avails of the light thrown by recent historical studies of Bohr to pursue the possible theological relevance of Bohr's complementarity[71] – which can now be seen as an instrumentalist attempt to find classical pictures to describe a non-classical entity. Although accepting the ontological reality of the electron, Bohr is instrumentalist with respect to his search for a classical representation. Bohr essentially argues that two incompatible classical pictures supply different aspects of electron reality, and that neither alone is sufficient to provide a full picture. McGrath points to parallels noticed here by some scholars between Bohr on the one hand and Barth and Torrance on the other.[72] A religious phenomenon – such as Christ – sometimes discloses itself in an irreducible bipolar manner – as two natures in one subject. Christianity in the early centuries struggled with two forms of reductionism – reducing Christ to the purely human and 'reducing' Christ to the purely divine. It eventually rejected both forms of reductionism, and even rejected any third compromise model. Jesus became fully human and fully divine.[73] Clearly, the complementarity of the human and divine natures in Christ is not instrumentalist, as it was with Bohr, but is much more fundamental.

McGrath concludes this volume by suggesting that one of the most significant differences between science and religion is not in how they begin, or even proceed, but in how they end. Perhaps theology helps us to look beyond the natural order, fully accepting its majesty, but does not stop there.

2. Science and Religion: An Introduction

McGrath here has written a book that aims to explore the interface between science and religion in an accessible manner, supplying all the knowledge readers will need of science, religion and philosophy. It provides numbered lists which break down issues into manageable pieces; boxed thumbnail sketches of various scientific and theological theories;

---

[71] Ibid., pp. 187–95.
[72] Ibid., pp. 198–201.
[73] Ibid., pp. 201–5.

biographical sketches; a study guide; and useful bibliographies at the end of each chapter. It covers much more historical and conceptual ground than *The Foundations of Dialogue in Science and Religion*, although at a far less detailed level, but preserving the same sophistication of analysis and the same clarity of style. I will discuss here only those themes that are not dealt with to the same extent in *The Foundations of Dialogue in Science and Religion*.

What I found most interesting in the *Science and Religion: An Introduction* is the greater emphasis placed by McGrath on the relationship between philosophy (including the philosophy of science) and religion. He studies the verificationism of the Vienna Circle,[74] and the falsificationism of Karl Popper (1902–94),[75] and their deployment in criticizing the validity of theological statements – by Anthony Flew, for example. McGrath lucidly summarizes criticisms of these theories that have emerged from within philosophy itself. In particular, Popper's attempt to exclude metaphysics from science – as unfalsifiable – is undermined by what is termed the 'tacking paradox': by conjoining a metaphysical statement to an empirical statement, the resultant statement is falsifiable (if the empirical component is), nevertheless the statement contains a metaphysical assertion.[76] In Thomas Kuhn he finds concepts useful to the understanding of doctrinal change, such as that of the 'paradigm shift'. He is more critical, however, of Kuhn's lack of sympathy with realism in scientific knowledge, since it seems to be unable to make sense of the concept of scientific progress.[77]

McGrath spends more time on Michael Polanyi (1891–1976), suggesting that he may have had a far greater impact on religious writers than on his fellow scientists.[78] One of Polanyi's fundamental assertions is that all knowledge – in the natural sciences, religion and philosophy – must involve personal commitment to what is known, and always contains strong tacit elements which may never be articulated. Contrary to a strong current in Western thought, according to which a personal commitment to knowledge was detrimental to objectivity in the pursuit of knowledge, Polanyi celebrates this commitment. McGrath argues that this has liberated theological writers from anxiety about their commitment to the ideas they were exploring. For Polanyi, all valid knowledge, both scientific and religious, is deeply fiduciary or credal.

---

[74] McGrath, *Science and Religion*, pp. 71–5.
[75] Ibid., pp. 76–80.
[76] Ibid., pp. 79–80.
[77] Ibid., pp. 80–3.
[78] Ibid., pp. 83–6.

Of equal interest is McGrath's examination of the relationships between science and the philosophy of religion. He discusses three general categories of argument for the existence of God: the cosmological argument (the argument from the necessity of a first cause), the kalam argument (developed by an early medieval school of Arabic philosophers) and the teleological argument. The cosmological and kalam arguments argue from the contingency of everything in the world to the necessity of a cause which is not contingent.[79] Science today in certain respects makes this argument more forceful, because of the discovery of the Big Bang, and the discovery of an extraordinary degree of fine tuning in the initial conditions of the universe. The cosmos certainly does look highly contingent, and it is more difficult today than at any previous period, perhaps, in the history of science to argue that the universe as we see it is self-explanatory and self-sufficient. Of course, it is not possible to infer with logical necessity that God, as understood in Christianity or Islam, is the immediate cause of the visible cosmos, but this inference is consonant with the evidence.

The teleological argument is also known as the argument from design. What was assumed to be designed in nature has shifted over the centuries. William Paley (1743–1805) in 1802 was highly impressed by the order and regularity of nature's laws as revealed by Newton, especially with respect to celestial mechanics, and also in living organisms such as the eye.[80] He saw all of this as implying a divine designer. However, within an eighteenth- and nineteenth-century science, with no knowledge of the Big Bang and fully aware of Aristotle's theory of the everlasting and unchanging nature of the universe, this argument was not compelling. Contrary to Newton's intentions, the Newtonian worldview led to a gradual rejection of the action of divine providence in the world, or even of a deity. Ironically, modern scientific discoveries – the Big Bang, the discovery of extraordinary fine tuning in the initial conditions and in the quantitative laws of the cosmos, and evidence that organisms have slowly evolved 'upwards' to the sophistication and complexity we see today – have inspired a vigorous reconsideration today of the argument from design.

McGrath also surveys the history of the more philosophical theories of God's action in the world.[81] In the tradition of Thomas Aquinas – who distinguishes between primary and secondary causes – God as primary cause does not act directly on the world, but through secondary causes.

---

[79] Ibid., pp. 89–98.
[80] Ibid., pp. 99–102.
[81] Ibid., pp. 102–9.

Aquinas uses this distinction to argue that suffering and pain are not to be ascribed to the direct action of God but to the frailty of the secondary causes through which he works. Nevertheless, for Aquinas God remains the 'unmoved mover': the primary but indirect cause of every action. God is the starting point of a great chain of causality, although he delegates divine action to secondary causes within the natural order.

McGrath also considers process theology, deriving from Alfred North Whitehead (1861–1947), which has points in common with Aquinas' conception of divine causality. Whitehead conceived reality as a process of becoming, change and event. He is concerned to allow for development within creation, subject to some overall direction and guidance, against a permanent background of order, which Whitehead identifies with God. Causation, both by natural objects and by God, is not coercion: it is influence and persuasion, and it is always both mental and physical, and the influence is in both directions. Just as God influences other entities, so he is influenced by them. God is a fellow-sufferer who understands. Theologians who have further developed process theology have argued that God is better thought of as a person than an entity. A great strength of process theology is that it respects free will. Indeed, all components of nature are free to ignore the persuasion of God. God is thus absolved from responsibility for both moral and natural evil. It also has no difficulty explaining God's action in the world.

McGrath points out that, for all its strengths, process theology abandons the powerful Christian intuition that God is transcendent and omnipotent.[82] It also has to meet the objection that, if God changes, how can he be perfect, since perfection seems to imply that there can be no possibility of change? Perhaps, however, that particular objection is now losing its force with the recognition that perfect entities can change and yet be perfect in a new and incommensurable way, without implying any qualitative comparison of better or worse. Nevertheless, for traditional Christian theists, the God of process theology seems to bear little resemblance to the God of the Old and New Testaments.

Turning to science and Christian concepts of creation, McGrath first points out that, in the Old Testament, nature is not divine. God created the heavenly bodies, which means that they are not divine and not to be worshipped. Also, creation is not simply a theme of Genesis: it can be found in other books of the Bible. McGrath also looks at the biblical concept of creation as ordering, and at 'righteousness' as conformity to the world ordering established by God. It was St Augustine who brought about the recognition that a doctrine of creation *ex nihilo* implies that

---

[82] Ibid., pp. 105–9.

time itself was brought into existence at the moment of creation, that it
too was created, and that creation did not occur within time. This idea is
employed in today's Big Bang cosmology, which argues that both time
and space were brought into existence at the moment of the Big Bang.

McGrath studies the issue of creation and ecology in more detail in
this text.[83] The starting point of such discussions is generally the accusation by the medievalist Lynn White (himself a committed Christian) that
Genesis encouraged humankind's dominion over, and exploitation of,
nature. However, a more careful reading of Genesis shows that, rather
than a lordship over nature, the concept of humanity as the stewards of
creation, and as the partner of God, are indicated by the text. A doctrine
of creation can thus act as a basis for an ecologically sensitive ethic. For
one scholar, Calvin B. DeWitt, this includes an 'earthkeeping' principle,
according to which humanity must sustain the Creator's creation; a
'Sabbath' principle allowing creation to recover; a 'fruitfulness' principle allowing the fruitfulness of nature to be enjoyed not destroyed; and a
'fulfilment and limits principle'. Also, the indwelling of God in nature
through the Holy Spirit indicates that the pillage of creation is, in a
sense, an assault on the Holy Spirit, and that nature is, in a sense, sacred.

Other scholars have pointed out that the exploitation of nature
reflects the emergence of a cultural mood of a desire to control – even of
a desire of mastery over religion – in the late nineteenth century, and the
attendant rise of technology. In 1923 Romano Guardini (1885–1968), a
Roman Catholic theologian, argued that the fundamental link between
culture and nature has been severed by the rise of the machine, allowing
humankind to impose its own authority on nature.[84] Blame for these
developments can hardly be placed at the door of Christianity.

Among the many special issues discussed by McGrath in this text, I
found his exploration of the relationships between religion and psychology of particular interest.[85] He begins with Ludwig Feuerbach
(1804–72), who argued in 1841 that God is a mistaken concept, which
arises quite understandably within human experience.[86] It is the projection of the desires and longings of humanity on an illusory transcendent
plane. In truth, we have made God in our own image. Feuerbach was
writing at a time when the liberal theology of Friedrich Schleiermacher
(1768–1834) tended to make the reality of God dependent on the

---

[83] Ibid., pp. 119–22; McGrath, *The Foundations of Dialogue in Science and
     Religion*, pp. 48–51.
[84] McGrath, *The Foundations of Dialogue in Science and Religion*, pp. 50–1.
[85] McGrath, *Science and Religion*, pp. 193–205.
[86] Ibid., pp. 194–7.

religious experience of the pious believer, and Feuerbach certainly offers a powerful critique of this position.

Feuerbach, however, generalizes in a very unscholarly way about world religions. Therevada Buddhism, for example, explicitly denies the existence of a God. Another weakness of Feuerbach's position is that, even if it is true that God is a projection of human longing, this does not imply that God does not exist. This kind of argument has become known as the 'genetic fallacy'. Furthermore, his arguments have reflexive implications – they can be turned against Feuerbach himself. His rejection of God may, perhaps, be a reflection of his own longing for autonomy. Nevertheless, many have found Feuerbach's argument, if not logically compelling, at least plausible and rhetorically very effective.

Others, such as Karl Marx (1818–83), have introduced different variants of Feuerbach's argument. Marx locates the origin of religion in socio-economic alienation. Religion is the 'opiate of the masses'. It is the result of a certain set of unjust social and economic conditions. Once these are removed, religion will cease to exist.[87] Again, the extraordinary variety of social and other circumstances in which religions exist and even thrive throughout the world make any simplistic causal analysis of their origins very difficult to sustain.

William James (1842–1910) brought a much more rigorous approach to the scientific study of religion.[88] He attempts an empirical study of the world religions, a study that is still authoritative. James is fully aware that religious experience is a private matter, difficult to articulate and codify, and equally difficult to analyse philosophically. All of this must be respected in the analysis of religion. He argues for a distinct quality in religious experience, distinguishing it from other forms of experience. It imparts a new quality to life, raises our 'centre of personal energy', giving rise to regenerative effects unobtainable in other ways. Furthermore, theology fundamentally owes its origin and form to these experiences. For James, the study of organized religion is a study of 'second-hand' religious experience, and has relatively little to offer those interested in genuine religious experience. In this interpretation, religion is best studied outside the framework of organized religious experience. This has not been found, subsequently, to be the best way of studying religion. Perhaps the institutionalization of religion brings the more extreme forms of religious experience under sober control.

A theme that might be very interesting to develop further here is the relationship between formal education in science and in religion. Much

---

[87] Ibid., pp. 196–7.
[88] Ibid., pp. 198–201.

of both scientific and religious knowledge begins as book learning, and is taken on trust from teachers. Are there similarities in the processes by which individual learners 'internalize knowledge', or take 'ownership' in both science and religion?

Perhaps the best-known variant of Feuerbach's analysis of religion is that introduced by Sigmund Freud (1856–1939), for whom religion is an illusion, the intrusion of repressed wishes into everyday life.[89] Religion has it origins in a prehistoric parricide resulting from sexual envy, giving rise to a collective sense of guilt which, in turn, leads to religious rituals. Religion is thus an expression of an Oedipus complex. The emphasis within Christianity on the death of Christ and the veneration of the risen Christ superbly illustrate for Freud his general principle. However, there is no foundation in anthropology or in history for these theories of Freud, and they are generally viewed today as highly speculative and even amateurish. Other psychological theories from that period, especially that of Carl Jung (1875–1961), had a much more open attitude to religion.

McGrath concludes the volume with seven case studies of major contributors to the field of science and religion in the twentieth century: Pierre Teilhard de Chardin (1881–1955), Charles A. Coulson (1910–74), Ian G. Barbour (1923–), Arthur Peacocke (1924–), John Polkinghorne (1930–), Wolfhart Pannenberg (1928–) and Thomas Torrance (1913–). The Methodist Charles Coulson – a brilliant mathematician, theoretical chemist and physicist – is well known for his vigorous rejection of the 'God of the Gaps': God is to be found in the remarkable order and beauty in nature rather than in the things science has not yet explained.[90] Coulson was a strong supporter of the equal validity of much of modern science and religion. Ian Barbour, physicist and theologian, with an interest in process theology, is today is regarded as the doyen of dialogue in the field of science and religion. John Polkinghorne, a theoretical physicist and Anglican priest, has contributed most, perhaps to making it publicly acceptable for scientists to declare an interest in science and religion. For McGrath, a major achievement of Polkinghorne's is to establish a firm place for natural theology in apologetics and theology.[91]

Wolfhart Pannenberg is a professional theologian who developed an interest in the natural sciences, and in particular in the theology of nature. He believes, for example, that scientific explanation of laws of

---

[89]   Ibid., pp. 201–5.
[90]   Ibid., pp. 210–12.
[91]   Ibid., pp. 207–10, 219–21.

nature need to be grounded in a deeper theological foundation.[92] For Pannenberg, it is meaningful and possible to think of reality as a whole, with the inclusion of the processes of nature as a history of the relations of God with his creatures. Arthur Peacocke, a physical chemist and Anglican priest, argues that both science and religion operate on the basis of 'critical realism', in which models are a partial, adequate, revisable and necessary means of depicting reality. He is also well known for his 'sacramental panentheism': that the transcendence of God acts within and under the processes the world.[93]

3. Thomas F. Torrance: An Intellectual Biography

The Scottish Barthian theologian Thomas Torrance is clearly the greatest single influence in McGrath's scientific theology project. In 1999 McGrath published an intellectual biography, partly as an act of piety, perhaps, and partly because it allowed him to deepen his own understanding and analysis of Torrance's work. Indeed, McGrath's study of Torrance sheds much light on the origins and commitments of his own project. Torrance has his own considerable scientific theology project. In 1978 he was awarded the Templeton Foundation Prize for Progress in Religion for his work on the interactions between Christian theology and the natural sciences.[94]

McGrath identifies a series of positions worked out by Torrance, which he endorses. Torrance seeks to reconstruct a natural theology immune from the criticisms levied against it by Barth and others.[95] For Torrance, natural theology has a proper and significant place within the ambit of revealed theology.[96] Torrance distinguishes between scriptural revelation, in which God reveals himself as a person, and nature, which, in the Reformed tradition, also reveals God, but only as mediated through the covenant of grace, and then not in a personal manner.[97] For Torrance, the doctrine of creation *ex nihilo* is the foundation of the idea that the world is contingent, and dependent upon God for its being and order. This means that nature is radically distinct from God. It also means that nature can be understood only by looking at nature, not by

---

[92] Ibid., pp. 213–15.
[93] Ibid., pp. 216–18.
[94] McGrath, *Thomas F. Torrance*, pp. 105–6.
[95] Ibid., ch. 9.
[96] Ibid., p. 185.
[97] Ibid., pp. 189–90.

looking at God.[98] This emancipates nature from philosophical preconceptions and from theology, and allows the notional separation of
science and theology. But it also implies that creation itself has revelatory potential; that a branch of theology is possible that may look
at, but through and beyond, nature, and obtain some insights about
God. Torrance criticizes a theological tradition deriving from late
Antiquity, which he describes as a 'deistic disjunction between God
and the world'.[99] He goes on to promote a reconstituted natural
theology within a Trinitarian context, linked both with revelation and
salvation through Christ. McGrath finds himself in greatest sympathy
with this project.

Torrance was also concerned to forge rigorous methodological
links between theology and the natural sciences, an area where he differs
from Barth, who was little interested in this issue.[100] Torrance regards
the natural sciences, rightly understood, as an immensely significant ally
in the struggle for theological integrity.[101] He sees science and theology
as complementary disciplines. An important distinction made by
Torrance, strongly influenced by Martin Buber's 'I-Thou' distinction,
and also by Michael Polanyi, is that science deals more with objects, theology deals with a person: it is more of a direct personal engagement
with God.[102]

For Torrance, theology is a science, in the sense of a rigorous intellectual discipline, and like every science requires its own forms of method
and analysis. There is no monolithic scientific method that defines what
is and what is not a science. Every reality is to be investigated according
to its own distinct nature. Theology is a human discipline that uses
human reason to produce, to the extent to which it is possible, an
ordered account of what can be known of its object – God. Also, for
Torrance as for Barth, theology recognizes the self-revelation of God in
Christ as its object, and hence as the sole criterion and foundation of its
affirmations.[103]

Torrance is credited by McGrath with having formulated the most
highly developed version of realism available in modern theology. Both
Christian theology and the natural sciences operate with an understanding of knowledge that has its ontological foundations in objective

---

[98] Ibid., p. 191.
[99] Ibid., p. 192.
[100] Ibid., ch. 9.
[101] Ibid., p. 198.
[102] Ibid., p. 202.
[103] Ibid., p. 208.

reality. Theology and the sciences share this carefully nuanced realist epistemology.[104]

An influence that Torrance derives particularly from Polanyi is his view that the universe discloses an ascending gradient of meaning in richer and higher forms of order. Instead of levels of existence and reality being explained reductively 'from below' in materialist and mechanist terms, the lower levels are found to be explained in terms of the higher often invisible and intangible levels of reality. For Torrance, Polanyi with this idea has created space for the 'spiritual' in the universe, by rejecting the reductionist position that all of nature is to be considered as existing at one level only. Polanyi's view also allows the integration of separate disciplines.[105]

4. A Scientific Theology Volume 1: Nature

Finally, we arrive at the carefully planned and detailed working out of McGrath's scientific theology project, which seeks to create an historically and philosophically informed synergy between the methods (and not the content) of theology and the natural sciences within an evangelical framework. Three volumes are planned, and two have been published. Anyone who hopes here for a grand new theological system in the German manner will be disappointed. McGrath's efforts are directed towards a more fundamental methodological programme:

> It is the contention of this work that the relationship of Christian theology to the natural sciences is that of two fundamentally related disciplines, whose working method reflect this common grounding in responding to a reality which lies beyond them, of which they are bound to give an ordered account.[106]

His concern is to equip a new kind of interdisciplinary theological laboratory, one that contains all of the tools necessary if the working interpretative, analytical and theory-building strategies developed by the natural sciences are to be systematically available to theology. Nevertheless, behind this methodological programme it is not difficult to detect a larger agenda. McGrath is concerned that theology should take a turn towards nature. He clearly feels that this dimension of theology has been neglected, throughout much of Christian history, perhaps.

---

[104] Ibid., pp. 211–13.
[105] Ibid., pp. 232–3.
[106] McGrath, *A Scientific Theology Volume 1*, pp. xviii–xix.

One is reminded a little here of early seventeenth-century scientists such as William Gilbert (1544–1603), Galileo (1564–1642), Francis Bacon (1561–1626) and René Descartes (1596–1650), who were as much concerned with creating new scientific methods as they were with creating new sciences, sometimes more so. Indeed, a new theological method is arguably more valuable than a new theological system, since a method can be very fertile in many systems. McGrath is offering to theology a workshop full of new tools. He is not claiming to have invented all of these tools, but he seeks to gather them together, refine them, and add to them where necessary. Nor is he claiming any kind of methodological identity between theology and the natural sciences. Indeed, from time to time, as we have already seen, he explores signifi-cant differences. Nevertheless, he is concerned to draw attention to important points of convergence.

The trilogy is written from an evangelical perspective, defined by McGrath as an approach to theology that is 'nourished and governed at all points by Holy Scripture', and 'seeks to offer a faithful and coherent account of what it finds there'[107] in dialogue with the central traditions of Christian theology, Catholicism, Orthodoxy and evangelicalism. Nevertheless, the tools he creates will be available to every tradition in theology. Also, the comparisons he articulates between science and theology can undoubtedly be illuminating to scientific method itself.

Volume 1, published in 2001, is devoted to an examination of the concept of nature, a concept of fundamental importance for both theol-ogy and natural science. McGrath is concerned to explore to what extent this concept is culturally and socially mediated, and the implica-tions of this for theology.

Volume 2, published in 2002, deals with realism in science and theol-ogy. McGrath articulates a nuanced 'critical realist' position, heavily influenced by the sociological philosopher Roy Bhaskar, and discusses how this may be applied to theology. He places a particular emphasis on theology as an a posteriori discipline that offers an account of reality.

Volume 3, which has not yet been published, will deal with the manner in which reality is represented, paying particular attention to the parallels here between theological doctrines and scientific theories.

These volumes partly represent much more carefully worked out versions of concepts and positions that we have already encountered, especially in *The Foundations of Dialogue in Science and Religion* and in the Torrance biography. However, there is also much that is new, and I will examine a selection of these features here.

---

[107] Ibid., p. xix.

As I have already pointed out, McGrath views the natural sciences as the *ancilla theologiae nova*.[108] Are there not dangers here? History provides examples of secular philosophy being allowed to play a magisterial role in theology, and this has sometimes had a decisive, and not always positive, influence over how the Christian faith is presented or conceived. Theologians have been aware of this since Antiquity. Augustine, for example, articulates most influentially the notion of the critical appropriation of classical culture. Providing the *ancilla* is understood, therefore, to function in a ministerial rather than in a magisterial capacity, the integrity of theology as a discipline can be maintained without too much difficulty. Of course, McGrath in no sense wishes to diminish the importance and autonomy of natural science by describing it here as an *ancilla theologiae*. Just as mathematics is a tool of physics, so McGrath understands the role of science in theology.

For some anxious critics, however, any form of positive interaction between Christian theology and the natural sciences is a Faustian pact in which Christian theology abandons its inner essence and identity in order to gain some slight credibility among its scientific despisers.[109] The admission of the natural sciences into the operative logic of Christian theology is undoubtedly dangerous if, together with methodology, provisional scientific judgements are admitted. There is a related danger in allowing transient trends in the content of philosophical theology into any scientific theology. Nevertheless, McGrath argues that the methodological dialogue he proposes is not merely a free arbitrary choice, compatible with Christian theology, but is actually demanded by the Christian understanding of reality. The Christian doctrine of creation demands a unitary understanding of knowledge, while being responsive to diversity within the creation. Furthermore, if God made the world, something of the character of God must surely be disclosed in creation, although not as fully as in revelation.[110]

This is an enduring theme in Christianity, and especially so in the early Reformed tradition. It has had an impact both on science and on theology in a great variety of ways. These include very general influences, such as the provision of a theological framework for viewing the world (God as the source of world order, or the contingency of the world), the provision of an indirect religious motivation behind scientific activities (as is claimed in the Merton thesis),[111] and a broader

---

[108] Ibid., pp. 7–20.

[109] Ibid., p. 19.

[110] Ibid., p. 21.

[111] Robert K. Merton, 'Science, Technology, and Society in Seventeenth Century England', *Osiris* 4 (1938), pp. 360–632.

cultural perspective in which Christian and theological ideas are absorbed into general scientific culture (such as Occam's principle of economy, originally theological in motivation).[112] There have also been many more specific influences in which the Christian doctrine of creation has influenced the very content of scientific theories, as in medieval cosmology[113] and early geology.[114] McGrath stresses that the Christian doctrine of creation was a factor here, among many others, on the emergence of Western science, and is not suggesting that it was the only or even the major influence. McGrath also stresses that the Christological dimensions of the doctrine of creation are such that, within this framework, divine rationality must be thought of as *embedded* in creation and *embodied* in Christ.[115] This leads to the powerful conclusion that a Christian understanding of the ontology of creation, therefore, *demands* a faithful investigation of nature.

All of this, for McGrath, leads on to the vision of theology which can be seen not of course as a natural science, but as a science more broadly understood (*Wissenschaft*), and related to other sciences, each of which has its own distinctive subject matter and means of investigation appropriate to that subject.[116] He explains how the perceived divide today between science and the humanities complicates this task. However, he raises the startling possibility that theology might again provide a unitary foundation for all of human knowledge.

More specifically, McGrath seeks to find illumination for theology from the manner in which the natural sciences have grappled with the question of how true knowledge is acquired and what form it takes.

McGrath also expands on his reasons for concentrating on the classic themes of Christian theology and on orthodoxy. He sees these as the most authentic and enduring forms of Christian theology.[117] They are securely based on apostolic experience and on Scripture, and represent the mature reflection of the faith community on its inheritance over a

---

[112] J.H. Brooke, M. Osler and J. Van der Meer (eds), 'Science in Theistic Contexts: Cognitive Dimensions', *Osiris* 16 (2001), p. 199.

[113] E. Grant, *Planets, Stars and Orbs: The Medieval Cosmos 1200–1687* (Cambridge: Cambridge University Press, 1996).

[114] M. Rudwick, 'The Shape and Meaning of Earth History' in D. Lindberg and R. Numbers, *God and Nature: Historical Essays in the Encounter between Christianity and Science* (Berkeley: University of California Press, 1986), ch. 12.

[115] McGrath, *A Scientific Theology Volume 1*, p. 25.

[116] Ibid., pp. 25–34.

[117] Ibid., p. 36.

period of 2000 years. It is unwise to treat this lightly. Radical alternatives to this central current tend to be transient responses to some contemporary crisis. The most recent theological pronouncements are not necessarily the best. Weakened statements of Christian orthodoxy often reflect a temporary change of cultural mood, with a resulting perception of the inadequacy of some feature of received theology, and may not be the result of a sustained theological critique of traditional doctrines. There was a period in the 1960s and 1970s, for example, which saw the abandonment of any element of the transcendent or the supernatural in certain circles in theology. This is now seen as a transient phase.[118]

McGrath emphasizes, however, that the maintenance of theological integrity is not equivalent to the wooden repetition of received doctrinal formulations.[119] There is a dynamic and ever-renewing process of the 'reception of doctrine'. There is quite a parallel here with the science of mechanics in that, since the seventeenth century, essentially the same foundational concepts and laws introduced by Newton again and again have been reformulated and renewed in different mathematical languages, using an evolving terminology and linked to the discovery of new concepts and varieties of application.[120] Theology, for McGrath, is essentially a communal attentiveness to Scripture; a desire to express what is found there to the church and the world, using conceptualizations accessible to envisaged audiences, in an auxiliary and not a foundational role.

From the perspective of his concern to respect and further perennial Christian theology, McGrath criticizes process theology quite severely as a passing fashion. He feels that the science and religion dialogue at present is in something of a 'Babylonian captivity' to process theology, equally unacceptable to orthodox theologians and to scientists.[121] Indeed, he insists that the dialogue should be direct and not mediated by any philosophical system, whether process philosophy or otherwise.

On a very general note, I believe that McGrath might have been a little more positive with respect to process theology here. All philosophical and theological systems, whether close to the central Christian traditions or not, seem to deliver useful ideas. When they become marginalized or disappear, some, at least, of the ideas explored so earnestly constitute a valuable residue and inheritance.

---

[118] Ibid., p. 38.
[119] Ibid., p. 42.
[120] John Roche, *The Mathematics of Measurement: A Critical History* (London: Athlone Press and Springer, 1998), chs 6, 8, 12.
[121] McGrath, *A Scientific Theology Volume 1*, pp. 38–41.

McGrath addresses the enormously important issue of how theology can use science in an auxiliary manner, without becoming trapped within a particular scientific theory. With the inevitable erosion of scientific theories, will not such a theology be itself eroded? McGrath's simple but powerful solution is not to rely on the specific understandings of nature, which science has arrived at by pursuing its methods, but to explore the methodological parallels between Christian theology and the natural sciences.[122]

It seems to me that this is a marvellous means of avoiding the importation of the 'transience' virus, when science is relied upon in theology. Methodologies may slowly evolve, or even fall out of fashion perhaps, but it does not seem to make historical sense to say that a certain scientific method was *false*. Furthermore, McGrath is careful to insist that it is used in an auxiliary and not in a constitutive role. If it is argued that some degree of 'contamination', however small, is nevertheless still possible and inevitable, then one must agree, but this can be avoided only if the whole enterprise of theological thinking is suspended and if all non-theological culture is ignored.

McGrath, perhaps, is playing too safe here, granting his commitment to critical realism. Surely a scientific theology can also rely safely on established scientific facts (the world is round; the blood circulates in the human body)? Of course, there will always be areas of science where what some scientists claim as facts others will be doubtful about, or where what is claimed to be a fact is, rather, in part an interpretation motivated by some hypothesis. Nevertheless, there are also very large areas of scientific data where one can only deny that a piece of scientific knowledge is a fact, if one heroically denies that there are any facts. I believe that theology can and should take account of these.

4.1. *Nature*

McGrath carries out a very thorough examination of the concept of 'nature' and its contrast with the concept of the supernatural.[123] He distinguishes a surface meaning – the observable world – and various philosophical meanings, ranging from naïve realism to full social constructivism. All of these have been shaped and given connotations by social experience and concerns, by science, and also by ideological agendas. Nature is a profoundly ambivalent concept ranging from

---

[122] Ibid., p. 50.
[123] Ibid., ch. 3.

sentimentalism to menace, reflecting the aspirations, longings and fears of those who appeal to it.

McGrath asserts that 'the concept of "nature" is a socially mediated notion, not an objective entity in its own right'.[124] McGrath's very interesting and extensive historical study of the concept of nature has convinced him that there is no self-evidently correct definition of 'nature': nature lies beyond definition in terms of its intrinsic identity. He demonstrates very persuasively that it may be 'the most socially conditioned of all human concepts'.[125]

While I agree fully that all concepts of nature are socially mediated, it does not follow that some of them, at least, do not have objective content. With sufficient scholarship and reflection we are often capable of seeing through the social dressing of a concept to the underlying objective reality. In physics, for example, we are perfectly capable of distinguishing between the algebraic expression of Newton's laws of motion – influenced as they are by social accidents such as the creation of writing, the Latin alphabet, the invention of upper and lower case letters, and a seventeenth-century battle over mathematical notation[126] – and the laws as they operate in nature independently of our notation, even though we invariably express those laws in an algebraic dressing.

I do see, however, that the extraordinary variety of meanings of the term 'nature', and the social and moral overtones of each of those meanings, often make it very difficult to see through the socially constructed content of the concept.

Surprisingly, perhaps, McGrath concludes his massive historical and 'postmodern' attack on the concept of nature by denying that 'nature' is totally socially constructed, but only partly so.[127] Nevertheless, it is so volatile a concept that it can only be properly rescued by the Christian category of creation. Again and again, I find that he employs a rhetorical strategy in which he defends so well the theory he is about to attack that it is sometimes not clear to me at the outset that he is about to demolish it.

For McGrath, a Christian theology of 'nature' is subsumed in the insight that the natural order, including humanity, is God's creation.[128] In the doctrine of creation, Christianity, therefore, already has a perfectly good 'theology of nature'. Nature is to be seen through the prism of

---

[124] Ibid., p. 87.
[125] Ibid., p. 88.
[126] F. Cajori, *A History of Mathematical Notations* (La Salle: Open Court, 1928–29, 1974 reprint), vol. 1, section B.
[127] McGrath, *A Scientific Theology Volume 1*, p. 133.
[128] Ibid., p. 137.

revelation as God's creation. In a particularly satisfying analysis, and drawing on a rich historical and contemporary literature, McGrath develops the implications of this concept in considerable detail.[129]

Creation *ex nihilo*, for example, allows the scientist committed to this doctrine to expect that divine rationality would somehow be reflected in the structure and workings of nature, but also to approach nature with the expectation that he does not have to look beyond the world of nature to find the proper object of his science. In an extended study of the doctrine of creation in Scripture, McGrath points out that, against any idea that the natural order is chaotic, irrational or inherently evil, the early Christian tradition affirmed that the natural order possesses an inherent goodness, rationality and orderliness, which derives directly from its creation by God. This also eliminated a radical difference between God and creation, and held that the truth, beauty and goodness of God could be discerned in creation. Aquinas, for example, develops the doctrine of creation to affirm both that God works within nature and within the autonomy of nature.[130]

For McGrath, we are authorized by Scripture to seek a partial disclosure of the glory of God through the works of God in creation. The mode of creation is conscious, ordered and deliberate, not arbitrary. Nevertheless, the Creator is to be regarded as free of limitations imposed by the inertia of a prior reality. Creation is, therefore, truly contingent.

Humanity also, though created in *imago Dei*, is not divine. It is part of the created order, but does bear a particular and significant relationship with the Creator. Furthermore, the Christian interpretation of *image Dei* is again Christological.[131] The Christian tradition has always insisted that Christ is the true *imago Dei*. For Calvin, redemption through Christ became necessary because of the fall of man and the consequent corruption of *imago Dei*, leading to a tendency towards idolatry.[132] Many theologians, particularly Augustine and Aquinas, have also identified *imago Dei* with human reason, thereby generating respect for reason and asserting that human rationality corresponds to divine rationality, giving us some knowledge of God. Developed reason can help us to know and love God better, and ultimately allow God to be grasped 'face to face' in the beatific vision.

Because of its correspondence with divine rationality, human reason, in the Christian doctrine of creation, also has the capacity to discover

---

[129] Ibid., pp. 138–91.
[130] Ibid., pp. 167–73.
[131] Ibid., p. 187.
[132] Ibid., pp. 173–6.

glimpses of the divine rationality in the created order. McGrath considers particularly how the extraordinary effectiveness of mathematics in nature[133] might reflect the divine beauty and ordering of nature, a conclusion many natural philosophers have come to, including Johann Kepler (1571–1630) and Galileo.

A Christian doctrine of creation, and of redemption, also affirms a congruence between the moral ordering of creation, including humanity, and the mind of God. The way the universe *is* determines how man *ought* to behave in it.[134]

As a footnote to the notion that imprints of the divine ordering can be found in nature, although in a very limited manner,[135] it is worth noting that modern science and technology offer some helpful analogies here. For example, the uninspiring and apparently random pattern of developed grains in a holographic film produce a clear, three-dimensional optical image when illuminated by coherent light, suggesting a significance to the pattern that cannot be obtained by direct observation. Even more remarkable, perhaps, is the manner in which modern physics often makes use of a mathematical formalism that is so remote from descriptive mathematics that it might be described as totally written in cipher, nevertheless it reflects important aspects of physical reality accurately.[136]

5. A Scientific Theology Volume 2: Reality

While the first volume of McGrath's trilogy deals mainly with a critique of the concept of nature and the importance to a scientific theology of the doctrine of creation, his second volume deals mainly with the epistemological and ontological status of the real world, including nature and human society. For McGrath, a scientific theology declines to make a priori judgements about what may be known of God, and the manner by which that knowledge should be established. It is an a posteriori discipline, responding to and offering a principled account of what may be known of God through revelation: a God luminously described by McGrath as 'embedded at different levels in the world'.[137]

---

[133] Ibid., pp. 209–14.

[134] Ibid., pp. 214–18.

[135] Ibid., pp. 218–30.

[136] See A. Einstein, H.A. Lorentz, H. Weyl and H. Minkowski, *The Principle of Relativity*, W. Perrett and G.B. Jeffrey (trs) (New York: Dover, 1952; first published by Methuen, 1923), pp. 109–64.

[137] McGrath, *A Scientific Theology Volume 2*, p. xi.

Here, as in his *Foundations of Dialogue in Science and Religion* volume, McGrath explores what is termed, in certain philosophical circles, 'the death of foundationalism', or 'the demise of the enlightenment project'.[138] For McGrath, 'Enlightenment foundationalism' was a philosophical movement, beginning with Descartes, which supposed that a valid philosophy of nature must be constructed deductively from true axioms and in a universalist manner that was independent of the social location of the philosopher.[139] This he criticizes severely and convincingly.

In preparing this chapter, I have read a fair amount of the literature describing and criticizing 'foundationalism', and I have encountered a rather different interpretation.[140] 'Foundationalism' is a pejorative term created and used polemically by a group of modern philosophers, and now theologians, to describe a presumed tradition of philosophical thought that they have superseded.[141] For this group of philosophers, at least, 'foundationalism' was once alive and is now dead. I readily accept that certain positions of some philosophers from Antiquity may be described without anachronism, in some sense, as 'foundationalist'. However, I have encountered no professional historical literature describing foundationalism,[142] and I am not at all convinced that the interpretation of foundationalism attributed to earlier philosophers by their modern critics is accurate or fair. Indeed, the term 'Enlightenment foundationalism' seems to have a polemical loading similar to the Renaissance coinage of the term 'Dark Ages'.[143]

---

[138] McGrath, *The Foundations of Dialogue in Science and Religion*, pp. 11–14; McGrath, *A Scientific Theology Volume 1*, pp. 20–39.

[139] McGrath, *The Foundations of Dialogue in Science and Religion*, p. 10.

[140] A. Plantinga and N. Wolterstorff, *Faith and Rationality: Reason and Belief in God* (Notre Dame: University of Notre Dame Press, 1983), pp. 16–93; W.P. Alston, *Epistemic Justification: Essays in the Theory of Knowledge* (Ithaca, New York: Cornell University Press, 1989), p. 19; P.K. Moser, 'Foundationalism' in R. Audi (ed.), *The Cambridge Dictionary of Philosophy* (Cambridge: Cambridge University Press, 1995), pp. 276–8; R.M. Chisholm, *The Foundations of Knowing* (Brighton: Harvester Press, 1982), ch. 1; N. Frankenberry, 'Functionalism, Fallibilism, and Anti-foundationalism in Wieman's Empirical Theism', *Zygon* 22 (1987), pp. 37–47; E. Sosa, 'The foundations of Foundationalism', *Noûs* 14 (1980), pp. 3–25; T.E. Uebel, 'Anti-Foundationalism and the Vienna Circle's Revolution in Philosophy', *British Journal for the Philosophy of Science* 47 (1996), pp. 415–40; John E. Thiel, *Nonfoundationalism* (Minneapolis: Fortress Press, 1991).

[141] Thiel, Nonfoundationalism, p. 2.

[142] The best historical summary I have come across is ibid., pp. 3–37.

[143] Philip P. Wiener (ed.), *Dictionary of the History of Ideas* (New York: Charles Scribner's Sons, 1969), vol. 3, p. 477.

I believe, however, that I may be able to make some useful remarks about a rather different question. Is mathematics and physics constructed in accordance with what I take to be the modified interpretation of foundationalism offered by McGrath, that is, actually based (and understood to be based) on true axioms or laws which are competent to deduce all of the properties and other laws from these axioms?

The Euclidean model of mathematics claimed, from a set of axioms regarded as basic (but not necessarily true),[144] to deduce and explain all of the properties of the mathematical objects presented to the axioms. However, an attempt to establish the consistency of the axioms of mathematics and logic by Gottlob Frege (1848–1925), Bertrand Russell (1872–1970) and others in the early twentieth century led to the recognition of deep difficulties in this approach.[145] More importantly, the exploration by Kurt Gödel (1906–78) of the axiomatic approach led him to recognize that mathematical truths 'emerge' in every mathematical system, which cannot be deduced from the axioms.[146] Mathematics, therefore, no longer claims that it can prove the consistency of all of its axioms, or that all of the properties of a mathematical system can be deduced from these axioms.

Physics is even more interesting. Newton's laws of motion are considered basic for mechanics, but they are inferred from experiment, not immediately given in experience. In physics what is basic is determined not by how it is arrived at, but by its location in an explanatory and deductive structure. Physics does hope, of course, and always has, that its observational data, definitions of physical properties, basic laws and hypotheses are true. From Newton onwards, the failure of quantitative laws in macroscopic physics has generally been a failure of accuracy or even applicability beyond a certain decimal place, rather than a total failure of the law. The measurement of physical constants similarly gradually improves in accuracy with advances in measurement technology. Some interpretations and hypotheses have, of course, failed, such as Newton's claim that the impenetrability of a macroscopic solid implies the impenetrability of its smallest parts.[147] A theory in physics is complex, including observational data, interpretations, empirical laws, hypothetical

---

[144] Roche, *The Mathematics of Measurement*, p. 36.
[145] M. Kline, *Mathematical Thought from Ancient to Modern Times* (New York: Oxford University Press, 1972), pp. 1187–97; McGrath, *A Scientific Theology Volume 2*, pp. 27–9.
[146] Kline, *Mathematical Thought from Ancient to Modern Times*, pp. 1206–7.
[147] I. Newton, *The Mathematical Principles of Natural Philosophy*, A. Motte (tr.) (London: Dawson's of Pall Mall, 1968), vol. 2, p. 203.

elements and useful constructs. It has become part of the culture of physics to expect that some of this will eventually fail, but that the empirical data and laws will endure, although within better-defined regimes. Physics has other basic principles, such as principles of symmetry and the principle of least action, which have considerable authority, but which are very difficult to categorize. They are not simple facts of nature or natural laws. They seem to be quite abstract, and yet valid and powerful.[148]

Modern physics presents an even more surprising picture. Schrödinger's equation, for example, is a basic principle of quantum theory, but it was not and cannot be established by experiment. It cannot even be given an empirical interpretation, since some of the symbols (the wave function, for example) have no assignable physical meaning. When we add to this the widespread importance given to intuitive knowledge in physics, we can see that the established empirical truth and even meaningfulness of all of the axioms of physics is not a necessity for physics to proceed successfully: what is useful, what is postulated, what is provisional, what is hypothetical, what is a recognized fiction, what is an idealization and even a mathematical artefact, all have a role to play in its basic principles. All, of course, have to be justified, but justification takes many forms.

It has also become clear in physics that while a derivation of properties from basic axioms seems to work quite well in classical mechanics, it works far less well in classical electromagnetism, where laws often 'emerge' in more complex systems (such as those of the electromagnetic field in solids)[149] which cannot be deduced from those of less complex systems. Electric circuit theory and its laws – such as Ohm's law – represent a subsystem in electromagnetism which is not deducible, either, from the basic laws of electromagnetism, although there are points of overlap with electromagnetism. There is also as much 'top-down' as 'bottom-up' derivation in physics. Physics is far more like a cathedral complex with added structures of different age, design, foundations and interconnections than it is like a pyramid.

I believe these remarks allow some nuancing of McGrath's discussion of Alvin Plantinga's argument that Christians are justified in treating God as a basic belief.[150] I do not believe it is necessary to appeal to the

---

[148] Roche, 'A critical study of symmetry in physics from Galileo to Newton'.

[149] John Roche, 'B and H, the Intensity Vectors of Magnetism. A New Approach to Resolving a Century-old Controversy', *American Journal of Physics* 68.5 (2000), pp. 438–49 (p. 445).

[150] McGrath, *A Scientific Theology Volume 2*, pp. 99–102; Plantinga and Wolterstorff, *Faith and Rationality*, pp. 59–63.

tradition-mediated character of knowledge to justify this, nor do I think it needs to be justified by challenging some rigid criteria for basic beliefs supposedly formulated by the 'foundationalist' philosophers. If we look to the structure of mathematical argument, basic beliefs or axioms are a priori constructs, used to deduce and explain the properties of a system of mathematical objects. From this perspective there is no challenge from mathematics to treating God as a basic belief. In physics, although many basic principles are inferred from experiment, others, such as Maxwell's equations in a medium, were not and are not. The predictive and explanatory success of a principle is commonly sufficient reason to give it support and treat it as basic. Also, qualitative hypotheses, such as the atomic hypothesis, have been supported, largely on intuitive grounds, for centuries. Again, some basic and highly useful physical principles have no clear physical meaning, and it remains something of a mystery how they were discovered and why they are so successful.

Analogy with mathematical and physical thinking suggests, therefore, that even if the concept of God is not derived from experience, this is not a ground for rejecting the concept. Alternatively, even if it is arrived at by inference from natural evidence, this does not make it logically derivative and dependent upon that evidence. It is a common experience of students of mathematics and physics, when they work through an argument for some theorem, that they may experience a 'rush' of understanding at the end of the argument, which seems to give them a direct intuition of the truth of the proposition. In other words, their grasp of the truth of the proposition is both immediate and mediated by argument at the same time. On the other hand, they may not experience this rush of understanding, and although they understand and accept the steps of the proof, they still do not grasp the truth of, or even properly understand, the proposition. It is also well known that brilliant mathematicians and physicists can sometimes directly intuit the truth of a proposition before they have found arguments to justify it.

I believe all of this supports McGrath's case that theology now needs to look at science for helpful concepts, and not so much at philosophy. I am utterly convinced that physics and mathematics – and, undoubtedly, other sciences as well – represent treasuries of concepts highly useful to theology, which has hardly begun to avail of them. Indeed, the resources of science here are so vast, and so well anchored in a highly successful investigation of nature, that in comparison the methodology of philosophy seems thin, abstract and uncertain. Philosophy, of course, continues to examine important questions.

McGrath explores in some depth a polarity within knowledge that he defines as that between the search for objectivity and that of the identification with community tradition.[151] He examines critically the view that communities create their own moral and other values and ideas and are not accountable to any external extra-linguistic objectivity for the outcome of this creative process. Just as McGrath finds the success of science a powerful argument for the defence of the objectivity of nature, he finds the unquestionable immorality of Nazism or Stalinism powerful natural arguments for the defence of moral objectivity.

In this text, McGrath passes beyond a study of realism in the natural sciences to its study in the social sciences, arguing that a scientific theology must draw on the sciences as a whole and not only on the physical sciences. To achieve this, he draws heavily on the writings of the philosopher of science Roy Bhaskar,[152] in particular on Bhaskar's insistence that each science develops methodologies appropriate to its ontology.[153] Furthermore, that method is not developed a priori, but is determined by the character of the object of investigation. Reality is stratified, and this is reflected in the stratification of the sciences.[154] By virtue of their subject matters a higher degree of constructivism is implicit in psychology and the social sciences than in the physics or biology.[155] McGrath insists, however, that both the socially constructed and the objective 'natural' component of scientific concepts have an equal claim to be regarded as 'real', and both are open to analysis.

The ontological stratification of reality is reflected in a scientific stratification working upwards from the molecular sciences, through the biological sciences, the social sciences, on to the psychological and symbological sciences.[156] Christianity is embedded at a number of levels within the world – ideational, cultural and historical. How do these different levels relate to each other, and how may a scientific theology represent them? It is problematic to suggest that theology can be treated as the direct equivalent – of physics, say – in terms of its method and ontology. Just because physics makes a very limited use of socially constructed realities, for example, we cannot argue the same for theology. A critical realism needs to be sensitive to this diversity, but can draw fruitfully on the experience of the natural sciences in their realist engagement with the world.

McGrath defines the cognitive goal of the programme of science as 'corresponding coherently with reality'. Ontological finality rests with

---

[151] McGrath, *A Scientific Theology Volume 2*, pp. xii–xiii.
[152] Ibid., p. xvi.
[153] Ibid., p. 12.
[154] Ibid., p. 12.
[155] Ibid., p. xiii.
[156] Ibid., pp. 12–13.

nature herself. One of the most serious weaknesses of the 'strong' theory of the social construction of knowledge is its failure to explain the importance of experimentation in the emergence of ways of thinking in science.[157]

Internal theoretical coherence and self-consistency are important in science, and represent an important method of testing the theory.[158] Nevertheless, the correspondence of the theory with reality is of primary importance for science. For McGrath, it is similarly important that Christian doctrines apply to an extra-systemic reality: the internal coherence of doctrines is not sufficient, since such consistency can be achieved without making significant contact with reality.[159]

McGrath discusses here a philosophical tradition that defines knowledge as 'warranted belief' or 'justified true belief'.[160] I find myself entirely out of sympathy with this tradition, because even to 'know' that a particular belief is 'warranted' already requires knowledge, and if a belief is known to be true then it is knowledge and not belief (we will no longer 'believe' in God, but know him, in the beatific vision). The 'warranted belief' definition collapses the distinction between knowledge and belief, and there is no longer a cognitive category – knowledge – radically distinct from that of belief. This is yet another refinement of Western philosophical scepticism: a philosophical tradition which here is unable to articulate a justification of an apparently given feature of our experience of reality, and ends up rejecting it. It is also an example of the manner in which a rather abstract intellectualism can so formalize its language that it loses contact with the experiences which originally grounded its terminology, and employs this same terminology to deny the very experiences which gave rise to it.

The distinction between knowledge and belief is derived from timeless human experiences; they are names given to cognitive states recognized by us as qualitatively distinct. We can name knowledge but we cannot define it – because it is a primitive given in experience. The very presumption that knowledge can be defined in terms of other categories, and therefore reduced to them, is ultimately incoherent. But how can we be sure that what we call knowledge really is knowledge? What is 'real knowledge' other than that which the denominating community has

---

[157] Ibid., pp. 14–15.
[158] Ibid., p. 16.
[159] Ibid., pp. 17–20.
[160] McGrath, *The Foundations of Dialogue in Science and Religion*, p. 89; McGrath, *A Scientific Theology Volume 2*, p. 3; W.V. Quine, *From a Logical Point of View* (Cambridge, MA: Harvard University Press, 1953), pp. 42–3.

chosen to name as 'real knowledge'? Do we have access to some higher meaning independent of experience? While we have an overwhelming experience of myriads of instances of knowledge that we have never found any reason to question, we can, of course, make mistakes and misdescriptions in assigning the term 'knowledge' to referents. However, we have also developed an enormous variety of strategies for avoiding or minimizing this.

The 'warranted belief' tradition frequently uses the word 'belief', where one would normally speak of 'knowledge', as in Willard Quine's expression 'growing up in a community of believers in stones and rabbits'.[161] I am increasingly convinced that the attempt to articulate a justification of our cognitive processes can very quickly upset the delicate balance between our language and what it refers to, and can easily lead into an almost empty verbal formalism. In consequence, I find a whole series of discussions on the foundations of knowledge which employ the concept of 'warranted belief' question-begging from the outset, lacking in concrete examples which clarify what is really being talked about, and generally quite unintelligible. McGrath valiantly attempts to engage all of this, and to distinguish valid from questionable positions, but I have not attempted to follow him into this troubled field.

5.1. Traditions

Theology, like science, has to be explored and advanced from where it is, from a tradition already in existence. There is no 'view from nowhere', from which we can evaluate our knowledge and theories.[162] The Christian tradition is already in existence, it does not need to be constituted. But we can, of course, carry out development and consolidation, and also make 'running repairs'. McGrath affirms that each tradition-constituted rationality, including, of course, theology, has every right to recognize and affirm its own distinctive foundations and criteria of judgement for its beliefs.[163] Recognizing and 'admitting' the tradition from within which one is conducting one's argument is remarkably clarifying, and generates sympathy, or at least tolerance, from readers operating from other traditions. Furthermore, it is remarkable how often it turns out that the case one is making is perfectly satisfactorily made within a given tradition, and does not require universal validation to be effective.

---

[161] D. Davidson and J. Hintikka, J. (eds), *Words and Objections: Essays on the Work of W V Quine* (Dordrecht: D. Reidel, 1969), p. 293.
[162] McGrath, *A Scientific Theology Volume 2*, pp. 57–60.
[163] Ibid., p. 71.

McGrath is also concerned that any valid Christian theology, although recognizing its own rootedness in a particular tradition, should be able to offer an account of the ideas and beliefs of other traditions and must be able to engage satisfactorily with them. It must not protect itself within an intellectual ghetto. McGrath explores the long history, beginning with Greek patristic theology, of attempts by Christian theologians to bridge traditions, in particular to explain other religions.[164] He sees natural theology as especially important for this role, as offering a trans-traditional resource.

Nature, a publicly accessible entity, is thus to be observed and interpreted in a scientific theology as God's creation. The function of natural theology is not to prove God's existence: this is accepted from the outset.[165] But from within this framework it can offer solutions to problems in other traditions, such as the uniformity, ordering and intelligibility of nature presupposed by science, without claiming that the second tradition will find this solution satisfying from within its own framework. Again, natural theology, by asserting that man is made in *imago Dei*, thereby asserts that some knowledge of God is to be expected outside the Christian tradition. McGrath also uses natural theology to explain the universal human ability to recognize beauty and wonder in nature and the presence and respect for goodness. He describes natural moral law at the 'cousin' of natural theology.[166] Natural theology thereby provides an account of how nature, when interpreted in a specifically Christian manner, can be held to possess a limited revelatory capacity that human reason is able to discern. It also allows Christian theology to position other disciplines and traditions in relation to itself, rather than to be forced into positions imposed by other traditions.

Pursuing the theme of trans-traditional rationality, McGrath explores the claims of mathematics to have access to universal verities. A Christian doctrine of creation offers an explanation of the realm of mathematical truths, of the extraordinary effectiveness of mathematics in nature, and of the success of the mathematical mind in discovering and applying them.[167] Nevertheless, even mathematics has tradition-specific beliefs. McGrath provides a well-known example from mathematics of an axiom that was thought to be universal, the parallel-postulate, which has turned out to be valid only within one mathematical 'tradition' –

[164] Ibid., pp. 72–8, 85–7.
[165] Ibid., p. 74.
[166] Ibid., pp. 87–97.
[167] Ibid., pp. 80–2.

Euclidean geometry.[168] Indeed, the shock of this discovery led to the decision to interpret the various mathematical systems not as descriptions of
features of empirical reality but as constructions of the mind with freely
chosen axioms as starting points. It has been a powerful lesson to the
whole of science not to assume too readily that its basic axioms are all
indubitable features of the natural world.

5.2. Interrogation of traditions

McGrath points to a long tradition in Christian theology that attempts
to clarify the manner in which affirmations about God are derived and
how they relate to analogous affirmations from the more familiar world
of the senses. What does the word 'God' stand for? How does the statement 'God exists' relate to the apparently analogous statement 'Socrates
exists'?[169] Similarly, how do moral statements about God relate to moral
statements about humans? This has led to the recognition that doctrinal
statements pass beyond themselves towards the greater mystery of God.
They are reliable yet incomplete descriptions of reality. Yet how are they
grounded in reality?

Theological interrogation is appropriate concerning the adequacy of
such representations, given their limitations. The Nicene controversy
was a dramatic example of the struggle to articulate insights in this
manner. These terms and representations are not an attempt to reduce
the experience to words, but an attempt to convey it through words. The
interrogation of received doctrines and theological positions is legitimate and necessary, given the historical and cultural rootedness of
Christianity. Have there been misinterpretations or misrepresentations
within Christianity of nature or historical events, or even of the significance of Jesus of Nazareth? This ongoing interrogation, a constant
feature of science at its best, is reflected in the historical development of
Christian doctrine.

McGrath views the Christian doctrinal and theological tradition both
as theory and practice, and as the actions of communities rather than
the ideas of detached individuals. He argues powerfully that for this
tradition to develop it must be stimulated, and that a part of that stimulus is interaction with other traditions. The interaction with the natural
sciences is perhaps the most powerful aid to theological development

---

[168] Ibid., pp. 97–8.
[169] McGrath, *The Foundations of Dialogue in Science and Religion*, pp. 151–2;
McGrath, *A Scientific Theology Volume 2*, pp. 44–6.

that is now available.[170] He interprets scientific theology, therefore, as a faithful and disciplined response to an encounter and engagement with reality, mediated by the methods of the natural and human sciences.

5.3. Realism

McGrath develops further his earlier discussions of realism.[171] As before, he bases it on the success of the natural sciences. McGrath spends much more time here refuting the 'epistemic fallacy', which confuses episte-mology with ontology by affirming that only what is known can be real. McGrath spends a lot of time critiquing the various forms of anti-realism, especially postmodernism and the 'strong programme' of social constructivism, which argue that social factors completely determine the perception and representation of reality. I would add here that a lot of the challenges to scientific realism have some plausibility only when one concentrates on the theoretical constructs of science and ignores the massive evidence or database commonly supporting the theory.

McGrath spends considerable time explaining how a critical realism can deal with a stratified reality, a reality that respects the emergence of genuine novelty at different levels in nature, and in theology. Social facts, such as one's citizenship, are to be regarded as existing on top of physical facts. They are not simply conventions; they are relational facts, although of a different kind from ordinary physical facts and relations. McGrath also asserts that his critical realism is compatible with the acceptance that, by knowing God, the knower is transformed. Critical realism might well hold the key to the reintegration of theology and spirituality, which some argue it has lost.

Again and again it is clear that, for McGrath, mathematics has con-siderable theological significance.[172] Mathematics enables the order within the world to be identified and seen as an aspect of the harmony within creation, grounded in the being of God. My own view of this is that the importance of mathematics here, though considerable, can be exaggerated. It has a limited scope in science, in that, as one moves away from physics and cosmology to biology, sociology, psychology and semiotics, its manifest significance seems to decrease.

McGrath carefully examines the tradition of Platonic realism in mathematics, according to which the truths of mathematics are claimed

---

[170] McGrath, *A Scientific Theology Volume 2*, p. 119.
[171] McGrath, *A Scientific Theology Volume 1*, ch. 10.
[172] Ibid., pp. 170–6.

to be timelessly existing 'out there', whether they are known or not. I am very unhappy about this form of mathematical realism. Does the non-denumerable infinity of non-Euclidean geometries, each with its own distinct curvature, actually exist? In what sense can abstract algebra be said to exist in some kind of Platonic realm: do the symbols of the Roman alphabet, for example, which are used in expressing this algebra, exist there? If it is claimed that the rules and relations obeyed by the symbols exist in abstraction from the symbols, this becomes very mysterious indeed.

Secondly, yes, many mathematical abstractions apply to nature and in extraordinarily unexpected and fertile ways. But there is a lot of artificial mental reworking in creating a mathematical fit to nature. Sometimes our mathematics does fit nature fairly descriptively, as in Maxwell's equations, for example, although even here an artificial construct – the axial vector – gives a false appearance of simplicity to the description.[173] More often, however, in modern physics, the mathematics we use to describe nature is so remote from description that it might be best described as an elaborate code which must pass through several decodings before a form of mathematics is arrived at which is truly descriptive. There is, indeed, a relation between this formalism and nature, but it is extremely oblique and abstract and it cannot be said to be a 'property' of nature in any ordinary sense. Of course, this in no way questions the theological significance of mathematics, but this should not be based on an exaggerated view of the fit between mathematics and nature.

Another major difficulty I have with Platonic realism in mathematics is that, at least in some interpretations of it, it makes mathematics a timeless, necessary, objective reality independent of the existence of any mind, or any universe or any God. I find this very odd.

McGrath again insists that critical realism is not being used in a foundational role for his scientific theology, but in an ancillary role, and also that it is an a posteriori discipline emerging from the sciences, and not a dogmatic a priori system. I would nuance the latter point as follows. Rather than drawing on any philosophical theory of realism, I think it is far better for a scientific theology to draw on the working praxis of science, within which an attitude towards what we can know about nature is discernable, and which has been sustained and refined through more than 2000 years of scientific research and reflection. This attitude can be

---

[173] John Roche, 'Axial Vectors, Skew-symmetric Tensors and the Nature of the Magnetic Field', *European Journal of Physics* 22 (2001), pp. 193–201.

of immense benefit to theology. For this reason, I feel that McGrath's scientific theology should derive its resources at least as much from the working methods of science as from philosophical theories about science, very fruitful though these have been. Certainly, the modern critical realist movement has the considerable advantage that it is closer to the spirit of science than any philosophical movement in the West for more than a century. It also challenges a narrow reductionism in science itself. But much of the positive achievement of critical realism is to address problems that have been generated within philosophy itself.

McGrath relies heavily on Roy Bhaskar, who has constructed a critical realism that gives equal weight to the realm of the socially constructed and the ontological given.[174] For Bhaskar, 'Perception gives us access to things, and experimental activity access to structures, that exist independently of us.' Mechanisms must be allowed to exist and operate without manifesting themselves in events, in that their existence cannot be held to depend on their being observed. This, a commonplace in science, is courageous philosophy, rejecting a current of scepticism in Western thought, which, chameleon-like, has reappeared in new colours every century since the Renaissance.

Bhaskar's realism embraces both the natural and social sciences.[175] The world must be regarded as differentiated and stratified and incapable of being adequately rendered by simple observations. Emergent strata in nature and in society possess features that are irreducible; that is, they cannot be conceived solely in terms of the lower levels. Bhaskar's critical realism thus rejects any reduction, scientific or philosophical, of nature just to one ontological level. He also rejects a sociological imperialism that insists upon the reduction of everything to social categories. Social and natural structures must be distinguished. Furthermore, methodology must be determined by ontology.[176]

Bhaskar rejects the 'epistemic fallacy'. This confuses epistemology with ontology by affirming that only what is known can be real, or that 'statements about being can be reduced to or analysed in terms of statements about knowledge'. He relates this to the ontic fallacy, which holds that knowledge is to be analysed as a direct, unmediated relation between a subject and being. The ontic fallacy ignores the cognitive and social mechanisms by which knowledge is produced from antecedent knowledge.[177] Clearly, this has profound theological implications.

---

[174] McGrath, *A Scientific Theology Volume 1*, pp. 209–14.
[175] Ibid., p. 224.
[176] Ibid., pp. 216–17.
[177] Ibid., pp. 218–19.

Stratification can also be recognized in theological reality.[178] God's revelation is to be located in nature, in history, in personal experience, in the life of the church and especially in Scripture. Within the Christian tradition, there is a created correspondence between creature and Creator. The reality of God is somehow rendered in the created order. Reflection on this reality through the parameters of the Christian tradition offers insights into the nature of God. The Christian doctrine of the incarnation affirms both historical and theological realities. Theological science, operating within its own very different tradition, addresses itself to God the Creator of this contingent existence, who is revealed through them. The distinctive role of theology here is to posit that the creative and redemptive being of God is the most fundamental of all strata of reality: it views nature through this lens. In this tradition, God must be distinguished from his creation. From this perspective, theology thus lies at the base, not the apex, of the sciences.[179]

McGrath, therefore, finds Bhaskar's critical realism helpful in offering a scientific theology resources to consolidate its position as a distinctive and legitimate intellectual discipline, to develop its own understanding of sources and methods, and to clarify its relationship to other disciplines in the natural and social sciences.[180]

He also finds Bhaskar's approach helpful in challenging reductionist approaches to theology in particular and to Christianity in general. It encourages a theological return to history, to viewing God's self-revelation as taking place, indirectly perhaps, in the arena of history. All levels of social experience and manifestations of religion, down to private religious experiences, also become of enormous significance to a scientific theology.[181]

McGrath continues with a summary of the impact of critical realism on the contours of a scientific theology. A scientific theology takes the form of a coherent and principled response to existing reality, it is an a posteriori discipline based on biblical witness, it takes account of the unique character of its object, and it offers an explanation of reality. He offers as a fifth postulate – that a scientific Christian theology is *Christocentric*.[182] McGrath here is not attempting to give the contours of a universal theology, but one operating within the central Christian traditions.

---

[178] Ibid., p. 226.
[179] McGrath *A Scientific Theology Volume 2*, p. 229.
[180] Ibid., p. 224.
[181] Ibid., pp. 239–44.
[182] Ibid., ch. 11.

A scientific theology is Christocentric for McGrath. Christ is the historical point of departure for Christianity, he is understood as revealing God, he is the bearer of salvation, and defines the shape of the redeemed life. There is a resonance between natural theology and the incarnation, since the rational ordering of creation is directly correlated with the incarnation. Human reason, creation and Christ are thus interlinked. This leads on to the question as to whether God is observable. God may be said to be observed in the person of Jesus Christ, who is God incarnate. God may also be observed indirectly in the world, through the lens of a natural theology. At the eschatological consummation God will be observed through the beatific vision.[183]

In his final volume, yet to appear, McGrath promises to demonstrate a direct convergence between scientific and theological communities, in the way in which they develop, formulate and confirm their theories.

His criticism of the Yale School of theology, which also offered a new methodology of theology, but did not produce a new theology employing these methods, places an onus on McGrath eventually to move on from his own retooling of the methodology of theology to a rebuilding of theology itself. This, of course, will take time, and ample 'leisure' to pursue research.

---

[183] Ibid., pp. 297–313.

4

The Uneasy Evangelical:
Alister E. McGrath on Postliberalism

Dennis L. Okholm

In many respects, Alister McGrath typifies the uneasiness with which evangelicals approach postliberalism. As we shall see, there are features of the postliberal agenda that warm the evangelical heart and even instruct the evangelical mind; yet there are tendencies that make the ever-jittery Fundamentalist-bred American evangelical and his or her polite British-bred counterpart suspicious. At the same time, McGrath's criticisms of postliberalism may be *too* typical of evangelical responses. That is to say, the common evangelical charge of anti-realism and the resistance to nonfoundationalism may be a majority position in need of reassessment.

1. Postliberalism

A few decades ago, a theological movement closely linked to Yale Divinity School answered the liberal trend in modern Christianity of accommodating the culture. Influenced by the thought of Ludwig Wittgenstein, Karl Barth, Michael Polanyi, Clifford Geertz, Peter Berger and others, Hans Frei and George Lindbeck set the agenda for what came to be known as 'postliberalism'.[1] In their wake followed theologians such as William Placher, Stanley Hauerwas and George Hunsinger.

---

[1] See Hans Frei, *The Eclipse of Biblical Narrative* (New Haven: Yale University Press, 1974) and *The Identity of Jesus Christ: The Hermeneutic Bases of Dogmatic Theology* (Philadelphia: Fortress Press, 1975) (originally published in *Crossroads* in 1967); and George Lindbeck, *The Nature of Doctrine: Religion and Theology in a Postliberal Age* (Philadelphia: Westminster, 1984). For the following summary, see Timothy R. Phillips and Dennis L. Okholm, 'The

Answering modernity's quest to ground the interpretation of reality in some universally accessible ahistorical reason or common pre-reflective human experience, the postliberals recalled the church in its postmodern context to something of the pre-modern agenda of catechizing Christians in the confessional faith that has grown out of the biblical narrative. Though, as William Placher has said, the death of modernity's totalizing agenda goes unnoticed in some universities, postliberalism appeals to the particularity of the biblical narrative as an interglossing, intratextual whole, which is focused on Jesus Christ, shapes the world of believers in their practice of worship, life and thought, and supplies the categories for understanding all of life. A religion, then, is like a language that:

> makes possible the description of realities, the formulation of beliefs, and the experiencing of inner attitudes, feelings, and sentiments. Like a culture or language, it is a communal phenomenon that shapes the subjectivities of individuals rather than being primarily a manifestation of those subjectivities.[2]

In this context religious doctrines function like rules of grammar that govern the way we use language to describe the world. Christian doctrines articulate the rules for using confessional language in defining the world we inhabit and the God we worship.

---

[1] (*continued*) Nature of Confession: Evangelicals and Postliberals' in Timothy R. Phillips and Dennis L. Okholm (eds), *The Nature of Confession: Evangelicals & Postliberals in Conversation* (Downers Grove: InterVarsity Press, 1996); and Alister McGrath, *The Genesis of Doctrine: A Study in the Foundations of Doctrinal Criticism* (Oxford: Basil Blackwell, 1990), pp. 14–34.

[2] Lindbeck, *The Nature of Doctrine*, p. 33. Accordingly, McGrath's goal in his more popular books, such as *Understanding Doctrine: What it is and Why it Matters* (Grand Rapids: Zondervan, 1990) and *Understanding Jesus: Who Jesus Christ Is and Why He Matters* (Grand Rapids: Zondervan, 1987), has been the theological task of facilitating the fixed reality of the narrative world to shape and inform the Christian's understanding of the 'real' world: 'Thinking people need to construct and inhabit mental worlds. They need to be able to discern some degree of ordering within their experience, to make sense of its riddles and enigmas. They need to be able to structure human existence in the world, to allow it to possess meaning and purpose, and to allow decisions to be made concerning the future of existence. In order for anyone … to make informed moral decisions, it is necessary to have a set of values concerning human life. Those values are determined by beliefs, and those beliefs are stated as doctrines. Christian doctrine thus provides a fundamental framework for Christian living' (McGrath, *Understanding Doctrine*, p. 2).

Lindbeck (the primary target of McGrath's assessment of post-liberalism)[3] labelled his approach 'cultural-linguistic' over against two approaches he rejected – namely the 'cognitive-propositional' theory typical of conservatives and the 'experiential-expressive' tack characteristic of liberals.

The cognitive-propositional approach to doctrine is an ahistorical view of doctrinal statements as 'informative propositions or truth claims about objective realities'.[4] Though Lindbeck does not believe the approach is wholly discredited (citing, as he does, examples such as Peter Geach, G.K. Chesterton, C.S. Lewis and Malcolm Muggeridge),[5] McGrath refers to Carl Henry as one who fits this category and whose method Lindbeck would describe as voluntarist, intellectualist and literalist (with reference to what is 'out there'). At the core of Lindbeck's dissatisfaction with this approach is its uselessness in furthering ecumenical discussions (the context within which Lindbeck made his proposals in his book *The Nature of Doctrine*). He is bothered by the fact that propositions within this view must always be either true or false, so that one cannot harmonize the historic affirmations and denials of, for example, transubstantiation.[6] While McGrath certainly does not view doctrines as literalistic propositions that exactly mirror reality,[7] he does want to rehabilitate the cognitive-propositionalist approach from what he argues to be Lindbeck's caricature of it. We shall deal with McGrath's objections to Lindbeck on this score in the third part of this essay. For now, we turn to McGrath's appreciation for Lindbeck's rejection of the experiential-expressive alternative.

McGrath exuberantly applauds Lindbeck's critique of the liberal option: it is 'fair, accurate, persuasive, and effective'; in fact, he suggests

---

[3] McGrath's exposé of postliberalism focuses almost exclusively on Lindbeck in *The Genesis of Doctrine*. Though the treatment of postliberalism is in large part verbatim in two later writings, namely 'An Evangelical Evaluation of Postliberalism' in Phillips and Okholm (eds), *The Nature of Confession* and Alister E. McGrath, *A Passion for Truth: The Intellectual Coherence of Evangelicalism* (Downers Grove, Illinois: InterVarsity Press, 1996), he does include other postliberal thinkers along the way in these more recent writings.

[4] Lindbeck, *The Nature of Doctrine*, p. 16.

[5] Ibid., p. 24.

[6] Ibid., p. 16.

[7] In fact, in a very helpful comment McGrath likens doctrine to a map: it represents the terrain, but it would be foolish to equate the map with the terrain. We might add that with this approach the history of theology involves attempts at revising the map to make it a more accurate representation.

that it 'may be the most significant long-term contribution he has made to the contemporary discussion of the nature of doctrine'.[8] Lindbeck criticizes the revisionists' understanding of religious language as a culturally conditioned expression of a universal prelinguistic consciousness. Doctrines are interpreted as 'noninformative and nondiscursive symbols of inner feelings, attitudes or existential orientations'.[9] This approach is unconvincing because it cannot specify or isolate a common core experience from religious language and then demonstrate that the language is an articulation or response to the experience, making the claim neither verifiable nor falsifiable. Either experience varies from culture to culture – and, therefore, from religion to religion – or it remains a subjective, vacuous and nebulous concept, the constancy of which cannot be established. In fact, this approach must admit the possibility that religious expectation 'creates' religious experience, rather than vice versa.[10]

McGrath does take issue with Lindbeck at one point in his critique of the experiential-expressivist approach for failing to distinguish those he criticizes from the tack taken by Schleiermacher, for whom Christian doctrine does not refer to pre-reflective experience, but to distinctively Christian and corporate experience. Still, McGrath enthusiastically enters into Lindbeck's attack on the liberal option by adding three more criticisms of his own.[11]

First, doctrine may not *articulate* experience; it may *contradict* it, as evident in Luther's 'theology of the cross'.[12]

Secondly, the assumption that an individual's personal experience constitutes the primary datum of religion does not allow us to distinguish between an atheistic and a born-again believer, even though empirical psychological studies indicate a marked difference in psychological qualities and social attitudes expressed at both cognitive and affective levels. This is due to what Lindbeck calls the 'homogenizing tendencies' of this view.[13]

---

8 McGrath, *The Genesis of Doctrine*, p. 20.

9 Lindbeck, *The Nature of Doctrine*, p. 16.

10 See McGrath's summaries of Lindbeck's criticism in *The Genesis of Doctrine*, pp. 25–6 and 'An Evangelical Evaluation of Postliberalism', p. 27.

11 See McGrath, *The Genesis of Doctrine*, pp. 22–5 for what follows.

12 In ibid., p. 25 McGrath writes: 'Experience … is the *explicandum*, rather than the *explicans*; it is what requires to be interpreted, rather than the interpreting agent itself. God is experienced as absent; doctrine affirms that God is present in a hidden manner. Theology engages with existential realities, yet is able to avoid being trapped by them, and being reduced to their level.'

13 See Lindbeck, *The Nature of Doctrine*, p. 128.

Thirdly, how can we know if the experience we are trying to capture in words or symbols really is an experience of God? McGrath asserts: 'Experience may indeed seek expression – but it also demands a criterion by which it may be judged.'[14]

The 'cultural-linguistic' theory of postliberalism, as already mentioned, treats doctrines as regulators of the religious language we use to describe the world and God. So the task of biblical and theological scholars becomes primarily practical: to edify the church by detecting distortions and deficiencies in the church's thoughts and actions. This means that Christian beliefs are fallible and reformable, an outlook that serves postliberalism's ecumenical purposes. Employing standards such as intratextual and Christological criteria and the upbuilding of the church, a hermeneutic results that acknowledges both diverse interpretations and unity. In this sense Lindbeck constantly reminds us that postliberalism is a formal research programme that can accommodate diverse theological traditions; it is engaged in prolegomena and not terribly interested in explicating doctrines themselves.[15] By treating doctrine as the rules or regulators of Christian language, it advocates the intentional catechization of Christians over against modernity's encroachment on the church. This is something McGrath appreciates; it resonates nicely with his agenda.[16] In fact, there is much in postliberalism to like for an evangelical like McGrath. To those features we now turn.

---

[14] McGrath, *The Genesis of Doctrine*, p. 25. See a similar critique with reference to Schleiermacher in Robert C. Roberts, 'The Feeling of Absolute Dependence', *The Journal of Religion* 57.3 (July 1977), pp. 252–66.

[15] See Phillips and Okholm, 'The Nature of Confession'. Of course, McGrath reminds us of Jeffrey Stout's description of postliberalism's preoccupation with methodology: it's like clearing your throat; you can only do it so long before losing your audience. See 'A Panel Discussion' in Phillips and Okholm (eds), *The Nature of Confession*, p. 250; also see McGrath, 'An Evangelical Evaluation of Postliberalism', p. 29. At the conference at which McGrath quoted Stout, Lindbeck presented an admirable paper on the atoning work of Christ, calling the church to correct a one-sided emphasis on the *Christus victor* theme by reaffirming Jesus as victim. His presentation should go far to answer McGrath's and Stout's criticism for not moving from a theological agenda to a theological statement – the pragmatic test for the reliability of a theological method. See Lindbeck's 'Atonement and the Hermeneutics of Intratextual Social Embodiment' in Phillips and Okholm (eds), *The Nature of Confession*, pp. 219–40.

[16] See his *Understanding* books (published by Zondervan) and *Evangelicalism and the Future of Christianity* (Downers Grove: InterVarsity Press, 1995), pp. 114–17.

2. What's Right about Postliberalism

The postliberal reaction against the homogenizing tendencies of liberalism is clearly voiced in the former's assertion of the centrality of Jesus Christ within the life and thought of the church. This emphasis on Christ's particularity is applauded by evangelicals against liberalism's 'abortive attempt to make theory (that all religions are saying the same thing) and observation (that the religions are different) coincide'.[17]

In addition to Christ's centrality, evangelicals can appreciate the liberation of Christian theology from extra-biblical presuppositions, the result of postliberalism's insistence on Scripture as the norm for belief and practice against the 'potential enslavement or debasement of Christian thought through a deficient theological method that allows ideas from outside the church to assume a controlling influence within it'.[18]

Of course, the evangelical doctrine of Scripture differs from the postliberal's in the former's commitment to some form of inerrancy or infallibility. But George Hunsinger admits that an evangelical like McGrath can maintain this commitment with a minimalist commitment to modernity.

At the same time, McGrath mitigates his appreciation of the postliberals' commitment to the authority of Scripture because they are not entirely free from dependence on extra-biblical foundations, such as Lindbeck's reliance on Clifford Geertz's cultural analysis and Stanley Hauerwas's on Yves Simon's analysis of political authority.[19] Yet evangelicals must also admit *their* commitment to extra-biblical paradigms in their evolving conceptions of biblical authority.[20]

Insistence on Christ's particularity and Scripture's normativity supports the postliberal emphasis on the distinctiveness of the Christian faith over against the prevailing culture. While McGrath believes that Lindbeck's categorization of the history of doctrine is 'seductive and misleading' for reasons that will become clear below,[21] he applauds

---

[17] See McGrath, 'An Evangelical Evaluation of Postliberalism', p. 35.

[18] Ibid., p. 25.

[19] McGrath, 'An Evangelical Evaluation of Postliberalism', n. 11, p. 258.

[20] See Stanley Grenz, 'Nurturing the Soul/Informing the Mind: The Genesis of the Evangelical Scripture Principle' in Vincent Bacotea and Laura Miguélez (eds), *Scripture in the Evangelical Tradition* (Downers Grove: InterVarsity Press, 2003).

[21] See McGrath, *The Genesis of Doctrine*, p. 18. To be fair, while I would not call *McGrath's* categorizations seductive or misleading, they can be confusing. For instance, to establish the fact that Lindbeck does not understand the cognitive-propositionalist appreciation of the referential sophistication of

Lindbeck's criticism of experientially oriented theories of doctrine. Postliberalism is commended for its 'studied and principled refusal to follow liberalism's headlong rush into the identification of the truth of the gospel with late twentieth-century liberal American cultural norms'.[22] Instead, it celebrates the distinctiveness of the Christian tradition and theology's role of articulating the distinctive grammar of the Christian faith.

In a somewhat similar vein, McGrath appreciates postliberalism's rejection of liberal foundationalism as a thing of the modernist past. Though, as we shall suggest later, his enthusiasm may be mitigated by a residue of foundationalism, McGrath believes it is wrong to criticize postliberalism for its abandonment of a universal discourse: it is like 'scolding a child who no longer believes in Santa Claus'.[23] For philosophical and religious foundationalism has been discredited. While liberalism's intent at this point is apologetic and while the concept may be a 'reassuring, cozy and useful illusion', it is still an illusion that can 'too easily become profoundly oppressive, forcing observation to conform to theory and repressing distinctiveness on the part of, for example, a particular religion on account of a prior dogmatic conviction that all are saying the same thing'. In fact, McGrath makes a similar argument against John Hick's pluralism, arguing that, in the end, the pluralist's claim that all religions are merely culturally conditioned understandings of salvation and of the same ineffable transcendent Real is an oppressive 'intellectual Stalinism'.[24]

---

[21] (*continued*) language (i.e. metaphor, analogy and so forth), McGrath cites in a footnote Sallie McFague's work on models. McFague is decidedly in Lindbeck's experiential-expressive camp, as clearly seen in her essay 'An Epilogue: The Christian Paradigm' in Peter C. Hodgson and Robert H. King (eds), *Christian Theology: An Introduction to Its Traditions and Tasks* (Philadelphia: Fortress Press, 1985 revised edition), pp. 377–90. Furthermore, the footnote couples McFague and Soskice – another strange categorization. See McGrath, 'An Evangelical Evaluation of Postliberalism', n. 25, p. 207.

[22] McGrath, 'An Evangelical Evaluation of Postliberalism', p. 35; also see p. 28.

[23] Ibid., pp. 24–5 for the quotes in this paragraph.

[24] See Alister E. McGrath, 'A Particularist View: A Post-Enlightenment Approach' in Dennis L. Okholm and Timothy R. Phillips (eds), *Four Views on Salvation in a Pluralistic World* (Grand Rapids, Michigan: Zondervan, 1996), pp. 206–9. It would be interesting to know exactly how McGrath would respond to Lindbeck's seemingly more tolerant approach to the availability of salvation in other religions (e.g., see *The Nature of Doctrine*, ch. 3), though I do not recall any place in which McGrath discusses this feature of Lindbeck's postliberalism.

Before turning to McGrath's criticisms of postliberalism, we should simply note three more evangelical appreciations.

First, evangelical heirs of the Protestant Reformation should welcome the trajectory postliberalism takes to wrench Scripture from the control of academic elites and return it to the church so that it can become world creating and identity forming for the laity. (One sees this, for instance, in the writings of Stanley Hauerwas.)

Secondly, the cultural-linguistic approach recognizes the fallibility of theological constructs and fosters a willingness to learn from various enduring grammars of faith (though McGrath argues that the cognitive-propositionalist approach *can* do this as well).

Thirdly, McGrath commends postliberalism for its strong sense of community, in contrast to evangelicalism's typical slide toward 'social atomism'.[25]

3. What's Questionable about Postliberalism

McGrath's commendations and appreciation of postliberalism does not stand alone. He has some grave misgivings and criticisms, which, in turn, are themselves called into question by other evangelicals.

McGrath's 'more general difference' with Lindbeck's postliberalism is the latter's resistance to viewing the three models as complementary.[26] For this reason, McGrath accuses Lindbeck of a reductionistic understanding of doctrine, based in part on what McGrath considers a 'more serious general criticism' – namely Lindbeck's highly selective, somewhat superficial and questionably reliable use of history to illustrate his points, usually depending on secondary sources rather than on primary material. McGrath argues that Lindbeck has really based his approach to doctrine on prior insights that find application in the social sciences (e.g., Geertz) and applied them to theological reflection. In contrast to such historically and socially abstracted theories, McGrath insists that any study of the development of doctrine as an historical phenomenon will lead one to realize the polymorphic and polyvalent character of doctrine. Lindbeck's decontextualized study 'does not coincide with the complex agglomerate of social, cognitive and existential parameters implicated in a fully nuanced account of doctrine as an historical phenomenon'. This explains our earlier observation about McGrath's

---

[25] See McGrath, 'An Evangelical Evaluation of Postliberalism', p. 35.

[26] See McGrath, *The Genesis of Doctrine*, pp. 32–7 for what follows; cf. Lindbeck, *The Nature of Doctrine*, p. 17.

disdain for Lindbeck's categorization of approaches to doctrine. It is McGrath's contention that an historical study of doctrine leads one to see the integrative nature of doctrine: it is cognitive, experiential, regulative and referential. McGrath makes his case in his four theses in *The Genesis of Doctrine* (chapter 3): doctrine is a social demarcator, interprets the Christian narrative, interprets our experience and makes truth claims. McGrath's historical approach is grounded in his insistence that doctrines are a response to the question posed to the community by the Christ-event: 'Truth is grounded in history and subsequent reflection upon an historical event.'[27] At the end of the day, McGrath would like Lindbeck to revise his thesis to incorporate aspects of the cognitive and experiential approaches to doctrine. He appreciates Lindbeck's concern for doctrine's internal regulative function as *one* of *several* functions of doctrine, but McGrath would like Lindbeck to admit that doctrine also has to do with veridicality and with effecting what it signifies.[28]

As mentioned, McGrath's concern to provide a history of the phenomenon of doctrine is evident in his insistence on the historical *cause* of the Christian doctrinal tradition. The 'proximate external referent' is the history of Jesus of Nazareth, which is mediated by the Christian tradition and *Lebensform* in such a way that it generates and regulates doctrine. This leads us to McGrath's central concern about post-liberalism. It is worth quoting at length:

> The chief difficulty raised by this approach concerns the origin of the cultural-linguistic tradition regulated by doctrines. Lindbeck seems to assume it is simply 'given' … The 'language' is just there … How does the Christian idiom come into being? Throughout his analysis, there seems to be a studied evasion of the central question of revelation – in other words, whether the Christian idiom, articulated in Scripture and hence in the Christian tradition, emerges from accumulated human insight or from the self-disclosure of God in the Christ-event. Yet Lindbeck's insistence on the primacy of 'the objectivities of religion, its language, doctrine, liturgies and modes of action' raises the unanswered question of how these primary data may be accounted for. Where do Christian doctrines come from? How can they be evaluated? To what is the Christian language a response? What extralinguistic reality is it

---

[27] McGrath, *The Genesis of Doctrine*, p. 74. This accords with McGrath's often-sympathetic treatment of Pannenberg.

[28] See ibid., pp. 60, 77–9. In affirming postliberalism's emphasis on the regulative function of doctrine, McGrath provides a nice excursus that calls attention to Schleiermacher's understanding of 'heresy' as opposed to 'unbelief': see p. 78.

attempting to describe or depict? Evangelicals find themselves in the position of being able to agree in broad terms with Lindbeck as far as he goes, yet wish that he went much further. For this reason, the *most fundamental evangelical critique* of postliberalism concerns the *inadequacy of its commitment to extralinguistic and extrasystemic realities.*[29]

McGrath's most serious criticism moves us to consider his suspicion of postliberalism's anti-realism and its concommitant disavowal of a correspondence theory of truth.

McGrath argues that the cultural-linguistic theory of postliberalism dispenses with external referents and reduces truth claims to mere 'intrasystemic consistency' or 'intrasystemic cohesion'. Is regulation of Christian discourse all there is to doctrine? Or is there some reality outside the biblical text to which the biblical narrative relates (whether or not we recognize this relation)? The postliberal approach appears to be a purely intratextual affair with little concern for its possible relation to external objective reality. One merely has to follow the rules, but does not need to accept their ontological implications.[30] McGrath goes so far as to say that, for Lindbeck, 'truth is firmly equated with – virtually to the point of being reduced to – internal consistency'.[31]

In fact, McGrath goes further in his accusation of postliberalism's anti-realism. He compares ('at least superficially') Lindbeck's approach to doctrine with Bultmann's approach to the *kerygma*, in that 'both are assumed just to be there, lying beyond challenge or justification'. McGrath wants both doctrine and *kerygma* not only to represent accurately the significance of an historical event but to be open to challenge regarding their adequacy in interpreting the event.[32] While McGrath's criticism must be taken seriously, still, if one function of doctrine is to

---

[29] McGrath, 'An Evangelical Evaluation of Postliberalism', pp. 34–5, italics mine. cf. McGrath's distinction between the 'event-character' of truth (which he endorses) and understanding revelation as the disclosure of general principles (which he does not endorse). Given the former, 'that doctrine comes into being in history renders it susceptible to historical investigation'. See McGrath, *The Genesis of Doctrine*, pp. 76, 93.

[30] McGrath, *The Genesis of Doctrine*, p. 29 and 'An Evangelical Evaluation of Postliberalism', pp. 28–36; references are made to Lindbeck, *The Nature of Doctrine*, pp. 32–41, 66–7, 106.

[31] McGrath, 'An Evangelical Evaluation of Postliberalism', p. 36.

[32] Ibid., pp. 38–9. He makes reference to his chapter on Ebeling and Bultmann in *The Making of Modern German Christology* (Grand Rapids, Michigan: Zondervan, 1994²), pp. 145–98.

correct our interpretations of experience, as in McGrath's citation of Luther's theology of the cross, then we must mitigate our claim to test in an *extra*-systemic manner the adequacy of our interpretation of an event. (For example, how does one test in an extra-systematic manner the theological claim that Jesus of Nazareth, who was crucified by Rome allegedly for political subversion, was in actuality the incarnate Son of God dying for our sins? Isn't this precisely Paul's point in 1 Corinthians 1:18–25? McGrath makes this case when he discusses the problem of moving from the historical event of the crucifixion to a specific interpretation of that event in *Intellectuals Don't Need God.*)[33]

But, again, McGrath's primary concern here is whether there is any event at all to which the postliberal is referring in making his or her confession of faith. It is not just the anti-realism that bothers McGrath; it is also the disavowal of a correspondence theory of truth. Just as 'intrasystematic consistency' belongs with 'coherence', so 'ontological reference' belongs with 'correspondence'. For the postliberal, theological statements are merely descriptive of the biblical material in much the same manner as Schleiermacher conceived of doctrine as descriptions of religious affections: 'Doctrine is descriptive, concerned primarily with intrasystemic cohesion.'[34]

In making his case against postliberalism at this point, we must return to McGrath's dissatisfaction with Lindbeck's caricature of the cognitive-propositionalist approach and to McGrath's charge of a reductionistic understanding of doctrine. McGrath distances himself from Carl Henry, whose type of cognitive-propositional approach is 'ultimately inadequate' because it fails to do justice to the full complexity of the biblical notions of revelation; nevertheless, McGrath wants to ensure that for evangelicals both revelation and doctrine have cognitive aspects. He surmises that Lindbeck's caricature may be due to a mistaken notion that evangelicals believe it is possible to 'definitively, exhaustively, and timelessly state the objective truth about God in propositional form'.[35] McGrath wants to assure (convince?) Lindbeck that the best practitioners of the cognitive-propositional approach can reformulate, amplify and supplement doctrinal statements. In fact, McGrath calls upon pre-moderns like Calvin, Zwingli, Luther and Vico to show how a cognitive account of experience can offer a sophisticated

---

[33] See Alister E. McGrath, *Intellectuals Don't Need God and Other Myths: Building Bridges to Faith through Apologetics* (Grand Rapids, Michigan: Zondervan, 1993), pp. 54–5.

[34] McGrath, 'An Evangelical Evaluation of Postliberalism', p. 36.

[35] Ibid., pp. 29–30.

rhetorical analysis of experience without in any way *reducing* experience to propositional form or degenerating into the pejorative sense of literalism that Lindbeck has in mind.[36]

It is at this point that McGrath prefers to talk about words 'signposting' a reality that they cannot capture.[37] That is, doctrinal statements possess a 'relative adequacy' both in terms of the original historical context of their formulation and in terms of the independent referent they are alleged to represent. Doctrines are 'reliable, yet incomplete descriptions of reality. Their power lies in what they represent, rather than what they are in themselves.' Doctrinal affirmations are perceptions, not total descriptions. They point beyond themselves to something inexpressible – something on the 'borderlands of experience'. (They also evoke experience and convey experiences the author wishes to share with readers.)

Actually, there are many levels at which cognitive or propositional statements work, and Lindbeck is to be commended for his valuable corrective to deficient cognitive models which suggest that 'an exhaustive and unambiguous account of God is transmitted conceptually by propositions'. In fact, all experience (not just religious experience) cannot be reduced to words. Every experience is modified by interpretive elements, as folks like Thomas Kuhn have made clear in the sciences. Experience is theory-laden. McGrath repudiates a 'brute empiricism'. Those who might influence postliberals (such as Polanyi and Berger) have taught us that prior knowledge and beliefs are constitutive in our experience. The cognitive dimension provides the interpretive framework (based on the biblical narrative) for Christian experience and the channel through which it is conveyed. But we cannot reduce Christianity to mere words or to inchoate experience.

This is precisely why McGrath is upset by Lindbeck's reductionism – why his antithetical posture towards cognitive *and* experiential models (McGrath is often favourably inclined toward Schleiermacher) is unsatisfactory. While an evangelical like McGrath insists that there is a genuinely cognitive dimension to doctrinal statements, such propositions 'need not and should not be treated as purely cognitive statements'. So, while McGrath is troubled by a complete surrender to a coherentist theory of truth, he is not advocating total capitulation to a correspondence theory:

---

[36] McGrath, *The Genesis of Doctrine*, p. 19.

[37] See ibid., pp. 17–20, 66–72 for what follows; cf. McGrath, 'An Evangelical Evaluation of Postliberalism', pp. 30–3.

> To speak of doctrine as making truth-claims ... is most emphatically not to commit oneself *exclusively* to a 'correspondence theory of truth,' or any other theory of truth; rather it is to observe the significant degree of isomorphism that exists between the inherently polyvalent concepts of doctrine and truth, and to register an historically-informed unwillingness to reduce either concept to univocity.[38]

McGrath has certainly represented the best of evangelical concerns in his rejection of anti-realism and his nuanced understanding of the cognitive-propositionalist approach. But we must ask whether he has treated postliberalism fairly. That is, *is* postliberalism *necessarily* committed to anti-realism?

First, McGrath's own language suggests that the answer is 'no'. McGrath either *suspects* that Lindbeck is an anti-realist or he merely *wishes* that Lindbeck would be more *forthcoming* in a commitment to realism. In other words, McGrath is uneasy at best and frustrated at worst.

McGrath's uneasiness is detected in the cautious language he uses to describe and critique Lindbeck's proposal. For instance, we have quoted McGrath saying that the postliberal approach '*appears* to represent a purely intratextual affair, with *little* concern for its possible relation to an external objective reality'.[39] His fundamental critique of post-liberalism is the '*inadequacy* of its commitment to extralinguistic and extrasystemic realities'.[40] Recognizing that Lindbeck believes first-order assertions make truth claims, McGrath concedes: 'An *implicit* commitment to views of truth with which evangelicals would find little to disagree underlies Lindbeck's analysis, even though he himself may not *explicitly* articulate this.'[41] In the same essay, McGrath makes statements such as 'This *apparent* evasion of truth claims can be seen in Lindbeck's discussion of ...' and 'Lindbeck, by accident or design, is *perhaps somewhat equivocal* over whether or not his cultural-linguistic approach to doctrine involves the affirmation or setting aside of epistemological realism and a correspondence theory of truth.'[42] And in one slightly different manner, McGrath mitigates his criticism of

---

[38] McGrath, *The Genesis of Doctrine*, pp. 79–80. Italics mine.
[39] McGrath, 'An Evangelical Evaluation of Postliberalism', p. 28. Italics mine (and in the following quotations in this paragraph).
[40] Ibid., p. 35.
[41] Ibid., p. 36.
[42] Ibid., pp. 37, 38. The latter quote ironically seems to be an equivocal accusation of equivocation!

Lindbeck's treatment of cognitive approaches to doctrine: 'there may be detected a persistent Wittgensteinian *reserve* concerning the external referent of doctrinal statements, and a perceptible *hesitation* over the claims of epistemological realism'.[43] At one point McGrath admits that even Lindbeck 'seems to concede implicitly' that religions do make truth claims.[44] McGrath wants Lindbeck to consider that his preoccupation with the regulative non-referential function of doctrine may refer to doctrines that are based on an historical misunderstanding or on a deliberate falsification, but McGrath can only admit Lindbeck 'seems unwilling and unable to consider' this option.[45]

McGrath's ambivalence is most clearly stated in the following: 'A sense of *unease*, similar to that associated with the instrumentalist approach, attaches itself within the community of faith to the suggestion that doctrinal terms are purely intrasystemic, having no referent outside the theoretical system itself.'[46] Lest one be accused of performing some kind of psychoanalysis here, the unease which McGrath expresses is, to his credit, perhaps due to his recognition that postliberals like Lindbeck are *not* committed to anti-realism. This is an ongoing discussion among interpreters of postliberalism that seems to have no end.

One interpreter who is sympathetic to a charitable reading of Lindbeck and concludes that postliberals are *neutral* in the realism–anti-realism debate is Jeffrey Hensley.[47] Such neutrality would indeed frustrate most evangelicals and make folks like McGrath uneasy.

Hensley argues that when a 'conceptual realist' states that concepts cut up the world, he or she is not denying the existence of material objects nor asserting that all existence is dependent on cognitive activity. Rather:

> it is asserted that the existence of kinds of entities, entities of those kinds and their interrelation are all relative to our human conceptual schemes or the ways in which we represent our experience. Humans are active in constructing their conceptual schemes, so, by inference, they are active in cutting up the world in the process of understanding the world through their various conceptual frameworks.[48]

---

[43] McGrath, *The Genesis of Doctrine*, p. 31.
[44] McGrath, 'An Evangelical Evaluation of Postliberalism', p. 37.
[45] Ibid., p. 38.
[46] McGrath, *The Genesis of Doctrine*, p. 32.
[47] See Jeffrey Hensley, 'Are Postliberals Necessarily Antirealists? Reexamining the Metaphysics of Lindbeck's Postliberal Theology' in Phillips and Okholm (eds), *The Nature of Confession*, pp. 69–80.
[48] Ibid., p. 74.

In the religious context, while the biblical narrative generates the grammar or conceptual framework of Christianity, still, there *is* a world that the text absorbs. There is also a text that absorbs the world, so that neither the world nor the text derive their *existence* from each other. It is meaning, not existence, that is conceptually relative. Or, said differently (and carefully), what is *taken* to be reality is socially constructed, but not reality or the world itself. What is denied is any Archimedian, concept-free standpoint – a denial we would have to concede is compatible with metaphysical realism.

Hensley goes on to argue that concepts are not so much screens or instruments through which we filter or make the world. Concepts are *bridges* between us and the world: 'We get to the objects *by way of* our concepts.'[49] The properties that objects possess is grasped and believed to be exemplified by our concepts. So the objects have natures and properties that are mind-independent, yet our perception of them is concept- or theory-laden. At this point, Hensley concludes that when Lindbeck asserts that all experience of reality is theory-laden, he is 'simply noting that we as human cognizers necessarily use concepts to describe and understand our experience. Concepts *bridge* rather than *screen* our idioms for understanding reality with reality itself.'[50]

But Lindbeck might still be susceptible to the claim that the *truth* of doctrine is independent of some correspondence to an external state of affairs, just as McGrath has suspected. Hensley claims this is true only to the extent that theology and doctrine are second-order activities – when theological utterances function as doctrines that govern Christian discourse. But when theological statements function as first-order assertions, such as in catechetical instruction or doxological acclamations, a truth claim *is* being made. As Hensley notes, the distinction between the two uses of theological statements is crucial (even though George Hunsinger has suggested that this is only a relative distinction that can easily be overdone,[51] and even though in a verbal exchange

---

[49] Ibid., p. 77.

[50] Ibid., p. 78.

[51] See 'Panel Discussion', p. 248. Taking into account this distinction, however, may explain McGrath's apparent concession in *The Genesis of Doctrine* (p. 65), when he writes: 'Lindbeck himself weakens his polemic against cognivist propositionalism by his insistence that the proposition "*Christus est dominus*" may be "not only intrasystematically but also ontologically true"' (ref. Lindbeck, *The Nature of Doctrine*, p. 65). See McGrath's discussion of Lindbeck's apparent concession in McGrath's assessment of Lindbeck's consideration of *homoousios* in *The Genesis of Doctrine*, pp. 29–30; cf. Lindbeck's

McGrath provocatively raised the possibility that this is an unhelpful artificial difference); Lindbeck maintains that doctrines have truth value when they function as first-order statements. Furthermore, Hensley notes that Lindbeck denies that correspondence to reality is a *sufficient* condition for truth, but he does not deny that it may be a *necessary* condition for truth, just as intrasystematic truth is a necessary but not sufficient condition for ontological truth. In fact, truth is understood to be a *combination* of an intersystematic coherence *and* a correspondence of the *entire* collection of statements with reality.[52] Hensley concludes:

> Consequently, while Lindbeck does not hold either a pure coherence or a correspondence theory of truth, it appears that nevertheless he maintains a realist or nonepistemic account of truth, whereby truth is thought of as an internal coherence of propositions which *as a whole* relate to particular states of affairs.[53]

---

[51] (*continued*) *The Nature of Doctrine*, pp. 92–6. If Hunsinger and McGrath are correct in weakening the first-order/second-order distinction, then Hensley's argument is seriously compromised *or* postliberals do indeed need to be more explicit as McGrath has suggested or revise their estimation of second-order assertions.

[52] Hensley's representation of Lindbeck here is supported by Lindbeck's discussion in *The Nature of Doctrine*, pp. 64–6. Lindbeck describes the difference between Christianity and maths in that the former is similar to a language, whereas the latter is an organized set of explicit statements (axioms, definitions, corollaries). In addition, in a religious system the right use of language cannot be detached from a particular way of behaving. The religious system is constituted by a *set* of stories used in specifiable ways to interpret and live in the world. Intrasystematic truth or falsity is a necessary but not sufficient condition for ontological correspondence, since the ontological (correspondence) truth of religious utterances is not an attribute they have *when considered in and of themselves*, but only as a function of their role in constituting a way of being in the world, which itself corresponds to the ultimate Real. Lindbeck appeals here to J.L. Austin's idea of the performatory use of language: a religious utterance *acquires* propositional truth of ontological correspondence only when it is a performance which helps create the correspondence, by which the utterance acquires propositional force. To say 'Jesus is Lord' is objectively real, but the only way to *assert* the *truth* is to do something about it – to commit to a way of life. E.g., citing Luther, Lindbeck says you cannot genuinely affirm 'Jesus is Lord' unless you make him 'your Lord'.

[53] Hensley, 'Are Postliberals Necessarily Antirealists?', p. 79, italics mine. One thinks here of Quine's 'web of belief'.

Hensley's analysis appears to be supported by some of Lindbeck's own statements, which, in the process, end up also mitigating McGrath's assertions that Lindbeck's treatment of doctrine is reductionist and that he does not appreciate the propositionalist approach.

At one point, Lindbeck insists that a statement is propositional (true or false) only in a determinate setting. In other words, stating 'The car is red' requires further specification and contextualization (such as identifying the car to which the statement refers). The same is true of the statement 'Jesus is Lord'. It is at this point that Lindbeck insists on the necessity of such a statement becoming a first-order proposition if it is to be capable of making an ontological truth claim:

> There is nothing in the cultural-linguistic approach that requires the rejection (or the acceptance) of the epistemological realism and correspondence theory of truth, which ... is implicit in the conviction of believers that when they rightly use a sentence such as 'Christ is Lord' they are uttering a true first-order proposition.[54]

In fact, Lindbeck explicitly accepts a 'modest propositionalism': 'There seems to be no reason why cultural-linguistic theories of religion need exclude, even though they do not imply, the modest cognitivist-propositionalism represented by at least some classical theists ...'[55] It appears from the sentiment expressed here that he is not as antithetical to the cognitive-propositional approach nor as monolithic in his appreciation of the functions of doctrine as McGrath suspects, though he certainly does not embrace either emphasis with the enthusiasm nor in the manner that would relieve McGrath's uneasiness.

But if Lindbeck's brand of postliberalism is, as Hensley argues in his essay, compatible in principle with metaphysical realism, McGrath's uneasiness remains to be assuaged, for Lindbeck remains a suspect of evangelicals who often, without logical necessity, couple anti-realism with anti-foundationalism.[56] It is understandable, then, that McGrath poses another challenge to postliberals.

In our enumeration of what is right about postliberalism from an evangelical perspective, we have already applauded its rejection of

---

[54] Lindbeck, *The Nature of Doctrine*, pp. 68–9.

[55] Ibid., p. 66. He has in mind the likes of Thomas Aquinas.

[56] See Hensley, 'Are Postliberals Necessarily Antirealists?', p. 80; and David K. Clark, 'Relativism, Fideism, and the Promise of Postliberalism' in Phillips and Okholm (eds), *The Nature of Confession*, pp. 107–20. Clark argues for a mild case of nonfoundationalism in combination with realism.

liberal foundationalism, as well as its insistence on the normative and shaping role the Bible plays in the church and the tension that creates over against the prevailing culture. But McGrath asks 'Why the Bible?' and 'Why Jesus?' That is, is the biblical narrative and the significance of Jesus Christ grounded in anything more than the community process of socialization? McGrath suspects the answer is 'no': 'the prioritization of Scripture is not adequately grounded at the theological level'. Instead, it appears to be defended on cultural, historical or contractual grounds.[57] The Qur'ân could be similarly grounded within Islam. But evangelicals have claimed that Scripture's authority is not derived from the community, but from some intrinsic property of the text – namely, the Bible's inspiration, apart from any human endorsements.

In related fashion, McGrath suggests that Lindbeck and Holmer emphasize intratextuality to the point that it runs the risk of focusing on the text to the extent that the reality of the person of Christ is obscured: 'The historical and theological priority of the person of Jesus Christ over his textual embodiment and interpretation must be acknowledged … Its [postliberalism's] emphasis on Christianity as a language with associated grammatical rules threatens to sever its vital connection with the person of Christ.'[58] Again, McGrath's use of the word 'threatens' makes this a possibility rather than an actuality, illustrating once again his frustration with a movement he wishes were more forthcoming.

McGrath does appreciate Hans Frei's emphasis on the text rendering the person of Jesus Christ. But McGrath argues that Frei does not take us far enough in grounding the narrative of Jesus Christ. Comparing Frei's approach to Albrecht Ritschl's in 1874, McGrath contends that the prioritization of the gospel narrative is grounded in Christ's temporal and archetypal priority in reference to the Christian community, but, though 'the approach does indeed allow us to identify a *Christian* approach to the identity and significance of Jesus Christ, it leaves us with the acutely difficult question of whether this approach is itself justified'.[59]

McGrath argues that Frei leaves us asking whether the story of Jesus is fiction or fact. How is one to know that this is not simply a piece of fiction claiming to be a 'self-warranting fact'? Frei has dismissed the history–faith relation in a Bultmannian manner. (Again, McGrath finds some options suggested in Pannenberg's work here.) Subsequent Christological claims are left unverifiable. What if our Christology rests upon a mistake?

---

[57] McGrath, 'An Evangelical Evaluation of Postliberalism', p. 40.

[58] Ibid., p. 40.

[59] Ibid., p. 42.

Evangelicalism has difficulty with any approach, whether originating with Bultmann or with Frei, that apparently weighs history so lightly .... It is not merely the internal logic of the New Testament that is regarded as important; rather, it is the demonstration that this logic can be shown to have arisen in response to genuine pressures as a consequence of what is known about the history of Jesus of Nazareth.... it attempts to uncover and explore the correlation between history and theology in the New Testament.[60]

At this point McGrath has entered into the fray of evangelical deliberations over foundationalism[61] (let alone about the relation between history and faith – a discussion that exceeds the limitations of this essay). Though, as we have noted, McGrath has applauded the rejection of any foundationalism whatsoever, one suspects from what he has argued here that he may harbour a bit of nostalgia for a mild foundationalism. Yet would the likes of John Calvin, a progenitor of the evangelical tradition, approve?

Calvin did not so much rest the authority of Scripture in some intrinsic property of the text (such as inspiration, as McGrath claims)[62] just as he did not ground it in some ecclesiastical sanction. For Calvin, Scripture's authority was grounded in the Spirit's authentication of the text:

Indeed, Scripture exhibits fully as clear evidence of its own truth as white and black things do of their color, or sweet and bitter things do of their taste ... the highest proof of Scripture derives in general from the fact that God in person speaks in it ... we ought to seek our conviction in a higher place than human reasons, judgements, or conjectures, that is, in the secret testimony of the Spirit ... the testimony of the Spirit is more excellent than all reason. For as God alone is a fit witness of himself in his Word, so also the Word will not find acceptance in men's hearts before it is sealed by the inward testimony of the Spirit. The same Spirit, therefore, who has spoken through the mouths of the prophets must penetrate into our hearts to persuade us that they faithfully proclaimed what had been divinely commanded ...

Let this point therefore stand: that those whom the Holy Spirit has inwardly taught truly rest upon Scripture, and that Scripture indeed is *self-authenticated*

---

[60] Ibid., p. 43.

[61] E.g. see John Franke's essay in the volume. Also see Stanley J. Grenz and John R. Franke, *Beyond Foundationalism: Shaping Theology in a Postmodern Context* (Louisville: Westminster John Knox, 2001).

[62] 'For Calvin, the authority of Scripture was grounded in the fact that the biblical writers were "secretaries ... of the Holy Spirit." ' Alister E. McGrath, *Reformation Thought: An Introduction* (Oxford: Blackwell Publishers, 1993[2]), p. 142.

[*autopiston*]; hence, it is not right to subject it to proof and reasoning. And the certainty it derives with us, it attains by the testimony of the Spirit ... Therefore, illumined by his power, we believe that neither by our own nor by anyone else's judgement that Scripture is from God ...[63]

In other words, Calvin *was* a nonfoundationalist when it came to rational or historical answers to the question 'Why the Bible?' In fact, in the *Institutes* Calvin *does* enumerate impressive arguments for Scripture's authenticity and authority, but, significantly, they are meant to further establish those who have *already* come to accept the divine authority of the Bible.[64]

Would Calvin agree that a preoccupation with the biblical narrative obscures the reality of Christ's person? Calvin insists that Jesus Christ comes to us clothed in Scripture. Certainly we meet him by the Spirit's use of the means God has provided the church for our spiritual benefit, but can we have a *meaningful* encounter with Jesus Christ apart from the text? McGrath has opened a line of inquiry here that is worth further pursuit, though, as he himself admits, it is hampered by the obscurity of Frei's text.[65]

We have argued that McGrath may not have sufficient cause to be uneasy over his suspicions of a postliberal commitment to anti-realism. He is certainly right to call for greater clarification. But whether or not his unease over their professed anti-foundationalism is warranted depends on the outcome of the current battle that rages on over this crucial issue in contemporary evangelical circles in our postmodern context.

Despite the fact that we have taken issue with some of McGrath's assessment of postliberalism, the fact that he has expressed an uneasiness rather than an outright dogmatic rejection of this movement models for us as evangelicals the graciousness and care with which we need to go about engaging our theological conversation partners in dialogue. My hope is that dialogues such as this one between articulate and sophisticated partners like McGrath and Lindbeck will enable us to

---

[63] John Calvin, *Institutes of the Christian Religion*, Ford Lewis Battles (tr.), John T. McNeill (ed.) (Philadelphia: Westminster, 1960), I.vii.2, 4, 5.

[64] See ibid., I.viii. To be fair, McGrath speaks of Aquinas's arguments for God's existence in a similar manner: they do not prove God's existence, but they point in God's direction and support those who already believe in God: see McGrath, *Intellectuals Don't Need God*, pp. 35–7.

[65] McGrath *does* say of Calvin's view in *Intellectuals Don't Need God* that 'God may thus be fully known only through Jesus Christ, who may in turn be known *only* through Scripture ...' (p. 216). McGrath appears to endorse this view.

defend a nonfoundationalist realism that seems most faithful to the theology of pre-modern evangelicals like Luther and Calvin.

Part II

Dynamics and Vitality of Evangelical Theology

5

Machen's Warrior Children

John M. Frame

1. Orientation

J. Gresham Machen, a lifelong bachelor, left no biological children, but many spiritual ones. The story of American conservative evangelical Reformed theology[1] in the twentieth century is largely the story of those children.

Machen (1881–1937) took degrees at Johns Hopkins University and Princeton Theological Seminary, then studied for a time in Germany. He returned to teach New Testament at Princeton Seminary. His faith and theological stability had been somewhat shaken by his experience with liberal German Bible critics and theologians, particularly Wilhelm Herrmann. But in time he became a vigorous and cogent defender of the confessional Presbyterianism taught at Princeton by such stalwarts as Charles Hodge, B.B. Warfield and Geerhardus Vos. In *The Virgin Birth of Christ*[2] and *The Origin of Paul's Religion*[3] he attacked (mostly German) critics of Scripture, arguing the historical authenticity of the

---

[1] I apologize for the large number of adjectives in this phrase, but it does state concisely the range of theology I will seek to analyse in this paper. 'Conservative' and 'Evangelical', of course, are terms variously defined. Here I will restrict my attention to those types of Reformed theology that credibly subscribe to historic Reformed confessions such as the Westminster Standards and the Three Forms of Unity. The theology of Karl Barth, though often described as conservative, Evangelical, and Reformed, does not fit this restriction because of Barth's view of Scripture, his denial of God's eternal decree and his refusal to identify the events of salvation directly with events of calendar time, among other things.

[2] New York: Harper, 1930.

[3] Grand Rapids: Eerdmans, 1925, 1947.

New Testament. In 1923 he published *Christianity and Liberalism*,[4] an attack on the liberal or modernist theology espoused by those critics and by many in American churches. This book argued not only that liberalism was wrong, but that it was a different religion from Christianity. According to Machen, Christianity and liberalism were antithetically opposed in their concepts of doctrine, God and man, the Bible, Christ, salvation and the church. The liberals taught that doctrine is secondary to experience, that God is Father to all apart from redemption, that the Bible is a book of mere human testimonies, that Christ is merely a moral example, that salvation is to be found by following that example, and that the church should accept this liberal gospel as orthodox.

Princeton Seminary was under the authority of the General Assembly of the Presbyterian Church, USA (henceforth PCUSA). In 1928 that body determined to reorganize the seminary to make it represent a broad range of opinion in the church, including the liberalism against which Machen had written. In response, Machen left the seminary, together with colleagues Robert D. Wilson and Oswald T. Allis. These scholars founded Westminster Theological Seminary in Philadelphia and added to its faculty such younger men as R.B. Kuiper, Ned B. Stonehouse, Allan A. MacRae, Paul Woolley, Cornelius Van Til and John Murray. Machen intended that Westminster would continue the confessional Presbyterian tradition of what would then be called 'Old' Princeton.

In 1936, Machen left the PCUSA after the denomination suspended him from the ministry for his involvement in the Independent Board for Presbyterian Foreign Missions. Machen and others had created that board to send out missionaries that could be trusted to preach the biblical gospel without any compromise with liberalism. Rather than accepting his suspension, Machen founded a new denomination, known first as the Presbyterian Church of America, later renamed the Orthodox Presbyterian Church (henceforth OPC).

Machen's movement represented numerically only a small proportion of Reformed believers in the USA. Many conservative Reformed people remained in the PCUSA. Many belonged to older, smaller denominations, such as the Reformed Presbyterian Church of North America (RPCNA) and Associate Reformed Presbyterian Church (ARP) that descended from the Scottish Covenanters. There is also a major wing of American Calvinism with Dutch roots. The Reformed Church in America (RCA) goes back to the founding of New Amsterdam (later New York) in 1626. The Christian Reformed Church (CRC) originated

---

[4] Grand Rapids: Eerdmans, 1923.

in a split from the RCA in 1822 and retained a more conservative stance than that body through much of the period since that time. In the last forty years, however, it has been troubled by debates over biblical inerrancy, women's ordination and homosexuality, leading many of its more conservative members to leave and form other denominations, such as the Orthodox Christian Reformed Church (OCRC) and the United Reformed Church (URC). These Scottish and Dutch groups, together with the conservatives in the PCUSA, respected what Machen and Westminster were doing, though they also supported their own denominational seminaries.

A small Reformed denomination of German background, the Reformed Church in the USA (RCUS) used Westminster for many years as the main institution for training its pastoral candidates.

There are also in the USA a number of people with Reformed convictions in Congregational, Independent and Anglican churches (both the large Protestant Episcopal Church and smaller bodies like the Reformed Episcopal Church). Many Baptists also embrace Reformed soteriology, with, of course, differing levels of appreciation for traditional Reformed views of covenant and church government. Some students from these traditions attended Westminster, and the seminary had some influence within these communities.

In 1973 there was a split in the Presbyterian Church US (PCUS), the southern counterpart of the PCUSA from which Machen departed, essentially for the same reason as the Machen split: opposition to liberal theology. Many of those who left the PCUS formed the Presbyterian Church in America (PCA).[5]

Machen's movement did not represent all of these elements of Reformed Christianity, but it had a major influence on all of them. Indeed, it can be argued that it provided their theological leadership. Machen himself made an effort to bring together American, Scottish and Dutch traditions at Westminster. The original faculty included R.B. Kuiper, Ned Stonehouse and Cornelius Van Til, all of whom were raised in the CRC. Another major influence on the seminary was biblical theologian Geerhardus Vos, another Dutchman from the CRC who taught at Princeton and remained there after 1929, though he had strong

---

[5] These names and initials can be confusing, of course. The denomination founded by Machen was originally called the Presbyterian Church *of* America, which differs from the PCA only by a preposition. In the present-day PCA, my own denomination, we try to remind people that as the church is in the world, but not of it, the PCA is *in* America, but not *of* it. Not that Machen would have had any other vision for his own denomination!

sympathies with Westminster. The Scots were also represented on the early faculty by systematic theologian John Murray, who maintained his British citizenship, though he taught in America until his retirement in 1967. Murray held to some of the distinctives (such as the exclusive use of Psalm versions in worship) of the groups in America influenced by Scottish Covenanters, such as the RPCNA, though he himself was a minister in the OPC.

There was also theological diversity in Machen's movement, which I believe he cultivated intentionally. Allan A. Macrae of the Westminster faculty was premillennial, later serving as an editor of the *New Scofield Reference Bible* (1967), a major work of dispensational theology. Paul Woolley was also premillennial, but without dispensationalist sympathies. Machen himself was postmillennial, the majority position on the Old Princeton faculty. The rest of the Westminster faculty was amillennial, so far as I can tell, though John Murray leaned in a postmillennial direction in later years. Other premillennialists served with Machen on the Independent Board for Presbyterian Foreign Missions. The premillennialists served as a link between Machen's confessional Presbyterianism and the broader currents of American evangelicalism.

This diversity, both ethnic and doctrinal, brought many influences to bear on Westminster and the OPC. It also helped Westminster to have significant influence upon many Reformed bodies and upon American evangelicalism generally. Old Princeton had already been regarded by many evangelicals as their theological leader. Even many non-Calvinists looked to the writings of Princeton professors B.B. Warfield, Robert Dick Wilson and Machen himself for scholarly defences of biblical authority and inerrancy. Lewis Sperry Chafer, President of Dallas Theological Seminary, corresponded with Machen, urging closer ties between the two seminaries (a desire that Machen did not reciprocate). Westminster also had a major influence upon the conservative wing of the CRC (and later the OCRC and URC), upon the Reformed Episcopal Church, among the Scottish bodies like the RPCNA, upon the PCA, and upon individuals and churches of Reformed Baptist persuasion.

Westminster graduates taught at seminaries such as Covenant, Gordon-Conwell, Trinity, Biblical, Mid-America and Reformed Episcopal. When Fuller Theological Seminary was organized in 1947 it used at first a curriculum very much like that of Westminster, and several Westminster graduates served on the early faculty. Reformed Theological Seminary, founded in Jackson, Mississippi, in 1966, now with three campuses and numerous extension centres, readily acknowledges a large debt to Westminster in curriculum, theological emphasis and faculty.

Westminster faculty and graduates have continued to provide leadership to the Reformed theological world. I believe it can be said that although Machen's Westminster was not a large seminary it was one of the most important influences, perhaps the most important institutional influence, upon conservative Reformed theology in the twentieth century.

Machen died of pneumonia in 1937, disappointed that his new denomination was already showing signs of division. Machen's children were theological battlers, and, when the battle against liberalism in the PCUSA appeared to be over, they found other theological battles to fight. Up to the present time, these and other battles have continued within the movement, and, in my judgement, that is the story of conservative evangelical Reformed theology in twentieth-century America. In the rest of this essay I will discuss that theological warfare, distinguishing twenty-two areas of debate.

2. Theological Warfare: Areas of Debate

2.1. *Eschatology*

The first theological battle in Machen's new denomination concerned the order of events in the last days, particularly the nature of the millennium, the thousand-year period mentioned in Revelation 20:4–6. Classic premillennialists, following some of the early church fathers, teach that the return of Christ will precede a thousand years of peace in which Christ would reign upon earth. Dispensational premillennialists hold that Christ's return will be in two stages: (1) secretly to rapture his saints, leaving all others behind, and (2) publicly, after seven years of tribulation, to institute his visible millennial reign. They also teach that during the millennium God will literally fulfil his promises to Israel, promises not given to Gentile believers. Amillennialists believe that the thousand years of Revelation 20 is a figurative number, indicating the whole period between Jesus' resurrection and his return, in which Christ rules from heaven and brings people to know peace with God through the preaching of the gospel.

In December 1935 John Murray began a series of articles called 'The Reformed Faith and Modern Substitutes' in *The Presbyterian Guardian*, then the organ of the Machen movement. These articles attacked dispensational premillennialism, as well as modernism and Arminianism, as heresy. They offended a number of people in the Machen movement who either (1) sympathized with dispensational theology, (2) were unable to regard it as heresy, or (3) who thought the debate about dispensationalism could lead to an attack upon non-dispensational premillennialists. This issue, together with the next to be mentioned, led to a split within the Machen movement, producing after Machen's death yet another new seminary (Faith Theological Seminary) and another new denomination (the Bible Presbyterian Church, BPC), which revised the Westminster Confession of Faith to make it premillennial.

Debate over eschatology has continued since that time among conservative American Calvinists. In 1957, Loraine Boettner's *The Millennium*[6] appeared, renewing discussion of the postmillennial position, which had been relatively unpopular in Reformed circles since the days of Old Princeton. Postmillennialists today usually agree with amillennialists that the thousand years of Revelation 20 designates the age between the resurrection and the return of Jesus. But they emphasize that during this period, or toward the end of it, the gospel will triumph, not only in bringing individuals to salvation, but also in dominating culture. In the 1960s and 1970s, postmillennialism became the dominant view of the Christian Reconstruction Movement, led by R.J. Rushdoony, Gary North and Greg L. Bahnsen. The reconstructionists argued that amillennialism and premillennialism, since they were pessimistic about the possibility of Christian cultural dominance, bore significant responsibility for the modern decline of Christian influence in society.[7]

Postmillennialists tend to hold preterist interpretations of many biblical texts dealing with the 'last days', such as Jesus' Olivet Discourse (Mt. 24; Mk. 13; Lk. 21) and the Book of Revelation.[8] Preterism holds that many (or, in an extreme form of preterism, all) of the events predicted in these passages have already taken place in the 'coming' of God to judge Israel, resulting in the destruction of the temple in AD 70. Recently, preterists (some affiliated with the Christian Reconstruction Movement, some not) have become very active, forming organizations, holding conferences and producing literature.[9] The extreme form of

---

[6] Philadelphia: Presbyterian & Reformed.

[7] See Gary North, *Dominion and Common Grace* (Tyler, Texas: Institute for Christian Economics, 1987); *Millennialism and Social Theory* (Tyler, Texas: Institute for Christian Economics, 1990); Rousas J. Rushdoony, *God's Plan for Victory: The Meaning of Postmillennialism* (Fairfax, Virginia: Thoburn Press, 1977).

[8] See, for example, David Chilton, *Days of Vengeance* (Fort Worth, Texas: Dominion Press, 1987), a commentary on the Book of Revelation.

[9] See, for example, < www.preteristarchive.com >.

preterism, sometimes called 'full' preterism, denies that Scripture promises a coming of Christ that is future to us.

In my judgement, and that of many others, extreme preterism is unorthodox. But partisans of the other eschatological views have exaggerated the importance of adopting one such position over another. It is not evident that Scripture is precise enough in this area to establish decisively one of these as the truth, let alone as a test of orthodoxy. And, contrary to the theonomic[10] postmillennialists, I think that eschatological positions have had very little to do with the cultural pessimism or optimism of their proponents. Many of the most politically active Christians in the USA have been premillennialists (Jerry Falwell, Pat Robertson) or amillennialists (James Skillen, the Association for Public Justice), contrary to the postmillennialist claim that these positions foster cultural irrelevance and impotence. For many Christians, biblical admonitions to seek justice in society are sufficient reason to become culturally and politically active, and these are far more weighty than the supposed implications of any eschatological view.

By the 1970s, for the most part, 'eschatological liberty' prevailed in most American Reformed denominations. Even the Reformed Presbyterian Church, Evangelical Synod (RPES), an offshoot of the BPC, which maintained the premillennial revisions to the Westminster Confession, came to hold that all three major positions could be tolerated in the church. But this developing consensus was not sufficient to erase the effects of the breach of 1937, which is still reflected in the denominational alignments.

2.2. *Christian liberty*

The other main issue that divided the OPC in 1937 was the issue of whether Christians should totally abstain from alcoholic beverages. Machen held that Scripture permitted moderate use of alcohol. Others in the Machen movement, however, held that the use of alcohol had produced so many evils in the modern world (such as destruction of individual lives, destruction of families, auto injuries and deaths) that conscientious Christians had no option but total abstinence. The moderationist position was the majority view of the Reformed tradition; abstinence the majority view of broader American evangelicalism, which had supported the prohibitionist amendment to the US Constitution. To the moderationists, the abstainers violated the principle of *sola*

---

[10] See later discussion of theonomy.

scriptura, elevating a cultural prejudice to the status of doctrine. To the abstainers, the advocates of moderation were refusing to apply broader Scriptural principles to a major social evil.

My impression is that the moderationists have pretty much won the day, although even now many American Reformed churches (usually in deference to recovering alcoholics) use unfermented grape juice in the Lord's Supper. One rarely hears the arguments for abstinence any more in Reformed circles, though the discussion continues in other forms of American evangelicalism.

2.3. The incomprehensibility of God

From around 1944–48 the OPC was troubled by a controversy between followers of Cornelius Van Til, Westminster's Professor of Apologetics, and those of Gordon H. Clark, Professor of Philosophy at Wheaton College, later at Butler University and Covenant College. The Presbytery of Philadelphia of the OPC ordained Clark to the ministry in 1944, but followers of Van Til complained against his ordination. Several issues entered this controversy, the main one described as the issue of the 'incomprehensibility of God'. Both sides agreed, of course, that God was incomprehensible to human beings. But they disagreed on the relation of God's thoughts to humankind's thoughts.[11] To Van Til, when God thinks 'This is a rose' the 'contents' of his thought are 'qualitatively different' from the contents of any human mind thinking 'This is a rose.' To Clark, the contents of God's thought and a human being's in this case are identical: both God and man are having the same thought. Van Til was trying to guard the Creator–creature distinction by saying that, just as God radically differs from humankind, so the contents of God's mind radically differ from the contents of humankind's mind. Clark was trying to avoid scepticism: for if God's thought is true, and human thought necessarily differs from it in every respect, then human thought cannot be true.

The debate was vigorous and voluminous. The key terms 'contents' and 'qualitative difference' were never very well defined, and the two parties regularly talked past one another. I think that in this discussion personal issues impeded conceptual clarity. And we must ask to what degree of precision may theologians seek to define the incomprehensibility of God without violating that very incomprehensibility?

---

[11] In my judgement, therefore, 'incomprehensibility' is a misleading term to describe the issue of the debate.

As I see it, however, Van Til, though he sometimes expressed his view in confusing language, did not deny what was most important to Clark, namely that God and man can believe the same proposition and thus can agree as to what is objectively true. Similarly, Clark expressed, in his discussion of the 'mode' of God's knowledge, what was important to Van Til, namely the radical difference between the nature and workings of the divine mind and the human.

The result of the controversy was that the General Assembly of the OPC did not revoke Clark's ordination, but Clark himself and many of his disciples left the denomination later over issues related to the controversy. Another battle, another split.[12]

2.4. Apologetics

Clark and Van Til battled over epistemology and therefore also over how people come to know God. Both men were 'presuppositionalists', in that they believed that God's revelation was ultimately authoritative for all human knowledge, rather than being subject to the higher authority of factual evidence. Becoming a Christian involves accepting God's Word as the supreme criterion of truth, that is, as one's ultimate presupposition. So the Word of God validates factual evidence, not the other way around.

Clark held that Christian theism, like other worldviews, was like an axiomatic system in mathematics: presupposing certain 'axioms' but validated by the criteria of logical consistency and adequacy for its tasks. The axiom of Christianity is the truth of the Bible, but the apologist can persuade enquirers that the Bible is logically consistent and is adequate to its redemptive task. Van Til resisted Clark's view of logic as a test of revelation, holding that logic itself, like factual evidence, is validated by Scripture, rather than Scripture by logic.[13] To Van Til, Clark was a rationalist. To Clark, Van Til was an irrationalist.

Others in Reformed circles rejected presuppositionalism altogether for more traditional apologetic approaches. Dr James Oliver Buswell, one of the premillennial group who broke with Westminster and the

---

[12] For a more thorough description and analysis of the controversy, with bibliography, see John M. Frame, *Cornelius Van Til: An Analysis of his Thought* (Phillipsburg: Presbyterian & Reformed, 1995), pp. 97–113.

[13] For Clark's position, see his *A Christian View of Men and Things* (Grand Rapids: Eerdmans, 1952), and *Religion, Reason and Revelation* (Philadelphia: Presbyterian & Reformed, 1961). For Van Til's position, see my *Cornelius Van Til*, especially pp. 141–84.

OPC, questioned Van Til from a largely empiricist perspective,[14] and several writers from the Christian Reformed Church questioned whether Van Til's approach was genuinely Reformed.[15] The 'Classical Apologetics' of John Gerstner, R.C. Sproul and Arthur Lindsley rejects Van Til in favour of an approach based on natural theology and historical evidences, presupposing certain 'basic assumptions', including 'the law of noncontradiction', 'the law of causality' and 'the basic reliability of sense perception'.[16] The debate continues into the present, with additional alternatives being offered and new voices being heard.[17]

One of those voices is that of philosopher Alvin Plantinga, who describes his position as 'Reformed Epistemology'.[18] This position says that people are rationally justified in believing in God without evidence or argument, though such rational beliefs are open to refutation by evidence and argument. In Plantinga's view, we come to know God when our faculties of knowledge, working rightly and placed in the proper environment, come naturally to form a belief in him. This position, I think, is largely right, but it seeks to answer different questions from those of Van Til, Clark, Gerstner and others. Therefore it isn't really

---

[14] See Van Til, *The Defense of the Faith* (Philadelphia: Presbyterian & Reformed, 1955), pp. 239–67.

[15] Ibid., pp. 4–20, 267–302. This and the previous section were dropped from later editions of *The Defense of the Faith*. See also James Daane, *A Theology of Grace* (Grand Rapids: Eerdmans, 1954) and Van Til, *The Theology of James Daane* (Philadelphia: Presbyterian & Reformed, 1959).

[16] John Gerstner, R.C. Sproul and Arthur Lindsley, *Classical Apologetics* (Grand Rapids: Zondervan, 1984), pp. 70–90. See also my review of this book, published as Appendix A of my *Cornelius Van Til*, pp. 401–22, and also as Appendix A of my *Apologetics to the Glory of God* (Phillipsburg: Presbyterian & Reformed, 1994), pp. 219–43.

[17] See, for example, Steven B. Cowan (ed.), *Five Views on Apologetics* (Grand Rapids: Zondervan, 2000). Prof. Alister McGrath, whom we honour in this volume, has made some helpful contributions to this literature, such as *Glimpsing the Face of God* (Grand Rapids: Eerdmans, 2002), *Explaining your Faith Without Losing your Friends* (Grand Rapids: Zondervan, 1989) and *Intellectuals Don't Need God and Other Modern Myths* (Grand Rapids: Zondervan, 1993). If I may say so, however, I think he is not at his best in the Appendix to the latter book that deals with Van Til.

[18] For the apologetic development of his ideas, see Alvin Plantinga, *Warranted Christian Belief* (New York: Oxford University Press, 2000). Kelly James Clark, a follower of Plantinga, has used this approach in *Return to Reason* (Grand Rapids: Eerdmans, 1990) and in Cowan (ed.), *Five Views on Apologetics*, pp. 265–312.

an alternative to these other views, though many consider it to be that. To borrow a distinction of William Lane Craig, Reformed epistemology is more concerned with how we can *know* the truth, whereas presuppositionalism and evidentialism are more concerned with how we can *show* it.

The discussion has, I think, been a useful one, leading the church to ask important questions (rarely asked in past centuries) about how Reformed theology bears upon epistemology and apologetics. But, as with the debates over eschatology, Christian liberty and incomprehensibility, the discussion has been far too shrill. It has led to the formation of factions in the Reformed community, each assured that it has the truth about apologetics and that the other factions have denied crucial aspects of Reformed theology. Van Til himself questioned the Reformed commitment of those who disagreed with his apologetic approach, and his opponents spoke equally strongly against him.

One may argue that the theology of Calvin and the Reformed confessions has apologetic implications. But the confessions do not deal specifically with apologetics or epistemology, so these should be regarded as open questions in the Reformed churches. Further, it seems to me that this is a subject on which more thinking needs to be done, before we attain a position worthy to be a test of Reformed orthodoxy.

2.5. Philosophy

Until about 1960, Van Til was associated fairly closely with the Dutch philosophical school of thought known as the 'philosophy of the idea of law'. The most famous member of this school was Herman Dooyeweerd,[19] but many others followed more or less the same approach, including D. Th. Vollenhoven, S.U. Zuidema, K. Popma, J.P.A. Mekkes, H. Evan Runner and H. Van Riessen. Around 1960, however, it became evident that Dooyeweerd disagreed with some aspects of Van Til's apologetic system and, more broadly, with the whole idea of making philosophy subject to the 'conceptual contents' of Scripture. Van Til, therefore, began to distance himself from the movement.

In the late 1960s some younger members of this philosophical school, including James Olthuis, Hendrik Hart and Calvin Seerveld, founded in

---

[19] Dooyeweerd's *magnum opus* is *De Wijsbegeerte der Wetsidee*, translated into English as *A New Critique of Theoretical Thought* (Philadelphia: Presbyterian & Reformed, 1953), in four volumes. A more popular presentation of his ideas is *In the Twilight of Western Thought* (Philadelphia: Presbyterian & Reformed, 1958).

Toronto the Institute for Christian Studies (ICS).[20] The ICS group published not only technical but popular articles on philosophical, political, social and theological issues. Conferences were held in many locations. As with other movements of the late 1960s and early 1970s, there was a radicalism about the presentations that inspired great zeal. The young audiences got the message that traditional Reformed theology was 'scholastic', 'dualistic', and thus not worthy of the Reformers. The only path to true reform, they thought, was to make theology, ethics, politics and all other spheres of life subject to a Christian philosophy, namely that of Dooyeweerd and his disciples. So the Reformed community went to war again, fighting battles in churches, seminaries and Christian schools over these issues.

The ICS leaned toward socialist politics and liberal views on many social and theological issues, but other followers of Dooyeweerd took more conservative positions. My impression is that by the late 1970s the battles in churches and institutions had petered out, though views on these matters continue to be exchanged in academic contexts.

2.6. Sabbath

Differences over the Sabbath began very early in the history of the Reformed community. Calvin held that in the New Covenant there was no special day divinely mandated for worship and rest. The Puritans and Scots, however, believed that the New Testament 'Lord's Day' (Rev. 1:10) is identical with the Old Testament Sabbath, except that it is observed on the first day of the week rather than the seventh.[21] Calvin's

---

[20] Some writings from the early North American phase of the movement: Hendrik Hart, *The Challenge of Our Age* (Toronto: Association for the Advancement of Christian Scholarship, 1968) and *Understanding Our World: An Integral Ontology* (Lanham: University Press of America, 1984); L. Kalsbeek, *Contours of a Christian Philosophy* (Toronto: Wedge, 1975); Calvin Seerveld, *A Christian Critique of Art and Literature* (Toronto: Association for the Advancement of Christian Scholarship, 1968). For my critique, see *The Amsterdam Philosophy: a Preliminary Critique* (Phillipsburg: Harmony Press, 1972) and *Cornelius Van Til*, pp. 371–86. For an attempt to apply Dooyeweerdian ideas to systematic theology, see Gordon J. Spykman, *Reformational Theology: A New Paradigm for Doing Dogmatics* (Grand Rapids, Michigan: Eerdmans, 1992).

[21] For a discussion of these positions, see Richard B. Gaffin, *Calvin and the Sabbath* (Fearn: Mentor, 1998). Still others hold that the New Covenant abrogates the Sabbath, but replaces it with the Lord's Day, a first-day celebration of the resurrection, but not a day of rest. See Donald A. Carson (ed.), *From Sabbath to Lord's Day* (Grand Rapids: Zondervan, 1982).

view is reflected in the Heidelberg Catechism, the Puritan view in the Westminster Standards. In the 1960s and 1970s, the OPC disciplined two ministers who held essentially Calvin's view of the Sabbath. These cases raised the question of whether Calvin himself would have been sufficiently orthodox to minister in that denomination and the more serious question of whether even the main historic divisions of the Reformed community are capable of ecclesiastical fellowship.

2.7. Charismatic gifts

Most Reformed believers hold that the New Testament gifts of tongues and prophecy ceased at the end of the apostolic age. The view that these gifts continue in the church has been thought to conflict with the Reformed view of *sola scriptura*, particularly the statement in the Westminster Confession of Faith (1.1) about 'those former ways of God's revealing his will unto his people being now ceased'. Nevertheless, some have argued that although Scripture is our sufficient standard of faith and life, God continues occasionally to reveal himself in other ways. John Calvin says Paul applies the term *prophet* in Ephesians 4:11 'not to all those who were interpreters of God's will, but to those who excelled in a particular revelation. This class either does not exist today *or is less commonly seen*' (emphasis mine). These prophets were 'instrumental in revealing mysteries and predicting future events', so 'now and again [the Lord] revives them as the need of the time demands'.[22] Later in the same discussion he says that God even raised up apostles (probably Calvin refers to Luther) in Calvin's time for extraordinary purposes. Samuel Rutherford, a member of the Westminster Assembly, reports supernatural predictions of the future among the Reformers.[23] Vern Poythress also cites reports of such extraordinary prophecies from John Flavel, various Scottish Covenanters, Peter Marshall, Cotton Mather and others.[24] Poythress argues that even given the cessation of the apostolic

---

[22] John Calvin, *Institutes of the Christian Religion*, John T. McNeill (ed.), Ford L. Battles (tr.) (Philadelphia: Westminster, 1960), IV.iii.4.

[23] Samuel Rutherford, *A Survey of Spiritual Antichrist* (London: Andrew Crooke, 1948), 1.7, pp. 42–4, cited by Vern Poythress: see following note.

[24] Vern Poythress, *Modern Spiritual Gifts as Analogous to Apostolic Gifts: Affirming Extraordinary Works of the Spirit within Cessationist Theology* (Glenside: Westminster Campus Bookstore, n.d.). See also Greg Barrow, *A Reformation Discussion of Extraordinary Predictive Prophecy Subsequent to the Closing of the Canon of Scripture* (Edmonton: Still Waters Revival, 1998). The latter author and publisher represent the Puritan Reformed Church, an

gifts it is still possible to recognize extraordinary works of the Spirit today that are significantly analogous to the apostolic gifts.[25]

Nevertheless, two OPC pastors have been disciplined for thinking it possible that the Spirit might do such things today, and many more in various Reformed denominations have been denied ordination on such grounds. A frequent argument is that the Reformed churches must 'bear witness against the modern charismatic movement'. It appears, however, that in taking this position the Reformed churches are also bearing witness against a part of their own history.

2.8. Theonomy

The publication in 1973 of Rousas J. Rushdoony's *Institutes of Biblical Law*[26] and in 1977 of Greg L. Bahnsen's *Theonomy in Christian Ethics*[27] created still another controversy. These books revived a position often held in Reformed history (but never unanimously) that present-day civil states should be governed by the Law of Moses. Specifically, the theonomists argued, the penalties for crimes in Old Covenant Israel should be applied to the same crimes today. So, now as then, adultery, homosexuality and blasphemy should be capital crimes. The theonomists were very militant in promoting their positions, and those in opposition were equally militant, if not more so. Churches and presbyteries were divided over this issue.

Opponents argued that God's relationship to Old Testament Israel was unique and that the specific laws given to Israel were not intended to rule all other nations. A moderate position[28] is that we must look at each of the laws God gave to Moses to determine the function of each in

---

[24] (*continued*) extremely small and highly traditionalist denomination that regards most conservative Presbyterian groups (such as OPC, PCA, RPNA) as apostate because they do not subscribe to the Scottish Solemn League and Covenant. In this case, ironically, their very traditionalism leads them to a position considered in the OPC to be a concession to the modern charismatic movement.

[25] Poythress, *Modern Spiritual Gifts*.

[26] No place of publication listed; Craig Press. I reviewed this book in *Westminster Theological Journal* 38:2 (Winter 1976), pp. 195–217.

[27] No place of publication listed; Craig Press. A second, expanded edition, including responses to critics, was published in 1984.

[28] For a more balanced discussion of the relevance of Old Testament law to the Christian, see Vern Poythress, *The Shadow of Christ in the Law of Moses* (Brentwood: Wohlgemuth & Hyatt, 1991).

redemptive history and civil society, and thus to determine the precise relevance of each statute for our society.

The theonomists, also called Christian reconstructionists, sometimes seemed to be offering a political programme for immediate implementation. Opponents were rather horrified at the idea that someone could take over the government and immediately institute death penalties for any number of actions that had until that time been treated lightly in society. As the discussion proceeded, however, it became evident that the theonomic thesis was actually somewhat more moderate, because (1) in their view, the Old Testament laws could not, and should not, be implemented in modern society until, through preaching of the gospel, those societies were dominated by regenerate people who loved God's law. Since most reconstructionists were postmillennial, they believed that one day Christianity would dominate human culture, but that that might not happen until many centuries into the future. And (2) they believed in a very limited state government, incapable of instituting anything like a reign of terror. In their view, the dominant government in society should be that of the family and the self-government of regenerate individuals.

My sense is that this controversy, like earlier ones, has wound down somewhat, though it continues to be much discussed in classrooms of Christian colleges and seminaries. More moderate positions, like that of Poythress referenced earlier, seem to be winning the day.

2.9. *Covenant and justification*

John Murray taught that the essence of covenant is God's gracious redemptive promise.[29] A younger colleague, Old Testament Professor Meredith G. Kline, argued in his article 'Law Covenant'[30] that the essence of covenant is law, not grace, though in the New Covenant Christ bears the penalties of the law as a substitute for his people, thus fulfilling the law covenant by grace. Thus our relationship with God is

---

[29] See his pamphlet *The Covenant of Grace* (London: Tyndale Press, 1954). See also 'Covenant Theology' in his *Collected Writings* (Edinburgh: Banner of Truth, 1984), vol. 4, pp. 216–40. In his lectures on systematic theology, he says that 'covenant in Scripture denotes the oath-bound confirmation of promise', *Collected Writings*, vol. 2, p. 49.

[30] *Westminster Theological Journal* 27 (1964–65), pp. 1–20. See also his *Treaty of the Great King* (Grand Rapids, Michigan: Eerdmans, 1963), *By Oath Consigned* (Grand Rapids: Eerdmans, 1968), and *The Structure of Biblical Authority* (Grand Rapids: Eerdmans, 1972).

based strictly on merit: either our own merits, which lead only to condemnation, or the merits of Christ imputed to us and received by faith, which bring us forgiveness and eternal life.

In the 1970s Norman Shepherd, one of Murray's successors in Westminster's systematic theology department, championed Murray's view of covenant. Shepherd emphasized especially that in the covenant God's grace and human responsibility are inseparable, as by God's Spirit we are united to Christ. In his view, our relationship to God is not based on merit: indeed, 'the very idea of merit is foreign to the way in which God our Father relates to his children'.[31] Rather, God 'promises forgiveness of sins and eternal life, not as something to be earned, but as a gift to be received by a living and active faith'.[32]

Since saving faith is living and active (Jas. 2:17), Shepherd emphasized that works are a 'necessary' evidence of justification by faith. The word 'necessary' led to much controversy at Westminster Seminary from 1974–82 and the reverberations from that controversy continue today. Shepherd's opponents said that he was making works necessary to salvation, compromising the heart of the Reformation, the doctrine of justification by faith alone apart from works. His defenders argued, however, that although works do not in any sense save us, any faith without works is a dead faith, a non-saving faith. Faith doesn't save because of the good works associated with it, but only because it embraces Christ alone as Saviour. But neither is saving faith ever without good works. To profess Christ with no interest in serving him is 'easy believism' or 'cheap grace'.[33]

A number of bodies (Westminster's faculty, its board, Philadelphia Presbytery of the OPC) studied Shepherd's position and did not officially pronounce him unorthodox. But the controversy would not quit, and in 1982 Shepherd was asked to resign his position for the good of the seminary community. In my view, that decision was an injustice.

Though Shepherd left Westminster for pastoral positions in the CRC, the controversy continues to this day. The website < www.trinity foundation.org > has published several articles accusing followers of Shepherd of denying the gospel. Westminster's California campus is now

---

[31] Norman Shepherd, *The Call of Grace* (Phillipsburg: Presbyterian & Reformed, 2000), p. 39.

[32] Ibid.

[33] This controversy somewhat parallels the controversy in broader Evangelical circles over 'Lordship salvation', the debate over whether one can confess Jesus as Saviour without confessing him as Lord. Shepherd's reasoning implies that one cannot.

dominated by those (including Meredith Kline, W. Robert Godfrey, Michael S. Horton and R. Scott Clark) who think that Shepherd's position is a serious error.[34] But some faculty members at Westminster in Philadelphia, which dismissed Shepherd in 1982, still endorse the main thrust of Shepherd's position.

2.10. Law and gospel

A number of Reformed writers in the 1990s have been attracted to a rather sharp dichotomy between law and gospel, a view historically more typical of Lutheran than of Reformed theology. On this view, the law consists exclusively of commands, threats and terrors, the gospel exclusively of promises and comforts. There are no comforts in the law, no commands in the gospel. Those who maintain this view say that, without a sharp distinction between law and gospel, the law is softened and the gospel is no longer good news.[35] Such a distinction between law and gospel, they believe, is implied by the doctrine of justification by God's grace through faith alone. These writers think that the views of Norman Shepherd mentioned earlier confuse law and gospel. The publication *Modern Reformation* has consistently maintained this position, and it is the dominant view of the Alliance of Confessing Evangelicals and Westminster Theological Seminary in California.

Opponents of this position in the Reformed community argue that the Bible itself does not take pains to separate law and gospel, though it does teach justification by grace through faith alone. The classic biblical statement of the law, the Ten Commandments, begins by proclaiming God's gracious deliverance of Israel from Egypt and tells Israel to keep the law out of gratefulness for that deliverance (Ex. 20:1–17). Among the commandments themselves are promises of blessing (vv. 6 and 12). God is gracious through his law (Ps. 119:29). Similarly, the 'gospel' in Scripture is the good news that God reigns; thus it includes the authority of God's law (Isa. 52:7). It includes the command to repent and believe (Mk. 1:14–15), and the belief it commands is a living faith, one that does good works (Jas. 2:14–26).[36]

---

[34] An error 'of Galatian proportions', according to one Westminster/California professor in correspondence.

[35] See, for example, Michael Scott Horton, 'The Law and the Gospel' at < www.alliancenet.org/pub/articles/horton.LawGospel.html >.

[36] For more discussion, see my 'Law and Gospel' at < www.reformationrevival.com/WeeklyE-News/Semper%20Archive/LawandGospel.html >, or < www.chalcedon.edu/articles/0201/020104frame.shtml >.

Those holding to the sharp distinction between law and gospel have been known to accuse their opponents of denying the gospel itself.[37] As with the other issues discussed here, this discussion has created a partisan division in the Reformed community.

2.11. Counselling

Jay E. Adams joined the Westminster (Philadelphia) faculty in the late 1960s, and in 1970 he published *Competent to Counsel*,[38] setting forth his theory of 'nouthetic' (later often called 'biblical') counselling. Adams was sceptical of secular psychology, believing that Scripture alone was sufficient for pastors to deal with the problems of counsellees. He questioned whether there was any such thing as 'mental illness', arguing that illnesses were either of the body (the sphere of medicine) or of the soul (the sphere of pastoral care). The biblical counselling movement grew rapidly. Now there are a number of churches, counselling centres and seminaries that maintain this viewpoint. Adams' movement seeks to bring the Bible to bear on counselling as Van Til brought the Bible to bear on apologetics and philosophy.

But like the other movements we have discussed, Adams' has provoked opposition. His opponents (sometimes called 'integrationists' or 'Christian'[39] counsellors) say that his counselling is not sufficiently responsive to the data of general revelation. His defenders argue that other forms of counselling substitute worldly wisdom for the teachings of Scripture. Differences also exist concerning the nature of science: is psychology a religiously neutral discipline, or does it operate on religiously significant presuppositions (note the Van Tillian term), antithetical to biblical teaching? The two schools also commonly differ as to the institutional status of counsellors: nouthetic counsellors argue that counselling is part of the pastoral ministry of the church. Integrationists often maintain that counsellors should be state-licensed professionals outside ecclesiastical jurisdiction.

I do sense some movement on both sides, especially in the last ten years or so: integrationists seem to be more and more impressed with insights from Scripture relevant to the problems of people; and nouthetics seem to recognize more and more the importance of general

---

[37] My basis for this statement consists of e-mail exchanges and personal conversations.

[38] No place of publication listed: Presbyterian & Reformed.

[39] As opposed to 'biblical'!

revelation.[40] Adams has always admitted the importance of medical care for physical problems. But the science of the last thirty years has found more and more links between the body and the mind, such as in the treatment of schizophrenia. But for all this rapprochement, the mutual suspicion and partisan divisions have been formed, and they do not seem to be going away.

2.12. The days of creation

As in the broader evangelical world, the interpretation of Genesis 1 has been controversial in Reformed circles. Nevertheless, there has been relative peace and tolerance over this issue until recently. A number of Old Princeton professors, including Charles and A.A. Hodge, B.B. Warfield, J. Gresham Machen and Oswald T. Allis, held that the days of creation were not literally twenty-four hours long. Edward J. Young, who taught Old Testament at Westminster for many years, held that the days referred to long ages of time.[41] In 1957, Meredith G. Kline published an article entitled 'Because it Had Not Rained',[42] arguing not only that the days were non-literal, but that the narrative does not even teach a temporal sequence of events. Following N.H. Ridderbos,[43] Kline argued that the list of days is a literary framework that has no implications for the length of time or the sequence of events. So in the Reformed community, some have held to literal days, others to age-long days and others to symbolic days. These positions co-existed fairly comfortably in Reformed churches until around 1980.

---

[40] For a review of developments since Adams' original work, describing recent rapprochement between the two schools and specifying the remaining differences, see David Powlison, 'Questions at the Crossroads: The Care of Souls and Modern Psychotherapies' in Mark McMinn and Timothy Phillips (eds), *Care for the Soul: Exploring the Intersection of Psychology and Theology* (Downers Grove: InterVarsity Press, 2001), pp. 23–61. See also David Powlison, 'Crucial Issues in Contemporary Biblical Counseling', *Journal of Pastoral Practice* 11:3 (1988), pp. 53–78.

[41] See *Studies in Genesis One* (Philadelphia: Presbyterian & Reformed, 1964).

[42] *Westminster Theological Journal* 20 (1957–58), pp. 146–57. Later he amplified his views in 'Space and Time in the Genesis Cosmogony', *Perspectives on Science and the Christian Faith* 48 (1996), pp. 2–15.

[43] N.H. Ridderbos, *Is There a Conflict Between Genesis 1 and Natural Science?* (Grand Rapids, Michigan: Eerdmans, 1957).

But since then, many have taken up the cause of twenty-four hour day creation,[44] and their disciples have followed the twentieth-century Reformed pattern of being militant about their views. Many Christian reconstructionists have embraced a literal position, joined by many strict subscriptionists (see later discussion) who base their argument on what the writers of the Westminster Confession are likely to have believed. Some presbyteries in the OPC and the RCUS have denied ordination to candidates who reject the literal view of Genesis 1.

Should one's view of the length of the creation days be a test of orthodoxy? I think not. The exegetical questions are difficult, and I don't believe that any other doctrinal questions hinge on them. A non-literal interpretation does not entail, for example, that Adam was anything but a real person, or that human beings evolved from animals.

2.13. Worship

The 'worship wars' of evangelicalism have also divided the Reformed community. Debate has centred on two specific issues.

1. *The regulative* principle this phrase denotes the way God regulates the worship of the church. Reformed theology has claimed to maintain a stronger view of *sola scriptura*, the sufficiency of Scripture, for worship than the Lutheran and Anglican traditions. That is the view that all elements of worship must be 'prescribed' in Scripture.[45] Not everything done in worship has the status of 'element'. The Westminster Confession of Faith (1.6) says there are some circumstances concerning the worship of God common to human actions and societies that are to be ordered by the light of nature and Christian prudence according to the general rules of the Word, which are always to be observed.

But what, precisely, is an element and what is a circumstance? Is the use of musical instruments an element or a circumstance? And what about the specific words of sermons, prayers and hymns? These are neither prescribed in Scripture, nor are they 'common to human actions

---

[44] Some recent examples: Noel Weeks, *The Sufficiency of Scripture* (Edinburgh: Banner of Truth, 1988), pp. 95–118; Robert Reymond, *A New Systematic Theology of the Christian Faith* (Nashville: Thomas Nelson, 1998), pp. 392–4); James B. Jordan, *Creation in Six Days* (Moscow, Idaho: Canon Press, 1999).

[45] *Westminster Confession of Faith*, 21.1. Compare 1.6, 20.2. Lutherans and Anglicans argue that we may do anything in worship that Scripture does not *forbid*, keeping in mind the overall biblical purposes of worship.

and societies'. Reformed theologians have taken various positions on these issues.

Some continue to defend the traditional Puritan-Scottish approach, which leads to the exclusive use of Psalm versions as worship songs (without musical instruments),[46] or some variant of that approach, with less drastic consequences.[47] Others hold that the 'prescriptions' of Scripture are fairly general, leaving a broader range of freedom than the tradition has recognized.[48] Those holding the latter view argue that, although God's prescriptions for the sacrificial ritual of the tabernacle and temple are very detailed and specific, the Bible prescribes nothing specific about synagogue worship, and little about the worship of the New Testament church.

2. *Worship style.* Some in the Reformed community advocate a very simple style of worship, focused on preaching, emulating the Puritans. Others have advocated a more elaborate ceremony, adapting the liturgies of Geneva and other Reformation churches. Still others have introduced elements associated with contemporary evangelicalism: three or four songs in a row, use of guitars, synthesizers and drums, use of contemporary worship songs, attempts to be sensitive to unchurched visitors. The first two groups have characterized the third as non-Reformed; advocates of contemporaneity accuse the traditionalists of ignoring the Pauline imperative that worship should be edifying (and therefore understandable) to the congregation, even to non-Christian visitors (1 Cor. 14; note especially vv. 22–25).[49]

2.14. Roles of women

As with other traditions, the Reformed community has been much concerned with the roles of women in family, church and workplace. The

---

[46] For example, Michael Bushell, *The Songs of Zion* (Pittsburgh, PA: Crown & Covenant, 1980).

[47] As in D.G. Hart and John Muether, *With Reverence and Awe* (Phillipsburg: Presbyterian & Reformed, 2002).

[48] See my *Worship in Spirit and Truth* (Phillipsburg: Presbyterian & Reformed, 1996) and 'A Fresh Look at the Regulative Principle' in David G. Hagopian (ed.), *Always Reformed*, forthcoming.

[49] The earlier-referenced book by Hart and Muether argues for traditional worship. My *Contemporary Worship Music: A Biblical Defense* (Phillipsburg: Presbyterian & Reformed, 1997) argues for a more contemporary approach.

ordination of women to church office has been particularly controversial. As I mentioned earlier, many conservatives left the CRC in the 1990s because that denomination opened all the offices of the church to women. Most of those I defined earlier as 'conservative' reject the ordination of women. But one group, the Evangelical Presbyterian Church (EPC), which left the PCUSA over its liberal theology, has women elders in some churches, though unlike the PCUSA the EPC does not require congregations to have women officers.

Even those denominations that reject women's ordination have not escaped controversy. One large congregation recently left the PCA because of controversy over their use of women in worship. A woman stood behind a pulpit and used Scripture in a way that some described as 'preaching'. So the controversy in the PCA has come down to the question of whether some biblical restrictions pertain to women that do not pertain to unordained men. That question turns largely on the interpretation of 1 Corinthians 14:33–35 and 1 Timothy 2:11–15. Some argue that these passages exclude women only from the teaching and ruling offices of the church. Others say that, in addition to this, women should either be entirely silent during meetings of the church, or at least should not be permitted to teach God's Word to a group that includes men.[50]

There has also been controversy over recent attempts to translate the Bible into 'gender-neutral' language, avoiding such things as generic masculine pronouns and the generic 'man'.[51] In 1997 there was an agreement between a group of evangelical leaders and the International Bible Society (IBS), together with Zondervan publishers, that the IBS would not proceed on a plan to revise the New International Version in a gender-neutral direction. But in 2001, IBS and Zondervan announced that they had not abided by this agreement, but were completing work on a translation called 'Today's New International Version' (TNIV), which follows a gender-neutral policy. This decision caused a great stir among evangelicals generally, the Reformed among them.[52]

---

[50] For these views and others, see Bonnidell and Robert Clouse, *Women in Ministry: Four Views* (Downers Grove: InterVarsity Press, 1989). The most helpful treatments of these issues in my view are James Hurley, *Man and Woman in Biblical Perspective* (Grand Rapids: Zondervan, 1981) and John Piper and Wayne Grudem (eds), *Recovering Biblical Manhood and Womanhood* (Wheaton: Crossway, 1991).

[51] Some feminists have advocated that God himself be designated without gender or even as a female. Zondervan and IBS did not go this far.

[52] For different viewpoints on this question, see D.A. Carson, *The Inclusive-Language Debate* (Grand Rapids: Baker, 1998), Mark L. Strauss, *Distorting*

Proponents of gender-neutral translations say that gendered generics are no longer understandable to contemporary readers of English. Opponents say that (1) these generics are understandable, though politically offensive to some, and that (2) replacing them inevitably depersonalizes the biblical message, replacing masculine generics with plurals and abstract terms.

2.15. Preaching and redemptive history

Though Geerhardus Vos, Professor of Biblical Theology, stayed at Princeton after Westminster was founded, many Westminster faculty members admired him and were highly influenced by his teaching. Vos taught that Scripture was not a book of doctrinal propositions or ethical maxims, but a history of redemption, narrating the mighty acts of God from creation to consummation.

In 1961 Edmund P. Clowney, Professor of Practical Theology at Westminster, published *Preaching and Biblical Theology*,[53] in which, following some Dutch writers of the 1930s and 1940s, he argued that the main purpose of preaching is to set forth that redemptive-historical narrative. Negatively, Clowney argued that sermons should not present biblical characters as moral examples (called 'exemplarism' and 'moralism' in the Dutch discussion), but rather should present the role of each character in the historical drama that leads to Christ. Thus preaching should always be centred on Christ and the gospel. This position was carried to an extreme by others who, unlike Clowney, argued that a preacher should never 'apply' the Scriptures to moral issues.[54]

Still others are not convinced by this argument. Though grateful for Clowney's drawing our attention to the redemptive-historical drama of Scripture and the centrality of Christ, some have noted that: (1) Scripture contains not only narrative, but also laws, proverbs, songs, letters and apocalyptic, all of which have distinct purposes that preachers should bring out. (2) The intention of biblical writers in describing biblical characters is in part, indeed, to present them as positive or negative examples for human behaviour (as Rom. 4:1–25; 1 Cor. 10:1–13; Heb. 11; Jas. 2:21–26, 5:17–18; 2 Pet. 2:4–10; Jude 8–13). (3) Scripture explicitly tells us to imitate Jesus (Jn. 13:34–35) and Paul (1 Cor. 11:1,2;

---

[52] *(continued)* *Scripture?* (Downers Grove: InterVarsity Press, 1998), and Vern Poythress and Wayne Grudem, *The Gender-Neutral Bible Controversy* (Nashville: Broadman & Holman, 2000). The last is most persuasive to me.

[53] Grand Rapids: Eerdmans, 1961.

[54] For this more extreme position, see the publication *Kerux*.

Tim. 3:10–11), indeed to imitate God the Father (Mt. 5:44–48; 1 Pet. 1:15–16). And Paul tells Timothy also to be an example (1 Tim. 4:12). Imitation is an important means to the believer's sanctification. (4) The whole purpose of Scripture is application: to our belief (Jn. 20:31) and our good works (2 Tim. 3:16–17). (5) Redemptive-historical preachers have sometimes been criticized for interpreting texts arbitrarily to maintain an artificial Christ-centredness.[55]

2.16. *Subscription*

The long-standing Reformed debate over the nature of subscription to confessions continued through the twentieth century. Reformed churches are traditionally confessional, requiring all officers (in some communions all members) to pledge agreement with historic Reformed confessions, such as the Westminster Confession and Catechisms, the Belgic Confession, and so on. The controversy over liberal theology convinced many conservatives that the confessions should be taken more seriously. Some warned, however, that there are dangers in a form of subscription that is too strict: if subscription means that one may never teach anything contrary to the confession, then for all practical purposes the confessions are unamendable and are placed on the same level of authority as Scripture. Reformed theology embraces *sola scriptura* and therefore must allow practical means by which the Bible can lead us to revise the confessions if need be.

Theologians have advocated different views of subscription, some more strict than others.[56] In my judgement, this debate has focused too much on history, not enough on theology. It has stressed too much the attempt to define the historic view of American Presbyterianism, too little the theological question of what kind of subscription is desirable: both to maintain orthodoxy in the church and to maintain the supremacy of Scripture above all secondary standards.

---

[55] For a longer discussion of these points, see my 'Ethics, Preaching, and Biblical Theology' at < www.thirdmill.org >.

[56] The case for 'full' subscription is made by Morton H. Smith in *The Subscription Debate* (Greenville: Greenville Presbyterian Theological Seminary, no date listed, published 1993 or later). A less conservative view is William S. Barker, 'System Subscription', *Westminster Theological Journal* 63 (2001), pp. 1–14. Four elders participated in a debate on subscription before the PCA General Assembly of 2001, which was published in the denominational web magazine, *PCA News*, at < www.christianity.com/pcanews >.

2.17. *Church unity*

Among the Reformers, Calvin was most concerned with the unity of the church, specifically with the visible unity of the Protestant movement. Resisting the tendency of Protestants to divide into Calvinist and Lutheran camps, Calvin subscribed to a revised version of the Lutheran Augsburg Confession. More recently, however, some Reformed thinkers have subscribed to the notion of 'pluriformity', the view that denominations are, on the whole, a good thing. On this view, denominations are God's way of dealing with diversity in temperaments, gifts and doctrines. They maintain peace in the body of Christ in the way that good fences make good neighbours.

Other Reformed theologians, however, have rejected pluriformity, believing that God never ordained denominational division and that he intends for differences among believers to be worked out within the church, not over good fences.[57] That position became more influential in the late twentieth century. Reformed denominations have formed organizations, such as the Reformed Ecumenical Synod, the International and American Councils of Christian Churches, the World Reformed Fellowship and the National Association of Presbyterian and Reformed Churches. They have sought 'fraternal' or 'sister church' relationships with other bodies. Some denominations have discussed union with others.

In 1982 the RPES 'joined' the PCA and was 'received' by it.[58] But the PCA turned down the application of the OPC to be received into the larger denomination. Four years later, the OPC, lacking the necessary two-thirds vote in the General Assembly, rejected a renewed invitation to union with the PCA. Pro-union and anti-union parties engaged in much ecclesiastical warfare during this period.

---

[57] See John Murray, *Collected Writings*, vol. 1, pp. 269–87 (Edinburgh: Banner of Truth, 1976), Edmund P. Clowney, *The Church* (Downers Grove: InterVarsity Press, 1995), John Frame, *Evangelical Reunion* (Grand Rapids, Michigan: Baker, 1991), also available at < www.thirdmill.org >.

[58] The process of 'joining and receiving' was a procedure designed to minimize pre-union negotiations, the idea being to work out differences after union rather than before. Arguably this is a more biblical procedure than the conventional negotiation, since Scripture tells Christians to work out their differences within the church rather than to shout at one another over denominational barriers. In practice, however, the RPES and PCA did engage in much negotiation and discussion before the union was approved.

It seems to me that, although Reformed churches are committed in theory to seeking union, there is a notable tendency for them to shy away from any actual union and indeed to create new divisions unnecessarily. Reformed churches tend to glory in their distinctives: their history, their ethnic origins, the theological battles of the past that have made them different from others.

Further, when groups of people leave a denomination over some issue, they tend to form new denominations rather than join denominations that already exist. So those who left the CRC over the issue of women's ordination did not, for the most part, join other Reformed or Presbyterian denominations, but formed new bodies. In my judgement, these new denominations were unjustified, and therefore add to the divisions in the body of Christ.

In the 1990s the Alliance of Confessing Evangelicals (ACE) brought together Christians from various confessional traditions: Lutheran, Reformed, Baptist, Anglican and others. Their emphasis was on the Reformation *sola*s: by Scripture alone, grace alone, faith alone, Christ alone, to the glory of God alone. The Alliance showed promise of bringing Christians together. However, to some extent it has itself become divisive, for it has become a party in evangelicalism advocating certain distinctives: a sharp distinction between law and gospel, a 'two kingdoms' view of Christ and culture, a history-centred approach to theology, strict subscription and traditional worship.

2.18. Tradition in theology

More should be said, therefore, about the role of tradition in the work of theology. Reformed theology has embraced *sola scriptura*, a principle Luther and Calvin used to carry out a radical critique of the ideas and practices of the church of their time. But these Reformers did respect their predecessors, making much use especially of the church fathers and Augustine. They accepted the teachings of the early creeds, and they purified worship in a thoughtful, cautious way, critical of the violent change advocated by others.

For thirty years or so there has been a movement in American evangelicalism to recover the past, to remedy the 'rootlessness' that many have felt in evangelical churches. In the 1950s and 1960s, the intellectual leaders of evangelicalism were for the most part biblical scholars, apologists and systematic theologians. But at the end of the twentieth century, church historians and theologians who do their work in dialogue with ancient and recent history have become more prominent. Reformed theology has participated in this development, so that many of its most prominent figures, such as David Wells, Donald Bloesch, Mark Noll, George Marsden, Darryl Hart, Richard Muller and Michael Horton, do theology in an historical mode. Many of these also advocate strict subscription and traditional worship, and they seek to renew an emphasis on Reformation distinctives: hence the discussions of covenant, justification, law and gospel, noted earlier. The ACE has supported this emphasis.

Though this emphasis has done some good by revitalizing interest in the Reformed heritage, some have found deficiencies in the theology emerging from this movement. The main issue is *sola scriptura*. The Reformed tradition consists not in merely repeating previous Reformed traditions, but, as with Calvin, in using the Scriptures to criticize tradition. The history-oriented theologians tend to be uncritical of traditions and critical of the contemporary church. But their arguments are often based on their preferences rather than biblical principle, and therefore fail to persuade. The Reformed community, in my judgement, needs to return to an explicitly exegetical model of theology, following the example of John Murray.[59] The exegetical approach is also (perhaps paradoxically) the most contemporary approach, for it applies Scripture directly to our lives today. This question is, of course, one of emphasis. We should never ignore our past. But my view is that the pendulum has swung too far in the direction of an historical emphasis.

2.19. Sonship

C. John Miller taught practical theology at Westminster Seminary in Philadelphia and planted the New Life Church (originally OPC, later PCA). He emphasized the importance of evangelistic, outward-facing ministry in the church, and founded World Harvest Mission.[60] He also began a ministry called Sonship, which through conferences and tapes presents a distinctive view of the Christian life: not only justification,

---

[59] I have argued these points at greater length in 'In Defense of Something Close to Biblicism', *Westminster Theological Journal* 59 (1997), pp. 269–318, with responses by Richard Muller and David Wells, reprinted as an Appendix to *Contemporary Worship Music*. See also my 'Traditionalism' at < www. thirdmill.org > and in *Chalcedon Report* 434 (October 2001), pp. 15–19, and 435 (November 2001), pp. 14–16.

[60] Among his writings are *Repentance and Twentieth-Century Man* (Philadelphia: Christian Literature Crusade, 1980), *Outgrowing the Ingrown Church* (Grand Rapids: Zondervan, 1986), *Powerful Evangelism for the Powerless* (Phillipsburg: Presbyterian & Reformed, 1997).

but sanctification too, by faith. The way to victory over sin, according to Miller, is not by the law, but by the gospel: looking to Jesus as the one who has borne the full guilt of our sins, 'preaching the gospel to yourself'. That involves a life of repentance, but also the recognition that Christ has set us free from sin to be his sons and daughters. Some have criticized the Sonship teaching as failing to understand the positive uses of the law in the believer's spiritual growth.[61]

Sonship has become a major renewal movement in conservative Presbyterian circles, especially the PCA. Those who have taken the Sonship course often emerge with a far more vital relationship with Christ. Nevertheless, advocates and opponents of Sonship have fought the typical Reformed battles. As with many of the movements and ideas discussed in this paper, I tend to agree with what Sonship affirms (the benefit of preaching the gospel to ourselves) but not with what it denies (that reflecting on God's law and striving to obey are somehow harmful to our sanctification).

2.20. *Christian hedonism*

John Piper's writings[62] have made a large impact on Reformed and other evangelical believers in the late twentieth century, and their influence continues unabated. Building on some ideas of Jonathan Edwards, Piper argues that the Christian life is essentially an enjoyment of God, for God is glorified when his people enjoy him. The Christian life gets out of kilter when we find ourselves enjoying other things in the place of God. Piper's work has generated a renewal movement similar to that of Sonship, though with a somewhat different message. Piper has been criticized for failing to recognize the theme of the Heidelberg Catechism: that our obedience to God is motivated by gratitude for what he has done for us. He has replied that he is not opposed to obedience motivated by gratitude. He rather opposes the 'debtor's ethic', the notion that we must somehow seek to pay God back for what he has done for us.

2.21. *Covenant and election*

In 2002, some lectures were given at the Auburn Avenue Presbyterian Church, Monroe, Louisiana, called 'The Federal Vision: A

---

[61] For a positive exposition of Sonship, read Neil H. Williams, *Theology of Sonship* (Philadelphia: World Harvest Mission, 2002). For a critique, Jay E. Adams, *Biblical Sonship* (Woodruff, South Carolina: Timeless Texts, 1999).

[62] See especially his *Desiring God* (Portland: Multnomah Press, 1996).

Re-examination of Reformed Covenantalism'.[63] These lectures created quite a stir in conservative Presbyterian circles. They argued that divine election should be understood primarily as an historical covenant, God's choice of people to belong to the visible church. Since baptism is the mark of entrance into the visible church, it is the inception of election. All baptized members of the church should consider themselves elect, as Paul in his letters addresses them as 'saints' and 'elect'. But election, like the covenant, is conditional. If people are so disobedient that they are excommunicated, put out of the church, then they are no longer to regard themselves as elect.

Critics of these lectures question (1) how this viewpoint does justice to the *eternal* character of election as described by Paul, for instance, in Ephesians 1:4, and (2) whether it makes election, and therefore salvation, dependent on human works. My own view is that the Bible teaches both historical election (God choosing individuals for tasks in history) and eternal election (God choosing individuals for eternal salvation).[64] When Paul addresses congregations as 'saints' and 'elect', he is speaking of eternal election. But he does not necessarily imply by these terms that every individual in the congregation is eternally elect. It would have been pedantic in such contexts for him to try to distinguish between those in the congregation who are, and those who are not, eternally elect.

The two sides should seek more pointedly to address the issues raised by their opponents. The Auburn Avenue group should focus on the two concerns noted above. Their opponents need to ask in what sense visible churches as such are the elect of God.

2.22. *Multi-perspectivalism*

Emerging from these battles, it has occurred to some of us that perhaps at least some of these conflicts have resulted from misunderstandings. Some of the disagreements may not be straightforward differences over truth versus falsity, but to some extent have resulted from people looking at biblical content from different angles or perspectives. The story of the blind men and the elephant is relevant here: one describes the elephant as shaped like a tree trunk, another like a great boulder, another like a thick cable because one focuses on the leg, the second on the torso, and the third on the trunk. Were they able to see, they would understand that

---

[63] The taped lectures are available from the church at < www.auburnavenue .org/past%20conf.htm >.

[64] For a discussion of this distinction, see Chapter 16 of my *Doctrine of God* (Phillipsburg: Presbyterian & Reformed, 2002).

there is truth in all three descriptions, that no description captures the whole animal, and that there is no cause for disagreement.

So I suspect, for example, that the disagreement over the incomprehensibility of God is a difference between some who focus on the continuity between God's thoughts and ours and others who focus on the discontinuity. I see no reason why we cannot affirm both, if we can escape our movement loyalties and read Scripture afresh. On the issue of confessional subscription, I think it possible to establish a form of subscription that will guard the church against heresy, while at the same time allowing Scripture to function as the church's primary standard, so that the church can, if necessary, revise the confessions according to the Word of God. On the issue of the dynamics of the Christian life, I'm inclined to think that Scripture teaches a number of factors in sanctification: not only reviewing the gospel (Miller) and scrutinizing our pleasures (Piper), but also asking God's grace to give us thankful hearts (the Heidelberg Catechism), seeking godly models to imitate (as discussed earlier), and reviewing the law to see how our Father wants us to behave (not only theonomy, but the traditional Reformed 'third use of the law').

Not every theological difference, of course, is a difference of perspective. Sometimes one must simply choose between one view that is true and another that is false. For example, either women should be ordained to church office, or they should not be. There is no middle ground on this specific issue, and the difference is not merely a difference of perspective. Even here, however, perspectival differences enter into the nature of the disagreement. Advocates of women's ordination tend to view the biblical data largely from the perspective of Galatians 3:28: 'neither Jew nor Greek, slave nor free, male nor female, for you are all one in Christ Jesus'. Opponents tend to focus on 1 Corinthians 14:33–35 and 1 Timothy 2:11–15. I doubt that unity will be restored on this issue until each group takes the perspective of the other group more seriously.

The main point of multi-perspectivalism is that only God is omniscient, seeing reality simultaneously from all possible perspectives. Because of our finitude, we need to look at things first from one perspective, then another. The more different perspectives we can incorporate into our formulations, the more likely those formulations will be biblically accurate.

Several of us have expounded this approach to theology in various places.[65] But alas, multi-perspectivalism itself has become a focus of

---

[65] See John Frame, *Doctrine of the Knowledge of God* (Phillipsburg: Presbyterian & Reformed, 1987), *Perspectives on the Word of God* (Eugene: Wipf & Stock, 1999), Vern S. Poythress, *Symphonic Theology* (Grand Rapids:

controversy in Reformed circles.[66] The usual criticism is that multi-perspectivalism is relativist, but multi-perspectivalists deny that criticism emphatically. In our view, there is one objective truth: the truth as God has made it. We can know much of that truth with certainty, based on God's revelation. But there are some matters, even in theology, about which many of us are uncertain. And especially in those cases it is important for us to cross-check our ideas by looking at the data from different perspectives.

3. Observations

I have enumerated twenty-two areas of conflict occurring in American conservative Reformed circles from 1936 to the present.[67] Under some of those headings I have mentioned subdivisions, subcontroversies. Most of these controversies have led to divisions in churches and denominations and harsh words exchanged between Christians. People have been told that they are not Reformed, even that they have denied the gospel. Since Jesus presents love as that which distinguishes his disciples from the world (Jn. 13:34–35), this bitter fighting is anomalous in a Christian fellowship. Reformed believers need to ask what has driven these battles. To what extent has this controversy been the fruit of the Spirit, and to what extent has it been a work of the flesh?

The Machen movement was born in the controversy over liberal theology. I have no doubt that Machen and his colleagues were right to reject this theology and to fight it. But it is arguable that once the Machenites found themselves in a 'true Presbyterian church' they were unable to moderate their martial impulses. Being in a church without liberals to fight, they turned on one another.

---

[65] *(continued)* Zondervan, 1987), Poythress, *God-Centered Biblical Interpretation* (Phillipsburg: Presbyterian & Reformed, 1999).

[66] Mark Karlberg, 'On the Theological Correlation of Divine and Human Language: A Review Article', *Journal of the Evangelical Theological Society* 32:1 (March 1989), pp. 99–105, and his review of my *Cornelius Van Til* (Phillipsburg, New Jersey: Presbyterian & Reformed, 1995) in *Mid-America Journal of Theology* 9:2 (Fall 1993), pp. 297–308. I have replied to both Karlberg pieces in Appendices to my *Doctrine of God* (Phillipsburg, New Jersey: Presbyterian & Reformed, 2002).

[67] Of course, between 1900–36 the chief battle was over theological liberalism. There was also a major conflict in the CRC over the doctrine of common grace, leading to the formation of the Protestant Reformed Church. I cannot enter into that controversy here, but I have addressed it in my *Cornelius Van Til* (Phillipsburg: Presbyterian & Reformed, 1995), pp. 215–30.

One slogan of the Machen movement was 'truth before friendship'. We should laud their intention to act according to principle without compromise. But the biblical balance is 'speaking the truth in love' (Eph. 4:15). We must not speak the truth without thinking of the effect of our formulations on our fellow Christians, even our opponents. That balance was not characteristic of the Machen movement.[68]

Reformed people need to do much more thinking about what constitutes a test of orthodoxy. Is it really plausible to say that, for example, Gordon Clark's view of incomprehensibility was unorthodox, when neither Clark's nor Van Til's positions are clearly set forth in the Reformed confessions? But again and again, through the history described above, writers have read one another out of the Reformed movement (and even out of Christianity) on such dubious bases. The assumption seems to be that *any* difference of opinion amounts to a test of fellowship, that *any* truth I possess gives me the right to disrupt the peace of the church until everybody comes to agree with me. But surely there are some disagreements that are not tests of orthodoxy, some differences that should be tolerated within the church. Examples include the disagreements over days and the eating of meat, described by Paul in Romans 14, and the disagreements about idol food, which he discusses in 1 Corinthians 8–10. In those passages there is no suggestion that people holding the wrong view should be put out of the church. Rather, Paul condemns the party spirit and calls the disagreeing parties to live together as Christian brothers and sisters. In my judgement, the Machen movement thought little about the difference between tolerable and intolerable disagreements in the church.

Scripture often condemns a 'contentious' spirit (Prov. 13:10, 18:6, 26:21; Hab. 1:3; 1 Cor. 1:11, 11:16; Tit. 3:9) and commends 'gentleness' (2 Cor. 10:1; Gal. 5:22; 1 Thes. 2:7; 2 Tim. 2:24; Tit. 3:2; Jas. 3:17). The Reformed community should give much more attention to these biblical themes.

With many, though not all, of the issues described above it is possible to see the positions as complementary rather than as contradictory.

---

[68] Machen, like others in the Reformed tradition, emphasized the 'primacy of the intellect'. See his *What is Faith?* (Grand Rapids: Eerdmans, 1925, reprinted 1962). As Ulrich Zwingli eliminated music from the worship service, turning it into a teaching meeting, Reformed leaders through history have tended to value intellectual rigour at the expense of people's emotions. In my judgement, this intellectualism is a mistaken emphasis and needs to be overcome. See my *Doctrine of the Knowledge of God* (Phillipsburg: Presbyterian & Reformed, 1987), pp. 319–46.

I believe that is true of the Van Til/Clark controversy, the counselling controversy, the Sonship controversy and some others. As I said earlier, I find these positions more persuasive in what they affirm than in what they deny.

With other issues there are genuine contradictions between the positions of the parties. But even in those cases, I think that often these parties are trying to express complementary biblical truths. Theonomy, for example, emphasizes the continuity between Old and New Testaments, anti-theonomy the discontinuity. A more adequate account will seek to do justice to both.

Overall, the quality of thought displayed in these polemics has not been a credit to the Reformed tradition. Writers have gone to great lengths to read their opponents' words and motivations in the worst possible sense (often worse than possible) and to present their own ideas as virtually perfect, rightly motivated and leaving no room for doubt. Such presentations are scarcely credible to anybody who looks at the debates with minimal objectivity.

The various anniversary celebrations and official histories in the different Reformed denominational bodies have been largely self-congratulatory.[69] In Reformed circles, we often say that there is no perfect church, that churches as well as individuals are guilty of sin and liable to error. But Reformed writers and teachers seem to find it almost impossible to specify particular sins, even weaknesses, in their own traditions or denominations, particularly in their own partisan groups. A spirit of genuine self-criticism (prelude to a spirit of repentance) is an urgent need.

Nevertheless, it is important to remember that there are some theological issues that really are matters of life and death for the church. In the PCUSA, as of the time of writing, there are controversies over whether church officers should be expected to observe biblical standards of sexual fidelity and chastity, over the ordination of homosexuals, and over whether Jesus is the only Lord and Saviour. The outrageous fact that such issues can actually be debated within the church places other controversies into perspective. The Confessing Church Movement within the PCUSA is fighting a courageous battle, and they deserve the prayers and encouragement of all Reformed believers.

---

[69] See, for example, Darryl Hart and John Muether, *Fighting the Good Fight* (Philadelphia: The Committee on Christian Education and the Committee for the Historian of the Orthodox Presbyterian Church, 1995). Though there is much useful information and reflection in this book, there is far too little recognition of possible inadequacies within the tradition.

My assignment was to write on Reformed theology. But I should note that the remedy for the divisions above is not merely better theological formulations. The almost exclusive focus on doctrinal issues in many Reformed circles is itself part of the problem. As Tim Keller advises, Reformed Christianity needs a vision that encompasses not only doctrinal statements, but also our piety, evangelistic outreach and missions of mercy.[70]

4. An Unrealistic Dream

- That Reformed thinkers continue to have bright, fresh ideas, but that they present these ideas with humility and treat with grace and patience those who are not immediately convinced.
- That Reformed thinkers with bright ideas discourage the rapid formation of parties to contend for those ideas.
- That those initially opposed to those bright ideas allow some time for gentle, thoughtful discussion before declaring the bright ideas to be heresy.
- That these opponents also discourage the rapid formation of partisan groups.
- That those contending for various doctrinal positions accept the burden of proof, willing to bear the difficulty of serious biblical exegesis.
- That we try much harder to guard our tongues (Jas. 3:1–12), saving the strongest language of condemnation (e.g., 'denying the gospel') for those who have been declared heretics by the judicial processes of the church.
- That Reformed churches, ministries and institutions be open to a wider range of opinions than they are now – within limits, of course.
- That we honour one another as much for character and witness as we do for agreement with our theological positions.
- That occasionally we smile and jest about our relatively minor differences, while praying, worshipping and working together in the love of Christ.[71]

---

[70] See 'The Vision of PPLN', available at < www.pastoral-leadership.org/articles/PPLNvision_Keller.pdf >.

[71] Thanks to Steve Hays, D. Clair Davis, David Powlison, John Muether and Greg Welty, who read an earlier draft of this paper and made helpful suggestions. I take all responsibility for the final formulation.

6

Evangelical Theology of Divine Openness

Clark H. Pinnock

1. Introduction

The term 'openness of God' is evangelical coinage for a model of deity
that belongs to what is called classical free will theism, which is a syner-
gistic tradition that goes back to the very origins of theology. It has
always resisted the theological monergism associated with the later
Augustine in favour of a more co-operative relationship between God
and humanity. The name 'openness of God' was selected because it was
unused, free of negatives, and suitable to the conviction that God is
'open' to his creatures and affected by them.[1]

In the contemporary context, open theism belongs to a family of
approaches known as relational or personalistic theism. It asks what
would happen to our understanding of doctrine if we considered that
God, for the sake of love, had given human creatures libertarian freedom.
What if God, seeking relationships of love, had given the creature the
freedom to enter into them? The open view contends that God, for the
sake of love, has indeed restrained his power so that a creation might
exist as a significant other to God and possibly be a partner of his. Open
theism is a theology of the living God, whose very being is self-giving love
and who is prepared to be vulnerable in engagement with the world. To
our way of thinking, God's steadfastness is not dead immutability but a
dynamic constancy of purpose; God's power is not raw omnipotence

---

[1] On the ancient synergist tradition from which every non-determinist theology derives, see Roger E. Olson, *The Story of Christian Theology: Twenty
Centuries of Tradition and Reform* (Downers Grove: InterVarsity Press,
1999), chs 17 and 28. For an exposition of open theism itself, see Terrance
Tiessen, critic of the model but a fine expositer of it: *Providence and Prayer:
How Does God Work in the World?* (Downers Grove: InterVarsity Press,
2000), chs 4–5.

but the sovereignty of love; and God's knowledge is not a trivial know-it-all-ness but deep wisdom which may even choose the foolishness of the cross.

In the year 1994, knowing that many inside the evangelical camp and many more outside it were hearing about the open model and expressing interest in it, a group of open theists who associate with evangelicalism decided it was time that more serious consideration be given to this proposal by scholars in the evangelical context.[2] We did not go forward with the book to cause a theological crisis but because we thought open theism was a promising line of enquiry that could enrich our discussions. From our standpoint, we thought it could even become a viable middle way between the immobilist theologies stemming from Augustine and Aquinas and the dynamism of process thought. Somewhat unexpectedly, what we thought would make a good discussion topic in the Evangelical Theological Society became for many an issue of theological boundaries. For us, in contrast, it has the appeal of a needed metaphysics of love grounded in the gospel and with relevance for the dynamic nature of modern science.[3]

---

[2] The book that launched the current debate among evangelicals was Clark Pinnock, Richard Rice, John Sanders, William Hasker and David Basinger, *The Openness of God: A Biblical Challenge to the Traditional Understanding of God* (Downers Grove: InterVarsity Press, 1994). A number of other scholars hold the open view of God position without using the language of openness: for example, Richard Swinburne, Pater Baelz, Vincent Brummer, John Polkinghorne, Nicholas Wolterstorff, Jürgen Moltmann, Hendrikus Berkhof, Paul Fiddes and Keith Ward.

[3] To get a feeling for the debate, see Christopher A. Hall and John Sanders, *Divine Debates: A Dialogue on the Classical and Openness Views of God* (Grand Rapids: Baker, 2002). Books in favour of open theism include Clark Pinnock, *Most Moved Mover: A Theology of God's Openness* (Carlisle/ Grand Rapids: Paternoster/Baker, 2001), John Sanders, *The God Who Risks: A Theology of Providence* (Downers Grove: InterVarsity Press, 1998) and Gregory A. Boyd, *God of the Possible: A Biblical Introduction to the Open View of God* (Grand Rapids: Baker, 2000). Books from evangelicals opposed to open theism include Bruce A. Ware, *God's Lesser Glory: The Diminished God of Open Theism* (Wheaton: Crossway, 2000), John M. Frame, *No Other God: A Response to Open Theism* (Phillipsburg: Presbyterian & Reformed, 2001), Douglas S. Huffman and Eric L. Johnson (eds), *God Under Fire: Modern Scholarship Reinvents God* (Grand Rapids: Zondervan, 2002), John Piper, Justin Taylor and Paul Helseth (eds), *Beyond the Bounds: Open Theism and the Undermining of Biblical Christianity* (Wheaton: Crossway, 2003) and Norman L. Geisler and H. Wayne House, *The Battle for God: Responding to the Challenge of Neotheism* (Grand Rapids: Kregel, 2001).

2. Growing as Hearers

Evangelicalism is a movement without a confession, though it has theological interests and a conservative ethos. An evangelical theologian can be expected to hold to sound doctrine and to contend for the faith once delivered to the saints, though in a trans-denominational way reflecting the coalition. Differences can be expected, given the ecumenical character of the movement, and even experiments in theological reform from time to time where new ground is broken. Though traditionalist, the movement is not completely stagnant theologically – new light is still allowed to pour forth from God's most holy Word and some room exists for theological creativity. In recent years, this anti-modernist coalition called evangelicalism has allowed for a measure of rethinking of issues, which (for some of us) is a sign of health, though for others a near disaster. In our perspective, reform is part of our search for a generous orthodoxy and an effective church-wide and world-wide witness. In this case there seems to be a need to enquire even further into the doctrine of God.[4]

Growing as hearers of the Word of God is basic to sanctification and is possible thanks to the work of the Holy Spirit. On the one hand, the Spirit binds us to the definitive salvific action of God in Jesus Christ, and, on the other hand, causes everything Jesus said and did to be seen in a new light. According to John, the Paraclete guides the community into more truth on the basis of the original gospel, so that we are able to reproclaim it in timely ways. The Spirit does not add to or surpass what Christ has revealed, but causes everything to be seen afresh. One could think of interpretation in musical terms as improvisation, where the performer discovers in the score a range of unexplored possibilities. As Webb puts it, 'to neglect re-applying the redemptive spirit of the text adds a debilitating impotence to a life-transforming gospel that should be unleashed within our modern world'.[5]

---

[4] For my reflections on Evangelical theology, see Clark H. Pinnock, 'Evangelical Theology in Progress' in Roger A. Badman (ed.), *Introduction to Christian Theology* (Louisville: Westminster John Knox, 1998), pp. 75–85.

[5] William J. Webb, *Slaves, Women, and Homosexuals: Exploring the Hermeneutics of Cultural Analysis* (Downers Grove: InterVarsity Press, 2001), p. 50. See also James D.G. Dunn, *Jesus and the Spirit: A Study of the Religious and Charismatic Experience of Jesus and the First Christians as Reflected in the New Testament* (London: SCM Press, 1975), pp. 351–3, Hans Küng, *The Church* (New York: Sheed & Ward, 1967), pp. 191–203 and Francis Martin, 'Spirit and Flesh in Doing Theology', *Journal of Pentecostal Theology* 18 (2001) pp. 5–31.

As we search the Scriptures and strive to hear what the Spirit is saying to the churches, we may be led to discern what truth matters most in the present situation. We might be enabled to understand what the signs of the times are telling us and what new treasures there are which can be brought out of the storehouse (Mt. 13:32). The Spirit makes theology such a delightful activity and so full of surprises. Theology is an ongoing discipline that gives rise to new ways of looking at old questions and brings into view previously undervalued aspects of our faith Occasionally it can even advance the church's knowledge of truth. In the tests for doctrinal faithfulness, it is all too often forgotten that the truth ought to engage the present situation. Biblical truth ought to be transforming truth. We ought to be saying what matters most in our proclamation.[6]

It is only right and proper that fresh proposals in theology sometimes be made, even when it concerns the nature of God. The reality of God is (after all) deep and inexhaustible. St Paul speaks of 'the depth of the riches and wisdom and knowledge of God' (Rom. 11:33) and of 'the love of Christ that surpasses knowledge' (Eph. 3:19). God is an inexhaustible mystery and the ways of responding to God are innumerable. Though we 'see in a mirror dimly' and 'know only in part', the doctrine of God always invites fresh thinking in a spirit of co-operation (1 Cor. 13:12). It is not enough just to rehearse the tradition – we welcome fresh acts of interpretation. Let us not be afraid of such exercises but be hopeful for enrichment to come out of dialogue.[7]

We need to remember too that there is not a single line of tradition when it comes to issues in the doctrine of God. The older theologians like Irenaeus, Augustine and Thomas Aquinas did not just say the same things exactly. They inquired into the mysteries and pondered how to take such truths as God's power, God's suffering and God's changing seriously. The tradition is not completely uniform and there is no law against considering and reconsidering matters. And do not think for a moment that open theists are the only ones doing so.[8]

---

[6] On the test of 'cruciality', see Christopher Morse, *Not Every Spirit: A Dogmatics of Christian Disbelief* (Valley Forge: Trinity Press International, 1994), pp. 65–6.

[7] S. Mark Heim applies this insight to our understanding of other faiths in *The Depth of the Riches: A Trinitarian Theology of Religious Ends* (Grand Rapids: Eerdmans, 2001).

[8] Just take a look at Calvinist John S. Feinberg's 900-page *magnum opus* to all that is being done: *No One Like Him: The Doctrine of God* (Wheaton: Crossway, 2001).

3. The Open View of God

The openness of God is a reading of Scripture that veers away from an abstract and impersonal approach to the divine mystery towards interactive, relational and personal categories. If classical theism's root metaphor is God as a stone pillar around which everything else moves, the root metaphor for open theism is a living personal God in loving relations with creaturely persons. God is thought of not as a metaphysical abstraction or all-determining power, but as a loving and caring parent (*abba*, Father) who interacts with his children. God is self-restrained for the sake of love and is our multi-temporal companion whose project world history is.

The open view in our way of presenting it is by no means a speculative proposal, but a Bible-based and Trinitarian theology, which features a God in whom Father, Son and Spirit are eternally giving and receiving love. Not a philosophical structure, this Trinitarian understanding lifts up the heart of the faith and projects a vision of God's graciously relational nature. We confess that God, in love and by sovereign power, created the world out of nothing, forming creatures capable of experiencing divine love. To this end, God gave them the capacity to enter into relationships with him and fellow creatures by granting them the freedom necessary for such relationships. And, despite the fact that we abuse our freedom by turning away from God, God remains faithful to his intentions for us.

When we speak of God as Triune, we mean that God is not a solitary monad but self-communicating love, not a supreme will to power but the will to community. God is the ultimate power whose very being consists in the giving, receiving and sharing of love. Thus the reign of the Triune God is a rule of sovereign love not a rule of brute force. God is not absolute power, or infinite egocentrism, or majestic solitariness, but creative, sacrificial and empowering love, whose glory consists not in dominating others, but in sharing life with them. Such love is precarious, involves vulnerability and runs the risk of rejection. It is quite different from inauthentic love, which seeks control like a possessive parent and holds on desperately to the offspring, denying it room to grow.

One way to understand the open view of God is to think of it as a theology of divine self-emptying (or *kenosis*). Though this is a term more often associated with Christology, it has wider implications.[9] Not

---

[9] Roland J. Feenstra, 'Reconsidering Kenotic Christology' in Ronald J. Feenstra and Cornelius Plantinga, Jr (eds), *Trinity, Incarnation, and Atonement: Philosophical and Theological Essays* (Notre Dame, Indiana: University of Notre Dame Press, 1989), pp. 128–52.

only does it express the notion of the Son of God surrendering divine glory in order to become human, of his choosing to enter fully into the human condition and even share in our suffering, it also points to the divine mystery underlying it, that God wants to be loved by us and willingly makes himself vulnerable. Though we are completely dependant on him, God is also willing to be dependant on us. Open theists see God's self-giving and self-sacrificing action for the good of others pre-eminently in Jesus Christ, who is the image and self-expression of the Father (Heb. 1:3). It is characteristic of love to be self-sacrificing and the incarnation reveals to us how God likes to use his power, not to dominate, but to love.[10]

This divine *kenosis* or self-emptying of God, in which God limits the exercise of his properties in order that significant creatures should exist, is balanced by a 'pleroma' or fullness of glory in which God experiences real gain and not diminishment as some say. The very act of self-emptying allows God to experience something truly wonderful – namely, loving relationships with creatures, which would otherwise have been impossible. We need to see that, alongside what looks like subtraction and loss, there is addition and gain, namely, the richness that is added to divine experience by enjoying these relationships. The self-limitation of God makes possible and renders visible wonderful new forms of divine glory. Open theists do not serve a diminished deity. God could have created a world whose future would be completely settled, but he chose something different. He made a world the future of which would not be totally settled and not be exhaustively foreknown just in order to let finite creativity flourish. There is no 'loss' here for God, since it is only a question of how God's power, which is his alone, is exercised.

Though he has power over the world, God lets himself be affected by creation, delighting in its beauty and grieving over its tragedies. God chooses self-limitation for the sake of having a covenant with humankind. Not like the God of Aristotle, indifferent to the world, thinking of nothing but himself, God in the gospel is completely aware of the finite world and intimately involved in the flow of events. Indeed, God is the supreme actor on the stage of history. He relates with us in temporal ways and experiences events as they occur. In creating the world, there

---

[10] It was a distinctive move on the part of Arminius to emphasize God's self-limitation. Reformed theologians had acknowledged condescension in God's revelation, but not self-limitation. See Richard A. Muller, *God, Creation and Providence in the Thought of Jacob Arminius: Sources and Directions of Scholastic Protestantism in the Era of Early Orthodoxy* (Grand Rapids: Baker, 1991), p. 281.

took place a *kenosis* of omnipotence in which God allowed a created order to exist alongside himself and let it function so that, while all that happens is permitted by God, not all that happens in it is in accordance with the will of God.

I do not see the biblical emphasis resting on God's omnipotence as much as resting on a kind of impotence by which God allows other significant agents to exist alongside himself, which can have positive or negative implications. God does not employ the kind of power that annihilates the other – rather he steps back and lets them be. Humanity can either respond in love and gratitude, or become a counter-player. This would not be possible unless humans had initiatives of their own with all the consequences. The tragedy is that humans became God's competitors instead of his partners. We see quality of God especially in the incarnation, where Jesus renounces earthly power and even becomes a victim of our rejection of him. Even the Spirit experiences this reality when over and over again he is resisted and grieved. As well, the Spirit seeks to form us after the pattern of the suffering servant. The open view of God is trying to pick up on these glorious themes.

By bringing into being a temporal creation, whose nature is expressed in its unfolding history, God granted reality to time and actualized in his own nature a temporal pole whereby he knows things and experiences things as they really are, that is, temporally in their succession. God is involved with time and in history, indicating that there is in God both that which is wholly free from variation (so that God's character is eternally unchangeable) but also that which corresponds to the changing circumstances of a temporal creation. The eternal God can embrace the experiences of time and, as the incarnation and salvation history shows us, time is not something foreign to him. God exists throughout all periods of time and is always our contemporary.[11]

In terms of the foreknowledge of God, in the boldest move by far in the open model, which is otherwise much like standard Arminianism, we take the Scriptures seriously which speak of God's being surprised by certain events.[12] Why, if God does not control the future in exhaustive

---

[11] John Feinberg agrees with us that God is temporal: see *No One Like Him: The Doctrine of God* (Wheaton: Crossway, 2001), pp. 427–33.

[12] For the biblical case for the future being partly settled and partly unsettled, see Terrance Fretheim, *The Suffering of God: An Old Testament Perspective* (Philadelphia: Fortress Press, 1984), ch. 4 and Boyd, *God of the Possible*, chs 1–2. Some critics ask us how we can hold to biblical inerrancy if we deny the teaching of Scripture that God knows all events of the future. The reason we can do so is because we do not find that the Bible clearly teaches it.

detail, would we imagine that God would know the future in exhaustive detail? If this is a world of real becoming, open to a future that is being brought about both by causal principles (such as natural law) and by human and divine agencies, it seems likely that the future of the world would be (to some extent) something still being decided. God's close engagement with time implies that he does not know all that will eventually happen at this point. God knows all that can be known, but, because he is engaged with history, does not know all that will eventually be known. If God's project is dynamic and the future open to what creatures (as well as what God) will decide to do, then the future is not yet fixed and may not be exhaustively foreknown. This does not imply that God is unprepared for any possible future or that God lacks the competence to face it. God knows all possibilities, but not as actualities. This is not only biblically sound and intellectually satisfying; it is immensely practical. Think of it – if we thought the future was still open to being changed, we might take a little more responsibility for changing it. If God knows everything that will happen in the future, what is the point to petitionary prayer? It is not surprising to me that practically oriented people seem to favour the open view of God over those for whom theological tradition matters most.

Please understand – all evangelicals affirm God's omnipotence and omniscience. The only disagreement is over *how* God is omnipotent and omniscient, which are matters for legitimate discussion. A question to critics might be: do you think it would be possible for God to create a universe the future of which he would not exhaustively foreknow? If it is possible, doesn't it appear that this is such a world? If it is not possible, who is limiting the sovereignty of God?

How truly beautiful God is! Though self-sufficient in glory and lacking in nothing, God nevertheless makes room for creatures and deploys his power on their behalf, not against them. For the sake of love, he self-limits and even self-sacrifices himself. If he had only love without power (as in process theism), God would be a compassionate but impotent spectator of the world. If he had only power without love (as in deterministic theologies), God would be a cosmic tyrant, holding the whole of history in an unrelenting grasp. As it is, God, the Father of our Lord Jesus Christ, is neither a bystander nor director of a puppet theatre. God is love and deploys his power for the good of humanity. God even permits the wayward freedom of his creatures and enters into their pain in order that, finally, they might share his bliss. The history of the world is the movement from divine self-emptying to our creaturely fulfilment in God. Open theists rejoice in this understanding, which understands God not as an indifferent metaphysical iceberg or a solitary narcissistic being who suffers from his own completeness, but as a free and creative Trinitarian personal God.

As I have said, these paths of (re)interpretation are not trodden by open theists alone. Other evangelical theologians too have noticed the problems in classical theism and have begun to address them. Indeed, most of the issues, apart from the question of omniscience, are discussed by critics of the open view themselves: such as the nature of divine immutability (Ware and Davis),[13] the divine pathos (Grudem and Erickson)[14] and the divine temporality (Nash and Tiessen)[15] and so on. Remarkably, John Frame says that God feels, like human beings, the flow of time from day to day – he can mourn one moment and rejoice the next. Frame also acknowledges give-and-take relationships between God and creatures and even agrees with Moltmann that God suffered in the suffering of Christ. In saying so, Frame opens up the rift between Calvinistic and the Thomistic versions of classical deterministic theism. Evidently, the issue is not whether to revise classical theism, but how best to revise it.[16] It is amusing and kind of sad to find one and the same scholar revising a hugely fundamental attribute like divine impassibility and then take great exception to our reconsideration of omniscience. It seems to me that, if impassiblity goes, the classical scheme collapses. On one level, evangelicals know that God loves and is loved, acts and is acted upon, moves and is moved (and so on), but on another level, they have trouble admitting it theologically. Somehow (and I think this gets to the heart of it) we must learn how to celebrate in our theology the beauty of God's perfection in changing as well as in unchanging ways.[17]

---

[13] Bruce A. Ware, 'An Evangelical Reformulation of the Doctrine of the Immutablity of God', *Journal of the Evangelical Theological Society* 29 (1986), pp. 431–46 and Stephen T. Davis, *Logic and the Nature of God* (Grand Rapids: Eerdmans, 1983), ch. 3.

[14] Wayne Grudem, *Systematic Theology: An Introduction to Biblical Doctrine* (Grand Rapids: Zondervan, 1994), pp. 165–6 and Millard J. Erickson, *God the Father Almighty: A Contemporary Exploration of the Divine Attributes* (Grand Rapids: Baker, 1998), ch 7.

[15] Ronald H. Nash, *The Concept of God* (Grand Rapids: Zondervan, 1983), ch. 6 and Terrance Tiessen, *Providence and Prayer* (Downers Grove: InterVarsity Press, 2000), pp. 321–5.

[16] Frame, *No Other God*, pp. 157–9, 175, 187.

[17] Richard Bauckham, *God Crucified: Monotheism and Christology in the New Testament* (Grand Rapids: Eerdmans, 1998), p. 79. Joseph M. Hallman, *The Descent of God: Divine Suffering in History and Theology* (Minneapolis: Fortress Press, 1991), pp. 125–7.

4. Reception of the Open View of God

Reception of (or better) reaction to the open view of God has been all over the map among evangelicals, but weighted on the negative side. At one extreme, missiologist Peter Wagner has hailed it as one of the most important theological discoveries since the Reformation. At the other end, Bruce Ware judges it to be a diminishing of God's glory and something close to idolatry. The former identifies with classical free will theism, originating in the early fathers, while the latter adheres to the deterministic theism of the later Augustine.[18]

It is typical among moderate critics to acknowledge that the open view of God has strengths. For example, it brings out the truth of God as a Triune person, picks up on the fact that God is moved by the suffering of his people and interacts dynamically with creation, and recognizes that God accommodates himself when relating to his people and holds humans accountable for what they do, and so on.[19] John Frame admits that our work has influenced him, forced him to think harder, and does greater justice to the responsiveness of God.[20] On the other hand, they rightly point out that the open view of God raises a lot of important questions and requires considerable rethinking. They see that it requires a paradigm shift in our thinking and worry about the many ramifications of such a change. At the same time, many want to engage it in

---

[18] C. Peter Wagner considers it the fourth most important theological insight since the Reformation because of its implications for world missions. (The other three insights are Wesley's teaching on holiness, Carey's sense that God needed people to evangelize and the recovery of the charismatic dimension.) See C. Peter Wagner (ed.), *Destiny of a Nation: How Prophets and Intercessors can Mold History* (Wagner, 2001). Others who are appalled by it include R.K. McGregor Wright, *No Place for Sovereignty: What's Wrong with Freewill Theism* (Downers Grove: InterVarsity Press, 1996), Robert A. Morey, *Battle of the Gods: The Gathering Storm in Modern Evangelicalism* (Southbridge, Massachusetts: Crown, 1989) and Douglas Wilson, *Bound Only Once: The Failure of Open Theism* (Moscow, Idaho: Canon Press, 2001).

[19] William T. Chandler speaks of strengths in open theism in *A Description and Assessment of Clark Pinnock's Openness View of God* (MTh, Southern Baptist Theological Seminary, 2000). Terrance Tiessen also models the kind of civil discussion we ought to be having: *Providence and Prayer: How Does God Work in the World?* (Downers Grove: InterVarsity Press, 2000). Helpful is Jon Balsersk, 'The God of Love and Weakness: Calvin's Understanding of God's Accommodating Relationship with his People', *Westminster Theological Journal* 62 (2000), pp. 177–95.

[20] Frame, *No Other God*, p. 211.

respectful dialogue, drawing upon the centuries of reflection on behalf of more traditional views, and they acknowledge that the discussions we have been having are stimulating.[21]

Our natural allies are theologians of the synergist tradition within evangelicalism, such as Wesleyan Arminians. Their criticisms are usually temperate, though I am puzzled by the reluctance of many of them to declare that the open view of God is a legitimate kind of synergist theology. Indeed, I am puzzled and a little dismayed by the strength of their opposition to it. I had thought they would have welcomed open theism more enthusiastically. And it strikes me as ironic that they seem to do it largely for the sake of their fondness for the exhaustive definite foreknowledge of God, which (as far as I can see) does them no good.[22] What I wish they would see is the reason why the high Calvinists are so worked up over open theism. It is because we have removed one of their most effective arguments against Arminian thought – that it is incoherent by its view of foreknowledge. It's a nightmare – here is a version of free will theism that makes sense even to them. At least raising this issue has opened up new horizons of possibility for evangelicals.

The open view of God is a version of free will theism. It is not identical with classical Arminianism and should be called neo-Arminian, since, though it shares a great deal with Arminianism (God's universal salvific will, genuine interactivity, real freedom, and so on), it does not share everything. What we want from them is just to be accepted by them as a legitimate expression of Arminian thought and not a danger to it, so that our common foe (theological determinism) may be effectively checkmated. What the Augustinians hope is that classical Arminians will join with them in condemning the open view of God and shut it out of the evangelical discussion. I hope that the Arminians do not let this happen. From my point of view, the open view of God is a stronger and more coherent form of Arminianism and therefore more of a threat to Augustinianism, provoking a stronger reaction from them than usual.[23]

---

[21] Two four-views books are a result of this debate: Gregory E. Ganssle (ed.), *God and Time: Four Views* (Downers Grove: InterVarsity Press, 2002) and Paul R. Eddy and James K. Beilby (eds), *Divine Foreknowledge: Four Views* (Downers Grove: InterVarsity Press, 2002).

[22] Simple foreknowledge only hurts and does not help relational theism because it sends a clear signal that everything is established by backward causation from the beginning. See Sanders, *The God Who Risks*, pp. 200–6.

[23] On whether open theism can be considered Arminian: Tony Gray, 'Beyond Arminius: Pinnock's Doctrine of God and the Evangelical Tradition' in Tony Gray and Christopher Sinkinson (eds), *Reconstructing Theology: A Critical*

It is the Augustinians who attack us mercilessly. These high or scholastic Calvinists wield considerable power in evangelicalism and are upset at the pressure that is being placed upon them by open theism. Albert Mohler writes concerning the open view: 'Evangelicalism faces a crisis of unprecedented magnitude. The denial and redefinition of God's perfections will lead evangelical theology into disintegration and doctrinal catastrophe. The very identity and reality of the God of the Bible is at stake.'[24] Such critics issue some very severe judgements. For example, Royce Gruenler says we are Pelagian, even though we affirm that grace precedes and fosters faith in us.[25] Robert Strimple says that we are Socinians, even though we are social Trinitarians.[26] Timothy George repeats the charge that we are process theists, in spite of our insistence that God's limitations are self-limitations and not necessary limitations.[27] Nicole calls the open view a 'cancer on evangelicalism', and Carson says it is 'amatereurish' and dressed-up Socinianism.[28] Evidently, we have touched a raw nerve, and become a threat to a group within evangelicalism who would like us out of the picture.

What can I say? First, we have run foul of a group of sectarian evangelicals. We find ourselves up against a vigorous paleo-Calvinistic credalism in evangelicalism, which places a great deal of stock in being intellectually and doctrinally just right. We have collided with devotees of a narrow branch of the Reformed faith, who claim to speak not only on behalf of the whole Reformed tradition, but also for all the rest of

---

[23] (*continued*) *Assessment of the Theology of Clark Pinnock* (Carlisle: Paternoster, 2000), pp. 120–46.

[24] In a comment supportive of Bruce A. Ware's book *God's Lesser Glory: The Diminished God of Open Theism* (Wheaton: Crossway, 2000). Since Ware's work, two more books hostile to the open view have appeared: Geisler and House, *The Battle for God* and Frame, *No Other God*. See also Robert A. Pyne and Stephen R. Spencer, 'A Critique of Free Will Theism' in two parts, *Bibliotheca Sacra* 158 (2001) for a calmer though still negative view.

[25] *Christianity Today*, 5 March 2001, p. 58. If the truth be told, we are semi-Augustinian synergists, like most Christians have always been.

[26] In John H. Armstrong (ed.), *The Coming Evangelical Crisis* (Chicago: Moody Press, 1996), ch. 2.

[27] Timothy George, *Amazing Grace: God's Initiative – Our Response* (Nashville: Lifeway Press, 2000), pp. 37–8. Thankfully, Pyne and Spencer rebut the charge: 'A Critique of Free Will Theism', note 5.

[28] His comment in support of Frame's book, *No Other God*. Funny thing: if we are Socinian because we share one point with them (present knowledge), then Calvinist Carson is an astrologer because he shares one point with them (a wholly definite future).

evangelicalism as well. It seems as if they think that God has no further light to bring forth from his Word other than what they themselves have received. One senses a hardening of the categories typical of fundamentalism and an excessive traditionalism. They find it difficult to admit that a number of different points of view might be valid, at least as positions to discuss, and difficult to admit that tradition might have erred. Is it too much to ask for a little less arrogance and zeal devoted to sorting out true evangelicals from pretenders, deviants and apostates?[29] Wouldn't it be better if these people would stop talking about non-Augustinian and non-Reformed theologies as necessarily flawed guides, even at their best? Is not the hallmark of authentic evangelicalism, not blind submission to tradition, but fresh biblical study? I wonder who is it who is troubling Israel really (1 Kgs. 18:18)?[30] Sometimes the flesh rather than the Spirit can dominate theology: the desire for power, an unwillingness to learn, a refusal to change, and so on. These are not of the Spirit and can lead to very bad judgements.

Trees appear strong when compared with wild reeds, but when the storm comes, it is the trees that are overturned, not the reeds, because reeds, flexible as they are, remain rooted. There needs to be more theological flexibility in evangelicalism. If we cling to our own positions and are not willing to be moved by the beliefs of others, we may fail in our theological work. Being a reed need not have to mean being wishy-washy – it can mean moving a little with 'the times and seasons' while being solidly anchored. An intense, humourless, opinionated rigidity about matters can break the spirit and make for bitter, ugly people. I say, let's be flexible, while being deeply rooted.

Secondly, at the same time, important issues are at stake. Bruce Ware put his finger on one of them in his title *God's Lesser Glory: The Diminished God of Open Theism*. He feels certain that we have overcorrected the tilt toward hyper-transcendence that is found in classical theism and as a result have brought the deity too much into the human sphere. We are debating nothing less than the nature of God's glory. Does it consist in exercising total control over the world as in Calvinistic determinism or is it more a matter of self-giving and self-sacrificing? Evangelicals of a certain type are strong on divine transcendence but weak when it comes to what we might call the divine condescension. Open theists want to

---

[29] So says John G. Stackhouse (ed.), *Evangelical Futures: A Conversation on Theological Method* (Grand Rapids: Baker, 2000), pp. 49–50, 57.

[30] So asks Roger E. Olson in ibid., pp. 205–6 and Stanley J. Grenz on 'the question of evangelical boundaries' in *Renewing the Center: Evangelical Theology in a Post-Theological Era* (Grand Rapids: Baker, 2000), pp. 175–83.

say that God is free and sovereign and does not need us, but also that God has decided not to be alone. (This too he is free to do.) We call for a better balance. Does God have to be presented as being far away, aloof and cold? Surely it cannot be right to admire a God with the properties of a tyrant and dislike a God with the properties of a lover. These critics sometimes remind me of Peter when he resisted the self-sacrificing vocation of Jesus. It was as if he could not accept Jesus stooping to such a degree. But was not God's glory revealed in him precisely in this decision to accept humiliation (Mt. 16:21–23)?

God's weakness was and is a scandal and an offence, but also the true glory of God and heart of the gospel. Luther warned against a theology of glory and advocated a theology of the cross.[31] It is a serious error, is it not, to resist the gracious condescension of God? While God is indeed the 'most' and the 'best', there are different kinds of goodness and greatness. Therefore, when we ascribe maximality to God, we need to understand what is involved. Is it not a divine perfection to be vulnerable? Is it not God's glory to want a relationship with creatures, a partnership in which God makes himself weak? I worry that some of my critics themselves lessen God's glory with their concept of an all-controlling and unconditioned deity. As Lucas remarks:

> Instead of the impassible Buddha, untroubled by the tribulations of mortal existence, Christians see God on a cross. Instead of the Aristotelian ideal of a self-sufficient God, who devotes his time to enjoying the contemplation of his own excellence, Christians worship a God who shared the human condition and came among us.[32]

The issue is not how much power God has (we agree about that), but how God chooses to use it. If God wanted to control everything, he could have done so. But he also has the power to create a world with free agents in it. To be glorious in power, God does not have to be a dictator. Obviously, open theists have reopened the old debate between monergists and synergists, which had been allowed to subside recently in the evangelical context, and they have added to its ferocity by suggesting how to make a better case for the Arminian side. From the point of view of fraternity, I am saddened, but from the point of view of truth, I

---

[31] Dennis Ngien, *The Suffering of God According to Martin Luther's 'Theologia Crucis'* (New York: Peter Lang, 1995).

[32] J.R. Lucas, *Future: An Essay on God, Temporality, and Truth* (Oxford: Basil Blackwell, 1989), p. 232.

am content. We have a fine opportunity to go forward together if we refuse to give in to fratricide.

Thirdly, I sense a degree of fear and fearmongering on the part of some. Confronted with the truth of God's self-sacrificing and self-limiting nature, they go about trying to stir up in people's minds an uneasiness about God's ability to reign over a world in which he does not exercise total control and does not have exhaustive foreknowledge. They ridicule the notion that God might actually have chosen to take risks for the sake of love. How (they insinuate) can God cope with a future that is partly open and unsettled? How could God be competent in the absence of a predestinarian blueprint? They call people to reject the open view of God not because it does not make good sense (biblically, theologically, philosophically and practically) but because of the alleged insecurity of trusting a God who has created a truly dynamic universe. What if God is not able to cope with a future that is partly open? What if his wisdom is not up to it? What if we can't trust him? I say shame on critics who play upon people's fears. I say shame too on those who want a God completely in control of everything but who makes no room for relationships of love. Control is not the highest form of sovereignty. Surely the need to control everything is a sign of weakness rather than strength. No – it takes a truly self-confidant God to give away some of his sovereignty and create a world with free agents in it. Fear can hide the glory of God and insecurity can drive the critique of the open view of God. Fear is also a visceral response and may explain the otherwise hard-to-understand misrepresentations and all the lies.

Of course, God cannot be ignorant of anything that he must know in order to realize his objectives, but that does not require that his foreknowledge be complete in every detail, which implies that the future is already determinate and human freedom illusory. The open view of God does not strike fear in us – it tells us that our lives and our prayers matter to God and contribute to the victory of God. According to the open view, God knows a tremendous amount about the future. He knows everything that will happen on the basis of what has already happened. He knows everything that could happen and might happen. He knows the whole range of what is possible and the relative likelihood of any particular event occurring. And God knows what his future plans call for and what things he intends to do that are not contingent on human decisions. I hope for an end to the misrepresentations and an end to the Arminians being fooled by them.

5. What do we do Now?

In an early review of *The Openness of God* Roger Olson wondered how
evangelicals would handle the proposal. He thought it might be a test of
the maturity of their work. In retrospect, I would say that we have not
handled it very well. On the other hand, I think we could handle it better,
if we would commit ourselves to 'open evangelicalism'. Our movement
is a loose family or coalition, centring upon several key commitments:
commitment to the biblical message, belief in a transcendent Triune
God, who interacts with creation and acts in history, celebrating the
transforming grace of God in human life and the importance of mission
to bring the good news to the whole world. Evangelicalism is a big tent
and (says Paul Hiebert) not so much a bounded set as a centred set,
involving an openness to the wider church and the practice of civility.[33]

As a trans-denominational and multi-confessional group, let Calvinists take seriously what Arminians say and let dispensationalists listen
respectfully to the Anabaptists. John Stackhouse writes:

> A perspective that starts from a given position but is inclined to appreciate,
> not merely guard against, other evangelical traditions, might lift us beyond
> inherited impasses and draw on fresh light regarding perennial mysteries
> such as original sin, the relation of the human will and divine providence,
> and the nature and scope of the atonement.[34]

Let's be honest, the theological boundaries of evangelicalism have
always been broad. They allowed a Zwingli to trash a 1,500-year-old
conviction about sacraments, a Calvin to devise a new theology of infant
baptism, and a J.N. Darby to propose a new dispensational theology.
The boundaries have been flexible and should remain so. Paradigm
shifts have taken place in Christianity over the centuries. It has not been
all smooth sailing.[35] The open view of God is just a variant of age-old free
will theism in theology. It need not cause such consternation. There have
always been two kinds of evangelical theology: one that promotes the
orthodoxy of old Calvinism (Puritan-Princeton: see George Marsden)
and one that gravitates to pietism and evangelism (see Donald Dayton).

---

[33] See Robert K. Johnson, 'Orthodoxy and Heresy: A Problem for Modern
Evangelicalism', *Evangelical Quarterly* 69 (1997), pp. 7–38.
[34] Stackhouse (ed.), *Evangelical Futures*, p. 57.
[35] To correct this mistake, see Hans Küng, *Christianity: Essence, History, and
Future* (New York: Continuum, 1996).

Some look to Calvin and regard monergism as the norm, while others look to Wesley and consider synergism an equally valid option. This debate, now having opened a new front, is not so alien and, besides, it is not going away – so we might as well get used to it.

Secondly, it would help if we could look at theology as unfinished business. Scholars, being limited in knowledge, need to learn from others, whatever their own convictions. Even if we think that God has given us a set of propositions in the Bible, there would still be much more to know about God than we presently know. So instead of trying to silence awkward voices, let's have new proposals and test them. Let us set for ourselves and for all people a rich feast. Let us not merely rehearse traditions, but welcome fresh acts of interpretation also. Doesn't one reformation call for another?[36]

It would help, too, if we could learn to disagree better. G.K. Chesterton once said that the trouble with quarreling is that it spoils a good argument. We need to learn to disagree civilly and learn from the other fellow. We can stir each other up to better ways of thinking. Like Paul says, let not the eye ever say to the foot, 'I have no need of you', or vice versa. Theologians need one another as members of the one body of Christ. The golden rule also applies: 'In everything, do to others as you would have them do to you' (Mt. 7:12).

Let us have an open evangelicalism and an open scholarship that allows openness theology a place at the table as an evangelically possible point of view. In a recent book, Roger Olson, an even-handed interpreter of evangelical thought, concluded that the open view of God is not heterodox, but a legitimate option for evangelicals.[37] An analogy to it might be the way in which the Evangelical Alliance (UK) has made a place at the table for proponents of the conditionalist approach to the nature and duration of hell.[38]

Make no mistake – this will be hard to accomplish. High Calvinism, which hardly exists outside what is called evangelicalism, considers the open view of God a cancer and blasphemy. It only had respect for Arminians previously because it deemed them misguided. But now that they are facing a form of this 'heresy' that really makes sense, the tight system that is their pride and joy is threatened. While I hope that the

---

[36] Roger E. Olson, 'Reforming Evangelical Theology' in Stackhouse (ed.), *Evangelical Futures*, pp. 201–7.

[37] Roger E. Olson, *The Mosaic of Christian Belief: Twenty Centuries of Unity and Diversity* (Downers Grove: InterVarsity Press, 2002), pp. 195–6.

[38] Evangelical Alliance, *The Nature of Hell* (Carlisle/London: Paternoster/ Evangelical Alliance, 2000).

discussion will continue under the umbrella of the evangelical big tent, I am not optimistic. We are willing – but are the critics willing? The situation could be calmed (and herein lies my hope) by the Arminians if they would join Olson (himself a classical Arminian) in recognizing open theism as a legitimate form of their position, or at least a new option that merits respect.

7

Toward a Trinitarian Evangelical Wesleyan Theology

Elmer M. Colyer

1. Introduction

My essay is autobiographical and programmatic. It summarizes the trajectory of my initial research into my own Wesleyan/Methodist intellectual heritage. The essay also indicates the direction I think evangelical Wesleyan theology needs to develop in. It stakes out the territory into which my own research and publications are headed: further work on the intellectual history of my own tradition as a prelude for constructive development of that tradition.

The title of my essay, 'Toward a Trinitarian Evangelical Wesleyan Theology', intimates one of my questions about my own American Methodist theological tradition. Has it been sufficiently Trinitarian? I have come to the conclusion that it has not, and that this may be its greatest failure as an intellectual tradition, though it is not the only Christian tradition that has had problems in this area over the same period of time.

I find it ironic that the Wesleyan theological tradition has been so insufficiently Trinitarian in light of the significantly Trinitarian character of the theology of the Wesley brothers, John and Charles. In fact, I wonder whether the Trinitarian insights of John and Charles Wesley have ever been fully developed and properly exploited within the tradition that claims them as progenitors, though there are encouraging recent developments.

My essay makes three basic points: (1) The deep-structure of the Wesley brothers' theology was thoroughly Trinitarian, though this is often missed or neglected in the intellectual history of American Methodism. (2) The deep-structure of American Methodist theology from the beginning has been insufficiently Trinitarian. It is astonishing how little has been written on the Trinity within the tradition and how little the doctrine of the Trinity has influenced wider theological conversation and construction. (3) The Trinitarian potential of evangelical Wesleyan theology needs to be fully realized. It is an encouraging sign that a growing number of Methodists today are deeply concerned about the Trinity.

I plan to follow up these theses in future publications in preparation for developing a thoroughly Trinitarian evangelical Wesleyan theology.

2. The Trinity in the Evangelical Theology of John and Charles Wesley

One of the curious discoveries in my initial research into Wesley's theology is how little has been written on Wesley's doctrine of the Trinity.[1] Indeed, there is scant discussion of the Trinity in many books devoted to Wesley's theology.

A recent example of this is Ken Collins' work, *The Scripture Way of Salvation: The Heart of John Wesley's Theology*.[2] There is no chapter, and not even subsection of a chapter, that deals with the Trinitarian deep-structure of Wesley's understanding of the *ordo salutis* (order of salvation).[3] In fact, there is no reference to the Trinity in the index, and hardly any mention of the Trinity anywhere in the book, despite the fact that Wesley understood the *ordo* in Trinitarian terms.

The chapter on Wesley's theology in Thomas Langford's book, *Practical Divinity: Theology in the Wesleyan Tradition*, provides yet another example. Read by virtually every United Methodist doctrine class across

---

[1] There have been several articles written on Wesley's doctrine of the Trinity in recent years, most notably by Geoffrey Wainwright. See his article 'Why Wesley was a Trinitarian', *The Drew Gateway* 59.2 (Spring 1990), pp. 26–43. Wainwright's article has been reprinted in Geoffrey Wainwright, *Methodists in Dialogue* (Nashville: Abingdon Press, 1995), pp. 261–74. Also see Seng-Kong Tan's article 'The Doctrine of the Trinity in John Wesley's Prose and Poetic Works', *Journal for Christian Theological Research* 7 (2002), at < www.home.apu.edu/~ctrf/jctr. >. Tan's article has a bibliography listing other recent publications on Wesley's doctrine of the Trinity.

[2] Kenneth J. Collins, *The Scripture Way of Salvation: The Heart of John Wesley's Theology* (Nashville: Abingdon Press, 1997).

[3] I am aware of the various criticisms against using *ordo salutis* to designate Wesley's soteriology, but I find them unconvincing.

North America, the chapter contains no discussion of the Trinity, not even a direct reference to the Trinity.[4]

An even more fascinating illustration of this lack of emphasis on the Trinity in Wesley's theology is Randy Maddox's book *Responsible Grace: John Wesley's Practical Theology*.[5] Maddox's study is extremely careful and comprehensive, arguably the best study of Wesley's theology to date. I have greatly benefited from it. The placement and brevity of his discussion of Wesley on the Trinity is especially curious, and somewhat symptomatic of Methodism's quandary over what to do with the Trinity.

The book has a chapter on 'The God of Responsible Grace', but this is not where Maddox discusses the Trinity. He thereby perpetuates the long-standing Western tendency to separate the discussion of the One God from the discussion of the Trinity. Maddox actually deals with the doctrine of the Trinity in a final subsection of his chapter on the Holy Spirit: Wesley's significant emphasis on the Holy Spirit is the occasion for a discussion of the Trinity, since Maddox correctly wants to emphasize the Trinitarian balance found in Wesley's theology.

The irony here is that Maddox sees the deeply Trinitarian character of Wesley's theology and perceptively points out that the Trinity served implicitly as 'the grammar of responsible grace',[6] a point we will examine more fully in a moment. But if the Trinity is the grammar of responsible grace, if the Trinity configures the shape and the content of responsible grace in all of its forms throughout the *via salutis*, must we not reflect this in the architectonic, in the structure and in the discussion of every aspect of Wesley's theology of grace?[7]

Yet Maddox does not reflect this in the architectonic of his book, and so his discussion of the Trinity ends up as a qualification of Wesley's emphasis on the Spirit and occupies just three pages, thereby structurally undermining the very insight he so eloquently articulates. It is as if Maddox sees the crucial character of the Trinity as the grammar or deep-structure of Wesley's theology, but has not found a way to integrate the insight into the architectonic and material discussion of the rest of

---

[4] Thomas A. Langford, *Practical Divinity: Theology in the Wesleyan Tradition* (Nashville: Abingdon Press, 1983).

[5] Randy L. Maddox, *Responsible Grace: John Wesley's Practical Theology* (Nashville: Abingdon Press, 1994). I have learned much from Maddox's various publications on the intellectual history of American Methodism. He is a groundbreaking scholar in this area.

[6] Ibid., pp. 139–40.

[7] See, for example, Maddox's account of Christian perfection which is insufficiently Trinitarian. Ibid., pp. 179–91.

Wesley's theology. Part of the problem here, of course, is that this is something Wesley himself really never fully developed, thereby forcing his interpreters to think out the interconnections and implications of Wesley's insights on the Trinity for the overall fabric of his theology.

Thus, from reading much of the secondary literature on Wesley's theology, despite deep insights from scholars like Maddox, one might get the impression that the Trinity is not all that prominent or important in Wesley's theology. There are a few notable exceptions, like Geoffrey Wainwright's article 'Why Wesley Was a Trinitarian',[8] which is probably the best published discussion of Wesley on the Trinity. The scholars who have written on Wesley's doctrine of the Trinity nearly all grant the importance of the Trinity in Wesley's theology even when they struggle to integrate Wesley's doctrine of Trinity into an overarching architectonic account of his theology.

Wesley's evangelical theology is far more deeply and comprehensively Trinitarian than is evident in much of the secondary literature. There are three bodies of evidence that support this point.

2.1. Wesley's explicit statements about the Trinity

Wesley did not write explicitly on the Trinity all that often and did not fully develop his Trinitarian insights. But what he does say is highly suggestive. The most significant of Wesley's explicit statements is his sermon 'On the Trinity'. Wesley opens the sermon with one of his recurring concerns:

> There are ten thousand mistakes which may consist with real religion; with regard to which every candid, considerate man will think and let think. But there are some truths more important than others. It seems that there are some which are of deep importance ... Surely there are some which it nearly concerns us to know, as having a close connection with vital religion. And doubtless we may rank among these that contained in the words above cited: 'There are three that bear record in heaven, the Father, the Word, and the Holy Ghost: and these three are one.'[9]

Wesley here asserts that the Trinity takes us to the very heart of vital Christian faith. In Wesley's mind, it is impossible to be Christian and not be in some sense Trinitarian.

---

[8]   See n. 1 above.

[9]   John Wesley, *The Bicentennial Edition of the Works of John Wesley*, Albert C. Outler (ed.) (Nashville: Abingdon Press, 1985), vol. 2, p. 376.

Wesley does not leave his readers in doubt about what he means, for he states his insight in strong and explicit terms:

> The thing which I here particularly mean is this: the knowledge of the Three-One God is interwoven with all true Christian faith, with all vital religion ... I know not how anyone can be a Christian believer till 'he hath' (as St. John speaks) 'the witness in himself'; till 'the Spirit of God witnesses with his spirit that he is a child of God' – that is, in effect, till God the Holy Ghost witnesses that God the Father has accepted him through the merits of God the Son – and having this witness he honours the Son and the blessed Spirit 'even as he honours the Father'. Not that every Christian believer *adverts* to this; perhaps at first not one in twenty; but if you ask any of them a few questions you will easily find it is implied in what he believes. Therefore I do not see how it is possible for any to have vital religion who denies that these three are one.[10]

Wesley here strongly asserts that Christian faith is intrinsically and aboriginally Trinitarian at the most basic level of our evangelical and doxological participation in the gospel. It is a participation, Wesley notes, that is rooted in the pattern of God the Father's reconciling activity through the incarnate Son, Jesus Christ, and his life, death and resurrection, a reconciliation realized in Christians through the person and activity of the Holy Spirit ('The Holy Ghost witnesses that God the Father has accepted him through the merits of God the Son').

Wesley says that it is a Trinitarian pattern that every Christian participates in and relives at the evangelical and doxological level ('the Spirit of God witnesses with his Spirit that he is a child of God'), even if he or she is not explicitly aware of it ('Not that every Christian believer *adverts* to this'). In short, our participation in the gospel and the gospel itself are both rooted in the patterned activity of the economic Trinity.

If you ask Christians about the core of their faith, Wesley thinks that this Trinitarian structure (what Maddox calls 'the grammar of responsible grace') quickly comes to the surface, for they say something like, 'Well, I came to believe that God loves me to the uttermost, and that God sent Jesus Christ to live the life of faith and love that I failed to live, and to die on the Cross for my sins so that I can be in right relationship with God.' And how do you know that? 'Because the Holy Spirit convicted me of my sin, enabled me to respond in faith and sheds God's love in Christ abroad in my heart so that I know I am a child of God.' Wesley's evangelical theology is thus intrinsically and thoroughly

---

[10] Ibid., pp. 385–6.

Trinitarian. Wesley understands the gospel itself and our participation in it in Trinitarian terms.

A second explicit statement on the Trinity is found in Wesley's famous 'Letter to a Roman Catholic'. In the letter, Wesley emphasizes what Protestants and Catholics believe in common. It is significant that he follows the Nicene Creed, repeating various phrases from it. In so doing, Wesley aligns himself with the most ecumenical and thoroughly Trinitarian creed in Christian history.

Here is what Wesley writes:

> As I am assured that there is an infinite and independent Being and that it is impossible there should be more than one, so I believe that this one God is the Father of all things, especially of angels and men; that he is in a peculiar manner the Father of those whom he regenerates by his Spirit, whom he adopts in his Son as co-heirs with him and crowns with an eternal inheritance; but in a still higher sense, the Father of his only Son, whom he hath begotten from eternity …
>
> I believe that Jesus of Nazareth was the Saviour of the world, the Messiah so long foretold … I believe that he is the proper, natural Son of God, God of God, very God of very God; and that he is the Lord … of all, having absolute, supreme universal dominion over all things; but more peculiarly *our* Lord …
>
> I believe the infinite and eternal Spirit of God, equal with the Father and the Son, to be not only perfectly holy in himself, but the immediate cause of all holiness in us: enlightening our understandings, rectifying our wills and affections, renewing our natures, uniting our persons to Christ, assuring us of the adoption of sons, leading us in our actions, purifying and sanctifying our souls and bodies to a full and eternal enjoyment of God.[11]

Once again, we find a soteriological matrix and the economic approach embedded in Wesley's Trinitarian talk: God is Father of those whom God regenerates by the Spirit, those whom God adopts in the Son as co-heirs with Christ. The infinite and eternal Spirit of God, equal with the Father and the Son, perfectly holy, is the immediate cause of all holiness in us, implying that the Father and the Son are also involved in the work of holiness in their own unique ways, as we already saw above in Wesley's sermon. For Wesley, this Trinitarian activity extends throughout the *ordo salutis*: enlightening our understandings, rectifying our wills and affections, renewing our natures, uniting our persons to

---

[11] John Wesley, 'Letter to a Roman Catholic' in Albert C. Outler (ed.), *John Wesley* (New York: Oxford University Press, 1964), pp. 494–5.

Christ, purifying and sanctifying our bodies to a full and eternal enjoyment of God.

Wesley also makes several important and interesting statements about the Trinitarian relations *ad intra*, within God's own internal life as the Triune God. The Spirit is infinite and eternal, equal with the Father and the Son. Jesus Christ is the proper natural Son of God, God of God, very God of very God. Most interesting of all is Wesley's statement that God's Fatherhood *in the highest sense* has nothing to do with God's relationship to us or the rest of creation, but rather is an intra-Trinitarian relation (God is 'in a still higher sense, the Father of his only Son, whom he hath begotten from eternity').

Like the Nicene Creed itself, the very structure of Wesley's series of affirmations is Trinitarian. But, as in his sermon, Wesley's approach is evangelical and doxological. His concern is not with an abstract concept of God, but with the understanding of God that arises out of the gospel itself within the evangelical and doxological faith and life of the church. So Wesley relates each section explicitly to soteriological concerns.

In comparing the sermon 'On the Trinity' and the 'Letter to a Roman Catholic', it is interesting that Wesley not only sees our basic evangelical and doxological soteriological encounter with the gospel in thoroughly Trinitarian terms; when he discusses the creedal Trinitarian faith held in common by Protestants and Catholics he instinctively does so in relation to soteriology and that same evangelical and doxological encounter with the gospel. The gospel and our participation in it is thoroughly Trinitarian and the doctrine of the Trinity is thoroughly evangelical and doxological.

This, I believe, is an important point and a defining characteristic of the theology of John and Charles Wesley that invites, if not requires, us to think of their theology in simultaneous evangelical and Trinitarian terms.

A third explicit statement of Wesley on the Trinity comes from his journal and is especially interesting because it deals with the Trinity in relation to Christian perfection. Here, Wesley defines Christian perfection in Trinitarian terms: '*Constant communion* with God the Father and Son *fills* their [Christians'] hearts with *humble love*. Now this is what I always did, and do now mean by [Christian] "perfection."'[12] We already saw above, in the 'Letter to the Roman Catholic', how Wesley

---

[12] John Wesley, *The Bicentennial Edition of the Works of John Wesley*, R.P. Heitzenrater and W.R. Ward (eds) (Nashville: Abingdon Press, 1992), vol. 21, p. 245.

says that the Holy Spirit is the *immediate cause* of this union and communion with the Son ('uniting our persons to Christ') and the Father ('to a full and eternal enjoyment of God'). Thus, even Christian perfection is understood by Wesley in radically Trinitarian terms: in the *koinonia* or communion of the Spirit we may enjoy constant communion with the Father and the Son, which fills our hearts with humble love for God and neighbour. Of course, this sounds a lot like what the Nicene theologians intended in their concept of *theosis* or *theopoiesis*.[13] Indeed, Wesley's doctrine of the Trinity bears marked similarities to certain strands of Nicene Trinitarian theology.

This Trinitarian understanding of Christian perfection is consistent with two additional statements by Wesley on the Trinity in relation to the church and eschatology noted by Wainwright. In the first, Wesley defines the church as those 'who have fellowship with God the Father, Son and Holy Ghost'.[14] I find even more fascinating Wesley's description of our Trinitarian eternal destiny in his sermon 'The New Creation': 'And to crown all, there will be a deep, an intimate, an uninterrupted union with God; a constant communion with the Father and his Son Jesus Christ, through the Spirit; a continual enjoyment of the Three-One God, and of all the creatures in him!'[15] It seems that the forensic categories found in Wesley's soteriology are in service of an ultimately participatory and Trinitarian understanding of salvation: our destiny in this life and the next is union and communion with the Triune God.

In light of Wesley's various explicit statements concerning the Trinity, it is clear that the origin and the *telos* or goal of Wesley's *ordo salutis* is the blessed Trinity: the love of the Father flows to us through the grace of our Lord Jesus Christ in the communion of the Holy Spirit. The Holy Spirit unites us to Christ and through Christ with the Father and progressively fills our hearts with love for God and neighbour. Our salvation is ultimately grounded in the differentiated activity of the Trinitarian persons and ultimately leads us to union and communion with the Triune God. We come to share in God's own life, the communion in being that the Triune God is as Father, Son and Holy Spirit.

Particularly noteworthy is the way in which Wesley's doctrine of the Trinity is so closely connected to the evangelical and doxological level of

---

[13] See Thomas F. Torrance's discussion in *The Trinitarian Faith: The Evangelical Theology of the Ancient Catholic Church* (Edinburgh: T. & T. Clark, 1988), pp. 138–42, 188–90.

[14] John Wesley, 'Letter to a Roman Catholic', p. 495. See Wainwright, 'Why Wesley was a Trinitarian', p. 40.

[15] Wesley, *Bicentennial Edition*, vol. 2, p. 510. See Wainwright, 'Why Wesley was a Trinitarian', p. 40.

the gospel itself and our participation in the gospel. The evangelical, doxological and Trinitarian dimensions of Wesley's theology are intimately interconnected and ultimately inseparable. Together, statements like these provide a significant body of evidence that the deep-structure of Wesley's evangelical theology, including the *ordo salutis*, is thoroughly Trinitarian. These same characteristics are reinforced in Charles Wesley's Trinitarian hymnody.

2.2. *Charles Wesley's hymns on the Trinity*

Given how little prose Wesley actually wrote about the Trinity, it may come as a surprise how much poetry his brother Charles composed on and to the Trinity. In fact, Charles published an entire collection of hymns in 1767 entitled *Hymns on the Trinity*.[16] The hymnal contains 136 hymns, divided into 4 parts. The fourth section has an interesting title: 'The Trinity in Unity'. Charles adds 52 'Hymns and Prayers to the Trinity', making a total of 188. Actually, Charles had previously published a collection of *Hymns to the Trinity* in 1746.[17]

Yet it is the content of Charles's hymns on the Trinity that is especially intriguing. Stanza two of his hymn 'And Can It Be' is a prime example: ' 'Tis mystery all th' Immortal dies! Who can understand his strange design. In vain the first-born seraph tries to sound the depths of love divine. 'Tis mercy all let earth adore, let angel minds inquire no more.'[18] Here, Wesley echos Gregory of Nazianzus's famous statement that we needed a God incarnate, a God put to death, that we might live. The cross, for Charles Wesley, is the event of a God who is free to love, free to enter a sin-stricken and broken world, free to suffer in order to redeem that world, because God does not want to be God without us. For the Wesley brothers, like the Trinity, this is a mystery that is more to be adored than explored. The idea that faith, worship and devotion are the appropriate forms of discourse on the mystery of God's suffering on the cross and blessed Trinity is found often in John's theology and in hymn after hymn of Charles Wesley.

Charles's hymn is also Trinitarian. Stanza three identifies the Father and the Son in the economy of salvation: 'He left his Father's throne

---

[16] Charles Wesley, *Hymns on the Trinity* (Bristol: Pine, 1767).

[17] Charles Wesley, *Gloria Patri, &c. or Hymns to the Trinity* (London: Strahan, 1746). See Barry E. Bryant, 'Trinity and Hymnody: The Doctrine of the Trinity in the Hymns of Charles Wesley', *Wesleyan Theological Journal* 25.2 (Fall 1990), pp. 64–73.

[18] *The United Methodist Hymnal* (Nashville: The United Methodist Publishing House, 1989), p. 363.

above (so free, so infinite his grace!) emptied himself of all but love, and
bled for Adam's helpless race. 'Tis mercy all, immense and free, for O my
God, it found out me!' The fourth stanza contains a poetic reference to
the Holy Spirit: 'Long my imprisoned spirit lay, fast bound in sin and
nature's night; thine eye diffused a quickening ray; I woke the dungeon
flamed with light; my chains fell off, my heart was free, I rose, went
forth, and followed thee.'[19]

I find the depth of theological content explicit and implicit in this
hymn most impressive and quite unlike what we find in much popular
Christian music today. Once again, it is a theological content embedded
within an evangelical and doxological matrix, embedded in our
encounter with the gospel, its Trinitarian deep-structure and our worship of the Triune God of grace elicited by that encounter. It is easy to
see how the early Methodists were infected with strong doses of deep
Trinitarian theology as much by singing Charles's hymns as from
reading John's sermons.

Let me intrigue you with a few more examples from Charles Wesley's
Trinitarian hymns: 'Jehovah is but One, Eternal God and true; The
Father sent the Son, His Spirit sent Him too, the everlasting Spirit fill'd,
And Jesus our salvation seal'd.'[20] This stanza is particularly interesting
because Charles writes of the Spirit, not simply the Father, sending the
Son, a most fascinating theological idea. This seems to indicate that
Charles does not restrict the *monarchia* (monarchy) to the Father alone.
Does the concept of 'Trinity in Unity' (the final heading in Charles's
Hymns on the Trinity) or *perichoresis* clarify and deepen the *monarchia*
along Trinitarian lines? Is Charles operating, at least implicitly, with a
concept of the *perichoretic co-activity* in which the Trinitarian persons
always and everywhere act together in such a way that their activities
co-inhere and interpenetrate one another without compromising each
divine person's distinctive mode of activity, in the same way that
the incommunicable characteristics of the three persons in no way
divide them but rather unite them in their differentiated oneness? There
is a growing consensus that Charles and John both operate with a
concept of *perichoresis* without explicitly using the term.[21] If so, might

---

[19] Ibid., p. 363.
[20] Charles Wesley, *Hymns on the Trinity*, p. 275.
[21] See Maddox, *Responsible Grace*, pp. 139, 322. Maddox refers to the work of
   scholars who agree on this point. The genesis of the concept of *perichoretic*
   co-activity and a shared *monarchia* seems to be found in one stream of Greek
   patristic theology in Athanasius, Epiphanius, Cyril of Alexandria and Gregory of Nazianzen, but *not* in Basil or Gregory of Nyssa, who both asserted the

this explain Charles's idea of the Spirit, as well as the Father, sending the Son?

The hymn continues by linking together the economic Trinity and the ontological Trinity: 'Senders and Sent we praise, with equal thanks approve; Th' economy of grace, The Triune God of love, And humbly prostrated before the One thrice holy God, adore!'[22] Charles states this connection even more forcefully in two other hymns. In the first he writes: 'Come, Father, Son and Spirit, give Thy love, – Thyself: and lo! I live Imparadised in Thee.'[23] The second comes from the 1780 *Collection of Hymns for the Use of the People called Methodist*: 'Send us the Spirit of thy Son, to make the depths of Godhead known. To make us share the life divine ...'[24]

Charles could not be more clear here that grace is not simply some benevolent attitude on God's part, not even some immaterial spiritual substance God provides. Rather, God's love *is* God's very self in concrete redemptive activity ('give Thy love, – Thyself', 'make the depths of Godhead known'). God's grace is *God* in redemptive Trinitarian activity on our behalf from the Father though the Son in the Spirit who lifts us up and unites us with the Son and through the Son with the Father, so that our salvation arises out of and leads to the union and communion of love that God is as Father, Son and Holy Spirit ('and lo! I live Imparadised in Thee', 'make us share the life divine'). Charles, like John, also views sanctification as sharing in God's Trinitarian life.

According to Charles, God sends the Spirit of the Son to make the depths of Godhead known. In Charles's perspective, when we know the love of God the Father through the grace of our Lord Jesus Christ in the communion of the Spirit, we actually do know something of the depths of the Godhead, while retaining the appropriate sense of mystery and worship. There is no dark inscrutable God, no *deus absconditus*, behind the back of the God we really know and worship through Jesus Christ in

---

[21] (*continued*) monarchy of the Father. See Thomas F. Torrance, *The Christian Doctrine of God: One Being Three Persons* (Edinburgh: T. & T. Clark, 1996), pp. 168–202. Seng-Kong Tan demonstrates the influence of the Athanasian Creed on Charles's 1780 *Collection of Hymns for the Use of the People called Methodist*. John said the Athanasian Creed was the best explication of the doctrine of the Trinity he ever saw. See Wesley, *Bicentennial Edition*, vol. 2, p. 377.

[22] Charles Wesley, *Hymns on the Trinity*, p. 275.

[23] Ibid., p. 327.

[24] John Wesley, *Works of John Wesley*, F. Hildebrandt and O.A. Beckerlegge (eds) (Oxford: Clarendon Press, 1983), vol. 7, p. 536. Wainwright cites this hymn in 'Why Wesley was a Trinitarian', p. 41.

the Spirit. This is, I believe, the Wesley brothers' ultimate theological ground for rejecting double predestination: how can there be an inscrutable double predestinarian deity behind the depths of the Godhead revealed from the Father through the Son in the Spirit?

There is much more in Charles Wesley's hymns on the Trinity and more work needs to be done here. In concluding this discussion, it is important to note that this Trinitarian fabric with its evangelical and doxological emphasis permeates all of Charles's hymnody, even in those general collections of hymns not explicitly devoted to the Trinity. David Tripp has published an interesting little study on the 1780 *Collection of Hymns for the Use of the People Called Methodist*, the closest thing early Methodism had to an official hymnal. Tripp found that nearly 25 per cent of the 1780 *Hymns* are explicitly Trinitarian.[25] This for me is very telling, for it reveals how deeply the Trinity is embedded in the minds and the evangelical theology of the Wesley brothers. It is the theological deep-structure that permeates not only their theological perspective, but also the entire *ordo salutis*, and their piety and worship.

2.3. *The letters and journals of the early Methodist laity*

There is a final body of evidence that points to the Trinitarian character of the theology of John and Charles Wesley: the letters and journals of the early Methodist laity.

Tom Albin, an expert on Charles Wesley and on spirituality in early Methodism, is the person who pointed out to me that the letters and journals of the early Methodist laity, most unpublished, contain many references to the Trinity in relation to their Christian lives and piety. Much work needs to be done here, for these letters and journals reveal something about how the Trinitarian evangelical theology of John and Charles actually gets embodied in the Wesleyan movement in the spirituality/theology of laity. Do the early Methodist lay persons understand their evangelical Christian faith and life in explicitly Trinitarian terms? Does John and Charles's emphasis on the Trinitarian deep-structure of Christian faith in general and the *ordo salutis* in particular find its way into the hearts, minds, lives and practice of the rank and file Christians involved in the Methodist movement? It seems that it does.

---

[25] See David Tripp, 'Methodism's Trinitarian Hymnody: A Sampling, 1780 and 1989, and Some Questions,' *Quarterly Review* 14.4 (Winter 1994–95), pp. 359–85. Tripp demonstrates that there is only half as many explicitly Trinitarian hymns in the 1989 official hymnal of the United Methodist Church as in the 1780 *Collection of Hymns*.

In his letters to various Methodist laypersons, John Wesley on occasion asks them if they have 'a clear sense of the presence of the ever-blessed Trinity'.[26] Of course, the intention of Wesley's question is clear from his sermon 'On the Trinity', and his statements on Christian perfection and the church examined above. He is asking about the 'knowledge of the Three–One God … interwoven with all true Christian faith, all vital religion'.[27] Wesley is questioning the state of this Methodist layperson's soul in explicitly Trinitarian terms, because he thinks that all true Christian faith, all vital religion, has its origin and its *telos* in the Three–One God. The early Methodist laity picked this up and embodied it as well. What follows is simply one example of what we find in the letters and journals of the laity.

In a letter dated in early 1777 to Hetty (Hester Anne Roe), a Methodist laywoman, John Wesley quotes from the papers of a Methodist layperson who recounts his evangelical and doxological encounter with the Three–One God:

> Just after my uniting with the Methodists, the Father was revealed to me the first time; soon after the whole Trinity. I beheld the distinct Persons of the Godhead, and worshiped one undivided Jehovah, and each Person separately … When I approach Jesus, the Father and the Spirit commune with me.
>
> Whatever I receive now, centres in taking leave of earth, and hastening to another place. I am as one that is no more. I stand and look on what God has done; his calls, helps, mercies, forbearances, deliverances from sorrows, rescues out of evils; and I adore and devote myself to Him with new ardor. If it be asked how, or in what manner I beheld the Triune God, it is above all description … I was overwhelmed with it; body and soul were penetrated through with the rays of Deity.[28]

Of course, this early Methodist brother could benefit from knowing how to manipulate the Trinitarian symbols with a bit more precision. But I dare say that I do not know of many Methodists today who talk about their Christian life in such vivid and consciously Trinitarian terms as communion with the Triune God that fills our hearts and

---

[26] See Wesley's letter to Jane Bisson dated December 1787 in John Wesley, *The Works of John Wesley* (Grand Rapids, Michigan: Baker, 1986³), vol. 13, p. 107. I know of at least seven of Wesley's letters where he asks this same point in various ways.

[27] Wesley, *Bicentennial Edition*, vol. 2, p. 385.

[28] Wesley, *The Works of John Wesley*, vol. 13, pp. 79–80.

minds and lives with praise and love for God and love and concern for
our neighbour.

When we combine all this evidence, it presents a rather intriguing
image of the evangelical theology of John and Charles Wesley. It seems
that the doctrine of the Trinity permeates Wesley's theology and early
Methodist worship and piety more than is often acknowledged. The
connection is crucial, for it is a Trinitarian theology that is evangelical
and doxological in orientation. I find this Trinitarian emphasis in early
Methodism fascinating and suggestive of a far more Trinitarian expression of evangelical Wesleyan theology and practice than we have thus
far realized in the history of American Methodism. What would a fully
Trinitarian evangelical Wesleyan theology look like if we took Wesley's
comments about the Trinitarian deep-structures of the *ordo salutis*, the
church and all Christian faith and vital religion seriously? Why did the
Methodists who followed not work this out more fully, especially in
light of the Trinitarian evangelical and doxological life of the early
Methodists who sang about the Trinity, worshipped the Trinity and
talked about their union and communion with the Triune God? Why did
Wesley's Trinitarian understanding of Christian perfection and the
church not receive more attention and development? We now turn our
attention to the Trinity in American Methodism.

3. The Trinity in the Intellectual History of American Methodism

Francis Asbury is characteristic and symptomatic of the intellectual
history of early American Methodism. Asbury had no formal theological education. Nevertheless, he quickly rose to prominence and became
the leader of American Methodism throughout his lifetime. Asbury
read widely, including many of Wesley's works. But he lacked Wesley's
immersion in the great tradition of the church. In fact, there were very
few American Methodists at any time during the nineteenth century
who were as deeply immersed in classical theological literature as
Wesley was.

This means that, from the very beginning, American Methodists read
Wesley without the benefit of his immersion in the great tradition of the
church. Asbury simply reiterated the main themes of Wesley's theology
and wrote practically no materials for the new American church. The
same is true of the early circuit riders. While they certainly shaped the
theological convictions of their hearers, they wrote little, and showed

minimal interest in the careful grounding in classical theological literature that Wesley required of lay preachers in England.[29]

This minimal reading of theological classics also reveals the impact of one of the common tendencies among Christian groups during the antebellum period: 'restorationism'.[30] The New World, an ocean away from Europe and the tyranny of tradition, provided a fertile new context within which to reinstitute the simple belief and practice of the New Testament. The irony is that most American Methodists saw this biblical primitivism (Albert Outler's term) as simply continuing Wesley's interpretation of Christian faith, minus some of Wesley's Anglican high church tendencies, like his view of the sacraments.

4. Asa Shinn: The Genesis of a New Tradition in American Methodism

The methodological implications of restorationism are clearly evident in one of the first theological monographs by an American Methodist, Asa Shinn. In his work, entitled *An Essay on the Plan of Salvation: In Which the Several Sources of Evidence are Examined, and Applied to the Interesting Doctrine of Redemption, in its Relation to the Government and Moral Attributes of Deity*, Shinn writes:

> Each one is bound under sacred obligation, to go to the Bible for his system of divinity, and so far as any man is governed by a regard to any human creed, in the formation of his religious opinions, so far he is deficient in the very principle of Christian faith; and pays that homage to human authority that is due only to the Divine.[31]

It is noteworthy that, while Shinn invokes a rather narrow and naïve reading of the *sola scriptura* principle, the initial discussion of his book deals with epistemology and he builds his position upon the Scottish

---

[29] Maddox documents the minimalist reading of the early circuit riders. Randy Maddox, 'Respected Founder/Neglected Guide: The Role of Wesley in American Methodist Theology', *Methodist History* 37.2 (January 1999), p. 73.

[30] Ibid., p. 74.

[31] Asa Shinn, *An Essay on the Plan of Salvation: In Which the Several Sources of Evidence are Examined, and Applied to the Interesting Doctrine of Redemption, in its Relation to the Government and Moral Attributes of Deity* (Baltimore: Neal, Wills & Cole, 1813), p. 230.

common sense philosophy pervasive in American culture at this time.[32] Furthermore, the essay is highly apologetic, rather than expository in character: it is a defence of the Wesleyan *ordo salutis* and its understanding of the relationship between divine and human agency ('the Government and Moral Attributes of Deity') over against the Calvinists, who were a chief cause for Methodist theologizing through much of the nineteenth century.

In this apologetic, Shinn's appeal to Wesley is minimal, and he cites John Fletcher far more frequently. Fletcher's writings are almost exclusively an apologetic for the Methodist perspective on entire sanctification and the relation between divine and human agency in the order of salvation (co-operant grace).[33] The doctrine of the Trinity is of little significance in Shinn's work, despite the fact that the book deals with God's sovereignty and attributes.

The book illustrates seven developing tendencies that become characteristic of much of American Methodist theologizing: (1) Shinn goes outside the Wesleyan tradition for intellectual resources, but not to the great tradition of the church. (2) Shinn utilizes a foundational appeal to philosophy to undergird his theological endeavour, rather than develop the intrinsic interrelations in the theological verities of the Wesleyan expression of Christian faith. (3) Cultural concerns and theological debates set the agenda for theological reflection. (4) Apologetics become the form and the standard of serious theology. (5) There is only minor appeal to Wesley, and that appeal is to Wesley as a *source* rather than a *model* for theology. (6) The *ordo salutis* begins to lose the Trinitarian deep-structure so evident in Wesley's theology. (7) When God is discussed, the focus is on the God–world relation (God's sovereignty and agency in the world) and divine attributes to the one God, rather than the Triune God, as if the one God can be abstracted from the Triune God and treated as a distinct reality.

There is a complex skein of reasons for these developments, which I do not have space to discuss here. Some of them go back to Wesley himself. But these seven tendencies develop markedly throughout the nineteenth century and some become *the* dominating characteristics of whole

---

[32] Langford, *Practical Divinity*, p. 82.

[33] See Randy Maddox, 'An Untapped Inheritance: American Methodism and Wesley's Practical Theology' in D.M. Campbell, W.B. Lawrence and R.E. Richey (eds), *Doctrines and Discipline* (Nashville: Abingdon Press, 1999), p. 25. Maddox documents this same pervasive supplementation of Wesley by Fletcher in monographs by other American Methodists. See Maddox, 'Respected Founder/Neglected Guide', pp. 74–6.

streams of the American Methodist theological legacy. The following section will first note several general trends related to these seven characteristics of American Methodist theology during the nineteenth and early twentieth centuries and then examine several theologians who illustrate these trends.

5. Clashes with the Calvinists: Philosophical Anthropologies to the Rescue

The Methodist debate with the Calvinists over God's sovereignty and moral attributes in relation to human sin and freedom continues unabated throughout much of the nineteenth century. In this debate, Methodist appeal to philosophical resources, especially philosophical anthropology, as the basis upon which first to defend and then later actually to construct a Methodist theology, grows dramatically throughout this period.

Over the same period of time, direct appeal to Wesley even as a source declines precipitously. Randy Maddox documents this decline and demonstrates that Wesley was not valued *as a theologian* throughout much of the past two centuries, until about 1960, when a few American Methodists began to reclaim Wesley as a theological mentor, a number that has grown since then.[34] His conclusion is that, while Wesley bequeathed to American Methodism the 'core of the Christian theological heritage' and 'a multi-level model of the "practical theologian"', 'the history of American Methodist theology has been one of progressive neglect (and occasional rejection of portions) of this inheritance'.[35]

During this same period in the nineteenth and early twentieth centuries, the Trinity suffers significant or entire neglect among nearly all American Methodist intellectuals. While these Methodists still affirm the doctrine of the Trinity, it plays little or no role in their actual theologizing. A significant reason for neglect of the doctrine of the Trinity, according to Sam Powell, was the foundational appeal to a philosophically defined 'personality of God' as the key concept (rather

---

[34] No one has documented this history more fully and insightfully than Maddox. See Maddox, 'Respected Founder/Neglected Guide', pp. 71–88, Maddox, 'An Untapped Inheritance', pp. 19–52 and Randy Maddox, 'Reclaiming an Inheritance: Wesley as Theologian in the History of Methodist Theology' in Randy Maddox (ed.), *Rethinking Wesley's Theology for Contemporary Methodism* (Nashville: Kingswood, 1998), pp. 213–53.

[35] Maddox, 'Respected Founder/Neglected Guide', p. 72.

than the Trinity) among American Methodist theologians in their defence of Methodism against Calvinist criticism.[36]

The problem, explicitly addressed by Edwin Sherwood in the *Methodist Quarterly Review* in 1894, is that, once a foundational appeal is made to the 'personality' of the one God, how is the 'personality' of the one God related to 'three persons' of the Triune God?[37] Powell argues that the philosophical concept of personality adopted by these American Methodists was incapable of bearing a Trinitarian interpretation, and he documents the difficulty this created for appropriating and utilizing the Trinity in theological construction.[38] The doctrine of the Trinity has never fared well in theologies that first develop a philosophically defined concept of the one God and then try to relate it to the doctrine of the Trinity defined by special revelation. This development of the doctrine of the one God in separation from the Triune God is theologically and methodologically problematic, yet characteristic of American Methodist theologians throughout the nineteenth and twentieth centuries.

One of the most damaging and disconcerting results of this focus on the personality of the one God and resulting neglect and marginalization of the doctrine of the Trinity in American Methodism is that the *ordo salutis* gradually loses the conscious Trinitarian deep-structure characteristic of the Wesley brothers. This opens the door for the *ordo* to be grafted into different theological deep-structures. In more than a little of American Methodism from Borden Parker Bowne and Boston Personalism onward, the Trinitarian deep-structure is replaced by some form of panentheist God–world relation. This regrafting, of course, inevitably transposes the order of salvation into something quite different from what we find in Wesley's theology.

Thus, it is no coincidence that this same stream of American Methodist theology, as it passes through these transmutations, gradually loses its 'evangelical' character. Toward the end of the nineteenth century in American Methodism, it is possible to be 'Wesleyan' and not be 'evangelical', something unthinkable for early Methodists in England and America. We will now examine several concrete examples of these changes: first Daniel Whedon is this section, and then Bowne and John Cobb in the next.

---

[36] See Sam Powell, 'The Doctrine of the Trinity in 19th Century American Methodism 1850–1900', *Wesleyan Theological Journal* 18 (Fall 1983), pp. 33–46.

[37] Edwin Sherwood, 'The Mystery of the Trinity', *Methodist Quarterly Review* 76 (1894), pp. 584–8.

[38] Powell, 'The Doctrine of the Trinity', pp. 39–44.

All of the seven tendencies identified above are present in Nathan Bangs and especially in Wilbur Fisk, both leaders in the Methodist confrontation with the Calvinists in the first half of the nineteenth century. These same characteristics are even more marked in Daniel Whedon, editor of the *Methodist Quarterly Review* from 1856–84. By this time, Methodism was no longer insulated from wave after wave of new intellectual currents surging through American culture, including the Enlightenment, with its various emphases that further challenged traditional Wesleyan theology.

Whedon's work evidences Wesleyan convictions, but the centre of gravity shifts markedly in response to these various intellectual challenges. Whedon takes on the Calvinists, especially Jonathan Edwards, but on the basis of an even more fully philosophically defined and defended concept of human freedom than we find in his predecessors.

Whedon summarized Edwards' maxim, 'God judges us as he finds us to be, good or evil and holds us responsible without regard to the means by which we come to be so,'[39] and posed his counter maxim, 'To this maxim … we oppose the counter maxim that *in order for responsibility for a given act or state, power in the agent for contrary act of state is requisite*. In other words: "*No man is to blame for what he cannot help. Power underlies responsibility.*"'[40]

If there is any doctrine in American Methodism that has been effectively mediated down to the grass-roots level of the church, it is this concept of human freedom: no one can be blamed for what he or she cannot help. At least for Whedon, this freedom was still connected to prevenient grace, though the Christological foundation of prevenient grace disappears in some of Whedon's successors.

In his monograph *Freedom of the Will as a Basis of Human Responsibility and a Divine Government* Whedon argues from human moral consciousness (his philosophical anthropology) to his doctrine of God. Human moral consciousness not only implies human freedom and human immortality, but even a particular view of God as a 'person'.[41] The God demanded by human moral consciousness is 'an infinitely free, excellent, meritorious Person'.[42] For Whedon, 'The *necessary* CONDITION to

---

[39] See Daniel D. Whedon, *Essays, Reviews and Discourses* (New York: Phillips & Hunt, 1887), p. 110. This text is quoted by Langford in *Practical Divinity*, p. 104.

[40] Whedon, *Essays, Reviews and Discourses*, p. 110.

[41] Daniel D. Whedon, *Freedom of the Will as a Basis for Human Responsibility and a Divine Government* (New York: Carlton & Lanahan, 1864), p. 110.

[42] Ibid., pp. 315–16.

the *possible existence of a true Divine Government is the Volitional* FREEDOM, *both of the infinite and the finite Person*' (emphases in Whedon's text).[43]

In Whedon, the past tendencies to go outside the tradition for resources to engage contextual and apologetic concerns, to appeal to philosophy (particularly to a philosophical anthropology), to focus on personality and attributes of the one God, come to even fuller expression. Whedon begins with a philosophical interpretation of human nature as a fact of human experience. This philosophical fact, in turn, becomes the point of departure for the theological construction of the other loci in his theology, as is evident in the quotations above. Wesley and the Trinity find little place within Whedon's purview. There are only two references to Wesley in Whedon's book *Freedom of the Will*. There is not even a sub-section of a chapter on the Trinity, despite the fact that chapters and sub-sections are devoted to God's existence and various divine attributes.[44]

Neither Whedon nor the other intellectuals in this stream of Methodist intellectual history reject the doctrine of the Trinity. Rather, the Trinity simply fades into the background, as the philosophical anthropology and the doctrine of the one God they develop move into the foreground of theological construction. The Trinity is not really the deep-structure of Whedon's theology and plays little role in his actual theologizing.

6. Philosophical/Wesleyan Synthesis

One could even say these tendencies to go outside the tradition, particularly to philosophy and philosophical anthropology, for intellectual resources with which to engage contextual and apologetic concerns, to focus on the attributes and personality of the one God with minimal attention to the Trinity so that the *ordo salutis* loses its Trinitarian deep-structure, have actually become *the* defining characteristics of a major stream of the American Methodist theological tradition. Thus this culmination of previous tendencies in Whedon ends up constituting the point of departure for complete philosophical-Wesleyan syntheses

---

[43] Ibid., p. 436.

[44] For similar analyses, especially the eclipse of the doctrine of the Trinity in nineteenth-century American Methodist theologians William Nast, John Miley, D.W. Clark, W.P. Odell and James Strong, see Powell, 'The Doctrine of the Trinity', pp. 33–44.

by generation after generation of American Methodist theologians right up to the present day,[45] despite the fact that these syntheses bear little connection to, or resemblance of, Wesley's own Trinitarian evangelical theology.

In fact, many if not most of the greatest intellectuals in American Methodism stand in this stream of wedding Wesleyan theology with a particular philosophy, nearly always some form of panentheism. Borden Parker Bowne, the greatest intellectual in American Methodism in the late nineteenth and early twentieth centuries, forged Boston Personalism by synthesizing a particular form of neo-Kantian idealism with themes inherited from his Methodist heritage, and turned Boston University into arguably the greatest intellectual centre of American Methodism for the first half of the twentieth century.

Bowne found personal idealism, with its stress on personality as the fundamental reality, to be the best philosophical position available and the philosophy most congenial to Christian faith.[46] Albert C. Knudson, chief theological successor to Bowne, provided perhaps the best succinct definition of Personalism as 'That form of idealism which gives actual recognition to both the pluralistic and monistic aspects of experience and which finds in the conscious unity, identity, and free activity of personality the key to the nature of reality and the solution to the ultimate problems of philosophy'.[47] Bowne used Personalism to combat the growing naturalism and materialism of modern scientific and secular Western culture.

The philosophical theism developed by Bowne (and other Boston Personalists) radically transformed the vestiges of Wesleyan theology carried into this philosophical synthesis. In fact, as Maddox astutely points out, this transformation was a major agenda of Boston Personalism, for Personalism's goal was to 'rationalize and moralize modern religion by purifying it of all mystical and ceremonial overlays'.[48] Since much of Wesley's evangelical theology fell under the domain of these 'overlays', it is little wonder that his work held little promise for the Personalists. Many traditional doctrines, like the Trinity, could only be radically reinterpreted, if retained at all, in order to bring them into line

---

[45] See Langford, *Practical Divinity*, p. 105.
[46] See Borden Parker Bowne, *Metaphysics* (New York: Harper, 1882), *Philosophy of Theism* (New York: Harper, 1887), and *Personalism* (Boston: Houghton Mifflin, 1908).
[47] Albert C. Knudson, *The Philosophy of Personalism* (Boston: Boston University Press, 1927), p. 87.
[48] Maddox, 'An Untapped Inheritance', p. 47.

with the Personalist God–world relation. For example, there is no discussion of the Trinity at all (hardly even an allusion to the Trinity) in Bowne's book *The Immanence of God*.[49] Thus the marginalization of the Trinity is even more profound in Bowne than in Whedon, for Bowne systematically replaces the Trinitarian deep-structure of Wesleyan theology with a Personalist God–world relation.

Despite American Methodism's tolerance for the erosion of its own theological legacy, Bowne's radical reinterpretations led to charges of heresy. George Cook claimed that Bowne's teachings on many of the themes of the *ordo salutis* (sin, salvation, justification, repentance, regeneration and assurance) were at odds with Methodist doctrine, and that Bowne actually denied the Trinity and substitutionary atonement. Bowne, however, was acquitted at the resulting trial.[50]

No one within Methodism has worked out more consistently and fully across the spectrum of loci the theological implications of a particular panentheist God–world relation as the deep-structure of theology than has John Cobb, whom I regard as the most brilliant United Methodist theologian in the second half of the twentieth century. Cobb develops a similar style of philosophical-Wesleyan synthesis as the Boston Personalists, but forges the synthesis on the basis of the process philosophy of Alfred North Whitehead and Cobb's liberal expression of the Methodist theological heritage.

Read, for example, his important book *Christ in a Pluralistic Age*,[51] in which Cobb cleverly, carefully and consistently reworks every aspect of Christology in order to bring into harmony with 'Creative Transformation ... the immanence of God in the world ... life itself, the life by which all that is alive lives'.[52] Cobb affirms, but radically redefines, the Trinity in light of his process panentheism. He identifies the *logos* with Whitehead's primordial nature of God and the Spirit with God's consequent nature.[53] The doctrine of the Trinity as affirmed by Wesley is not the deep-structure of Cobb's theology, rather it is the process panentheist God–world relation, and it plays a crucial defining role in the other theological loci.

---

[49] Borden P. Bowne, *The Immanence of God* (Boston: Houghton Mifflin, 1905).

[50] See Langford, *Practical Divinity*, p. 123.

[51] John B. Cobb, *Christ in a Pluralistic Age* (Philadelphia: Westminster, 1975).

[52] Cobb provides this summary thesis of his earlier book: John Cobb, 'Christ Beyond Creative Transformation' in Stephen T. Davis (ed.), *Encountering Jesus: A Debate on Christology* (Atlanta: John Knox, 1988), p. 144.

[53] See Cobb, *Christ in a Pluralistic Age*, pp. 70–7, 259–64, especially pp. 70, 262. Also see Cobb, 'Christ Beyond Creative Transformation', pp. 152–3.

Of course, Cobb can claim that he is simply following the lead of countless other American Methodist theologians back to Bowne and even Whedon and Shinn. The list of panentheist synthesizers from Bowne to Cobb is impressive and long: Knudson, Brightman, DeWolf, Schilling, Rall, Harkness, Ramsdell and Ogden, to mention only the more prominent figures in this stream of American Methodist intellectual history.

7. Systematic Theologies

One other stream of American Methodist theology is important for this essay, since it actually discusses the Trinity, but also helps explain the fading influence of Wesley as a theological mentor in American Methodism. The best way to approach these systematic theologies is in light of a recurring criticism of Methodist theology given perhaps its clearest formulation by a Calvinist, E.P. Humphrey, in his address at the 1852 Presbyterian General Assembly. Humphrey argued that Methodist theology was unworthy of serious consideration because it:

> has yet to be reduced to a systematic and logical form ... We have its brief and informal creed in some five and twenty articles; but where is its complete confession of faith, in thirty or forty chapters? ... Where is its whole body of divinity, from under the hand of a master, sharply defining its terms, accurately stating its belief, laying down the conclusions logically involved therein, trying these conclusions, no less than their premises, by the Word of God, refuting objections, and adjusting all its parts into a consistent and systematic whole?[54]

Of course, Humphrey was correct in one sense, for Wesley and early Methodism developed nothing like Calvin's *Institutes*. I think that Humphrey identifies a task that still needs to be pursued within Methodism in our own day, though on the basis of a Trinitarian deep-structure grounded in Scripture, in Wesley's Trinitarian theology, and in dialogue with the great tradition of the church. But it is a task that must be pursued in a rather different form than the one implied in Humphrey's statement, for the standard he upholds is Reformed scholasticism.

Actually, this scholastic form of theologizing had already been employed by a British Methodist, Richard Watson, in his multi-volume *Theological Institutes*, completed in 1828. Watson's *Theological*

---

[54] E.P. Humphery, *Our Theology and its Development* (Philadelphia: Presbyterian Board of Publication, 1857), pp. 68–9. Maddox cites this text in Maddox, 'An Untapped Inheritance', p. 33.

Institutes became *the* most read and influential systematic theology in American Methodism throughout much of the nineteenth century and the main theological text required in the course of study for fifty years. Virtually all Methodist preachers read it.

The sub-title is revealing: *A View of the Evidences, Doctrines, Morals, and Institutions of Christianity*. Even more illuminating is the quantity and role of evidence, for the work opens with 150 pages of 'Evidences of the Divine Authority of the Holy Scriptures', a rationalist apologetic for acceptance of Scripture as divine revelation. The assumption behind this, of course, is that epistemological foundations have to be established before an examination of the Christian web of belief can begin.[55]

Throughout the work there are polemical defences of disputed Methodist doctrines, often contra the Calvinists, but also contra deists and Anglicans. The deductive use of Scripture is defended and consistently employed. Watson draws on a variety of sources, but rarely ever refers to Wesley.

Of the work's seven hundred and fifty pages, less than forty are devoted to the Trinity. Thirty of those forty pages attempt to deduce the doctrine of the Trinity from Scripture. This leaves only a couple of pages that actually discuss the content of the doctrine. There is no appeal to Wesley in this entire section. Most telling of all is that the economic, evangelical and doxological approach of the Wesley brothers is completely absent in Watson, save for a single quotation from Dr Waterland (who Watson labels 'one of the Athanasians') under the sub-heading of 'The Importance of the Trinity':

> While we consider the doctrine of the trinity as interwoven with the very frame and texture of Christian religion, it appears to me natural to conceive that the whole scheme and economy of man's redemption was laid with a principal view of it, in order to bring mankind gradually into an acquaintance with the three Divine persons, one God blessed for ever ... Such a redemption was provided, such an expiation for sins required, such a method of sanctification appointed, and then revealed, that so men might know that there are three Divine persons, might be apprised how infinitely the world is indebted to them, and might accordingly be both instructed and inclined to love, honor, and adore them here, because that must be a considerable part of their employment and happiness hereafter.[56]

---

[55] Maddox 'An Untapped Inheritance', p. 34.

[56] Richard Watson, *Theological Institutes: Or, A View of the Evidences, Doctrines, Morals and Institutions of Christianity* (Nashville: Publishing House of the Methodist Episcopal Church, South, 1906), p. 262.

It is a fascinating quotation, since Watson seems oblivious to the fact that it undermines his approach to the doctrine of the Trinity, indeed the entire architectonic fabric of his *Theological Institutes*. If 'the doctrine of the Trinity is interwoven with the very frame and texture of Christian religion' (this sounds amazingly similar to Wesley),[57] if 'the whole scheme and economy of humanity's redemption was laid with a principle view of it', then must we not reflect this not only in our discussion of the Trinity, but also in the entire architectonic or structure of our theology? Must not the doctrine of the Trinity be carefully related to and integrated with the other loci of theology, especially of the *ordo salutis*, and not simply left isolated within the structure of theology as just one more doctrine among others?

This is my main criticism both of Watson and the various systematic theologies written by American Methodists who follow his lead throughout the nineteenth century and the first half of the twentieth century (even those who are clearly evangelical): these Methodist systematicians draw their model for systematic theology from outside the tradition, and then force Wesleyan theology into that mould, which I am becoming more and more convinced does violence to Wesley's theology in the process.

Watson and many other American Methodist systematicians who recast Wesleyan theology in this scholastic mode consistently uproot the doctrine of the Trinity from its soteriological, evangelical and doxological matrix. They isolate the doctrine of the Trinity in the dogmatic structure of theology where it is no longer integrally related to other loci of theology, especially the *ordo salutis*. This, in turn, renders the doctrine of the Trinity just one more Christian belief among others, and therefore the Trinity no longer functions as the deep-structure of theology, nor does the Trinity bear the forthright relation to all vital religion as in the case of the Wesley brothers.

Thus even though Watson and the systematicians who followed him, like Miley for example, affirm the Trinity and even discuss the doctrine in their works, I am not satisfied with the way this stream of American Methodism deals with the Trinity, both in terms of content and in terms of placement within the dogmatic structure of theology. Their treatments are not in keeping with the place and the content of the Trinity in the theology of John and Charles Wesley, and actually subvert the spiritual/theological Trinitarian dynamism of early Methodism, one of the real treasures that the Wesleys bequeathed to their followers. Here I

---

[57] Wesley had read Waterland's work. See Bryant, 'Trinity and Hymnody', p. 65.

agree with Thomas F. Torrance that method, form and content are inseparable in theology.[58] This isolation of the Trinity with the dogmatic structure of theology means that it is difficult for the Trinity to operate as the deep-structure of these Methodist systematic theologies and/or influence the life of the church, for as simply one more belief among others left unrelated to other loci of theology like the *ordo salutis*, the Trinity no longer functions as the origin and goal of all vital religion, interwoven with all true Christian faith.

On this point, of course, Wesley was part of the problem, since he provided no model of how to express his theology in a rigorous form. But there is an alternative to borrowing forms from outside the tradition, though it is much more difficult: that is to develop a dogmatic structure or architectonic from within the tradition in such a way that method, form and content unfold together. Why not go back to the Wesleys, appropriate their Trinitarian insights, and then develop a theological architectonic that more accurately reflects the Trinitarian deep-structure of theology to which their insights point, especially in relation to the *ordo salutis*? Why not develop a theology, including method, content and form, in relation to Trinitarian knowledge of God as it actually arises at the evangelical and doxological level on the basis of the economic Trinity, as Wesley tried to describe it in his various discussions of the Trinity? Has any American Methodist, evangelical or otherwise, really attempted this thus far?

8. The Neo-Wesleyan Movement and the Present Context

The stream of American Methodist theology where one might most expect this kind of Trinitarian evangelical Wesleyan theology to find expression and development is the Neo-Wesleyan movement. As the Neo-orthodoxy of Barth and Brunner among others reverberated on American shores, some American Methodists were quick to see its implications for Methodism. So they also began to reassert traditional Protestant themes in protest against what they perceived to be the deformation of the Wesleyan heritage by liberal American Methodism.[59]

Most important among the early Neo-Wesleyans was Edwin Lewis, followed by a number of others (George Cell, William Cannon, Franz Hildebrandt, John Deschner and Robert Chiles, among others).

---

[58] See chs 1–4 of Torrance, *The Christian Doctrine of God*.
[59] See *Religion in Life* 29.4 (1960), which is devoted solely to 'Neo-Wesleyanism'.

These scholars reaffirmed traditional themes. Some of them produced studies of Wesley often emphasizing parallels between Wesley and the Magisterial Reformers.[60]

The Neo-Wesleyan movement, along with the ecumenical dialogues in the middle of the twentieth century (that pushed Methodists to reflect upon their ecclesial identity), both led to growing interest in reappropriating Wesley and recovering a more distinctively 'Wesleyan' tradition. It was Albert Outler who led the charge to recover Wesley as a serious theologian in his own right. A crucial milestone in this movement has been the development of the definitive critical text of Wesley's works (*The Bicentennial Edition*), a project still in progress.

Neo-Wesleyanism and the broader movement to recover Wesley as a theologian have generated a wealth of studies of Wesley's theology, well over a hundred book-length works since 1960 alone.[61] It has encouraged a number Methodist theologians today to return to Wesley as a theological mentor.[62]

The curious thing for me is how little publication on the doctrine of the Trinity in general and on the Trinity in Wesley in particular has come from Neo-Wesleyanism and the broader movement to reclaim Wesley. There is significant talk about the Trinity in Methodist circles these days, but it has been generated primarily by ecumenical dialogue and encounters with Trinitarian theologies outside the Wesleyan tradition. I find this conversation extremely encouraging.

9. Toward a Trinitarian Evangelical Wesleyan Theology

It should be clear from the preceding discussion that the intellectual history of American Methodism has not really appropriated and developed the Trinitarian insights of the Wesley brothers' evangelical theology. In fact, more than a few American Methodist theologies have been anaemic on the doctrine of the Trinity.

Furthermore, I am sympathetic with Maddox's plea that Methodists retrieve Wesley's *form* of theological activity: *scientia practica.*[63] Wesleyan theology needs to be pursued within the evangelical and doxological life of the church, and the production of rich and theologically

---

[60] See Langford, *Practical Divinity*, pp. 208–9, and Maddox, 'An Untapped Inheritance', pp. 48–9.
[61] See the bibliography in Maddox, *Responsible Grace*, pp. 375–408.
[62] Maddox, 'Respected Founder/Neglected Guide', p. 87.
[63] Maddox, 'An Untapped Inheritance', pp. 50–2.

sound materials for Christian formation is a crucial task for theologians, other scholars and pastors.

Yet we need to go further than this. Indeed, the form of Wesley's theological activity in sermons, journals, songs and so on is part of the problem, for, as noted above, he did not provide his followers with a distinctively Wesleyan *Institutes* or *Summa*. I see no reason why the Wesleyan 'body of divinity' cannot be given careful, comprehensive and architectonically rigorous expression in a way that both discloses the distinctive theological patterns of that theology and comes to expression as an evangelical and doxological activity in praise of the Triune God, for the edification of the church, and for the transformation of the world.

As I have delved into Wesley's thought, I have begun to share Outler's excitement regarding the theological possibilities latent in Wesley's theology, possibilities largely unrealized within the intellectual history of American Methodism. I have become more and more convinced of Outler's thesis that Wesley has been unjustly dismissed as a theological popularizer unworthy of serious study by both those outside and within the Wesleyan heritage.

Here in Wesley I find an unashamed evangelical focus on the gospel, a broad catholic sensitivity and sensibility, and evidence for a deeply Trinitarian theology. More and more I have come to see latent in the work of the Wesley brothers a fully Trinitarian evangelical Wesleyan theology yet to be given comprehensive and architectonically rigorous expression, something John Wesley never attempted himself, and something American Methodism has generally neglected because of its foundational appeal to philosophical first principles and borrowing of theological form from outside the tradition, both of which have marginalized or eclipsed the Trinitarian insights of the Wesley brothers.

What follows are several of what I consider to be indispensable defining elements for the development of a thoroughly Trinitarian evangelical Wesleyan theology:

1. We need a faithful and critical reappropriation of Wesley's theology (read in light of the great tradition of the church), especially the Wesley brothers' Trinitarian insights. This must include carefully thinking through the architectonics latent in those insights.
2. We must reclaim the evangelical and doxological matrix of the Wesley brothers' theology, for knowledge of God and the entire Christian faith are biblical *and* participatory. This evangelical and doxological matrix is missing from more than a little of the theological work in the history of American Methodism.

3. Since the Trinity is the origin and the *telos* of Christian faith and practice in Wesley's theology, the doctrine of the Trinity needs to configure the entire architectonic shape of Wesleyan theology and the content of the various loci covered. The doctrine of the Trinity must not be isolated in the dogmatic structure of theology and treated as just one more Christian belief as in Watson's *Theological Institutes* and other American Methodist theologies. The early Wesleyan expression of Christian faith was aboriginally and intrinsically Trinitarian. This should be true of all Christian faith, for it is the differentiated *perichoretic* co-activity of the Triune God that establishes the constitutive relations that makes the gospel what it is. It is especially important for theology to give account of God's Trinitarian economy (*oikonomia*, the divinely ordered pattern of God's ongoing reconciling and redeeming interaction with Israel and preeminently embodied in Jesus Christ and the outpouring of the Holy Spirit at Pentecost), and give a Trinitarian account of the *ordo salutis*, our participation in God's economy. This, I believe, is what Wesley is pointing to when he says that 'knowledge of the Three–One God is interwoven in all true Christian faith, with all vital religion'.

4. Thus it is foremost the knowledge of the Triune God arising out of evangelical and doxological participation in the gospel that ought to be carefully developed in theology, whatever else we can learn about God from other sources. Theology ought to refine, extend, correct, unify and develop the knowledge of God that arises out of the church's indwelling of the Scriptures and participation in the reality of the gospel to which Scripture bears witness.

5. American Methodism's tendency to allow contextual and apologetic concerns (as crucial and unavoidable as these concerns are) to be the key defining focus of theological reflection and discourse is imbalanced and ultimately unhelpful. These concerns must be addressed, but out of a Wesleyan theology first pursued in its own right in a manner that does not do violence to the verities of the faith. If Wesley's example demonstrates anything, it demonstrates both the possibility and desirability of this kind of theological integrity *and* contextual relevance.

6. American Methodism has been insufficiently critical in its foundational appeal to philosophy and insufficiently critical in its borrowing of theological forms from outside the tradition. I have no problem with *ancilla theologiae*, but if the intellectual history of American Methodism teaches us anything, it is the grave danger involved in insufficiently critical foundational appropriations of philosophy (and any other *ancilla*). Theology can and should learn from many other disciplines.

But this needs to be done with far more sophistication, rigour and integrity than we find in some of the intellectual history of American Methodism. While there is much of great value to be learned from this history, when we examine that history from the perspective of the doctrine of the Trinity, the problems and dangers involved with philosophical *ancilla* are particularly highlighted.

The time is ripe in many respects for the development of a thoroughly Trinitarian evangelical Wesleyan theology. The ecclesial health of the family of churches that make up the Wesleyan/Methodist tradition is not exactly at a high point. There is a deep need for theological and spiritual renewal. The *Bicentennial Edition* of Wesley's works and the burgeoning secondary literature on Wesley's theology over the past four decades have provided many of the tools necessary for the task, as has the burgeoning interest in and literature on the Trinity in evangelicalism and the wider Christian community. My hope is that this essay will encourage the development of Trinitarian evangelical Wesleyan theology.

8

Karl Barth's Evangelical Principles: Reformation Legacy in his Theology

Sung Wook Chung

This paper aims to explore evangelical principles of Karl Barth by investigating the Reformation legacy in his theology. Many evangelical theologians have recently been endeavouring to integrate the strengths and merits of Barth's theology into their theological construction. For example, Donald Bloesch has repeatedly affirmed that his theological work has been deeply indebted to Karl Barth.[1] Although Bloesch has expressed his reservations about some aspects of Barth's theology, he has continued to maintain an appreciative attitude toward him. Among other examples, we have Bernard Ramm, Kevin Vanhoozer, Stanley Grenz, T.F. Torrance and Miroslav Volf.

I view this trend as a healthy development. But we need a more mature and sophisticated understanding of Barth's evangelical legacy for a more helpful interaction with his theology for the purpose of constructing evangelical theology with dynamics and vitality. I am convinced that Barth's evangelical principles originate mainly from the Reformation legacy in his theological formulations. On the basis of this foundational insight, I will explore Karl Barth's reception of theological fundamentals of the sixteenth-century European Reformation by focusing on major slogans associated with the Reformation. Among those slogans are *sola scriptura*, *sola fide*, *sola gratia*, *solus Christus*, *sola crucis*, *soli deo Gloria*, the priesthood of all believers, *coram deo*, *semper reformanda*, the idea of calling, the communitarian and ecumenical character of the church, and so on.

---

[1] See Donald Bloesh's systematic theological work *Christian Foundations* (Downers Grove: InterVarsity Press, 1992–present).

At the outset, it is crucial to appreciate that Barth was not a slavish imitator of Luther and Calvin in his appropriation of Reformation principles. As Hans Urs von Balthasar has stated:

> As a Reformed theologian, Barth would modify or entirely drop crucial points in Luther's doctrine ... But he has also done the same with Calvin himself. Can we even conceive of Calvin without a natural theology? Well, Barth works through these implications more consistently than Calvin! Did not Calvin explain the connection between divine righteousness and human justification? Then, the point is to show what Calvin neglected to show! Calvin's doctrine of double predestination contradicts the central meaning of redemption in Christ? Then Barth drops it without hesitation![2]

Although he enthusiastically accepted the evangelical tenets of the Reformation, Barth maintained a critical and creative attitude toward the Reformers. Sometimes he unhesitatingly criticized the Reformers' failures while creatively and innovatively developing their foundational insights in accordance with his own distinctive theological and philosophical presuppositions. I will focus on these aspects of Barth's innovative advancement of the Reformers' wisdom.

1. *Solus Christus*

Martin Luther was a Christocentric theologian. He believed that only Jesus Christ saves sinners. For Luther, sinners can obtain their peace of mind and eternal salvation in Jesus Christ alone. Jesus Christ himself is our salvation, reconciliation, justification and sanctification. Calvin accepted Luther's foundational insights into the relationship between Jesus Christ and human salvation. Calvin repeatedly affirmed that Jesus Christ is the only mediator between God and humanity.

Barth also recognized the significance of Jesus Christ for creation, reconciliation and redemption, acknowledging that both Luther and Calvin were Christocentric theologians. As Hunsinger has argued:

> not least among the many powerful themes that Barth would absorb from Luther is that of 'christocentrism,' perhaps the most basic point in all of Barth's theology. Indeed, Barth not only owed this point to Luther but went on to radicalize it. In this respect he would remain truer in some ways to the

---

[2] Hans Urs von Balthasar, *The Theology of Karl Barth*, E.T. Oakes (tr.) (San Francisco: Ignatius Press, 1992), p. 22.

spirit than to the letter of Luther's thought. But the original impulse had come from Luther and can be traced back to him alone.[3]

It is crucial, therefore, to understand that Barth pressed his Christocentric concern further and constructed a Christological dogmatics. In so doing, Barth often criticized Luther and Calvin for not being sufficiently Christocentric, especially in relation to the doctrine of election, reconciliation and the knowledge of sin. Barth criticizes Calvin, saying:

> It is when we look at Jesus Christ that we know decisively that God's deity does not exclude, but includes His humanity. Would that Calvin had energetically pushed ahead on this point in his Christology, his doctrine of God, his teaching about predestination, and then logically also in his ethics! His Geneva would then not have become such a gloomy affair. His letters would then not have contained so much bitterness.[4]

For Barth, Calvin's doctrine of election was not solidly grounded upon the person and work of Jesus Christ as the sole mediator and reality of the covenant between God and humanity. Moreover, Barth argues, Calvin's concept of God, who predestines some to eternal salvation and others to eternal damnation before the foundation of the universe, was coined totally out of the context of Christological determinations of divine nature and work. Furthermore, Barth claims, it was invalid for Calvin to argue that the knowledge of sin comes through the law rather than through the knowledge of Christ.

It is important to understand that Barth's critique of Luther and Calvin aimed not to dismiss all the legitimate insights of the two Reformers, but creatively to expand and refine them. As Barth has stated:

> We do not have teaching by repeating Calvin's words as our own or making his view ours ... Be they never so devout and faithful, those who simply echo Calvin are not good Calvinists ... The aim, then, is a dialogue that may end with the taught saying something very different from what Calvin said but that they learned from or, better, through him.[5]

As Hunsinger has stated:

---

[3] George Hunsinger, *Disruptive Grace: Studies in the Theology of Karl Barth* (Grand Rapids: Eerdmans, 2000), p. 283.

[4] Karl Barth, *The Humanity of God* (Richmond: John Knox Press, 1960), p. 49.

[5] Karl Barth, *The Theology of John Calvin*, Geoffrey W. Bromiley (tr.) (Grand Rapids: Eerdmans, 1995), p. 4.

the centrality of Jesus Christ in this strong soteriological sense is something that Barth most certainly learned from Luther. That Christ alone is our salvation, that he is no an incomplete but a perfect savior, that he is our righteousness on account of his obedience, that he is not the source of our righteousness without also being its reality and ground ... the christocentrism for which Barth is so famous would scarcely have been thinkable without Luther's Reformation breakthrough.[6]

Barth's Christological framework was a product of his endeavour to integrate innovatively and critically the Reformers' Christocentric insights into his own dogmatics. Thus, we can regard Barth's Christological concern as a reflection of his evangelical legacy handed down from the Reformers. If we acknowledge that the centrality of Christ is one of major features of evangelical theological tradition, then we should embrace Barth as an evangelical theologian.

2. *Sola Scriptura*

Luther's Reformation movement was grounded upon the Scripture principle. For Luther, Scripture is the only authority in Christian faith and life. Luther claimed that God speaks in and through Scripture. Calvin also accepted this principle and argued that Scripture is the only source for the true knowledge of God and ourselves. For Calvin, Scripture alone is God's revelation and God's Word.

Karl Barth was also emphatic upon this principle of Scripture alone. As Bruce McCormack has argued, Barth advocated the Reformed Scripture principle while he was working at the University of Göttingen.[7] In the first book of the *Church Dogmatics*, Barth also discussed the three-fold Word of God. The primary Word of God is the person of Jesus Christ as God incarnate, while Scripture witnesses to the primary Word of God. For Barth, Scripture is the written Word of God and the only material source of the knowledge of God. Barth was convinced that faithful exegesis of Scripture could provide us with true knowledge of the Triune God.[8] If we acknowledge that the Scripture principle is one of

---

[6] Hunsinger, *Disruptive Grace*, p. 286.

[7] Bruce L. McCormack, *Karl Barth's Critically Realistic Dialectical Theology* (Oxford: Oxford University Press, 1997), pp. 305–7, 317–18.

[8] For more detailed discussion, see my book *Admiration and Challenge: Karl Barth's Theological Relationship with John Calvin* (New York: Peter Lang, 2002), ch. 4.

major characteristics of evangelical theological tradition, then Barth must be regarded as an evangelical theologian.

3. Word and Spirit

Along with the Scripture principle, both Luther and Calvin were emphatic upon the fact that the written Word of Scripture cannot be the living Word of God without the mysterious work of the Holy Spirit upon human hearts. The Word and the Spirit always work together. As Paul Althaus has argued:

> We must now ask about the relationship between the external word and the inner word which God speaks to the heart. For Luther they are most intimately connected. His expressions on this can be summarized in two sentences: (1) The Spirit does not speak without the word. (2) The Spirit speaks through and in the word.[9]

For Luther, the Spirit never speaks about things that are contradictory to what Scripture witnesses, and the written Word of God must be enlivened by the Spirit to have effect upon human hearts.

Calvin advocated the same idea. In the *Institutes*, he says:

> Let this point therefore stand: that those whom the Holy Spirit has inwardly taught truly rest upon Scripture, and that Scripture indeed is self-authenticated; hence, it is not right to subject it to proof and reasoning. And the certainty it deserves with us, it attains by the testimony of the Spirit. For even if it wins reverence for itself by its own majesty, it seriously affects us only when it is sealed upon our hearts through the Spirit.[10]

By saying this, Calvin wants to affirm the importance of the mysterious work of the Spirit in confirming that Scripture is the Word of God. For Calvin, only when the Spirit enlightens and inspires us can we accept Scripture as the living Word of God. Only through the mysterious witness of the Spirit can we confirm that 'God in person speaks in'[11] Scripture.

---

[9] Paul Althaus, *The Theology of Martin Luther*, Robert C. Schultz (tr.) (Philadelphia: Fortress Press, 1966), p. 36.

[10] John Calvin, *Institutes of the Christian Religion*, John T. McNeill (ed.), Ford L. Battles (tr.) (Philadelphia: Westminster, 1960), I.vii.5.

[11] Ibid., I.vii.4.

Karl Barth accepted the Reformers' insights wholeheartedly. Discussing the role of the Holy Spirit in the revelation of God and for the possibility of the knowledge of God, Barth argues that the Holy Spirit enables human beings to hear the Word of God and to know God. In other words, the Holy Spirit plays a role as the subjective reality and possibility of the human encounter and knowledge of God by empowering human beings to acknowledge God's revelation in faith and obedience:

> According to Holy Scripture God's revelation occurs in our enlightenment by the Holy Spirit of God to a knowledge of His Word. The outpouring of the Holy Spirit is God's revelation[12] ... Where it is believed and acknowledged in the Holy Spirit, the revelation of God creates men who do not exist without seeking God in Jesus Christ, and who cannot cease to testify that He has found them.[13]

In this connection, one may raise a further question as to what makes the human witness to revelation in Scripture be heard, obeyed and confirmed as the Word of God and the revelation of Christ. How can the divinity of Scripture be realized subjectively in the mind of human beings? Answering this question, Barth appeals to the secret work of the Holy Spirit. 'If the church lives by the Bible because it is the Word of God, that means that it lives by the fact that Christ is revealed in the Bible by the work of the Holy Spirit.'[14] Just as the Holy Spirit is the subjective reality and possibility of revelation, so his secret work makes possible for man to hear the Word of God in the Scripture. Barth appeals to Calvin's foundational insight in making this point:

> And it was on the same point that Calvin expressed himself so vigorously. As he worked it out in *Inst.*, I, 7, 4 and the Commentary on 2 Tim. 3:16, his view was this. There exists an exact correspondence between the certainty with which the word of the apostles and prophets was the Word of God in itself, or for them, and the certainty with which it as such illumines us. In both cases only God can bear witness to God ... And in both cases the God who attests Himself is the Spirit: no one else, but the same Spirit.[15]

---

[12] Karl Barth, *Church Dogmatics*, G.W. Bromiley (tr.) (Edinburgh: T. & T. Clark, 1961), I/2, p. 203.

[13] Ibid., I/2, p. 362.

[14] Ibid., I/2, p. 513.

[15] Ibid., I/2, p. 521.

Hence, without the Holy Spirit's secret work of illumination upon the human mind here and now, no one can hear the Word of God in Scripture or know God through Scripture. The Holy Spirit who inspired the human writers of Scripture in the past must do the same work in the present for a human being to recognize and obey the Word of God in and through Scripture. By appealing to Calvin here, Barth seeks to legitimate his endeavour to support his argument for the indispensability of the Spirit's work of internal testimony upon the human mind.

If we acknowledge that the principle of Word/Spirit is one of the major hallmarks of evangelical theological tradition, we should accept Barth as an evangelical theologian.

4. *Sola Gratia*

Luther's discovery of the gospel of grace drew him to the Reforming movement. Luther rediscovered the good news that sinners are saved by grace alone. For Luther, human beings are totally unable to save themselves. They need an external help. God, by his grace, has prepared a way for salvation through the death and resurrection of Jesus Christ. Divine grace, Luther argues, liberates sinners from the bondage of sin, death and the Devil. Sinners can never contribute to the work of salvation. They just receive salvation as God's gracious gift. Calvin was also emphatic upon the grace of God. Human beings cannot earn salvation through their own works. They should depend upon God's pure mercy and abundant grace for their salvation.

Barth also stressed the importance of divine grace. For Barth, grace is the central motif of the gospel. Election of grace is the sum of the gospel. The gospel is the news of undeserved grace. Barth extended the theme 'grace alone' into the area of knowing God. For Barth, not only salvation but also the true knowledge of God is by grace alone. By grace God makes himself an object of human knowledge. God reveals himself to humanity. Unless God discloses himself, it is impossible for humanity to know God. So, human beings' true knowledge of God is totally dependent upon God's revelation and self-disclosure.

Barth believed that the very action of God's self-disclosure is a gracious act for humanity. So, the possibility of knowledge of God totally depends upon God's gracious determination to reveal himself and to encounter human beings personally. God graciously approaches humanity and draws it to himself.

In terms of the relationship between the law and the gospel, Barth formulated an innovative idea. Barth critically revised the theme of law and gospel advocated by both Luther and Calvin. He reversed the traditional order of 'law and gospel' into 'gospel and law'. Barth argued that the law does not bind, accuse and kill, nor is it prior to the gospel of grace. Rather, the gospel of grace always precedes the law, containing the law in itself. For Barth, the law is the necessary form of the gospel, and the gospel is the basis, the ground and the content of the law. Thus, he argues, both Luther and Calvin are wrong in their argument that the law opposes the gospel, and they are mutually exclusive in certain contexts.

By reversing the traditional order of 'law and gospel', Barth wanted to affirm the absolute primacy of God's grace over humanity's ethical responsibility. For Barth, the God of Christians is the God of grace revealed in the Lord Jesus Christ. If we acknowledge that the emphasis upon the primacy of God's grace is one of the major features of evangelical theological tradition, then we should embrace Barth as an evangelical theologian.

5. *Sola Fide*

Martin Luther's theological breakthrough came from his discovery of the doctrine of justification through faith alone. Luther agonized over the question of how a sinner can have a loving relationship with the righteous God. Through meticulous exegetical engagement with Scripture, Luther realized that the righteousness of God is not a condemning righteousness, but a forgiving and reconciling righteousness. God declares sinners righteous on the basis of the vicarious death and resurrection of Jesus Christ. God remains righteous in reconciling sinners with him because sinners are proclaimed righteous through faith in the Lord Jesus Christ. Faith is the channel through which sinners participate in God's work of justification. Ever since Luther found out this liberating truth, the doctrine of justification through faith alone has become one of the most significant benchmarks of the evangelical tradition.

In terms of the doctrine of justification by faith, Calvin was a faithful disciple of Luther. Calvin repeatedly stressed the importance of the doctrine of justification. As Calvin states, 'the theme of justification is the main hinge on which religion turns'.[16] Although Calvin's approach to the doctrine of justification was a bit different from Luther's, it is undeniable that Calvin wholeheartedly accepted Luther's groundbreaking insights into justification by faith alone.

---

[16] Calvin, *Institutes of the Christian Religion*, III.xi.1.

It is important to note that Barth creatively reappropriated the Reformers' doctrine of justification by faith alone. For example, we can find numerous appreciative quotations from Luther and Calvin in relation to the theme of justification in Barth's lectures on ethics delivered in Münster in 1928–29.[17] Barth expressed frequently his agreement with Luther and Calvin that sinners are justified through faith and by grace alone. In the *Church Dogmatics*, Barth devoted numerous pages to the discussion of the theme of justification and faith. Barth radicalized the Reformers' foundational insights into the fact that human faith cannot contribute to justification by saying, 'of the Reformers Calvin made this distinction with particular sharpness. Faith as such cannot contribute anything to our justification ... It is not a habitus. It is not a quality of grace which is infused into man.'[18] For Barth, faith is God's gracious gift, not human work. So justification is by grace and through faith alone. Barth presents a positive evaluation of the Reformation as follows:

> The strength of the Reformation exposition of righteousness by faith alone consisted in a word in this, that it saw and made plain that the living Jesus Christ – and His righteousness as man's righteousness – is the scarlet thread which runs through Galatians and therefore through the rest of Holy Scripture ... That is why in the substance of our understanding of this matter we definitely have to take our stand with them.[19]

If we acknowledge that the doctrine of justification by faith alone is a hallmark of evangelical theological tradition, then Barth should be embraced as an evangelical theologian.

6. *Sola Crucis*

'The cross alone is our theology.' By saying this, Luther sharply distinguished *theologia crucis* from *theologia gloriae*. For Luther, the God of Jesus Christ is revealed in the paradox of the cross. Through the cross of suffering, humiliation and death, God discloses his power, glory and eternal life. God reveals himself in a paradoxical situation of the crucifixion of his beloved Son. Thus Luther 'deserves to be called a

---

[17] For a detailed discussion, see my article 'Creative Reappropriation: Barth's Use of Calvin in the Münster *Ethics* (1928/29)', *International Journal of Systematic Theology* 2.2 (July 2000), pp. 204–18.

[18] Barth, *Church Dogmatics*, IV/1, p. 617.

[19] Ibid., IV/1, p. 642.

theologian, who comprehends the visible and manifest things of God seen through suffering and the cross'.[20]

While Luther stressed the theological implications of the cross, Calvin emphasized ethical implications of the cross. Calvin argued that the sum of the Christian life is the denial of ourselves, and bearing the cross is a part of self-denial. For Calvin, Christians are to take up their cross, as followers of Christ. The cross leads Christians to perfect trust in God's power and permits them to experience God's faithfulness. The cross, Calvin claims, gives Christians hope for the future by training them to patience and obedience.[21]

As George Hunsinger has argued:

> another powerful theme that Barth absorbed from Luther involves the theology of the cross ... The God of the New Testament has been belatedly rediscovered as a God of suffering love. This striking rediscovery has arisen, it would seem, largely from the impulse of Karl Barth, and the most important source for Barth in the history of theology was undoubtedly Martin Luther.[22]

In an echo of Luther, Barth stated, 'in this humiliation God is supremely God, that in this death he is supremely alive, that He has maintained and revealed His deity in the passion of his man as His eternal Son'.[23] Barth accepted Luther's insights that God reveals himself through paradoxes.

Barth dealt with the theme of bearing the cross in the context of his discussion of sanctification in the *Church Dogmatics* IV/2. For Barth, the cross is an 'indispensable element in any Christian doctrine of sanctification'.[24] In echo of Calvin, Barth stated, 'we refer to the cross which everyone who is sanctified in Jesus Christ, and therefore every Christian, has to bear as such, the people of God in the world being ordained to bear it'.[25] For Barth, Christians must bear the cross since Christ, their Lord and Master, suffered on the cross. Barth made an appreciative comment on Calvin:

> Calvin was at his best in this context. In what has to be thought and said concerning the Christian's cross, it is not for him a question of manufacturing

---

[20] *Luther's Works* (American edition) (St Louis/Philadelphia: Concordia/Fortress, 55 vols, 1955–86), vol. 31, p. 52.

[21] Calvin, *Institutes of the Christian Religion*, III.vii, viii.

[22] Hunsinger, *Disruptive Grace*, p. 287.

[23] Barth, *Church Dogmatics*, IV/1, pp. 246–7.

[24] Ibid., IV/2, p. 598.

[25] Ibid., IV/2, p. 599.

a violent paradox, but of an *altius conscendere*; of the recognition of the point where the sanctification of man points beyond itself from its root in the Holy One.[26]

If we acknowledge that the centrality of the cross is a hallmark of evangelical tradition, then Barth should be viewed as an evangelical theologian.

7. *Soli Deo Gloria*

Luther repeatedly affirmed that sinners are justified before God through faith and by grace alone. So, only God can be glorified for the work of salvation. God would not give his glory to any other people or gods. Salvation is given to sinners as a gift, so they must praise and glorify God alone. Salvation is not a human achievement, so human beings should not be glorified for their salvation. God does everything for the salvation of human sinners.

Calvin accepted Luther's profound insights into the gospel of grace. He repeatedly argued that the creation proclaims God's glorious wisdom and power. For Calvin, natural order is the theatre or mirror of God's glory. Human beings have been created to know, serve, enjoy and glorify God alone.

Although Barth did not use frequently the phrase *soli deo gloria*, it is not difficult to confirm that he would agree with Luther and Calvin that only God should be honoured and glorified for his work of salvation. For example, discussing the reality and possibility of the knowledge of God in *Church Dogmatics* II/1, Barth affirms that the possibility of human knowledge of God is totally dependent on God's sovereign and gracious determination to let human beings know him.

8. The Priesthood of All Believers

Luther advocated the principle of the priesthood of all believers by stating as follows:

> Christ is a priest together with all his Christians ... This priesthood cannot be made or given by ordination. Here no one is made a priest. He must be

---

[26] Ibid., IV/2, p. 606.

born a priest and bring it with him as the inheritance with which he has been born. The birth of which I am speaking is the birth of water and the Spirit. Through this all Christians become priests of a great high priest, children of Christ and fellow heirs with him.[27]

Luther based his idea of the priesthood of all believers on several important texts of the Bible, such as 1 Peter 2:5 and 2:9. Since all Christians are royal priests of God, they enjoy privileges to 'stand before God, pray for others, intercede with and sacrifice ourselves to God and proclaim the Word to one another'.[28] Christians do not need any human mediators or intermediaries since all Christians with no exception have become priests through faith in Christ. Christ alone is our mediator. Christians united with Christ, who is the head of the church, participate in his priesthood. The church as the community of believers enjoys the privileges of priesthood. As a community of priesthood, the church can have access to and worship God in spirit and truth.

Karl Barth wholeheartedly accepted the Reformers' idea of the priesthood of all believers and expanded it in accordance with his own theological presuppositions. He advocated the idea of the theologianhood of all believers. He believed that every Christian should be regarded as a theologian because every Christian has been called to know and have relationship with God. For him, 'theology is a function of the Church'[29] as a community of believers. The church as a community of saints 'produces' theology.[30] Barth continues to argue:

> The Church confesses God as it talks about God. It does so first by its existence in the action of each individual believer. And it does so secondly by its specific action as a fellowship, in proclamation by preaching and the administration of the sacraments, in worship, in its internal and external mission including works of love amongst the sick, the weak and those in jeopardy.[31]

Just as all the members of the church are spiritual priests, so all the members of the church are theologians and dogmaticians. All Christians have privileges to be engaged with theological work, that is, listening to and proclaiming the Word of God. As Barth has stated:

---

[27] *Luther's Works*, vol. 40, p. 19ff.
[28] Althaus, *The Theology of Martin Luther*, p. 314.
[29] Barth, *Church Dogmatics*, I/1, p. 3.
[30] Ibid., I/1, p. 4.
[31] Ibid., I/1, p. 3.

theology is not a private subject for theologians only. Nor is it a private subject for professors. Fortunately, there have always been pastors who have understood more about theology than most professors. Nor is theology a private subject of study for pastors. Fortunately, there have repeatedly been congregation members, and often whole congregations, who have pursued theology energetically while their pastors were theological infants or barbarians. Theology is a matter for the church.[32]

If we acknowledge that the principle of the priesthood of all believers is one of major theological legacies of evangelical tradition, then we should embrace Barth as an evangelical theologian.

9. *Ecclesia Semper Reformanda*

'The church once reformed must be always reforming.' This is one of the most important and foundational insights of the Reformers. In particular, Calvin was emphatic upon this principle. He encouraged his disciples and descendants to continually be involved in the work of reformation because we cannot have the perfect church here on the earth. All individual Christians are in the process of being conformed to the image of Christ and all Christian churches are in the process of becoming the perfectly holy temple of God. So, Calvin understood the task of reformation not to be finished within the sixteenth century, but remaining until the second coming of the Lord Jesus Christ.

Karl Barth accepted this principle of *semper reformanda* wholeheartedly. He repeatedly stressed the ongoing need of reformation of the church. He had an historical consciousness that he was involved in another 'reformation' of the church through his theological and dogmatic engagement. So, he often compared his theological work in the twentieth century with the Reformer's theological work in the sixteenth century.

It is important to appreciate that Barth applied this principle to the task of theologization. In other words, he stressed the ongoing need of theological reformulation and revision. There is no absolutely perfect system of theology that does not need any revision or refinement. In this connection, it would be pertinent to quote one of his statements in regard to this idea:

---

[32] Karl Barth, *God in Action*, Elmer G. Homrighausen and Karl J. Ernst (trs) (New York: Round Table Press, 1963), pp. 56–7.

It is the case, that the recognition of the ecclesiastical authority of a teacher not only does not exclude but strictly demands a critical, and even a very critical attitude to him. When we hear him, that means that we have to pay attention to the lines of his exposition and make them our own. But when we do that, we cannot simply repeat what he has drawn. We have to copy it in responsibility to the Scriptures and confession which have spoken to us through him. And that means that we have to draw it out and develop it. And that means also that we have also not to listen to him: at those points, that is, where everything considered we do not find that this voice agrees with the voice of Scripture and the voices of the Church speaking independently in the confession. There can be as little question of a repristination of the teaching of Luther and Calvin as of the orthodoxy of the 17th century.[32]

This long passage shows the principle according to which Barth holds a general attitude toward the theological forefathers, including Calvin and Luther. Barth maintained a critical attitude toward Luther and Calvin because he believed that his own interpretation of Scripture and church confessions could be more faithful to Christianity than theirs. For Barth, the possibility of the theological advancement by the later generation must be conceded and promoted explicitly. All theological formulations and constructions are subject to the ongoing need of re-evaluation, revision and even rejection. For Barth, the standard against which the existent theological constructions must be evaluated is Scripture alone. Since no theological formulation can exhaust the entire teaching of Scripture, every theological formulation must be always in the process of revision.

10. The Importance of the Church as the Community of God

Luther put a great stress upon the importance of the church. For him, the church was the communion of saints (*communio sanctorum*), the body of Christ, the bride of Christ, the pillar of the truth and the family of God. He repeatedly emphasized the centrality of the church for Christians.

Calvin was also emphatic upon the essentiality of the church. Calvin accepted Cyprian of Carthage's idea that the church is the mother of the saints. For him, Christians whose spiritual Father is God should have the church as their mother. Calvin understood the church's major functions to be teaching, educating, training and nurturing believers on the basis

---

[32] Barth, *Church Dogmatics* I/2, pp. 618–19.

of the Word of God, that is, the Scripture. So he regarded the preaching ministry as the most crucial task of the church.

Karl Barth was also a church theologian. He was engaged with pastoral and preaching ministry for a long time in Geneva and Safenwil. In the context of his pastoral ministry, he rediscovered the primacy of the Word of God. In particular, Barth emphasized the communitarian character of the church. For him, the church was, more than anything else, the community of believers. It is also very important to appreciate that Barth understood theological work not to be the individual theologian's work but to be the church's work as a community. So he named his theological masterpiece 'Church Dogmatics' rather than 'Christian Faith' or 'Systematic Theology.' For Barth, dogmatics is a science that critically analyses and synthesizes the proclamation of the church as a community of faith. Barth also understood theology and dogmatics to be of service to the health of the church. He rejected the ideal of 'a purely academic theology'. For him, theology must play a role as a servant of the church. Theology must be connected with various ministries of the church.

For Barth, the church is neither a human organization nor a religious society. Rather, the church 'arises from the election, decision, and disposition of God toward man. In revelation they have become an event. There God meets men and communicates Himself to men.'[33] Barth also accepted Calvin's insights that the church exists where the Word of God is properly preached and heard. He argues:

> the constitution and preservation of the church rests in this, that man hears God. This is what makes it truly great and truly little. In the church man hears God because He has spoken, and he gives ear to what God has spoken. The church exists wherever this is done, even if it consists of only two or three persons.[34]

If we acknowledge that the centrality of the church is one of major emphases of evangelical theological tradition, then we should embrace Barth as one of the evangelical theologians.

11. The Ecumenical Character of the Church

The Roman Catholic polemic against Luther's Reforming movement was characterized by the accusation of Luther being a separatist. According to the polemic, Luther was advocating a schism, regarded as

---

[33] Barth, *Church Dogmatics* I/1, p. 21.
[34] Ibid., p. 22.

one of the most unpardonable sins. However, if we scrutinize historical evidences, we can easily refute the Roman Catholic polemic against Luther. Simply enough, Luther was never a separatist. He always strived to reform the church from within. Whenever he talked about his church, it meant the current Roman Catholic Church. There was no other church than the late medieval Roman Catholic Church for Luther. Although his church had fallen into moral corruption and spiritual confusion, Luther still loved his own church. And he repeatedly affirmed his intention to devote his life to the work of reformation of the current Roman Catholic Church. Although Luther's intention was clear, the Roman Catholic Church's response to Luther's reformation initiative was problematic. Luther was finally excommunicated and dismissed and his followers were condemned as heretics.

It is also important to remember that Calvin was a genuinely ecumenical theologian. As F. Wendel has stated:

> Calvin was much preoccupied with the unity of the visible Church. This unity existed between all the Churches that based themselves upon the pure Gospel, whatever differences there might be among them concerning customs, ceremonies and organization. Even divergences of doctrine should not necessarily break this unity.[35]

As is well known, Philipp Melanchthon, who was a close colleague of Luther, was a close friend of Calvin. On many occasions, Calvin strived to bring doctrinal unity or consensus between the Lutheran church and the Reformed church during the sixteenth-century Reformation. Calvin believed in the crucial importance of maintaining unity, both external and internal, between the churches. In particular, Calvin did not give up in his effort to produce a doctrinal formulation of the Sacraments, agreeable to both the Lutheran and the Reformed church.

Karl Barth, more than anything else, was an ecumenical theologian. As Clifford Green has stated:

> The burgeoning ecumenical movement enlisted his interest and help, particularly for the assemblies of the World Council of Churches in Amsterdam (1948) and Evanston (1954); he took a lively and hopeful interest in the Second Vatican Council, studying all its documents, and visited the Vatican in 1966.[36]

---

[35] F. Wendel, *Calvin: The Origins and Development of his Religious Thought*, Philip Mairet (tr.) (New York: Harper & Row, 1963), p. 310.

[36] Clifford Green (ed.), *Karl Barth: Theologian of Freedom* (Minneapolis: Fortress Press, 1991), p. 21.

12. The Idea of Calling

Both Luther and Calvin were emphatic upon the idea of calling. They rejected the traditional Roman Catholic idea that only priests, monks and nuns have special callings and vocations from God. Rather, Luther and Calvin universalized the idea of calling, arguing that all stations of life must be regarded as divine callings. For Luther and Calvin, not only specifically religious service but also general jobs and careers must be regarded as God's sacred callings. By working faithfully in his or her vocation, every Christian can serve, please and glorify God. Just as all Christians are spiritual priests, so all Christians have sacred callings. As Paul Althaus has stated, 'since God has established and ordered our vocation, the works which we do in our vocation are pleasing to him'.[37]

Following the Reformers' foundational insights, Barth put a special stress upon the idea of calling. But Barth creatively expanded the idea of calling into one of the major aspects of Christian life, which forms the concentrated midpoint between justification and sanctification. As William Stacy Johnson has stated:

> in his earlier treatment of creation Barth had also spoken of vocation, but only in the broad sense of pursuing an occupation or a particular form of work (*Beruf*). Here in IV/3 the meaning is different. Here vocation is not, in the first sense, the calling to be a monk or a minister but the calling to be a Christian.[38]

This means that, although Barth appreciated the Reformers' fundamental understanding about the importance of the general idea of calling, he creatively and innovatively extended the idea into a new concept. Just as he universalized the idea of 'being a theologian' by advocating the principle of the theologianhood of all believers, so he universalized the concept of 'being called by God'. For him, every Christian, without exception, is called to be a true Christian in his or her life. In other words, every Christian is given a vocation to be a true and faithful witness to the gospel of grace revealed in Jesus Christ.

---

[37] Paul Althaus, *The Ethics of Martin Luther*, Robert C. Schultz (tr.) (Minneapolis: Fortress Press, 1972), p. 41.

[38] William Stacy Johnson, *The Mystery of God: Karl Barth and the Postmodern Foundations of Theology* (Louisville: Westminster John Knox, 1997), p. 144.

13. Concluding Remarks

In evangelical theological circles there has been a dispute over the question of whether Barth should be embraced to be an evangelical theologian or not. Brothers and sisters in the conservative Reformed theological camp have been criticizing the demerits and dangers of Barth's theology. One good example would be Cornelius Van Til, who accused Barth of new modernism. Besides, Barth's view of Scripture as human witness to revelation and his allegedly universalistic tendency have been the objects of criticism.

Even though we could appreciate the value and validity of those critiques, it seems undeniable that Barth's theology embodies numerous aspects of evangelical theological ideals. As I have argued in this paper, Barth learned many valuable lessons from Luther and Calvin, although he was not a slavish imitator or duplicator of the Reformers. In sum, he was an innovative refiner and a creative developer of the Reformers' evangelical legacy.

9

An Evangelical Narrative Christology for a Religiously Plural World

Gabriel Fackre

'Who do people say I am?' Jesus' question was the subject of the 1995 Wheaton College colloquy of 'evangelicals and postliberals in conversation'.[1] Alister McGrath and I were the initial team of evangelical presenters in dialogue with postliberals George Lindbeck and George Hunsinger. In the closing panel, I asked Professor Lindbeck about the saving significance of confessing Christ: 'I want to stay on this one more inch: Does the proclamation of the gospel ... have soteric weight for the postliberal project? Or is it something else? I think that's what Alister was pressing ...'[2]

This chapter is a continuation of that Christological inquiry by way of an evangelical reading of the biblical narrative that both parties in that conversation put to the fore. More specifically, it is an evangelical narrative Christology against the background of today's religious pluralism, with a firm commitment to the saving particularity – the 'soteric weight' – of Jesus Christ, to which Alister McGrath has so faithfully witnessed in his writings and his life.[3]

The religious response to 9/11 sharpens the question of our commitment to the salvation wrought in Jesus Christ. It came to the fore in the rush to generic prayer by many Christians in interfaith services and other settings out of a fear of the religious antagonisms that the attack on

---

[1] Timothy R. Phillips and Dennis L. Okholm (eds), *The Nature of Confession: Evangelicals & Postliberals in Conversation* (Downers Grove: InterVarsity Press, 1996).

[2] Ibid., p. 252.

[3] The following is an adaptation of a paper delivered at the 2002 meeting of the American Academy of Religion in the Christian Theological Research Fellowship.

the Twin Towers might generate. No offence given to fellow mourners, Muslim, Jewish or otherwise, as would be the case if we interceded 'in Jesus' name'? No talk of 'the scandal of particularity', following the advice of *New York Times* columnist Thomas Friedman, who asks, 'Can Islam, Christianity and Judaism know that God speaks Arabic on Fridays, Hebrew on Saturdays and Latin on Sundays?'[4] If poll results are to be believed, the 2002 *US News/PBS Religion & Ethics Newsweekly* findings confirm this confidence in an indulgent and multilingual deity.[5] Widespread is a 'plural shock' that makes for Christological heart failure.

A comment in passing on the irony entailed in this current relativist orthodoxy. Christians whose interfaith sympathies prompt generic prayer, or alternately, hold that God gives equal linguistic time to these three Near Eastern faiths, actually demean the other religions they are seeking to honour. By disallowing particularity, we deny to them the universal epistemological and soteriological claims that make them what they are.[6] Generosity to the religious 'other' has to do with *how* we make such claims, not foregoing them, speaking the truth in love, not hate, with a commensurate listening to the prayers and testimonies of alternate faiths.

Of a piece with our faith is that well chosen 'the' of John 4:42[7] – Jesus Christ, *'the* Saviour of *the* world'[8] – for all, not the 'for me' or 'for us' of

---

[4] Thomas L. Friedman, 'The Real War', *New York Times*, 27 November 2001.

[5] Detailed in Jeffrey Shetler, 'Faith in America', *U.S. News and World Report* 132.14 (6 May 2002), pp. 40–9.

[6] As in S. Mark Heim's insightful critique of a pluralist threesome, Wilfred Cantwell Smith, John Hick and Paul Knitter, in *Salvations: Truth and Difference in Religion* (Maryknoll, New York: Orbis, 1995), pp. 13–126.

[7] The biblical citations throughout are from the NRSV.

[8] The issue of 'the' was noted by Al Krass in earlier debates on religious pluralism, as in his comment 'In the minds of the early Christians there was no doubt but that *their* Lord was *the* Lord' in 'Accounting for the Hope that is in Me' in Donald G. Dawe and John B. Carman (eds), *Christian Faith in a Religiously Plural World* (Maryknoll, New York: Orbis, 1978), p. 158. See also Russell F. Aldwinkle, *Jesus –A Savior or The Savior?* (Macon: Mercer University Press, 1982). Diane Eck's recent work, *A New Religious America: How a Christian Country has now become the World's most Religiously Diverse Nation* (San Francisco: Harper, 2001) is an argument for removing the 'the', indeed, from all the claims of the Johannine text to be discussed. Her evidence for the extensiveness of the change in the new America in terms of the number of adherents of other religions is directly challenged by the recent detailed study by Tom W. Smith, 'Religious Diversity in America: The

today's modernisms and postmodernisms. Here is a universal truth claim for Christ's scandalous particularity.[9] But Jesus, the Saviour of the world from what? The answer can be found in another Johannine text, 'I am the way, and the truth, and the life. No one comes to the Father except through me' (Jn. 14:6). This encompassing verse is the declaration that Jesus is the way/*hodos*/path that God makes into the world to save us from sin, thereby bringing *reconciliation* with God; to rescue us from error, bringing the *truth* of the knowledge of God, *revelation*; to deliver us from death, bringing *life* with God in all its aspects, *redemption*.[10] Of such is the work of the Saviour, the last two derivative from the first, following theologically the epexegetical role in the text of *aletheia* and *zoe* vis-à-vis the primary predicate, *hodos*.[11]

What of this three-fold claim in the midst of today's religiously plural world? It provides us with an illuminating framework for interpreting a range of perspectives in the current theological debate. Each, in its own fashion, takes a position on how Jesus Christ is reconciler, revealer and

---

[8] *(continued)* Emergence of Muslims, Buddhists, Hindus and Others', National Opinion Research Center, University of Chicago, Internet available. Generalizing from a multitude of recent surveys and studies, Smith concludes: 'This indicates that non-Judaic-Christian religions are much smaller than frequently cited high-end estimates and have hardly transformed the religious landscape as much as often portrayed … Non-Judeo-Christian religions make up a small, but growing share of America's religious mosaic. In 1973–1980 the General Social Survey (GSS) indicated that they accounted for 0.8% of the adult population. This grew to 1.3% in 1981–1990 and 2.6% in 1990–2000 … The Muslim population is commonly overestimated by a factor of 3–4 … Impressive as the actual changes in non-traditional religions have been, they can not match these and many related claims about the growth and size of these religions' (pp. 5, 1, 4).

[9] Kathryn Tanner notes the transformation in contemporary theology of Luther's *pro me* from its focus on 'a dimension of the reality of Christ's working' to the 'modern penchant for making questions of human subjectivity paramount'. Kathryn Tanner, 'Jesus Christ' in Colin Gunton (ed.), *The Cambridge Companion to Christian Doctrine* (Cambridge: Cambridge University Press, 1999), pp. 253, 264. In the case being here considered, the subjectivity is given a postmodern turn expressed in its pop phrase, 'it works for me' (while something very different may 'work for you').

[10] The distinction between 'reconciliation' and 'redemption' follows, roughly, that made by Karl Barth in his *Church Dogmatics*. A detailed exegesis of this verse is found in Gabriel Fackre, *The Christian Story: A Pastoral Systematics – Authority: Scripture in the Church for the World* (Grand Rapids: Eerdmans, 1987), vol. 2, pp. 254–341.

[11] The case made by Raymond Brown and others. See Fackre, *The Christian Story*, vol. 2, p. 262.

redeemer: where the reconciling *deed* is done, where *disclosure* of the same is made, where *deliverance* happens. The diversity of views goes well beyond the familiar but inadequate typology of exclusivism, inclusivism and pluralism. After a thumbnail sketch of each, with documentation in the endnotes, I shall develop the last one, an evangelical 'narrative' view of the person and work of Christ. In what follows, the use of taxonomy, a chart, pictorials, alliteration, metaphor and the master metaphor, story, reflect my long-time effort in 'pastoral systematics', striving to make the complexities of the discipline accessible to working clergy.[12]

1. A Range of Current Views[13]

1.1. *Pluralist Perspectives*

The first five views are 'pluralist' in that they put to the fore a commonality shared by Christ with other religions.

Common Core
At the centre of all the great religions of humankind is found a common core of divine (however conceived) doing, disclosing and delivering. Each faith approaches it through its own heroes, expresses it in its own language, celebrates it in its own rituals, formulates it in its own rules of behaviour and passes it on in its own communal forms. While the rhetoric of each religion may claim that its way, truth and life are for all, these absolutist professions are, in fact, 'love talk', the metaphors of commitment, not the metaphysics of reality. Jesus is, therefore, *'my* Saviour', not *'the* Saviour'. In pop idiom, 'you do your thing and I'll do mine'. Christian faith and other religions are different routes to the same core Reality. Often added as a test of validity is the norm of ethical fruitfulness, judged to be universal. Thus a C is assigned to each of the three claims in the accompanying chart.[14]

---

[12] A chart accompanies the presentation.

[13] This more complex spectrum of views began with an early sifting and sorting in 'The Scandals of Particularity and Universality', *Midstream* 22/1 (January 1983), pp. 32–52 and runs to a recent version in 'Christ and Religious Pluralism: the Current Debate', *Pro Ecclesia* 12/4 (Fall 1998), pp. 389–95.

[14] The 'love talk' characterization is that of Krister Stendahl in 'Notes from Three Biblical Studies' in Gerald H. Anderson and Thomas F. Stransky (eds), *Christ's Lordship and Religious Pluralism* (Maryknoll, New York: Orbis,

Common Quest

Perspective 2 makes no claim for a reachable core, as perspective 1 does. Postmodern ambiguity rather than modern foundational certainty is the order of the day. Religions are quests for self-understanding, not paths to Reality. Like the relativism of the common core view, this too is describable in popular idiom as 'different strokes for different folks'. Unlike it, perspective 2 judges that the common quest provides no way to an ultimate truth and life. Rather, 'my Saviour' is the profession and practice of 'what works for me' in the midst of my day-to-day penultimacies; a pragmatic test in a postmodern world for what is self-referentially adequate. Thus all the Cs are followed by question marks.[15]

Common Pool

Like its predecessors, perspective 3 gives pride of place to religious commonalities, but seeks to respect the uniqueness of a religion and not dissolve it into a common core, contra perspective 1, and insists that such is in touch with Reality, not just involved in a quest for it as in perspective 2. It does this by maintaining that each is its own distinct reconciling way to ultimate Reality, disclosing some needed aspect of ultimate truth, delivering its devotees to saving life through its own means. The way of Christ grants to Christians access to Reality, offers a distinct illuminating take on the truth, and delivers ultimate life through its unique portal. The challenge is to pool the best from each with the goal of a 'world faith'. Thus a C is assigned to each, but an add-on revelatory P of particularity in revelation, recognizing the contribution Christ makes to a fuller disclosure.[16]

---

[14] (*continued*) 1981), pp. 13–15. A terse formulation of the core as the 'pattern of the new being encoded 'in the name of Jesus' for Christians, but in other names for other religions' appears in the Dawe essay, 'Christian Faith in a Religiously Plural World' in Donald G. Dawe and John B Carman (eds), *Christian Faith in a Religiously Plural World* (Maryknoll, New York: Orbis, 1978), pp. 13–33. John Hick, Wilfred Cantwell Smith and Paul Knitter probably are the best known twentieth-century exponents of this view, others expressing it in one form or another in John Hick and Paul Knitter (eds), *The Myth of Christian Uniqueness* (Maryknoll, New York: Orbis, 1987).

[15] See Richard Rorty, *Objectivism, Relativism and Truth: Philosophical Papers* (Cambridge: Cambridge University Press, 1991), vol. 1 for the philosophical underpinnings of this view.

[16] Although John Hick's writings can be associated with variations on View 1, his argument in *Death and Eternal Life* New York: Harper & Row, 1976) falls into this category. Gavin D'Costa has traced Hick's developing point(s) of view in *John Hick's Theology of Religions* (Lanham: University Press of America, 1987).

Common Community

Challenging the individualism of the foregoing options, the common community view sees us as creatures of formative cultures. Our communal destiny is normative for us as well as descriptive of us, a call to know who we are, and live out of the traditions in which we are immersed. For Christians, this means clarity about our defining characteristics, knowing our ecclesial language and lore and respecting our community's rules of believing and behaving. Christ can be no other than the way, truth and life for us. Given our postmodern circumstances, we can lay no claim to reaching ultimate Reality through our way, or assert such to be true and saving for everyone. Hence, Christians are to 'keep the faith', but acknowledge that they share with others the common condition of ambiguity, with a question mark placed after each CP.[17]

Common Range

The fifth perspective shares the pluralist premise of the former options. The religions are on common ground in matters of way, truth and life, all providing reconciliation, revelation and redemption. However, when it comes to disclosure of the Really Real – accessible here too, as in perspectives 1 and 3 – Jesus' light is the brightest and best. To change the figure, Jesus is on the same mountain range as Mohammad, Buddha, Moses – or, for that matter, other great prophets from Socrates to Gandhi and Martin Luther King, Jr – but is the Mount Everest among the peaks of human experience. The difference is in degree, not kind, for Christ offers the same saving benefits as other high religions. A higher degree of truth is signified by placing a P before the C of the revelatory category.[18]

---

[17] Another 'narrative' view, associated with Hans Frei and George Lindbeck and a notable company of their students, is regularly under discussion as in the critique by I.M. Wallace, 'The New Yale Theology', *Christian Scholars Review* 17.2 (December 1987), pp. 154–70. However, Bruce Marshall has shown that Lindbeck's communal narrativity does include a claim of 'correspondence to the real order'. 'Aquinas as Postliberal Theologian', *The Thomist* 53.3 (July 1989), pp. 353–402. For the struggle of postliberal theologians to come clear on this issue, see Garrett Green (ed.), *Scriptural Authority and Narrative Interpretation* (Philadelphia: Fortress Press, 1987).

[18] See W. Norman Pittinger's oft-referenced development of degree Christology in *The Word Incarnate* (New York: Harper & Brothers, 1959) and his later development of this view vis-à-vis the specifics of religious pluralism in 'Can a Christian be a Buddhist Too?' and 'Can a Buddhist be a Christian Too?', *Japanese Religions* 11.2 & 3 (September 1980), pp. 35–55.

1.2. Particularist Perspectives

The next five views declare for the definitive singularity of the deed God does in Jesus Christ to reconcile the world. How that impacts disclosure and deliverance distinguishes the perspectives from one another.

Anonymous Particularity

Only at one point in human history does God come among us to do the necessary deed of reconciliation. Jesus is the 'absolute Saviour' not a relative one, the singular incarnate Word, reconciler of God and the world. However, this particularity has a universal scope. The power from the Christological centre of history radiates everywhere in incognito fashion, giving all humans and their diverse religious traditions a sense, to one degree or another, of the divine purposes, the option of responding aright and the offer of grace to do so. With that right response, they become 'anonymous Christians'. While so granting the universal possibilities of both revelation and redemption, only in the privileged church of Christians is there the clear knowledge of the divine and assurance of the path to salvation.[19] Thus a P for reconciliation, a PC for revelation, and a PC for redemption.

Revelatory Particularity

God comes to reconcile the alienated world in only one way and gives ultimate truth only in one place: in Jesus Christ. This divine deed is so radical that all human beings are reconciled to God in this central event, dying with Christ in his humiliation and rising with him in his exaltation. The church is uniquely given the revelation of this truth and called to get the message out to the human race of 'virtual believers' so reconciled. Are all then finally redeemed by the reconciling way of God in Christ? We have a right to *hope* that is so based on the deed done, but not to assert a universal homecoming as an article of faith. Only the

---

[19] Expounded in Karl Rahner, *Theological Investigations*, Margaret Kohl (tr.) (New York: Crossroads 1981), vol. XVII, pp. 24–50 and his *Foundations of Christian Faith: An Introduction to the Idea of Christianity*, William V. Dych (tr.) (New York: Seabury Press, 1978), pp. 138–321. A variation on this theme is developed in evangelical idiom by John Sanders in the sections of John Sanders (ed.), *What About Those Who Have Never Heard? Three Views on the Destiny of the Unevangelized* (Downers Grove: InterVarsity Press, 1995).

sovereign God decides the final outcome. Hence a solitary P appears at both way and truth and a C? at life.[20]

Pluralist Particularity

Christ is the defining particular way that God makes into the world, giving a unique truth and special saving life. Yet the generosity of God provides in different religions other ways, truths and aspects of ultimate life ('religious fulfilments' in conformity with their desires). Christians believe that the one to whom they testify is the supreme deed, disclosure and deliverance of the Triune God, inclusive of the partial goals of other religions, and seek to witness that superiority to all. A primary P is placed under the way alongside a secondary C, and similarly ordered PCs under truth and life.[21]

Imperial Particularity

Christ is the particular way God came into the world to bring the only truth and only saving life to be had. The elect and/or those who decide for Christ during their time on earth know the truth and are saved. Those passed over and/or who do not decide for Christ perish eternally. Christians are charged to preach the gospel so that those called may respond in saving faith. Therefore a singular P as deed, a primal P under truth with a C that recognizes non-salvific general revelation and a solitary P under deliverance.[22]

---

[20] Karl Barth's *Church Dogmatics*, 4/1–4 is the most detailed outworking of this view, with *apokatastasis* as an 'article of hope' described in *Church Dogmatics*, 4/3.1, G.W. Bromiley (tr.) (Edinburgh: T. & T. Clark, 1961), pp. 477–8. Whether Barth departs significantly from his revelatory exclusivity with his discussion of 'free communications' and 'parables of the Kingdom' in *Church Dogmatics* 4/3.1 is a matter of continued debate. For a discussion of this see the writer's *The Doctrine of Revelation: A Narrative Interpretation of Revelation* (Edinburgh/ Grand Rapids: Edinburgh University Press/Eerdmans, 1997), pp. 136–7, 143–5.

[21] A view given prominence initially by Joseph DiNoia in 'The Universality of Salvation and the Diversity of Religious Aims', *World Mission* (Winter, 1981–1982), pp. 4–15, but developed in detail by S. Mark Heim in his two works, *Salvations* and *The Depth of the Riches: A Trinitarian Theology of Religious Ends* (Grand Rapids: Eerdmans, 2001).

[22] With a qualification here and there, but substantially a detailed exposition of the imperial views, is Ronald H. Nash's *Is Jesus the Only Savior?* (Grand Rapids: Zondervan, 1984), and his sections in Sanders (ed.), *What About Those Who Have Never Heard?*

Narrative Particularity[23]

A narrative is 'an account of characters and events in a plot moving over time and space through conflict toward resolution'.[24] The defining deed, disclosure and deliverance take place in the central chapter of a grand narrative that runs from creation to consummation. But as the story of God, the chapters that lead up to and away from the centre play their role in the plot of reconciliation, revelation and redemption, as reflected in a P for way, a PC for truth and a PC? for life. To that centrepoint we turn, the person and work of Jesus Christ, situating its exposition narratively, with a quick comparison at appropriate points of the views just canvassed.

2. Narrative Particularity: The Person and Work of Christ

Locating who Christ is (the person) and what Christ does (the work) in the setting of the biblical macro-story provides a framework for grappling with the concerns of the pluralist options without eroding the scandalous particularity of John 14:6. Jesus Christ is *the* Saviour of *the* world. At the same time, the story requires both a width and length to the divine mercy that makes for a 'generous orthodoxy' in a religiously plural world.

The Christian story begins with a prologue, the eternal being of the tripersonal God. The loving Life Together of Father, Son and Holy Spirit – the immanent Trinity – sets the stage for a journey toward a comparable end *ad extra*, the unfolding of the plan and plot of the economic Trinity. Stated in terms of its background portrayal, the drama happens in the Grand Narrative of Scripture, from creation to consummation. In that story, who God is is disclosed by what what God does.[25] With

---

[23] The postmodern veto of metanarratives of the sort to be discussed is rejected for these reasons: (1) Postmodernity as an intellectual construct is itself a metanarrative. What sauce for the goose is sauce for the gander; (2) The imperiousness and violence attributed to metanarratives depend on the contents of same, not their character as cosmic story. Postmodern ideology has its own history of imperialism when it achieves power, as in sections of academia. J. Richardson Middleton and Brian J. Walsh, *Truth is Stranger Than it Used to Be: Biblical Faith in a Postmodern Age* (Downers Grove: InterVarsity Press, 1995), pp. 75–9 and *passim* take up some of these matters.

[24] Gabriel Fackre, 'Narrative Theology: An Overview', *Interpretation* 37.4 (October 1983), p. 341.

[25] Gabriel Fackre, *The Christian Story: A Narrative Interpretation of Basic Christian Doctrine* (Grand Rapids: Eerdmans, 1996³), vol. 1, pp. 245–6.

regard to the person of Christ, the tale told in the Johannine language of Theophilus of Antioch's is illuminating. It begins with the indwelling Word of the divine Life Together, the *logos endiathetos*.[26]

Reflecting the divine being and purpose, God wills the coming to be of a covenant partner, the outgoing work of the *logos prophorikos*, sourced by the Father and empowered by the Spirit. Thus, chapter 1 of the story: the world is brought out of nothing into created being for a life together with God, and with itself. Within creation, the creature with the human face is in special relationship and responsibility to God (Gen. 1:26, 2:15–17), called and capacitated (the double meaning of the *imago Dei*)[27] to respond in kind to God's loving reach. (So God and Adam as portrayed on the ceiling of the Sistine Chapel.) The invitation to life together with the Creator includes a comparable outreach to one another (Gen. 1:27, 2:18) and to creation. Thus the charge: 'Adam, trust and serve God', do not 'play God'. (Gen. 3:5). Except for the ministry of angels, whatever an atom, an animal or other created beings are given and called to be, as in Barth's wise agnosticism, we can only guess.[28]

As the story unfolds, what God wills for us and what we will toward God go on collision course. So comes 'sin', the self's idolatrous curve inward (Luther) rather than outward toward God, the human other and creation itself. The result is a life self-sufficently *alone*, not a life together (Gen. 3:6–13). Chapter 2 is about the stumble and fall of the world, our alienation from God and its derivative estrangements from neighbour and nature (Gen. 3:14–24). Thus the Christian problematic of sin: our

---

[26] See Theophilus of Antioch, *Ad Autolycum*, for the journey of the *logos* to be tracked here. William Placher notes, however, that ' "Wisdom" … has some claim to be the earliest term Christians used for the relation of Jesus Christ to the one he called "Father" ' and that 'in a number of texts from shortly before the time of Jesus, "Word" and "Wisdom" are used more or less interchangeably'. William C. Placher, *Jesus the Savior: The Meaning of Jesus Christ for Christian Faith* (Louisville: Westminster John Knox, 2001), pp. 22, 25. Given the feminine gender of Wisdom and thus its deconstruction of a too simple masculine characterization of the Triune God, and the precedent of interchangeability with Word, there is no reason to deny the journey of the second person as describable also as that made by Wisdom. It may have special resonance when considering the work of common grace. For all that, we honour the insight of Theophilus by using his own language.

[27] Fackre, *The Christian Story*, vol. 1, pp. 68–71.

[28] On the modesty counselled, see Karl Barth, *Church Dogmatics*, 3/2, pp. 78, 374, 395, 521. On the ministry of angels, see the writer's 'Angels Heard and Demons Seen', *Theology Today* 51/3 (October 1994), pp. 345–58, much in debt, again, to Barth.

breach of the intended relationship between God and the world and the loss of its accompanying light and life. To turn the world around requires a saving way of reconciliation with God with its derivative revelation and redemption.

The purposes of God are stronger than our perverse powers. So chapter 3 in the story, the renewal of our Maker's bonding with the world. Its first phase is the covenant with Noah, the pledge of the long-suffering Creator to stay with creation even in its rebel state, signalled by the rainbow promise of divine perseverance (Gen. 9:12).[29] Sealing the promise is the giving of sufficient light and power to keep the Grand Narrative going forward.[30] Christologically viewed, this is the sustaining largesse of the *logos spermatikos* with a variety of gifts to know and do things that are true, good, beautiful and holy, a 'common grace' that discloses something of the path ahead and delivers its receivers from impediments on that journey (Gen. 9:1–7, 14:18–20; Heb. 7:1–17).[31] Amidst the distorting effects of the fall on our efforts to pursue that goal, genuine evidences of this preserving Word are manifest wherever truth enlightens and life is made livable. To anticipate, why would this universal grace not be at work in many and diverse ways within the world religions?

Chapter 3, part two in the narrative can be pictorially described as an end point of the rainbow that settles among a particular people. God makes a special covenant of grace with Abraham, whose graced faith makes him 'father of us all' (Rom. 4:17). This singular covenant includes its Mosaic form of the light of law and its Exodus deliverance of life for the chosen people, embodying the ministries of prophets, priests

---

[29] See David Novak, *Image of the Non-Jew in Judaism: An Historical and Constructive Study of the Noahide Laws* (Edwin Mellen Press, 1983). C.H. Dodd's durable study of 'the Noachian covenant' is in 'Natural Law and the Bible', *Theology* (May and June 1946), reprint. A recent review of Reformation thought on the natural law aspects of the Noachic covenant vis-à-vis aspects of the theology of Thomas Hooker is found in the monograph by W.J. Torrance Kirby, *The Theology of Richard Hooker in the Context of the Magisterial Reformation*, Studies in Reformed History and Theology 5 (Princeton: Princeton Theological Seminary, 2000). For an extended discussion of covenant with Noah as it relates to contemporary theologies, see Fackre, *The Doctrine of Revelation*, pp. 61–102.

[30] Anticipated in the time between the fall and Noachic covenant by the sustenance of the world to that point, interpretable as the broken but not destroyed *imago*, now confirmed and extended to the End by the covenant with Noah.

[31] For an interesting discussion of 'common grace' and the 'Melchizedek factor', see Gordon Spykman, *Refomational Theology: A New Paradigm for Doing Dogmatics* (Grand Rapids: Eerdmans, 1992), pp. 320–21, 424–7.

and kings, and the dream of a *shalom* to be. In Pauline retrospect, this people with its special graces of revelatory disclosure as well as covenantal deed and deliverance participates proleptically in the central scandal of particularity to come, warranting an anti-supersessionist understanding of the place of the Jewish people in Christian faith.[32] Indeed, the opened book of this people gives us the story we are telling, pointing, again in Christian retrospect, toward chapters yet to be.

In one Jew, a Galilean carpenter, the rainbow end becomes an intersection, a cruciform representation of the doctrine of the person and work of Christ: *incarnation* as the deep drive of God into our world, and *atonement* – at-one-ment – as the bringing together of the alienated parties to God's purposes.

3. Incarnation

An evangelical narrative interpretation of the incarnation, as given in the patristic formulation of the journey we are following, points to the *logos ensarkos*, the enfleshed Word. Theophilus' trajectory throughout is based on the prologue of John's narrativity with the metaphors of 'light' and 'life' we have borrowed from its account. Thus, 'in the beginning was the Word and the Word was with God and the Word was God … All things came into being through him … in him was life and the life was the light of all people … and the Word became flesh and lived among us …' Missing often in traditional and even credal accounts is the story's chapter on Israel (as in the prologue's references to Moses and the prophet John),[33] but otherwise, the path of the *logos* is that traversed in the story we are here following. Its contribution to a narrative interpretation of the person of Christ is its Trinitarian refinement of the who of the incarnation. Not the Father, not the Spirit, but the Son becomes flesh. The intersection of God with the world is the Word

---

[32] For commentary on the state of the question see 'A Symposium on *Dabru Emet*: A Jewish Statement on Christians and Christianity', *Pro Ecclesia* 11/1 (Winter 2002), pp. 5–19. For a review of current supersessionist and anti-supersessionist views, and the author's position, see 'The Place of Israel in Christian Faith' in Markus Bockmuehl and Helmut Burkhardt (eds), *Gott lieben und seine Gebote halten: In memoriam Klaus Bockmuehl* (Basel: Brunnen Verlag Giessen, 1991), pp. 21–38.

[33] The chapter missing in too much traditional Christian teaching has contributed to the terrible legacy of anti-Judaism. Interesting, however, Theophilus did see the *logos* at work in the Old Testament theophanies.

incarnate. For all that particularity, the Word is the Word of the Father, enfleshed by the power of the Spirit, and thus, the issue of the Father of the Son by the Holy Spirit.[34]

By the divine action Jesus Christ is 'true God from true God … incarnate from the Virgin Mary' (Nicene Creed). The second person of the Trinity 'became' Jesus of Nazareth (Jn. 1:14). No qualified or compromised entry of deity here.[35] With the multiple meanings of *logos* in the ancient world in mind, we can say the eternal Word, purpose, plan, reason, vision … came to dwell among us. The divine intention for creation's 'life together', the Word of the Life Together of the Triune God, lived and breathed in this Nazarene. His words and deeds embodied the *agape* and *shalom* that God is and wills. Nothing less than God among us can deal with the alienations to which we are heir.

As important as the divine initiative, no less consequential is the reality of the 'among' us and 'became' one of us. No illusory flesh here diminished or dissolved by deity, as the church's credos and definitions of the first four centuries of Christological debate were at pains to assert.[36] The Word-in-the-flesh meant God taking on our finitude: in matters of the mind not being a 'know-it-all' but rather learning to 'grow in wisdom'; in matters of the body, urinating and defecating, sweating in a carpenter shop and bleeding on a cross; in matters of the soul, wrestling with doubt on that same tree. The person of Christ is truly human as well as truly God, yet truly one, 'without confusion, without change, without distinction, without separation'.[37]

When lodged in a narrative framework these standard assertions of classical Christian faith have implications for our spectrum of options on the issues of religious pluralism. For one, the narrative reading is placed among the particularist views regarding the first rubric, 'way'. As the once-happened incarnate Word, Jesus Christ is the singular way God makes into our world to reconcile it to its Creator. Here is the decisive turning point in the story, God among us first-hand.

The Word made flesh, however, is no bolt from the blue. The *logos* is the architect of creation. The Word that 'was God … was in the

---

[34] A formulation (Moltmann) that attempts to maintain the Christological accent of the West, but recognize the parity of the Persons more clearly stated by the East's single procession.

[35] Contra the Ebionisms, Adoptionisms, Arianisms and Nestorianisms of the Christological controversies.

[36] Contra the Docetisms, Modalisms, Appolinarianisms and Monophysitisms of the same controversies.

[37] Formula of Chalcedon.

beginning with God [and] all things came into being through him'
(Jn. 1:1, 2, 3). The same Word, after the fall, graces the world with
Noah's rainbow. Wherever creation displays marks of its Creator,
visible by the preserving light and power of common grace, the second
person of the Trinity is the mediator of that disclosure. Wherever truth is
known or life made livable, the hidden Christ is present. This is a work
of the person, a matter to be developed in the section on the atonement.

The rainbow of universality, however, touches down at a point of
particularity. Two-thirds of Christian Scripture witness to the special
graces of disclosure and deliverance given to a chosen people. Who
Christ is and what Christ does cannot be understood or come to be without this trajectory toward the story's centre, recorded in the Hebrew
Scripture within the Christian Bible. Paul's declaration of Abraham as
the 'father' of faith and his assertion that 'the gifts and the calling' given
to this people are irrevocable place the Jewish people in unique relation
to God's saving purposes (Rom. 4:16, 11:29).[38] The final soteriological
implications will be taken up below.

The accomplishment of the purposes of God happens when the rainbow arc is driven deep at the particular point of one Jew. What is done in
this enfleshment of the Word is the work of Christ, the reconciliation of
the alienated parties to the divine purposes.

4. Atonement

The work of the person is to transform the condition of the world from
separation to communion. The central chapter of the Christian story
tells us that the at-one-ing charge from the Father to the Son by the Holy
Spirit is carried out in the life, death and resurrection of Jesus Christ.
From Bethlehem's person comes the work of Galilee, Calvary and Easter
morning. This micro-narrative, set within the context of the macro-
narrative we have been tracing, is our framework for interpreting the
doctrine of the atonement. That is, traditional concepts associated
with the doctrine, such as the three-fold office of Christ, redemption
accomplished and applied, the finished and continuing work of Christ,
and so on, are construed narratively, providing the perspective on the
issues of religious pluralism framed by John 14:6.

---

[38] Bockmuehl and Burkhardt (eds), *Gott lieben un seine Gebote halten.*

4.1. The Three-fold Office of Christ

The *munus triplex*, developed in detail by John Calvin but also in wide ecumenical usage,[39] provides a framework for interpreting the Jesus story, as it bears on the claims of reconciliation, revelation and redemption.

The Prophetic Office

The life of the prophet Jesus discloses who God is. His Galilean ministry is a demonstration of the agape/shalom of God. His being, his relationship to others, to creation and to the Father, his healings, his preaching and teaching concerning the yet/not yet reign of God, all bespeak and embody the Life Together that God is.

Prophecy is 'forth-telling' the Word about God encompassing the 'foretelling' of the outcome of the purposes of God in the kingdom to come. As such, the knowledge of the fullness of who God is and what God wills, hidden from view in a fallen world, is revealed in the prophetic ministry of Jesus, who as the Word enfleshed makes that ultimate disclosure. The first office, correlated narratively with the Galilean ministry, is the *revelation* of ultimate truth about God and the Kingdom of God, obscured elsewhere by the pervasive error of sin (more than the ignorance of finitude) that damages (but does not destroy) our *imago Dei*, making available the rudiments by a preserving grace. Only at the revelatory Centre are to be found the fundaments, the fullness of 'truth' in the prophetic office.[40]

The radical nature of the fall is such that the world is enraged by the presence in its midst of a loving Word over against all that the world is in its hates and hurts. Evoking that wrath, absolute love as 'burning coals' (Rom. 12:20), the prophetic office *exposes* the depth of human sin as well as *discloses* the heights of the divine *agape*. The life of the prophet ends in crucifixion. Yet the cross opens a new sub-chapter in the Jesus story. With it comes the priestly ministry.

---

[39] From John Calvin's *Institutes of the Christian Religion*, vol. 1, Henry Beveridge (tr.) (Grand Rapids, Michigan: Eerdmans, 1957), II.xv, pp. 425–32 to the Second Vatican Council's 'Decree on the Apostolate of the Laity' in Walter Abbott SJ (ed.), *Documents of Vatican II* (New York: Guild Press, 1966), p. 491 and *passim*.

[40] The three offices are themselves a 'life together' reflecting their Trinitarian origins. Hence, the priestly and royal ministries of Christ also participate in the prophetic office, and vice versa, even as each has its distinctive role. See Fackre, *The Christian Story*, vol. 1, pp. 149–50.

The Priestly Office

A priest sacrifices for sin. Jesus, our high priest, sacrifices for the sin of the world. This priest is like no other for he is the victim that he, the priest, lays on the altar. And, like no finite other, as God enfleshed on that altar, the victim-priest has an infinite capacity to confront and overcome the infinite magnitude of the world's sin. The person of Christ takes into the divine being the full measure of judgement we are due, and thus 'the cross in the heart of God' (Charles Dinsmore), the godly mercy that overcomes the divine wrath (Luther), the crucified God (Moltmann).[41] No God 'up there' exacting punishment on Jesus 'down here', as in pop piety or child abuse ideology,[42] but the crucified deity who takes away the sin of the world. Thus the Johannine assertion that Jesus is 'the way' that God, the Son, makes toward us in order to overcome sin and reconcile the world.

We linger a bit longer at this central office in wonder at what happened on the cross to turn the world around. Can a story Jesus tells shed light on the narrative of his own death? The tale of the running father and the returning son hints strongly of what was to come (Lk. 15:11–24). Where did the expected Semitic punishment of an ungrateful offspring go? Where else but into the father's own heart? There, acceptance absorbed anger in a suffering love that made for a spurt forward to greet the wayward offspring. And the parental run was on while the son was 'far off', an unconditional (*agape*) welcome, innocent of the whys and wherefores of the returner.

How can we not have here a portent of the divine mercy that on the cross takes into itself the divine judgement against sin? A Word that God's suffering love welcomes those who return in the faith that a sinner can be received? A trust in a spontaneous and unconditional *agape*? The tenth view of the saving work of Christ turns to story to express God's own story. And this small tale also illustrates the interpenetration of the offices of Christ, for the priestly and royal ministries are required to illuminate the latter, and the latter to interpret the former.

---

[41] In addition to the well-known work by Jürgen Moltmann, *The Crucified God*, R.A. Wilson and John Bowden (trs) (London: SCM Press, 1974), see also Richard Baukham, *God Crucified, Monotheism & Christology in the New Testament* (Grand Rapids: Eerdmans, 1999 and Carlisle: Paternoster Press, 1998).

[42] cf. Placher, *Jesus the Savior*, pp. 112–13.

The Royal Office

The accomplishment of the work of Christ requires confrontation with the 'last enemy', death. Death is mortality and more, including as it does all the sin, evil and suffering that militate against life. Easter morning announces the defeat of that final foe. The resurrection confirms the victory of the victim's sacrifice and gives assurance of the things hoped for, the world's future healing.

Regents rule their terrain. The resurrection announces that the kingdom will have its ruler, the divine–human person. Christ the risen king is the surety that reconciliation has come to be and that redemption, as the 'application' of its 'benefits' by the Holy Spirit, is assured. Christ is the deed that delivers as well as discloses. Thus the Johannine assertion that Christ is the defining 'life' as well as the way and the truth.

The threefold office makes possible a full-orbed understanding of the work of Christ as portrayed in the biblical account of this central chapter. It is an ecumenical formula that challenges the reductionisms that tend to be embodied in historic traditions, ones that focus exclusively on the prophetic Jesus who saves from error/ignorance, the priestly Jesus who saves from sin, and the royal Jesus who saves from death.

4.2. The Continuing Work

The work of Christ as revelation, reconciliation and redemption is accomplished in the life, death and resurrection of Jesus Christ. For the Grand Narrative to move toward its conclusion, the world must share in the consequences of the deed done. The 'finished work' requires a 'continuing work'; atonement accomplished moves to atonement applied. The ascension of Jesus Christ to the right hand of the Father extends the royal reign, stretching it toward the finale when Christ 'hands over' his rule to the Father (1 Cor. 15:24).

The ascended Christ continues all three ministries in the time between the times of Easter and Eschaton. Wherever the fruits of reconciliation – revelation and redemption – are given, Christ is present and active. Their central locale is described in the story of Pentecost.

On that Day, the ascent of Christ manifests itself by the descent of the Spirit, the light of the risen Son bursting toward us in tongues of fire settling upon disciples that, so graced, become apostles (Acts 2:1–4). The gift of *kerygma* given by Christ the prophet opens the mouth of Peter to tell the story (Acts 2:15–36). The charism of *leitourgia* given by Christ the priest empowers the community to celebrate the story in baptizing and breaking bread (Acts 2:41–42). So the church's means of grace – Word and sacrament – for disclosing the final truth of the reconciling deed of God in Christ, and offering ultimate life-giving deliverance to those who receive the Word audible and visible through justifying faith.

The gifts of *koinonia* and *diakonia* join *kerygma* and *leitourgia* in the continuing work of the in-Spirited Son of the Father (Acts 2:42, 44). As the sanctifying power of love that mirrors the Life Together of both God's being and doing, the life together of the Christian community and its service to the neighbour in need are charisms of the kingship of Christ that defeat death-dealing powers.

The continuing prophetic, priestly and royal work of Christ ranges over the world beyond the borders of church. Wherever any truth is disclosed, any life is granted by deliverance from evil and suffering, Jesus Christ exercises his three-fold office incognito (Mt. 25:31–46). The Noachic covenant is the gift of a Christological common grace, as earlier noted. So the New Testament assurance that God has 'not left himself without a witness in doing good ... so that they would search for God and perhaps grope for him and find him ...' (Acts 14:17, 17:27). Of such is the derivative disclosure and empowerment to pursue it of the 'absolute Saviour'. These gifts given by the hidden Christ are the temporal truth and life generously distributed so that the Grand Narrative can go forward to its goal. Common grace does not save the world from sin. Only one incarnate and atoning Way does that. And its reception by justifying faith is the only life worth living eternally. Documenting the distinction here made is an edition of *Cruden's Concordance*, which notes the two meanings of salvation in Scripture, 'deliverance from sin and its consequences', the basic Christian problematic, as distinguished from the sense we are describing here in the grace of preservation as 'preservation from trouble or danger'.[43] The Johannine 'life' in its ultimate sense as *eternal* life, here and hereafter – the creed's life *everlasting* – is the More not to be confused with the temporal life 'lasting' given by common grace.[44]

Christ's Noachic arc over our fallen world, with its universal grace, includes a rainbow of world religions, instruments of his preserving purposes. Within them are manifest truth that enlightens and life that empowers their adherents in the world's journey on its way, as measured by the norm of Christ.[45] In this respect, the narrative view is distinguished

---

[43] On the various meanings of salvation in Scripture, see Aldwinkle, *Jesus – A Savior or the Savior?* pp.19–85.

[44] Fackre, *The Christian Story*, vol. 1, pp. 190–207, 227–30.

[45] As measured by Christ, and also as potentially enriching our very understanding of Christ, drawing out what is implicit in his person and work, as Christian faith enters new contexts shaped by diverse religious traditions.

from perspective 7 with its denial of truth beyond the exclusive disclosure in the event of Christ and thus excision of the world's religions from the purposes of God. 'Common' grace, it should be noted, does not mean the sameness of religious truth known and done, given the variety of differing charisms available through this generous universality.[46] Contra perspective 9, 'general revelation' means a rich grace at work in the truth known and life given in the world's religions that keep the story going forward (as well as the universality of Christ's offer of salvation to be discussed in the consummation of the story). On the other hand, an evangelical narrative view of the gifts of these common Christological graces is tethered to the biblical storyline and does not make the speculative leap of perspective 8 that takes the humanly enriching religious insights and experiences (the 'horizontal' graces) into the trans-historical 'vertical' and eschatological realms as varied (albeit lesser) religious fulfilments; only a graced justifying faith can give eternal life. Nor can it raise the significance of common grace to offer anonymously the eternal deliverance claimed for such by perspective 6. In all cases, what measure of light and life are granted to any one world religion can only be judged by the defining disclosure at the centre of the story.[47] The wider ministries in the

---

[45] (*continued*) While the narrative perspective here developed differs from the point of view argued in *The Depth of the Riches* regarding the diversity of eternal religious fulfilments, based on a different judgement regarding the depth of the fall and its consequences, and the relation of the immanent to the economic Trinity, Heim, following A.F. Walls and L.O. Sanneh, lays out persuasively how 'translations' of the gospel in contexts shaped by other religions can enlarge the understanding of our own faith. Heim, *The Depth of the Riches*, pp. 139–140.

[46] Common grace and general revelation do not require equivalency of disclosure and deliverance as might be concluded from the language of 'common' and 'general'. The latter refer to the universal grace at work beyond the historical particularity of Jesus Christ, and can accommodate the idea of differing dimensions of that grace present in varied religious traditions, 'revealed types', as argued by Gerald McDermott in *Can Evangelicals Learn from World Religions?* (Downers Grove: InterVarsity Press, 2001), pp. 113–19.

[47] So Barth's helpful investigation of the same in *Church Dogmatics*, 4/3.1, pp. 125–8. Gerald McDermott also deploys this Christological norm, while giving attention to the 'light' God gives to other religions, one that can even enrich the understanding of the truth in Christian faith itself, drawing out its implications. See McDermott, *Can Evangelicals Learn from Other Religions?*, *passim*. By using the biblical distinction between the two forms of deliverance, this paper speaks of the 'life' possible as well in salvation from earthly evil through non-Christian religions.

continuing work of Christ are made possible by the once-happened accomplishment of atonement, the defeat of sin at the centre of the story in the life, death and resurrection of Christ.

4.3. The Consummating Work of Christ

The continuing work is consummated by Christ, the Hound of Heaven, who pursues us beyond the gates of death and to the very End. As the whole world has been reconciled by the saving way God has made into our midst, and is given the promise of God's universal salvific will (1 Tim. 2:4), we have grounds for believing the Word of final truth with its offer of eternal life will be heard by all. The divine perseverance is such that Christ 'descends to the dead' (Apostles' Creed) and proclaims the Good News 'even to the dead' (1 Pet. 4:6), those whose earthly journey has not been graced by hearing the Word.[48] This is the length to which God's mercy will go.

In the closing chapter of the story, Christ's invitation becomes adjudication. 'He will come again to judge the living and the dead' (Apostles' Creed). Eschatological consummation is closure, a reminder of the gravity of choices made. Returning to our present 9/11 context, it is Christ the judge of the quick and the dead whom the suicide bombers will meet at the Great Assize, as will all of us who contributed to the circumstances that brought that day to be. Of course, given the trajectory of the story, as perspective 7 rightly maintains, we may consider the possibility of a final penitent and believing 'yes' to all who have not

---

[48] The concept of divine perseverance beyond the gates of death is carefully surveyed by John Sanders in *No Other Name: An Investigation of the Destiny of the Unevangelized* (Grand Rapids: Eerdmans, 1992), pp. 177–224, reviewing its appearance in early patristic thought up through nineteenth- and twentieth-century theologians, both evangelical (Donald Bloesch) and ecumenical (George Lindbeck). I develop the point of view as an inheritance from the nineteenth-century 'Andover theory' in the sections of Sanders (ed.), *What About Those Who Have Never Heard?*, pp. 56–61, 71–94, 150–5, in a trialogue with Ronald Nash and John Sanders. The New Testament evidence is hotly debated by biblical scholars. For more recent 'pros', see Bo Reicke, *The Disobedient Spirits and Christian Baptism A Study of 1 Peter 3:19 and its Context* (Lund: Ejnar Munksgarrd, Kobenhavn, 1946) and Leonhardt Goppelt, *A Commentary on 1 Peter*, John E. Alsup (tr.) Ferdinand Hahn (ed.) (Grand Rapids: Eerdmans, 1993), and 'cons', Paul J. Achtemeier, *1 Peter: A Commentary on 1 Peter* (Minneapolis: Fortress Press, 1996) and Wayne A. Grudem, *The First Epistle of Peter: An Introduction and Commentary* (Leicester/Grand Rapids: Inter-Varsity Press/Eerdmans, 1988).

heard aright the Word of truth from the all-loving and all-powerful God. A universal reach of the Good News is not universalism's assurances that all will be saved. The divine love is tough as well as tender, making such prognostications an article of hope, given the trajectory of the story, not an article of faith. Both the divine sovereignty to decide such and the freedom granted to resist the divine invitation preclude such claims.

What of Paul's confidence that 'all Israel will be saved' (Rom. 11:26)? Such suggests a different destiny from that of people of other religions who have not heard the Word. Might it be that these heirs of Abraham, the 'father' of saving faith, will learn on that final Day that the identity of the agent of their Abrahamic faith is the person of Jesus Christ? Not unlike what faithful Jews contend when they hold that Christians saved by their Noachic faith will learn of its source in the God of Abraham, Isaac and Jacob?[49]

5. Conclusion

To affirm Jesus as the Saviour of the world entails the telling of the great story, a plot with its characters and events moving over time and space through conflict to resolution. Our reading of the sequence of its chapters seeks to honour the wider grace at work in the covenant with Noah and the longer work of grace in the proclamation of the Good News by a perseverance that reaches beyond death itself, and this without eliminating the offence of a particularist gospel. How much we need a Christology sturdier than the weak accommodations current among the pluralists! Yet also a bold particularity ready to acknowledge the wider and longer mercies of the Triune God.[50] Of such is an evangelical narrative Christology that affirms Christ as the way, the truth and the life, in the context of today's religiously plural world.

---

[49] The writer engaged in just this exchange with Jewish philosopher Michael Wyschogrod during a two-year Jewish-Christian Theological Panel sponsored by the United Church of Christ. For a survey of its materials, see 'God's Unbroken Covenant with the Jews', *New Conversations* 12.3 (Summer 1990).

[50] Philip Jenkins in *The Next Christendom: The Growth of Global Christianity* (New York: Oxford University Press, 2001) documents the demographic changes of an eroding northern Christianity with its strong pluralist strains and an exploding Southern Christianity with its own orthodox but not so generous tendencies.

Appendix

	Way	Truth	Life
(1)	C	C	C
(2)	C?	C?	C?
(3)	C	CP	C
(4)	C?	P?	C?
(5)	C	PC	C
(6)	P	PC	CP
(7)	P	P	C?
(8)	PC	PC	PC
(9)	P	PC	P
(10)	P	PC	PC

10

Semper Reformanda in a Changing World: Calvin, Usury and Evangelical Moral Theology

Andrew Goddard

At the start of a new century it is clear that the Christian church and the growing and influential evangelical movement within it will face many challenges in the realm of moral theology. New issues will certainly arise that demand fresh serious thought and do not fit easily into traditional categories, but it is also likely that there will be calls for revision of the church's traditional ethical teaching in numerous areas. At one level this is nothing new. The church has constantly had to address new concerns and respond to changing culture. In the last half century it faced the challenges of the sexual and technological revolutions in Western society, and how faithful disciples of Christ should respond to these will remain areas of controversy for many years to come.

Within modern evangelicalism a number of different responses to moral disagreement and the possibility of change in moral teaching and practice can be discerned. Although for much of the twentieth century (particularly in more fundamentalist circles) there were some well-established moral codes for personal holiness, which demarcated evangelical culture from the wider church and the world, evangelicals have not generally made subscription to carefully defined moral positions central to their theological identity. There have, for instance, been long-standing differences among evangelicals on a wide range of important moral issues as varied as whether recourse to war is justifiable and Christians can fight in a just war and the legitimacy of remarriage during the lifetime of a former spouse.

Evangelicals have also shown themselves able to accept some changes in traditional Christian moral thinking with little or no serious dispute. We have seen, for example, the widespread privatization of decisions about contraception and the acceptance of most forms of artificial birth control without any great disagreement or, indeed, much argument.

While Roman Catholics are divided, 'among Protestants, it is not simply that the overwhelming majority of them come down on the same side of the issue, but that for most of them *there is no real issue here at all*'.[1]

Other radical changes to traditional ethical teaching have also been widely accepted, but have caused major disagreements and continue to divide evangelicals. Perhaps most notable here are questions surrounding gender equality and the role of women in marriage, society and especially the church. In yet other areas, such as homosexuality, recent decades have seen changes in evangelical understanding, but evangelicals as a whole have resisted (to my mind rightly) arguments undermining traditional teaching that all sexual conduct outside life-long heterosexual marriage is wrong.[2] Finally, faced with new moral questions for which Scripture and Christian tradition provide no immediate and obvious guidance, evangelicals have tended to be cautious and conservative, although they have, to varying degrees, tolerated those who advocate more open stances. For example, in an otherwise conservative book on reproductive technologies from an evangelical publisher, the author can write of surrogacy that 'we cannot ... say it is morally wrong in certain cases',[3] while D. Gareth Jones has, in several works, argued for greater openness to the possible acceptability of various technologies that most evangelicals strongly oppose.

As these examples illustrate, evangelical responses vary when faced with new moral questions or demands to rethink traditional moral positions. There is, however, little serious thinking about the *method* of response in such situations and, as recent history has shown, this produces a number of risks. Unless there is more thought and care, evangelicals could fragment and splinter as they reach different conclusions on issues, and leave some evangelicals feeling betrayed by changes in

---

[1] James Nuechterlein, 'Catholics, Protestants and Contraception', *First Things* 92 (April 1999), pp. 10–11. A helpful symposium had appeared earlier in *First Things* 88 (December 1998), pp. 17–29.

[2] Until relatively recently most Evangelicals would have taken a strong condemnatory stance, rejecting anyone identifying as homosexual. Recent Evangelical writers tend to embrace a more tolerant position, such as found in Stanley Grenz, *Welcoming but not Affirming: An Evangelical Response to Homosexuality* (Louisville: Westminster John Knox, 1998) or The Evangelical Alliance's report *Faith, Hope & Homosexuality* (Carlisle: Paternoster, 1999). Despite the attempts of significant Evangelicals such as Michael Vasey, Lewis Smedes and Roy Clements to be more affirming of some same-sex partnerships, this viewpoint has little wider support among Evangelicals.

[3] Brendan McCarthy, *Fertility & Faith: The Ethics of Human Fertilization* (London: Inter-Varsity Press, 1997), p. 224.

moral teaching they cannot accept. Alternatively, evangelical moral theology could lose coherence as conclusions are reached on each issue on a pragmatic and *ad hoc* basis by means of a 'moral majority', and consensus (not evangelical theological principle and method) therefore defines evangelical thinking. These risks are likely to increase in the coming decades, especially if evangelical theology and ethics remains true to its calling and allows the church's missionary task to shape its agenda and theological method. In a rapidly changing and pluralist society where Christian influence is in historic decline and Christianity increasingly subjected to moral criticism, many new converts will be ignorant of Christian moral reasoning. The traditional practices of Christian discipleship which previously appeared 'common sense' may be alien to them and questioned by them.

In such a context, it is vital that Christian identity and distinctiveness is maintained. As Alister McGrath has argued, 'the rise of aggressively secular cultures in the west obliges communities of faith to distinguish themselves from the prevailing secular order, unless they are to be absorbed by it'.[4] McGrath is arguing here that this will make doctrine of continued, perhaps increasing, importance in the church. His argument is even more powerful in relation to the imperatives that are bound together with the indicatives of Christian doctrine. Jacques Ellul was right when, after the Second World War, he wrote that what was most important for Christianity was 'to create a new style of life'. He continued:

> There used to be a style of life peculiar to the Middle Ages. In the sixteenth century, there was a style of life carried on by Reformed Church Christians … There is a bourgeois style of life … there is the Communist style of life; there is no longer a Christian style of life … A doctrine only has power (apart from that which God gives it) to the extent in which it is adopted, believed, and accepted by men who have a style of life which is in harmony with it.[5]

On the other hand, while maintaining a distinctive style of life, Christians must also seriously consider whether traditional moral teaching has to be rethought and adapted in the light of new knowledge and a different context.[6] As just one among a variety of moral communities and

---

[4] Alister E. McGrath, *The Genesis of Doctrine: A Study in the Foundations of Doctrinal Criticism* (Oxford: Blackwell, 1990), p. 196.

[5] Jacques Ellul, *The Presence of the Kingdom*, Olive Wyon (tr.) (Colorado Springs: Helmers & Howard, 1989[2]; original French first edition 1948), p. 120.

[6] Cyril S. Rodd, *New Occasions Teach New Duties?: Christian Ethics for Today* (Edinburgh: T. & T. Clark, 1995) addresses this question, taking its

viewpoints, when Christians enter public dialogue, their own moral conclusions will rightly come under scrutiny. Although a critique of common moral understandings will be a central part of evangelical engagement with contemporary culture,[7] it cannot be denied that Christian morality can itself become blinded by a depraved and corrupt culture.[8] Christian mission must therefore also constantly ask where the church's moral teaching is in error and causes an unnecessary scandal, repelling outsiders and preventing them hearing the real scandal of the gospel of Christ and him crucified.

In the light of this challenge, serious thought must be given not only to how to respond to new ethical challenges, but how to discern when traditional moral thinking needs to be revised and how to undertake such revision. Educated guesses could be made as to likely issues on the church's agenda in future years, but rather than highlighting these and assessing each in turn, it is better to develop a more general methodological framework which is of value whatever specific issue becomes the focus of challenge and controversy.

In asking how to evaluate criticism of the church's moral teaching and proposed revisions to it, two (surprisingly common) extremes in much popular Christian moral debate can be noted but summarily rejected.

At one extreme (broadly the more liberal), is a tendency to assume the worst about the church and its tradition and be rather uncritical of challenges to traditional moral teaching. This may be motivated by guilt for the church's evident past moral failings, by a simplistic hermeneutic which reduces the gospel to liberation from oppression and treats as valid all claims of oppression and all proposals for liberation from those

---

[6] (*continued*) title from James Russell Lowell's hymn, 'New occasions teach new duties, Time makes ancient good uncouth'. Alister McGrath contributed a chapter on the Reformation (pp. 47–60).

[7] Alister McGrath has addressed some of these issues in his lecture 'Understanding and Responding to Moral Pluralism', published by the Center for Applied Christian Ethics.

[8] To cite just one of numerous examples, the refusal of many Evangelical clergy in eighteenth-century England to oppose draconian capital punishment would rightly now be seen as a moral failure on the part of otherwise godly and wise Christian leaders. See Timothy Gorringe, *God's Just Vengeance: Crime, Violence and the Rhetoric of Salvation* (Cambridge: Cambridge University Press, 1996), who gives the example of the great John Fletcher of Madeley (d. 1785) refusing to 'meddle in the affair' of the nineteen-year-old brother of his servant girl sentenced to death for housebreaking and robbery by appealing to have the sentence commuted (pp. 1–3).

who identify themselves as oppressed, or by any other number of factors. Despite its apparently powerful rhetorical force, the premise 'Wrong on slavery, wrong on women' (even if accepted) does not enable us to conclude that the church is wrong on some other issue (say homosexuality).

At its worst, this approach represents an historicist progressivist attitude which Wycliffe Hall's consultation on the Future of Anglicanism described as a Western corruption of eschatology into a kind of doctrine of 'progress', which is not truly hopeful but merely presumptuous complacency because it defends the achieved position of the culture against any possible criticism out of the legacy of the past.

The response to moral critique is here determined by moral adaptation to the spirit of the age with the added tragedy that, given the pace of change, when the church marries herself to the latest trend she will now find herself widowed more often than the poor woman in the Sadduccees' parable.

At the other, conservative, extreme of reactions to pressure for rethinking (perhaps the stronger temptation for much evangelicalism) is a tendency simply to reassert what has always been said. Rather than serious listening, humble self-scrutiny, and a desire to be corrected where in error, there is a firm confidence not only in divine truth but in our current hold on that truth and hence the error of those advocating change. Here again one can discern an error that is in part due to eschatological corruption. There is a refusal to recognize the limits and fallibility of our contemporary knowledge and an apparent belief that we already see face to face and know as we are known. The words of Vanhoozer in relation to hermeneutics are applicable here:

> The truth of Christ is both gift and task. On the one hand, we have the Word written; on the other hand, we must interpret it. While its meaning has been fixed by the past, our grasp of that meaning is partial, and its significance is incomplete. There is an eschatological tension that must not be ignored, a tension that prohibits us from thinking that the truth – the single correct interpretation – is our present possession. It is a mistake, in other words, to confuse the content of tradition with any one moment of tradition. Truth … can neither be rushed nor coerced … Yes, it is difficult to wait, but it is worse to bring the quest for truth, for a final interpretive solution, to a premature conclusion.[9]

---

[9] Kevin Vanhoozer, *Is there a Meaning in this Text?* (Leicester: Apollos, 1998), p. 429. He later writes, 'That the meaning and significance of a text are never a present possession, but a partially fulfilled promise, is perhaps sufficient antidote to the poison of prideful interpretation' (p. 465).

If evangelical moral theology rejects these two extremes, where should it look for guidance on the way forward? There are few better resources in Christian history (especially in a Festschrift honouring Alister McGrath) than the Reformation and lessons from that period of church history. Among many possible insights for changes in moral teaching, two will be highlighted here, concentrating on the details of the second.

The first is a principle summing up the *via media* between the extremes outlined above: *ecclesia reformata semper reformanda*. The church, having been reformed, should always be open to further reformation. The opening clause reminds us that the test is not (as in the more liberal extreme) simply whether the church goes on being reformed. Future reformation must give due weight and recognition to the reform that took place in the sixteenth century. As David Wright puts it in his excellent article relating this to the contemporary homosexuality debate:

> It would be subversive of the truth of this principle if *semper reformanda* were applied in such a way as to undermine the historic Reformation ... Claims to be implementing *semper reformanda* along lines that do, despite the liberating principles of the sixteenth century – Christ alone, grace alone, faith alone, Scripture alone – are bound to ring hollow. This does not imply ... an assumption that the Reformers of that era always got things right, but rather, if *reformata* and *semper reformanda* are to hang together and mutually inform each other, that the continuing vocation of reform will be credible, especially if it seeks to reverse changes made at that time, only by entering more deeply into those sources of Reformation authority.[10]

The second clause reminds evangelicals that they cannot exempt themselves from the challenge of present reform. As Wright again comments, 'the church is always capable of falling into grave deformation so as to be in need of thorough reformation, and if that were true in the late medieval centuries there is no reason to believe that it may not be true in any age'.[11]

Although very important, this general principle provides little concrete guidance for the method of reforming moral teaching. To find this in the Reformation, a concrete example is required, and none is

---

[10]   David Wright, 'The Homosexuality Debate and the Reform of the Church', *Anvil* 15/1 (1998), pp. 22–33 (here p. 23).

[11]   Ibid., p. 22.

potentially more rich than that of John Calvin and his approach to the question of usury.[12] As our concern here is methodological rather than with the substantive issue, the details and validity of Calvin's arguments in relation to usury will not be closely examined. It is, however, vital to recognize what a radical change his work represented. In the words of John T. Noonan:

> Once upon a time, certainly from at least 1150 to 1550, seeking, receiving, or hoping for anything beyond one's principal – in other words, looking for profit – on a loan constituted the mortal sin of usury. The doctrine was enunciated by popes, expressed by three ecumenical councils, proclaimed by bishops, and taught unanimously by theologians. The doctrine was not some obscure, hole-in-the-corner affection, but stood astride the European credit markets, at least as much as the parallel Islamic ban of usury governs Muslim countries today ... The great central moral fact was that usury, understood as profit on a loan, was forbidden as contrary to the natural law, as contrary to the law of the church, and as contrary to the law of the gospel.[13]

It is also the case that this revision of moral teaching was not part of a wider Reformation trend. Luther, for example, famously stands in stark contrast to Calvin in his very negative attitude to usury[14] and 'it is generally acknowledged by those who have studied Calvin's economic and

---

[12] Alister McGrath has commented briefly on this in his *A Life of John Calvin: A Study in the Shaping of Western Culture* (Oxford: Blackwell, 1990), ch. 11 and 'Calvin and the Christian Calling', *First Things* 94 (June/July 1999), pp. 31–5.

[13] John T. Noonan, Jr, 'Development in Moral Doctrine' in James F. Keenan S.J. and Thomas A. Shannon (eds), *The Context of Casuistry* (Washington DC: Georgetown University Press, 1995), p. 188. For a helpful recent study of the background to Calvin, see Joan Lockwood O'Donovan, 'The Theological Economics of Medieval Usury Theory', *Studies in Christian Ethics* 14.1 (Edinburgh: T. & T. Clark 2001), pp. 48–64. I am also very grateful to Michael Wykes for sharing with me his work on this subject, 'Devaluing the Scholastics: Calvin's Ethics of Usury', to be published in *Calvin Theology Journal* (Spring 2003).

[14] Lockwood O'Donovan, 'The Theological Economics of Medieval Usury Theory', pp. 61–3, gives a sympathetic account of Luther, while many, including McGrath, dismiss him here ('that Luther's economic thought – if one can dignify it with such a title – was hostile to any form of capitalism largely reflects his unfamiliarity with the sophisticated world of finance then emerging in the great free cities' – *A Life of John Calvin*, p. 231).

political views that he was the first of the Reformers to give a *theological* defence of the practice of lending money at interest'.[15]

Calvin's treatment of the subject is limited, but appears in a number of places. Three of his commentaries discuss biblical texts that speak on the subject of usury:[16] his harmony of the four last books of the Penta-teuch (1554), which discusses Exodus 22:25, Leviticus 25:35–38 and Deuteronomy 23:19–20 with reference to the eighth commandment; his 1557 commentary on Psalm 15:5; and his posthumously published commentary on Ezekiel 18:8–17. The most important text, however, to which reference is most often made below, is a personal letter on usury written in 1545 to his friend Claude de Sachin, although only published (by Beza) in 1575.[17] These texts, rather than a wider account of Calvin's moral theology, form the basis for the discussion of ethical method that follows.

The aim now is to discern the lines of argument Calvin developed as he revised traditional church moral teaching on usury in order to see what guidance these give to evangelicals and others faced with new appeals for further changes in Christian moral teaching. Often such

---

[15] Guenther H. Haas, *The Concept of Equity in Calvin's Ethics* (Carlisle: Pater-noster, 1997), p. 117, in a chapter devoted to 'Equity & Usury'. The best dis-cussion of Calvin's economic thought remains André Biéler, *La Pensée Economique et Sociale de Calvin* (University of Geneva, 1959) where pp. 453–76 focus on the subject of usury.

[16] The Old Testament texts have been helpfully divided into three broad catego-ries – (a) those which prohibit usury in loans to the poor (e.g. Ex. 22:25; Lev. 25:35–38), (b) those which include all Jews (not just the poor) in their prohibi-tion but exclude outsiders (e.g. Dt. 23:19–20), and (c) those which condemn usury by relating it to avarice, greed and oppression (e.g. Ezek. 18:5–18) – by T.F. Divine in his *Interest: An Historical and Analytical Study in Economics and Modern Ethics* (Marquette University Press, 1959), pp. 5–11. For a more recent discussion by an Old Testament scholar, see 'Lending at Interest' in Cyril S. Rodd, *Glimpses of a Strange Land: Studies in Old Testament Ethics* (Edinburgh: T. & T. Clark, 2001), pp. 142–57.

[17] The original French text is found in OC 10.245–9 and reproduced in J.B. Sauer, *Faithful Ethics According to John Calvin* (Lewiston, New York: Edwin Mellen Press, 1997), pp. 255–8. The translation cited here is in Mary Beaty and Benjamin W. Farley, *Calvin's Ecclesiastical Advice* (Edinburgh: T. & T. Clark, 1991), pp. 139–43 and reproduced in Oliver O'Donovan and Joan Lockwood O'Donovan, *From Irenaeus to Grotius* (Grand Rapids: Eerdmans, 1999), pp. 682–4, where the editors justify inclusion 'not only because it bears slightly on the monumental debate about the role of Calvinism in the advent of modern capitalism, but as demonstrating his ethical method' (p. 666).

debates become heated not only because of the substantive issue over which there is disagreement but because of a lack of agreement as to how the church *could* faithfully revise its teaching on an issue. Often those opposing change and upholding tradition find the very *form* of arguments advanced by revisionists to be invalid, and so the stakes are raised to encompass deeper issues, such as authority in the church. If, however, there is to be constructive moral debate and dialogue on any issue, then people on each side must 'take up the arguments that others have raised against them, and try to give serious answers' and 'to do that they must think their opponents mistaken, certainly, but not wholly foolish or malicious'.[18] Those involved must therefore discern 'a language in which to disagree rather than speaking two incompatible or mutually exclusive tongues'.[19] Some agreement as to what forms and structures of theological argument are legitimate patterns of Christian moral reasoning is therefore essential. Such agreement would enable us, when we reach different conclusions on any particular matter, to address the methodological question of *how* differences arose, where people have parted ways in their moral judgements, and whether a particular stance represents a fundamental deviation from orthodox Christian moral theology.

Given that the focus here is methodological, three limits need clearly to be stated. First, Calvin himself is most likely to prove an ally of traditionalists on the *substance* of our debates about moral change. So, for example, in relation to both the role of women in the church and homosexual behaviour – two examples to which we regularly return – his substantive views will legitimately be claimed on the side of those in the argument who oppose calls for change. Secondly, the simple fact that a claim for revising the church's moral teaching uses the *forms* of argument Calvin utilized in relation to usury does not in and of itself demonstrate the cogency or acceptability of that claim. It is false to assert that, because certain forms of argument Calvin advanced in relation to usury are paralleled in recent arguments in favour of women's leadership or homosexuality, then those arguments must be convincing. Thirdly, despite the near-universal contemporary Christian acceptance of lending money at interest, some may believe Calvin's move was a false step within the tradition and/or that his ethical method in making that step is a flawed precedent.

---

[18] Oliver O'Donovan, 'Homosexuality in the Church: Can there be a Fruitful Theological Debate?' in Timothy Bradshaw (ed.), *The Way Forward?: Christian Voices on Homosexuality and the Church* (London: Hodder & Stoughton, 1997), p. 20.

[19] Rowan Williams, 'Knowing Myself in Christ' in ibid., p. 12.

1. Approaching Moral Change

Before outlining the central features of Calvin's arguments for revising traditional moral teaching on usury, it is helpful to examine some broader contextual features of the debate and Calvin's role within it. These shed light on how evangelicals today can best approach discussions about moral change.

First, although Calvin's thinking on this must be located in the context of the social and economic changes of his time and, in the opinion of some, proved to have a significant impact on the development of Western economic thought and practice, the issue is not particularly prominent in his writing or ministry as a whole. It arises and is addressed by him in an ecclesial context as he reads and expounds Scripture (his commentary discussions) and offers pastoral advice to Christians seeking to serve Christ in the world (his private letter on usury). This acts as an important reminder for all involved in often heated discussions about ethical matters. There is a need for Christians to keep a proper sense of proportion. Questioning of accepted moral teaching should be expected to arise primarily from the reading and applying of Scripture to the church's contemporary life and from the questions and struggles of Christian disciples as they seek to discern the will of God in their daily lives.[20]

This focus on the ecclesial context stands as a challenge to much contemporary church life. It is comparatively rare for serious, open and honest discussion (let alone disagreement) to be aired among evangelicals on moral issues. Often there is a simple trumpeting by leaders of a clear traditional position as an expected public standard which cannot be questioned and/or an effective privatization of moral decision making in which little moral guidance or support is provided to Christians struggling with such issues as possible recourse to reproductive technologies, marriage after divorce, or cohabitation before marriage. Calvin's modes of addressing the issue of usury – clear public teaching of Scripture and private pastoral counsel – draw attention to these (rather than say political campaigning) as the best ecclesial context for developments in Christian moral thinking to arise and be tested and weighed by the Christian community.

---

[20] For a discussion of this in relation to the ordination of women, see the sermon of R.T. France, 'It seemed good to the Holy Spirit and to us?' *Churchman* 108.3 (1994), pp. 234–41. France explains why he does not think his method here entails acceptance of homosexual practice in 'A Slippery Slope? The Ordination of Women & Homosexual Practice – A Case Study in Biblical Interpretation' (Cambridge: Grove Biblical Series 16, 2000).

Secondly, Calvin opens his letter with the words 'I have not personally experienced this.' Such a confession is even more important in our
contemporary context, where pronouncements on moral issues from
people apparently aloof from the concrete reality they are addressing are
often felt to lack authority. It would, of course, be foolish to suggest that
one can make sound and serious moral judgements on a subject only if in
one's own life there has been personal deliberation on acting in that
particular sphere. This would mean that only infertile couples can speak
about the morality of IVF, or divorcees about the rightness of remarriage after divorce, or women who sense a call to ministry about the
rightness or otherwise of limits on which church offices it is right for
women to hold. As the rest of the letter makes clear, Calvin felt perfectly
capable of offering clear moral counsel despite his opening disclaimer.
Nevertheless, even if personal experience is not necessary before reaching moral judgements, a refusal to listen to and learn from those for
whom the issue is a real, live and pressing one – and they are perhaps the
most likely initial source of pressure for changes in traditional moral
teaching – will seriously undermine, in some contexts even discredit,
moral teaching.

In Acts 15, where the early church is considering changing the
requirements to be made of Gentile converts, the testimony of Peter's
experiences in mission to the Gentiles is of crucial importance. This
incident has recently been applied (often illegitimately) to contemporary
discussions about revising church teaching on homosexuality,[21] but it
does remind us of the limited but important role of Christian experience
in moral deliberation. Stephen Fowl has drawn attention to the need to
be able to read the Spirit at work in a situation in order to read Scripture
aright and argues that one of the reasons we fail here is that we are not
good at forming and nurturing the patterns of relationship and types
of common life which enable us to perform this vital task. So, if we
lack direct personal experience in an area of moral disagreement, it is
important to seek out and learn from those Christians who have such
experience. Fowl explains what this might mean in relation to the homosexuality debate:

> Any analogous application of Acts 10–15 to issues of homosexual inclusion
> will need to be grounded in testimonies of 'homosexual holiness' ... It is
> crucial that Peter, Paul, and Barnabas were all circumcised Jews testifying

---

[21] I have discussed the parallels between Acts 15 and the contemporary gay
debate in *God, Gentiles and Gay Christians: Acts 15 and Change in the
Church* (Cambridge: Grove Ethics Series 121, 2001).

about the work of the Spirit in the lives of uncircumcised Gentile believers ... It should not, then, be the responsibility of homosexual Christians to provide 'narratives of homosexual holiness' ... The onus is on other Christians who may enter (or have already entered) into friendships with homosexual Christians out of which they might offer testimony of their friends' holiness. Alternatively, it may be the case that such friendships generate calls to repentance from one friend to another ... Christians have no reason to think they understand how the Holy Spirit weighs in on the issue of homosexuality until they welcome homosexuals into their homes and sit down to eat with them.[22]

Thirdly, issues of moral character are important in approaching moral disagreement and weighing arguments for changing moral teaching. Calvin speaks highly in his letter of its recipient's 'prudence and the moderation of your heart'. It is this that gives Calvin a great confidence in his correspondent's moral discernment and probity that is often lacking in others. As the recent revival of virtue ethics has reminded the church, the character of those engaging in moral evaluation must not be factored out of discussion as of no importance as if we best evaluate moral proposals and actions simply by abstract, supposedly objective, act analysis. As Oliver O'Donovan reminds us, 'information about the agent's character is necessary for an evaluative process of moral thought in which the thinker stands at an observer's distance from the agent and her acts and assesses them'.[23]

In making moral judgements on actions, and especially when considering possible reform of traditional teaching, the character of those proposing changes must be considered. Clearly, personal virtue cannot be decisive, as those who are virtuous can misconstrue the world and make wrong moral judgements. Nevertheless, a person's way of looking at the world and his or her considered moral judgements on contentious issues carry more weight when that person displays Christian virtue in their life.

Fourthly, Calvin reveals a strong awareness of the dangers of church pronouncements on complex and disputed moral issues. After confessing his own personal inexperience, he continues:

---

[22] Stephen Fowl, *Engaging Scripture: A Model for Theological Interpretation* (Oxford: Blackwell, 1998), pp. 121–2. A powerful example of this is the discussion of homosexuality in Richard Hays, *The Moral Vision of the New Testament* (Edinburgh: T. & T. Clark, 1996), pp. 379ff., based on his friendship with Gary.

[23] Oliver O'Donovan, *Resurrection and Moral Order: An Outline for Evangelical Ethics* (Leicester: Inter-Varsity Press, 1986), p. 211.

I have learned from the example of others how perilous it is to respond to the
question for which you seek my counsel. For if we should totally prohibit the
practice of usury, we would restrain consciences more rigidly than God himself. But if we permit it, then some, under this guise, would be content to act
with unbridled license, unable to abide any limits.

Towards the end of his letter, before delineating the limits he himself
places on usury, he again reiterates the need to 'proceed with caution, as
almost everyone is looking for some word to justify his intention'.

Calvin here implies (and his writing and practice elsewhere confirms)
that there are situations where God himself clearly binds human con-
science. In such situations the church can presumably speak with great
confidence and boldness. There are, however, moral issues where the
church in its public teaching must proceed with great care. In these, the
church must walk a narrow tightrope, avoiding apparent encouragement of moral laxity, while not falling into a rigorist legalism that
demands more of Christ's disciples than God himself requires. As in
relation to usury, most appeals to change Christian moral teaching seek
to loosen traditionally strict prohibitions and argue that there are some
situations and forms of action where what was previously considered
wrong is, in fact, licit. Calvin's careful and cautious approach highlights the great care needed by the church in speaking on such issues. He
warns those seeking change that they must define new clear limits, while
challenging defenders of the status quo that they must not always view
any and every relaxation of long-standing norms as a sign that the
church is rejecting God's will.

Fifthly, Calvin takes an unashamedly theological approach to moral
decision making. Biéler, opening his study of Calvin's economic and
social thought, reminds readers that:

it is not possible to speak of Calvin's social and political thought without
linking this to the theological premises on which it rests. To detach it from
these foundations would quite simply betray its author. One runs the risk of
understanding nothing of the practical morality of the reformer, of completely distorting the meaning of his thought, if one does not go back to the
spiritual sources of his doctrine and action.[24]

---

[24] Biéler, *La Pensée Economique et Sociale de Calvin*, p. xiii (own translation).
Biéler begins his discussion on Calvin and usury by summarizing his theology
of money in society (pp. 453–4).

So, in his commentary on the relevant texts in the Pentateuch, the discussion of usury 'is not initially treated in terms of economics or even of general economic ethics, but the giving of interest free loans is based on 'the rule of love', for the sake of the poor'.[25] This again presents an important challenge to Christian ethicists and church leaders that in their preaching and pastoral counsel and their engagement on moral issues in wider public life it is necessary to develop a theologically attuned mind and not simply approach questions in the terms of secular discourse and as defined by economists, sociologists or 'experts' in other disciplines.

The structure of Calvin's own theological engagement with the moral question of usury must now be examined in some detail in order to find guidance for contemporary evangelical moral theology as it proposes, weighs and passes judgement on moral issues and changes in traditional Christian teaching.

2. Debating Moral Change

Turning to the detail of Calvin's treatment, it is important to reiterate that what follows is concerned with methodology. It is necessary to determine neither the persuasiveness of the specifics of Calvin's arguments for his view on usury nor the strength of the forms of argument advanced in that particular case. The aim is, through uncovering the structure and forms of Calvin's moral persuasion, to discover and map out some basic principles and rules that could guide evangelicals as they reach moral judgements, particularly when they assess the legitimacy of proposals to reform the Christian moral tradition. Although unable comprehensively to cover all Calvin's arguments across his writings on usury, the traditional three-fold division of Scripture, reasoned analysis and Christian tradition is easily discernible in his letter on the subject and provides a helpful framework for analysis of the structure of Calvin's moral reasoning. The first of these is by far the weightiest in Calvin's discussion, and will be for all evangelicals, and is therefore given much more extensive treatment.

---

[25] T.H.L. Parker, *Calvin's Old Testament Commentaries* (Edinburgh: T. & T. Clark, 1986), pp. 158–9.

2.1. Scripture

In his moral theology, as in his dogmatics, 'in the first place, it must be stressed that Calvin is a biblical theologian'.[26] In relation to usury, as in other areas, Calvin gives clear primacy to Scripture as the means through which God speaks and as the locus of divine commandments. We have already seen the importance of biblical commentary in his writing on usury and in his letter on the issue, after his preliminaries, the substance of his argument begins, 'First, there is no scriptural passage that totally bans all usury.'[27] The first half of that letter is devoted to Scriptural exegesis and interpretation in which he makes it clear that the Holy Spirit speaks through Scripture, which contains 'the clear commandment of God'.

The modern evangelical insistence that the Bible is the supreme authority in all matters of behaviour here finds support in Calvin and this belief must remain at the heart of evangelical moral theology. Closer study of his argument shows, however, that Calvin cannot be claimed for a simplistic 'The Bible says ...' approach to Christian moral reasoning. Eight features of his appeal to Scripture prove of great value to evangelicals struggling with how to relate Scripture to complex contemporary moral issues.

First, Calvin's bold assertion that 'no scriptural passage ... totally bans all usury' is not obvious, and so requires detailed explanation in both his letter and commentaries. On the surface, it is a claim many would question, and so specific passages are carefully studied in their own right and in the light of Scripture's teaching as a whole.

It is important to realize that implicit in this statement would appear to be a principle that were one to conclude that scriptural passages did totally ban all usury then the debate would effectively be closed. Whether or not to accept the teaching of God's Word is not something that should be open to debate among Christian ethicists. However, recalling the tightrope Calvin's letter identified him as self-consciously walking and his concern not to bind consciences more rigidly than God himself, the commentary on the Pentateuch makes clear that Scripture at times leaves matters open for further debate when it comes to moral

---

[26] McGrath, *A Life of John Calvin*, p. 150.

[27] Biéler comments 'As usual, Calvin turns in the very first place to the teaching of the holy Scriptures' (*La Pensée Economique et Sociale de Calvin*, p. 457), having earlier made clear that 'We must first of all note that Calvin, in order to justify the taking of interest, does not simply leave on one side the biblical texts used as a foundation by other Christian teachers to condemn it' (p. 455).

discussion: 'I do not dare to pronounce upon so important a point more than God's words convey.' As his delineation of limits to usury and his appeal to scriptural principles makes clear, the Bible's failure to categorically and comprehensively forbid something does not entail silence on the part of the church. However, those giving clear, firm and wide-ranging prohibitions must be confident that they derive from God's Word and are not simply human traditions.

This leads, secondly, into Calvin's clear and vital distinction between the authority of Scripture and the authority of the Christian tradition's reading of Scripture. In relation to usury, the central biblical text appealed to in support of the Christian prohibition was the words of Christ in Luke 6:35, calling on his followers to lend without expecting to get anything back. Calvin therefore begins with this text in his discussion of Scripture, immediately following his rejection of a scriptural prohibition with the claim: 'For Christ's statement, which is commonly esteemed to manifest this [the total ban on all usury], but which has to do with lending, has been falsely applied to usury.'

Here we are reminded of the simple but often neglected fact that just because Christians have (perhaps for centuries) related a saying of Scripture to discussion of a particular moral issue does not infallibly prove that such a text is being correctly interpreted or that it is right to appeal to it in their moral argument. From an evangelical perspective, tradition has authority, but the authority of any tradition – even an evangelical tradition of reading Scripture in a certain way – is only and always subordinate to the authority of Scripture itself. One must be able to appeal to Scripture itself over and against the church's traditional interpretation of Scripture.[28]

So, in relation to one of the many contemporary debates where appeal to Scripture is vitally important, even most upholders of traditional views on homosexuality now acknowledge that the Sodom narrative in Genesis 19 gained a wholly unjustifiable prominence within the Christian tradition's understanding of homosexuality. While few have been convinced by arguments that seek to remove all references to illicit

---

[28] Some stimulating writings on the authority and interpretation of Scripture linked to the postliberal school rightly draw attention to the ecclesial context and tradition-shaped pattern of our interpretation of Scripture, but can become problematic to the extent they are unable to make sense of this fundamental principle that Scripture stands over and must correct the church. The work of Kevin Vanhoozer in *Is there a Meaning in this Text?* and *First Theology: God, Scripture & Hermeneutics* (Leicester: Apollos, 2002) provides a helpful counterbalance to that tendency.

sexual conduct from the narrative, most view any relevance it has to contemporary discussions of same-sex partnerships as comparatively small, and even then only when this text is set within the wider biblical teaching concerning human sexuality.[29]

Thirdly, in any appeal to Scripture, particularly an appeal that seeks to overturn traditional interpretations, close attention must be paid to the plain sense of the text in its original language and in the original context of that text. Careful, close biblical exegesis is certainly not sufficient for good Christian moral reasoning,[30] but it is necessary. Calvin's argument against a blanket prohibition on usury is therefore in part a careful study of key Hebrew terms showing that because the Hebrew word *tok* can generally mean 'defraud', 'it can be translated otherwise than "usury"' and that other terms refer to usury which "eats away at its victims"'.

Once again, there are obvious parallels here with contemporary discussions. Evangelical discussion about the role of women in marriage and the church has focused on careful study of the Greek word *kephale* and the meaning of the man/husband as the head of the woman/wife.[31] A similar debate has arisen in recent years in relation to the scope of Paul's terms traditionally understood as referring to homosexuality.[32] Despite the tediousness of some of this work and the weariness such studies can

---

[29] Richard Hays, one of the best defenders of traditionalist views, boldly asserts, 'The notorious story of Sodom and Gomorrah – often cited in connection with homosexuality – is actually irrelevant to the topic' (*The Moral Vision of the New Testament*, p. 381). Even Gagnon, while not going so far as Hays, admits that, 'to the extent that the story does not deal directly with consensual homosexual relationships, it is not an "ideal" text to guide contemporary Christian sexual ethics' (Robert A.J. Gagnon, *The Bible and Homosexual Practice: Texts and Hermeneutics* (Nashville: Abingdon Press, 2001, p. 71).

[30] Hays, *The Moral Vision of the New Testament*, p. 3 cites a remark by Oliver O'Donovan in a 1987 Yale Divinity School lecture that 'interpreters who think that they can determine the proper ethical application of the Bible solely through more sophisticated exegesis are like people who believe that they can fly if only they flap their arms hard enough'.

[31] The *kephale* debate has tended to revolve around whether the term signifies leadership and authority (so most fully Grudem in various articles) or source/origin (as argued by Fee and Witherington). For a survey of the debate and a different proposal, see Andrew Perriman, *Speaking of Women: Interpreting Paul* (Leicester: Apollos, 1998), especially ch. 1.

[32] In relation to *arsenokoitai* the major work is that of David Wright (references in 'The Homosexuality Debate and the Reform of the Church', p. 23, n. 1). On both that term and *malakoi*, see discussion in Gagnon, *The Bible and Homosexual Practice*, pp. 303–39.

evoke, they have a proper, if limited, role in evangelical discussions about what is faithful change in moral teaching.

Fourthly, great care needs to be taken to avoid over-interpretation of biblical prohibitions, especially where strong negative language is used in Scripture. Calvin is quite frank about the strength of biblical opposition to usury, speaking in his letter of 'the Holy Spirit's anger against usurers' displayed in the prophets and Psalms, and even acknowledging that 'the Holy Spirit ... advises all holy men, who praise and fear God, to abstain from usury'. His commentary on Psalm 15:5 admits that David seems to condemn all kinds of usury in general, and without exception. Nevertheless, despite statements such as these, his letter still maintains that 'we need not conclude that all usury is forbidden'.

Part of the explanation for this tension (even apparent contradiction) in Calvin's analysis is to be found in the careful exegetical study of terms which narrows their apparent scope and shows them to be less universal than they may initially appear to the naïve reader. However, four other more significant hermeneutical moves are made in reaching his conclusion, which could disconcert some contemporary evangelicals due to the potential for their abuse, but appeal to which could facilitate a dynamic evangelical approach to biblically based moral reasoning.

Fifthly, attention must be paid not simply to Scripture's prohibitions but to Scripture's intention in issuing prohibitions. Following his admission about the apparent universality of Psalm 15:5, Calvin's commentary turns to the rationale offered in Leviticus 25:35, 36 to argue that 'the end for which the law was framed was that men should not cruelly oppress the poor'. This then qualifies Ezekiel, who 'seems to condemn the taking of any interest whatever upon money lent; but he doubtless has an eye to the unjust and crafty art of gaining, by which the rich devoured the poor people'.

Calvin here follows a form of what Charles Cosgrove's recent work identifies as a basic hermeneutical rule found in much appeal to Scripture in moral debate – the rule of purpose. This Cosgrove states as 'the purpose (or justification) behind a biblical moral rule carries greater weight than the rule itself'.[33] Parallel forms of argument are easily discerned in other areas of contemporary moral disagreement. Those, for example, who do not see Jesus' words as prohibiting all forms of remarriage after divorce (except perhaps – the Matthean exception – on

---

[33] Charles H. Cosgrove, *Appealing to Scripture in Moral Debate: Five Hermeneutical Rules* (Grand Rapids: Eerdmans, 2002), p. 12. The chapter includes a discussion of this in relation to interest (pp. 34–7), which, although not referring to him, argues in a similar vein to Calvin.

the grounds of *porneia*) include among their arguments the claim that Jesus' primary concern in the relevant sayings (Mk. 10:2–12; Matthew 5:31–32, 19:3–12; Luke 16:18) is to criticize the inequalities of a male-dominated society and to protect the weaker partner in a system where Jewish men easily divorced and discarded their wives in order to marry other women.[34] Similarly, the texts limiting the roles of women in church leadership (for example 1 Cor. 14:34; 1 Tim. 2:11–15) are often argued to have as their underlying rationale the prevention of false teaching or disruption of public worship and that the formulation of that concern in terms of limitations being placed on women teaching need not therefore be understood as a blanket rule. As these cases perhaps illustrate, problems can arise for those who wish to broaden traditional moral limits by appeal to this rule when either no rationale is explicitly offered in Scripture or the rationale itself appears to be one which, as with homosexuality, could be held to apply with equal force today.[35]

Sixthly, despite a concern for careful and close exegesis of relevant passages in Scripture, Calvin ultimately does not focus his attention solely on these in reaching his conclusion about the specific issue of usury. He is far from being a literalist or legalist who derives his ethical judgements from a sophisticated form of biblical proof-texting. In words that perhaps stand out most starkly in his letter for most evangelicals, Calvin argues that 'we ought not to judge usury according to a few passages of scripture, but in accordance with the principle of equity'.[36] Similarly in his commentary on the Pentateuch, Calvin is adamant that 'if they object that usurers are absolutely condemned by David and Ezekiel I think that their declaration ought to be judged of by the rule of charity'. Although there is truth in the claim that 'methodologically, his argument is as much dependent on philosophical concepts … as on

---

[34] So, for example, David Atkinson, *To Have and to Hold* (London: Collins, 1979), ch. 4 and Greg Forster, *Healing Love's Wounds: A Pastoral Response to Divorce and to Remarriage* (Marshall Pickering, 1995), ch. 4.

[35] Cosgrove shows (*Appealing to Scripture in Moral Debate*, pp. 37–44) that Romans 1 by providing a creation norm for rules against homosexual practice 'warrants a blanket form of the rule' and so 'the justification is therefore a reason (insofar as we grant authority to the Bible at the level of its rule justifications) in favour of our adopting a moral rule against homosexuality' (pp. 42–3).

[36] Haas therefore rightly argues 'It is the principle of equity that allows Calvin to analyse the social and economic realities of his day, that transcends a rigid biblical literalism … Equity allows Calvin to read the Bible with new eyes' (Haas, *The Concept of Equity in Calvin's Ethics*, p. 121).

biblical injunctions',[37] it would be wrong to say that Calvin here turns his back on Scripture and biblical authority. Rather, he has let Scripture shape his thinking at the level of moral and theological principles as shown by his letter's closing limits on usury. There he insists that 'everything should be examined in the light of Christ's precept: Do unto others as you would have them do unto you. This precept is applicable every time', and argues that what is lawful in regard to usury is to be based on 'a principle derived from the Word of God'.[38]

In a world where the spectre of liberal consequentialist situation ethics regularly rears its ugly head and appeals are frequently made to Christian love as the sole guide for Christian moral reasoning in each and every situation, statements such as 'our determination must be derived from nowhere else than … the declaration of Christ, on which hang the law and the prophets – Do not unto others what ye would not have done to thyself' normally set evangelical alarm bells ringing. That these are, in fact, the words of the great French Reformer as he sets about rethinking (in a way we now accept almost without thinking) the tradition's long-standing ban on usury should remind us that within the right context such a form of moral argumentation and appeal to Scripture may have a certain place and a level of validity within evangelical moral reasoning and revision of tradition.[39] Similar methods of moral persuasion are easily identifiable (and often critiqued) in two recent debates: the appeals to justice and equality (perhaps with reference to Gal. 3:26) in relation to gender[40] and the appropriation of a

---

[37] O'Donovan and O'Donovan, *From Irenaeus to Grotius*, p. 666.

[38] In relation to Cosgrove's hermeneutical rules, this would appear to be one possible form of his fifth rule of moral-theological adjudication, namely that 'moral-theological considerations should guide hermeneutical choices between conflicting plausible interpretations' (Cosgrove, *Appealing to Scripture in Moral Debate*, p. 154).

[39] There are, of course, strong reasons why simply reducing Christian ethics to one single principle (whether love, equity, liberation or something else), although surprisingly common, both distorts Scripture (see Hays, *The Moral Vision of the New Testament*, ch. 10) and limits and misunderstands Christian moral understanding and reasoning about human action (see Charles R. Pinches, *Theology and Action: After Theory in Christian Ethics* (Grand Rapids: Eerdmans, 2002), especially ch. 2 on monism in Protestant ethics).

[40] One among many examples here is the work of Paul K. Jewett, first in his *Man as Male and Female* (Grand Rapids: Eerdmans, 1975), and in his later *Who We Are: Our Dignity as Human – A Neo-Evangelical Theology* (with Marguerite Schuster) (Grand Rapids: Eerdmans, 1996), especially pp. 166–72.

range of biblical principles claimed to entail greater acceptance of homosexual practice.[41]

Seventhly, due recognition needs to be given to differences between the world for which Scripture was first given and our own cultural situation. This is perhaps the most significant of Calvin's hermeneutical moves in reworking the tradition. The crucial paragraph in his letter follows his discussion of Ezekiel, which concluded that 'the prophets only condemned usury as severely as they did because it was expressly prohibited for Jews to do'. It reads as follows:

> Today, a similar objection against usury is raised by some who argue that since the Jews were prohibited from practicing it, we too, on the basis of our fraternal union, ought not to practice it. To that I respond that a political union is different. The situation in which God brought the Jews together, combined with other circumstances, made commerce without usury apt among them. Our situation is quite different. For that reason, I am unwilling to condemn it, so long as it is practiced with equity and charity.

At least two different senses can be given to Calvin's decisive argument 'our situation is quite different'. On the one hand, it could represent a distinction based on a biblical theology of salvation history and progressive revelation in which earlier legal prohibitions within Israel are no longer binding on those in Christ.[42] Calvin's commentary on the Exodus text, where lending without interest is viewed as 'a political law … a part of the Jewish polity' now abrogated and replaced by Christian charity which was always its fundamental rationale, appears to appeal to this form of argument. Many evangelicals accept not only the long-standing theological hermeneutic that reads the Old Testament in this way, but also now acknowledge wider dynamic developments within Scripture as a whole that can legitimately be extrapolated further into our contemporary cultural context in a way that goes beyond the strict letter of Scripture.[43]

---

[41] Stanley Grenz, *Welcoming but not Affirming*, critiques a number of these (covenant, love, justice and liberation) in a section headed 'The Bible Versus the Texts' (pp. 90–5), while the recent strange theology of revisionist Elizabeth Stuart offers a stinging critique of much liberal and liberationist gay and lesbian theology in her *Gay and Lesbian Theologies* (Aldershot: Ashgate, 2002).

[42] McGrath discusses Calvin's understanding of the relationship between Old and New Testaments in his discussion of *Institutes* II (*A Life of John Calvin*, p. 157ff.).

[43] An interesting proposal here is the 'redemptive movement hermeneutic' developed by William J. Webb in his recent study, *Slaves, Women & Homosexuals:*

There is also, however, a second and potentially much more wide-ranging meaning in this statement that 'our situation is different'. This would enable such judgements on the relevance and applicability of biblical material to be made on the basis of changing culture and our understanding of the contemporary form of moral problems. So Biéler comments that, more aware of economic realities than many of his predecessors, Calvin 'realised very quickly that these biblical texts are not able to be properly applied to certain new realities of financial life'.[44] It is, in other words, partly Calvin's understanding of the new phenomenon in question that leads him to conclude that the practice of usury in ancient Israel is different from the practice of usury in his own time, and so enables a greater freedom in interpretation of the relevant biblical texts than previous generations of Christians had permitted.

This whole method in moral argument is based on the need for appeals to Scripture in contemporary moral reasoning to be analogical in form because 'we reason from like to like, not from identical to identical'.[45] Calvin here argues that social and economic change has made the issue of usury in his day less and not more like the phenomenon Scripture condemns, and that as a result there needs to be change in the church's moral tradition. Most contemporary Christians, including probably a majority of evangelicals, now follow a similar hermeneutic in relation to biblical texts that place restrictions on women's ministry. They argue that in an egalitarian society with well-educated women, our situation is 'quite different' from that of the biblical world, and so some if not all of the Pauline and other prohibitions are no longer absolutely binding.[46] Although they have convinced fewer, those arguing

---

[43] (*continued*) *Exploring the Hermeneutics of Cultural Analysis* (Downers Grove: InterVarsity Press, 2001).

[44] Biéler, *La Pensée Economique et Sociale de Calvin*, p. 455.

[45] Cosgrove, *Appealing to Scripture in Moral Debate*, p. 53. His second chapter gives as his second hermeneutical rule, the rule of analogy – 'analogical reasoning is an appropriate and necessary method for applying scripture to contemporary moral issues' (p. 51) – and provides a helpful discussion of this form of reasoning.

[46] Even those who oppose some of these trends find themselves accepting others (e.g. few insist on head coverings as required in 1 Cor. 11:5ff., while John Stott and others who uphold a view of female submission now permit women to teach despite 1 Tim. 2:12) while the unavoidability of analogical reasoning is evident by the need for those who wish to uphold a view of male headship to discern which roles and functions today (bishops, presbyters, cell group leaders, and so on) are properly limited to men.

for changes in relation to homosexuality similarly argue either that the biblical prohibitions are not universal moral laws and so no longer binding[47] or that homosexuality today is something so different from that found in the biblical world that we cannot treat it as requiring a similar response to that found in Scripture.[48]

It is vitally important to note that Calvin does not use another common but subtly different argument found in his appeal to rethink Christian moral judgements on usury. His argument is that he understands his current situation to be different from that of the biblical writers. This is not the same as an argument that he in his current situation knows better than the biblical writers. Calvin will use a form of the latter argument in his critique of the Christian tradition, but his high view of the inspiration and authority of Scripture means that he will not simply dismiss its moral teaching on the grounds of a more enlightened understanding of the phenomena about which it speaks. Evangelicals today must also reject this method of superior judgement over God's Word rather than subjecting oneself to the judgement of God's Word.

Eighthly, rather than simply focusing on prohibitions and warnings, it is necessary to develop a fully rounded appreciation of Scripture that highlights its positive and distinctive theological perspective on the broad issue under discussion. Throughout his writing on the subject of usury, Calvin is eager to set Scripture's specific and explicit teaching on usury within its broader understanding of riches and poverty and Christian responses to these. Only in the light of this biblical and theological interpretation of human economic life can the specific subject of usury be properly addressed. So his letter's rejection of the tradition's appeal to Luke 6:35 as referring to usury highlights Christ's command 'to lend to those from whom no hope of repayment is possible' and calls on Christians 'to help the poor' as 'Christ's words far more emphasize our remembering the poor than our remembering the rich'. His concluding limits on usury also stress this, insisting that nobody should take interest

---

[47] This argument is most fully developed in William Countryman, *Dirt, Greed and Sex* (Philadelphia: Fortress, 1988). A strong argument against his reading of Romans 1 is presented in Thomas E. Schmidt, *Straight & Narrow?: Compassion and Clarity in the Homosexuality Debate* (Leicester: Inter-Varsity Press, 1995), ch. 4.

[48] Such a social constructionist understanding of homosexuality is an important element in Michael Vasey's arguments to his fellow Evangelicals that they need to rethink this issue (*Strangers and Friends* [London: Hodder & Stoughton, 1995]), summarized in his contribution to Bradshaw, *The Way Forward?*, pp. 60–70.

from the poor and those lending must not neglect their duties or disdain
their poor brothers. As already noted, what is lawful for Christians in
their monetary dealings is to be determined not by 'the common practice
or the iniquity of the world', but rather 'a principle derived from the
Word of God'.

This final characteristic of Calvin's method returns us to where this
section began and the heart of Calvin's approach to moral questions that
must remain the heart of any genuine evangelical approach to ethics –
biblical and theological study. Calvin's own proposals for moral revision avoid wooden, naïve and fundamentalistic appeals to biblical texts,
and so must contemporary evangelical responses to proposals to modify
traditional Christian moral teaching. It is also clear that if Calvin's
methods of arguing his case in relation to usury are held to be within the
bounds of evangelical orthodoxy then care must be taken before rejecting out of hand and *tout court* those who use similar hermeneutical tools
in their appeal to Scripture in order to challenge long-held moral beliefs
within the church today. Nevertheless, a clear boundary is set by Calvin,
and must remain a hallmark of evangelical ethics. In relation to ethics, as
in relation to doctrine, the fundamental method he calls us to follow is
the same: 'we shall have to turn back to the Word of the Lord, in which
we have a sure rule for the understanding. For Scripture is the school of
the Holy Spirit.'[49]

All appeals to change moral teaching must therefore be brought
under the authoritative witness of Scripture. Scripture as the *norma
normans* must judge all proposals for reforming the Reformed church,
for it (not evangelical tradition nor church authority nor contemporary
consensus) is the final and supreme authority.

2.2. Reasoned analysis

The stress of Calvin and the wider Reformation on *sola scriptura* did not
entail rejection of either careful moral reasoning or appeals to tradition.
It simply held that 'the practices and beliefs of the church should
be grounded in scripture. Nothing that could not be demonstrated to be
grounded in scripture could be regarded as binding upon the believer.'[50]
In discussing usury, one of Calvin's recurring pleas is the need for careful, considered analysis of the actions being subjected to moral scrutiny.

---

[49] John Calvin, *Institutes of the Christian Religion*, Ford Lewis Battles (tr.),
John T. McNeill (ed.) (Philadelphia: Westminster, 1960), III.xxi.3.

[50] McGrath, *A Life of John Calvin*, p. 275.

So, his letter requests his friend to 'always keep in mind that what we must bring under judgement are not words but deeds themselves'.

Calvin's argument in favour of certain forms of usury could be expressed in terms of a method common and important in thinking through moral questions: a reconceptualization of the economic phenomenon in order to show that part of what was regularly universally categorized as forbidden usury is in fact significantly different in practice from Scripture's concerns and so cannot simply be subsumed in the standard moral descriptions and condemnations. This, he insists, is not simply changing the name of the practice in order to avoid the biblical teaching, but rather a more careful reasoned analysis of the phenomenon under investigation.

Calvin's method highlights the importance of moral description and the dangers in establishing and applying loose, all-embracing prohibitions on certain forms of human conduct or too quickly subsuming new issues within older categories. In contemporary debates the significance of this is evident in relation to certain forms of contraception (should the morning-after pill be classified as a licit form of contraception or as an illicit early abortion?) and in some of the debate over homosexual practice where the stronger arguments in favour of some modification and nuancing of the church's traditional prohibition are those which wish to argue that expressions of sexual love within quasi-marital same-sex relationships are not to be included within the category of acts subject to biblical condemnations.[51]

Related to this insistence on careful analysis of the human actions being condemned or approved, Calvin reminds us that evidence of abuse and evil in conjunction with a certain form of life does not necessarily require total rejection of it. Seemingly weakening his argument, Calvin is astonishingly frank about his assessment of the general practice of usury, which his letter acknowledges 'almost always travels with two inseparable companions: tyrannical cruelty and the art of deception', such that he considers it 'desirable if usurers were chased from every country'. His commentaries similarly do not seek to condone the general practice, admitting in relation to Psalm 15 that 'it is scarcely possible to find in the world a usurer who is not at the same time an extortioner, and addicted to unlawful and dishonourable gain'. Nevertheless, despite

---

[51] The two strongest advocates of such a view are Jeffrey John, *'Permanent, Faithful, Stable': Christian Same Sex Partnerships* (London: Darton, Longman & Todd, 1993, 2000), summarized in Bradshaw, *The Way Forward?*, pp. 44–59 and Eugene F. Rogers, Jr, *Sexuality and the Christian Body* (Oxford: Blackwell, 1999).

these observations, Calvin concludes that reason does not suffer us to admit that all usury is to be condemned without exception. Good Christian moral reasoning needs to see beyond abuses in order to discern whether there is nevertheless a good use which is acceptable to a faithful disciple of Christ. Here the development of moral imagination can play an important role by presenting cases for reflection. Calvin's letter follows this method by presenting an example of what he considers to be a situation in which it would be perfectly acceptable to practise usury. In relation to one area of contemporary debate, Oliver O'Donovan's fairytale about a childless woodman and his wife entertainingly sheds light on important moral issues surrounding in vitro fertilization (IVF), and illustrates why although many evangelicals object to IVF as currently commonly practised, they could, unlike most Roman Catholic opponents of the procedure, approve certain forms of this technology, most notably if they did not lead to the discarding of spare embryos.[52]

2.3. Tradition

Calvin is generally well versed in and respectful of the church fathers, recognizing the importance of engaging with the Christian tradition, especially if one is seeking to revise it.[53] In relation to usury, however, his treatment of the tradition must be considered a very weak part of his argument. In his letter he refers to St Ambrose and Chrysostom but swiftly dismisses their argument about the non-productivity of money as 'too frivolous' and then lists a string of rhetorical questions caricaturing their understanding of economics.[54]

Sadly, a similar lack of careful and sympathetic reading of Christian tradition often marks many contemporary debates where traditional

---

[52] Oliver O'Donovan, *Begotten or Made?* (Oxford: Oxford University Press, 1984), ch. 5. Others have, less convincingly, argued that there may similarly be a limited licit role for human cloning as a therapy for infertile couples, e.g., Gareth Jones, *Clones: The Clowns of Technology?* (Carlisle: Paternoster, 2001), ch. 3.

[53] For Calvin and the Fathers, see Anthony N.S. Lane, *John Calvin: Student of the Church Fathers* (Edinburgh: T. & T. Clark, 1999). McGrath's passion for this method is evident in, for example, 'Engaging the Great Tradition: Evangelical Theology and the Role of Tradition' in John G. Stackhouse (ed.), *Evangelical Futures: A Conversation on Theological Method* (Grand Rapids: Baker, 2000), pp. 139–58, which includes a discussion of Calvin.

[54] For better accounts of the much richer Christian tradition against usury, see the articles of Lockwood O'Donovan and Wykes cited above.

teaching is being questioned.[55] Part of the reason for this might be found in the fact that those who are seeking change know the tradition is opposed to their conclusion (so they tend to dismiss or ignore its arguments), while, paradoxically, when the tradition is closely examined it can provide less support for its ostensible upholders than might be expected. So, to return to evangelical disagreements over gender, Kevin Giles has argued at some length that a recent defence of limiting women's roles represents a novel interpretation of Scripture.[56] He claims its authors disregard the traditional understanding of the text of 1 Timothy 2 (that women were created second and are inherently more liable to deception and error than men) and defend the 'traditional' view of female subordination in a novel manner.[57] Similarly, those who defend the traditional prohibitions on homosexuality find many arguments defending this view in the tradition are less persuasive today. In contrast, a central contemporary argument in support of the tradition – the created order of humans as complementary sexual beings, male and female – is less prominent in much historical Christian discussion.[58]

Despite the limitations in Calvin's treatment of the Christian tradition, his fundamental perspective on tradition must not be forgotten. Evangelical moral theology must increase its knowledge of and respect for the Christian heritage of moral thinking and beware of assuming that simply repeating the conclusions of the tradition is sufficient. It must, however, always understand tradition to be subject to Scripture and so open to reform. This can be easy to acknowledge in relation to

---

[55] In contrast, one of the strengths of Gordon J. Wenham and William E. Heth, *Jesus and Divorce* (Exeter: Paternoster, 1984 and Carlisle: Paternoster, 2002) is their opening critique of the well-established Evangelical consensus allowing some remarriage after divorce through a careful study of the views of the early church.

[56] A.J. Köstenberger, T.R. Schreiner and H.S. Baldwin (eds), *Women in the Church: A Fresh Analysis of 1 Timothy 2:9–15* (Grand Rapids: Baker, 1995).

[57] Kevin Giles' 'A Critique of the "Novel" Contemporary Interpretation of 1 Timothy 2:9–15 Given in the Book, Women in the Church' appeared in two parts in the *Evangelical Quarterly* during 2000 – *Evangelical Quarterly* 72 (2) (pp. 151–67) and *Evangelical Quarterly* 72 (3) (pp. 195–215). *Evangelical Quarterly* 73 (3) (2001) contains a reply from Köstenberger (pp. 205–24) and a final response from Giles (pp. 225–45).

[58] The recent work of Gagnon, *The Bible and Homosexual Practice*, although flawed in a number of places and sometimes unpleasant in tone, offers the most substantial argument yet for created order as the consistent underlying biblical rationale for the texts condemning homosexual conduct.

past changes, so most accept that the distinguished nineteenth-century evangelicals who defended slavery and condemned liberal, progressive Christians who opposed it were wrong to think and act as they did.[59] It is, perhaps, more difficult to relate the corrigibility of tradition to contemporary debates such as homosexuality and so acknowledge (as Oliver O'Donovan does in his discussion of the important St Andrew's Day Statement) that a central evangelical argument is in fact based on well-supported and biblically grounded tradition rather than the explicit teaching of Scripture.

> The faithful homosexual Christian, however, is in a situation which the church cannot recognise as one of 'two forms or vocations' within which a 'life of faithful witness in chastity and holiness can be lived'. As it stands, the claim that there are two and only two such forms, though well supported, as the authors think, from Scripture, is not directly a biblical one but claims the authority of unbroken church tradition. If that tradition were shown to be essentially defective (i.e. without the supposed support of Scripture) or (less implausibly) to be more accommodating than has been thought (e.g. including homosexual unions as a valid variant of marriage), then, of course, there would be no general difficulty. But that supposes a radical development in the church's understanding of the tradition. The Statement does not rule such a development out a priori; in principle, no Anglican who believed, as Anglicans are supposed to believe, in the corrigibility of tradition *could* rule it out a priori. Yet the authors do not entertain the suggestion that such a development is in train or can be anticipated, and so they conclude: 'there is no place for the church to confer legitimacy upon alternatives', i.e. to marriage and singleness.[60]

---

[59] Willard M. Swartley's important *Slavery, Sabbath, War & Women: Case Issues in Biblical Interpretation* (Scottdale: Herald Press, 1983) summarizes the pro-slavery arguments and includes among their advocates Charles B. Hodge. Those wondering how Evangelicals could support such a position should see Kevin W. Giles' provocative piece, 'The Biblical Argument for Slavery: Can the Bible Mislead? A Case Study in Hermeneutics', *Evangelical Quarterly* 66:1 (1994), pp. 3–17.

[60] Oliver O'Donovan, 'Reading the St. Andrew's Day Statement' in Chris Sugden and Vinay Samuel (eds), *Anglican Life and Witness* (London: SPCK, 1997). Quotations from the St Andrew's Day Statement published in Bradshaw, *The Way Forward?*, pp. 5–11.

3. Conclusion – Living with Change

That the world is likely to remain marked by continued, perhaps increasing, change appears as certain as any statement can be about the future. Among the theological sub-disciplines, moral theology is an area most likely to feel those 'winds of change' rushing through it. New issues will need to be addressed and old certainties will be challenged.

In some circles, evangelicals and evangelical theology are understood as inherently conservative (even reactionary), with part of their popular appeal allegedly lying in the constancy and certainty they offer in a world of rapid change. Although there are elements of truth there, if evangelicals are serious about being heirs of the Reformation who seek to conform their lives and the life of the church to the voice of the living God, then mature evangelicalism should be a vital and dynamic theological movement neither resisting all challenges to its traditions (as if all challenges were a sign of unfaithfulness) nor adapting uncritically to trends in society. Rather, it must live out its conviction that *ecclesia reformata, semper reformanda.*

In fact, evangelicalism should go further and expect to find itself, as Calvin did, advocating reform in both church and world, rather than simply responding to the agendas of others whether within or without the church. It should do this through bringing together reasoned reflection and respect for tradition, but placing both under the supreme authority of Scripture. Above all, it must be convinced that although care must be taken not to bind consciences more rigidly than God nor to evade difficult hermeneutical debates, God rules us through the Word of God in Scripture. Evangelicals must therefore not be afraid to confess in relation to their ethics *Scriptura sacra locuta, res decisa est* (Scripture has spoken, the issue is decided).

11

Revelation and Natural Theology

William J. Abraham

Science impinges on the Christian faith at two distinct levels. First, in so far as science is taken as a standard of justification or knowledge, epistemologies of science set the standard for the epistemology of theology. This can be a blessing or a curse. It is a blessing if it provides a genuine and illuminating account of the epistemology of theology. It is a curse if it introduces an alien vision of epistemology into theology.

Much British theology has been deeply concerned about this issue. In part this stems from the incredibly privileged position granted to science in the culture as a whole. The cognitive status of theology has been so uncontested in high culture, in part due to the intellectual privileging of science, that it is very tempting to resolve the ensuing dissonance by assimilating theology to science. Anyone educated in Britain or Ireland cannot escape the shadow of science and its special status in elite culture.[1] In North America, theologians have until recently been much less worried about the epistemological relation between science and theology. Mainstream theology has been preoccupied not so much with questions of the truth or rationality of theology as it has been with the moral health of theology. It has been worried about how far theology has been involved in the oppression of various minorities and how far its themes can be reworked to bring about genuine liberation.[2]

At a second level, science and theology can relate not epistemologically, but materially. Both science and theology speak of, describe and in some sense explain the same phenomena, namely, the world, its nature and its history. This more mundane relation can work in one of two ways. Positively, theology and science can complement each other in their

---

[1] See, for example, John Polkinghorne, *Belief in God in an Age of Science* (New Haven, Connecticut: Yale University Press, 1998).

[2] For a recent example, see Joerg Rieger, *God and the Excluded* (Minneapolis: Fortress, 2001).

descriptions and explanations of the world. Thus a scientific vision of the sheer magnitude and complexity of the world can deepen a theological rendering of the power and providence of God. Negatively, they can run into conflict. Thus a scientific account of the origins of human agents can clearly contradict a theological account, as when theories of evolution and certain doctrines of special creation conflict. It is the latter kind of relation that has been predominant in North America as compared with Britain and Ireland. Cultural factors clearly play a role at this point. In North America, populist forms of evangelicalism and the educational institutions they have developed give voice to proposals that would not make it into the bloodstream of the academy in the British Isles.

Given Alister E. McGrath's training and cultural formation, given his ready acquaintance with the Anglo-American scene, and given his voracious appetite for every and anything related to the relation between science and religion, it is not surprising that he has taken up both these kinds of issues with irrepressible enthusiasm. They have, in fact, now become front and centre in his work. Here one has to make a confession. Reading McGrath is a unique experience. There are times when he settles into the topic in hand and it is relatively easy for the informed reader to know where he is going and to follow the arguments that get him there. There are other times when he wanders up so many historical and philosophical highways and byways that one is breathless before the journey is over. One is never quite sure what to make of the argument either in detail or as a whole.

In this paper I shall ignore material relations between science and theology; my interest is in the epistemological relation between science and theology. I want to explore and evaluate some limited aspects of McGrath's proposals in this domain. I make no claim to be comprehensive in the exegesis of his work; nor am I always certain about the interpretation I explore. However, the issues I take up in McGrath's work are of enormous importance for our understanding of theology in the immediate future. While I shall argue that there are as yet unresolved difficulties in McGrath's programme as a whole, there are two crucial insights he enumerates that must be carried forward into any future epistemology of theology.

Taking his cue from the work of Thomas F. Torrance,[3] McGrath has now embarked on an ambitious project to develop a three-volume work

---

[3] McGrath describes Torrance as 'the leading British theologian of the Twentieth century'. See *A Scientific Theology Volume 1: Nature* (Grand Rapids: Eerdmans, 2001), pp. 77, 280. He has written a fine biography of Torrance in *T.F. Torrance: An Intellectual Biography* (Edinburgh: T. & T. Clark, 1999).

in scientific theology.[4] The first volume, which will be our concern here, weaves back and forth between epistemological issues and material theological issues. Yet this is a misleading characterization. Precisely what makes McGrath so interesting is that he advances a bold epistemological thesis about the relation between theology and science on the grounds that both disciplines share the same subject matter, namely, the created order made *ex nihilo* by the God and Father of our Lord Jesus Christ.[5] His aim is not just to retrieve a positive account of the relation between theology and other sources of truth enshrined in the various academic disciplines that currently exist. His aim is to provide 'a unitary foundation of human knowledge' on the basis of Christian theology.[6] On the way to this goal he intends to bring in what we can only describe as a new revolution that undercuts or dissolves the standard distinction, say, between the natural sciences and the humanities. What this signals from the outset is that McGrath's project is epistemological through and through. His 'scientific theology' is one more exercise in the epistemology of theology.

We can see this epistemological orientation most clearly when we begin at the end of McGrath's inquiry. The conclusion he drives home is that it is possible to have a genuine natural theology so long as we relocate natural theology within revealed theology. Over against natural theology as an autonomous, independent exercise, we can bring new life

---

[4] See McGrath, *A Scientific Theology Volume 1*. McGrath makes clear that similar themes are pursued in his *The Foundations of Dialogue in Science and Religion* (Oxford: Blackwell, 1998), but it is not entirely clear how these two texts are to be related. The internal development of both texts is very similar; at times whole passages of the latter text show up unchanged in the former text. One gets the impression that McGrath has started all over again to work out a vision of the relation between science and theology and that he has shifted away from dialogue between science and religion to a positive correlation of science with Christian theology. In order to limit the potential confusion, I shall focus on the first of these two texts in order to do justice to his most recent ideas and arguments. It should also be said for the sake of clarity that McGrath has a distinctive style in which he constantly loads the text with forays into the history of theology and with extensive polemical and *ad hominem* asides. Both these can be a serious distraction to the reader; it is far from easy at times to be sure that one has captured his proposals and arguments. This too should be borne in mind in what follows.

[5] McGrath has throughout the natural sciences in mind. I shall follow him in this, referring at times to the natural sciences in order to let this designation not slip from view.

[6] McGrath, *A Scientific Theology Volume 1*, p. 34.

back into it by reconstruing it as an appeal to the order of creation that confirms what God made known in special divine revelation through Jesus Christ. Thereby we can overcome Karl Barth's veto on natural theology, vindicate T.F. Torrance's extension of Barth's epistemological vision, and open up a fresh engagement with the natural sciences.

With this in place we can trace the journey through McGrath's volume as a whole. The first chapter clears the decks in two ways. First, it roots the whole project in those patristic sources that allow philosophy into theology so long as it remains a handmaid to Scripture and special divine revelation. Secondly, it provides warrants for the appeal to natural science as *ancilla theologiae* by appeal to special revelation itself; that is, by insisting that the divine revelation embedded in creation is embodied in Christ. Accordingly, whatever the differences between the various disciplines, there is 'a unitary conception of the human intellectual enterprise'.[7] Hence there are good reasons from within divine revelation to engage in interaction with the natural sciences. The second chapter completes this foregrounding by a kind of double anchoring. The theology with which science engages is that supplied by classical Christian orthodoxy; the science with which theology engages is that of a robustly realist cast. Neither designation should be seen as requiring commitment to an essentialist conception of theology or science.

Chapter three supplies the reasons for rejecting any neutral conception of nature. Given that all conceptions of nature are socially constructed if not socially determined, Christians are free to think of nature as the outcome of divine action: nature is a form of creation. The theme of creation is then given explicitly Christian content in a fascinating historical account of the origins of the Christian doctrine of creation *ex nihilo* in chapter four. This is followed by an exceptionally long exposition of the doctrine of creation that is related to human agents and their rational capacity to discern the rationality of God in creation. The rationality of God is witnessed to by the human ability to discern moral order and by the prevalence of mathematics, order and beauty enshrined in scientific explanations of creation.

As already noted, chapter four provides the capstone. Recent natural theology, represented as an attempt to prove the existence of God from premises that do not presuppose any religious belief, is really a recent, late seventeenth- and eighteenth-century invention, and one that 'our age finds no pressing reason to follow'.[8] It was misguided polemical

---

[7] Ibid., p. 25.
[8] Ibid., p. 259. This is a very weak and odd rejection of Alston, but I shall not chase that hare here.

enterprise that fitted the social agenda of the day. However, back of that kind of bad natural theology, there is a good form of natural theology that antedates it. That earlier natural theology is legitimated by the Bible, can withstand the Barthian assault on natural theology, and has been championed and restored in the theology of T.F. Torrance. In this new natural theology, on the other side of commitment to the full and final revelation of God in Jesus Christ, appeal can rightly be made to the witness to God in the natural order as God's creation and to humanity as made in the image of God. This new natural theology is not undermined by the consequences of sin. Rather, it supplies points of contact with unbelievers in the work of apologetics, and it provides a comprehensive means by which theology may address the world in the public arena.

Given McGrath's tendency to meander, it is crucial to keep our eye on the quarry. It would be very easy to get caught in a whole nest of interesting issues. Is McGrath right in his reading of the many figures that show up in the narrative? Has he systematically suppressed the more pietistic side of evangelicalism in favour of a generic creedal version? Has he really solved the Euthyphro dilemma on the epistemology of moral discourse? Is he right in his remarks about the late Jewish commitment to the doctrine of creation *ex nihilo*? Can his Anglican biblicism be sustained? We could multiply the questions in many directions. The crucial issue we need initially to address, however, is whether this programme is a viable one. Is it a coherent project? Will it withstand critical scrutiny? Is it an advance on earlier developments?

In pursuing our quarry, let us assume that McGrath is correct about the central place of divine revelation in the epistemology of theology. Let us go further. Let us assume that the early doctrinal and creedal developments he has incorporated into his version of evangelicalism are correct. Can we relocate natural theology within this arena and make epistemological progress? Much hinges here on how we conceive of natural theology, on whether divine revelation supplies McGrath the warrant he needs, on how we think through the 'rationality' of science and theology, and on whether the 'data' to which appeal is made on the other side of divine revelation provide genuine support for McGrath's form of theism in the way he envisages. These are very demanding conditions of success.

As McGrath rightly recognizes, natural theology is a complex and contested enterprise. At this point we need to set aside the historical survey and get ruthlessly clear about the options. We can helpfully distinguish between three very different conceptions of natural theology. Let's simply call them conceptions A, B and C.

In conception A, natural theology means the intellectual attempt to provide support for any form of theism by means of deductive or inductive appeal to premises that do not presume the truth of the theism in question. Here the concern is with legitimate and valid inference; the premises are examined for truth, and the inferences are examined for cogency. Much contemporary natural theology in the analytical tradition, brilliantly represented by Richard Swinburne, represents this version of natural theology.[9] How far it was or was not represented by earlier figures is a matter for historical investigation. Moreover, to dismiss this version of natural theology on the grounds of it being motivated by polemical or social agendas in the eighteenth century is to commit the genetic fallacy; it is to seek to undermine the validity and soundness of an argument by drawing attention to the inappropriate motives of its proponents. This is an old ploy in the history of philosophy and theology, and it is so obviously flawed that it needs no refutation here. The proper and legitimate way to refute a bad argument is to argue against its soundness and validity; everything else is a distraction.

In conception B, natural theology means the attempt to argue for the justification of theistic belief on the grounds of apparent awareness of the divine in nature and in personal experience. Here the relevant mode of cognition is not inference but perception; what is at stake is not the soundness or validity of various inferences but the reliability of our belief-producing mechanisms represented by religious perception, or the *sensus divinitatus*, or the inner witness of the Holy Spirit. The revival of this kind of natural theology, represented respectively by William Alston[10] and Alvin Plantinga,[11] is an astonishing turn of events. Again, we need not worry overmuch about how far this kind of natural theology is to be found, say, in John Calvin, Jonathan Edwards, John Wesley, Frederick Schleiermacher, John Hick and the like. Moreover, the proper way to refute this kind of natural theology is to undermine the theory of perception, or of belief production, or of proper function, on offer.

In conception C, natural theology means the appeal to various features of the universe as confirmation of a prior appeal to special divine revelation. In this instance the propriety of the privileged site and articulated content of divine revelation is assumed. Thick religious and theological descriptions of various features of the universe are then

---

[9] See especially his *The Existence of God* (Oxford: Clarendon Press, 1979).

[10] See especially his *Perceiving God* (Ithaca, New York: Cornell University Press, 1991).

[11] See especially his *Warranted Christian Belief* (New York: Oxford University Press, 2000).

assembled in such a way that they support or confirm the prior commit-ment to divine revelation. In reality, this form of natural theology might legitimately be described as a disguised appeal to general divine revela-tion. Having agreed, or assumed, that God is revealed in Jesus Christ, and that the truth of that special revelation is appropriately expressed in the ancient faith of the church, one further discerns the activity or presence of God in the created order, both physical and human. God, it is said, is now manifest in the created order and can be discerned to be manifest to some degree even by sinful human agents. Moreover, the data invoked are logically dependent on prior theological doctrines of creation and redemption; indeed without these doctrines, the appeal to the relevant data is considered to be illegitimate and unwarranted. The way to refute this kind of natural theology is to show that the appeal to special revelation is arbitrary; or to argue that the data supposedly confirming the appeal to special revelation do not exist; or the data do not logically support special revelation. While any one of these moves would be highly damaging, a convergence of arguments along these lines would be fatal.

Permit a couple of hermeneutical comments before we return to the exposition of McGrath. First, there is an interesting progression from type A through type B to type C. Type A eschews any initial commit-ment to theism; type B may or may not involve an initial commitment to theism; type C requires not just an initial commitment to theism but to special revelation. Note, secondly, that there is both continuity and discontinuity between type B and type C. The affinity is in the appeal to perception, discernment or awareness of the presence or activity of God in the created order, whether non-human or human; the discontinuity is that in type B natural theology there need be no prior commitment to special divine revelation in Jesus Christ. Thirdly, it is important to ask what status is ascribed to any of these types of natural theology either in the economy of theology or in the life of the church as a whole. Certainly, proponents of natural theology have often insisted on a very high status for each of these types: however, this cannot be assumed; it must be argued for in detail.

McGrath rejects natural theology A and natural theology B, but he subscribes to a version of natural theology C. He rejects the first two because they fall foul of the objections Barth levelled at all natural theo-logy. Thus they involve an unacceptable autonomy, a false intellectual dualism, and cannot be legitimized by the divine revelation given in Jesus Christ, the foundation of all proper Christian theology. Natural theology C avoids autonomy and dualism; in addition, it is itself man-dated by divine revelation. The latter is worth explicating further. The core of the argument is that the divine *logos* embodied in Jesus Christ is embedded in the very structures of the universe.

> the Christian understanding of the ontology of creation demands a faithful investigation of nature. For this reason, the exploration of the interface between theology and the natural sciences is to be regarded as ontologically motivated and legitimated. Yet the Christian doctrine of creation is not limited by the demand that we see nature as creation; it has a highly signifi-cant Christological component. The New Testament identifies an implicit continuity between creation and redemption, focused on the person and work of Christ. The Christological dimensions of the doctrine of creation are such that divine rationality – whether this is conceptualized as *logos* or *ratio* – must be thought of as being embedded in creation and embodied in Christ. The same divine rationality or wisdom which the natural scientist discerns within the created order is to be identified within the *logos* incar-nate, Jesus Christ. Creation and redemption ultimately bear witness to the same God, and the same divine rationality.[12]

We can spell out this argument as follows. The embodiment of the divine *logos* in Jesus Christ is God's own decision and doing; it is an act of sheer grace. Because the life, death and resurrection of Jesus Christ are consti-tuted by God's own electing decision, that act of God in Jesus Christ per-mits the true nature and character of God to be represented in our obedient cognitive response to God, as enshrined in the Scriptures and the creedal tradition of the church. In submitting our lives, including our cognitive life, to the saving and sanctifying work of God in Jesus Christ through the Holy Spirit, our discourse about God replicates in a genuine way the very character of God. Thus the object known, God the blessed Trinity, shapes and mirrors our discourse about the divine, so as to provide an objectively true and non-arbitrary depiction of God. From this same revelation we know that the God of redemption is the God of creation and that the *logos* or rationality present in Jesus Christ is embedded in creation. Thus we should expect that a true and proper natural science that submits itself in humility to be shaped and formed by creation would also objectively represent the truth about creation. Thus the mathematically precise and intrinsically beautiful depiction of the world truly and objectively represents the order of the world as it is. In this case the object known, namely the world, forms what is known in science. Hence there is a single rationality at work in both theology and science. To be sure, different disciplines will have their own unique

---

[12] McGrath, *A Scientific Theology Volume 1*, pp. 24–5.

features depending on their subject matter and their specific means of investigation, but across the disciplines there is a unitary rationality grounded in a robust Christian theology. Moreover, the truth derived from divine revelation is confirmed by the fact that human agents made in the image of God have the capacity to engage in science and by the fact that the science they develop turns out to be faithful to reality.

This epistemological vision has proved to be exceptionally attractive in wide tracts of North America and Europe over the last generation. Its influence helps to explain the pervasive hostility to natural theology A and natural theology B within many theological circles. This version of natural theology is grounded in divine revelation; in its realism, it is resolutely non-subjectivist and appropriately objectivist in orientation; it is stated in terms of the classical Christology of the church, and hence it is thoroughly Trinitarian in content; it can be argued to have clear continuity with the best insights of the leading theologians across church divisions prior to the Enlightenment; and it not only finds a home for a realist understanding of natural science, it also appeals to the work and results of natural scientists for confirmation. Neither natural theology A nor natural theology B can provide these kind of gains; worse still, they usually involve forms of autonomy and dualism that are intellectually otiose both intrinsically and theologically.

Attractive as this epistemological vision may be, I now want to argue that the difficulties in it far outweigh the gains. There are, however, at least two crucial insights within it that can and should be rescued from the surrounding theory. I happen to think that they can only be salvaged if we can take on board the work of natural theology A and natural theology B. Any argument for that thesis must await another occasion.

The chief and arresting initial difficulty with natural theology C is that it has no way of securing its initial commitment to the divine revelation from which it derives its theory of universal rationality. It simply has to begin with the assumption that the Fathers of the church got it right on both the identity and content of divine revelation; that they were correct in identifying Jesus of Nazareth as the one and only Son of God, as worked out at Nicaea and Chalcedon; and that they were correct in insisting that this same Jesus Christ is the one and only source of truth about God. Now we can well grant that theologians are at liberty to work from within this circle of faith. However, they surely need to provide some account as to why we should enter this circle of faith in the first place. These are massively substantial proposals that cannot simply be built into the operation at the outset. Yet this is precisely what Torrance and McGrath do.

It is not enough at this point to be told that the object of knowledge should determine the form and content of our knowledge. This is an epistemological platitude that has been around since Aristotle. More precisely, we need some account as to how Torrance and McGrath know that, over against other claims to possess and properly interpret divine revelation, they have the real goods. We need some kind of assuring word that God is indeed known in and through Jesus of Nazareth; to claim that this is the case because it was God's choice thus to be made known is to repeat exactly what is at stake and to stall the conversation indefinitely. The account of rationality and justification Torrance and McGrath supply already presupposes that they have access to the truth about God; it is totally parasitic on that claim; hence we are no further along than when we started. Indeed Jews, Muslims and Mormons can make precisely the same move by meshing the Aristotelian epistemological platitude that the object known must determine our thinking about what is known with their commitments to the locus of divine revelation. We are left with any number of circles of faith that can deploy the very same epistemic principles to arrive at radically different theologies.

The upshot of this is simple. Natural theology C may operate for a time as a stopgap epistemology in a world where the academy at large dismisses all claims to revelation as spurious. It cannot begin to work in a world where secularism is under stress from postmodernism, or where rival claims to divine revelation have dramatically hit the world stage. Returning to the epistemological vision worked out by Barth in the 1930s and later updated by Torrance is simply no longer viable.

One senses that McGrath may be half aware of this. Thus when it comes to his defence of realism in natural science, his initial vision of rationality derived from divine revelation is idling. His arguments in favour of realism in natural science are in fact attractive. His realist reading of science is derived from the explanatory and predictive power of scientific theory, from its use of experimental confirmation, and from the technological control that it furnishes. He also adds an argument from testimony, providing his own word from his hard-won training in chemistry and biophysics as evidence. While the latter cannot be set aside cavalierly, it has very limited value, simply because scientific training does not in itself provide immediate justification for epistemological proposals on the status of scientific theory. Scientists, like historians who write on the epistemology of historical investigation, are deeply divided among themselves; their testimonies are far from unanimous. Happily, McGrath does not rely overmuch on this kind of evidence for his scientific realism; it becomes something of an aside. Moreover, his scientific realism does not at all depend on his theological realism.

Indeed if it did, it is hard to see how it could supply support for the latter, in that, if it depended on his prior theological realism, the whole argument would be circular. Furthermore, note that the data derived at this point from his scientific realism are not at all couched in theological categories or descriptions. And this too is significant, for if McGrath was to provide a description of science that depended on prior commitment to and deployment of the very theological categories for which he is supplying confirmation, then the whole argument would once again be circular.

What is at issue here is that the case for realism in the natural sciences really borrows next to nothing from the case for theological realism. We might express this by saying that the rationality embodied in natural science is indeed subject-relative. Moreover, the crucial features securing the scientific realism are not at all available to theology as represented by McGrath. Leaving aside the issue of explanatory power, theology produces neither predictive power nor technological control of the kind provided by science. Nor is theology in any way dependent on the results of carefully constructed experiments. Christian theology depends crucially on special divine revelation in history and on divinely inspired witness and interpretive assistance to the church inaugurated by Jesus Christ through the work of the Holy Spirit.[13] Equally, the work of the theologian depends on the radical renovation of our sinful cognitive capacities and dispositions. At this point, the connection between theology and spirituality is far deeper than any aesthetic or ascetic analogies in the life and work of scientists might at first suggest. Moreover, divine revelation requires an absolute but not unconditional or indefeasible commitment that is not matched by the provisional and studiously conditional practices of science. Furthermore, divine revelation takes one into a world of ineradicable mystery all too visible in the doctrines of the incarnation and the Trinity that would never be taken as a mark of success in science. By its very nature science seeks to explain the mysteries and wonders of the created order in mathematically precise theorems that are indeed mysterious to the uninitiated but that provide illuminating explanations to those in the know. Finally, to crown it all, there is a degree of unavoidable offence in both the site and interpretation of divine revelation that would be a scandal to the kind of

---

[13] This moves calls for a radical rejection of the modified biblicism that remains central to McGrath's vision of Evangelicalism. In my judgement we need a much more soteriologically oriented vision of scripture. See my *Canon and Criterion in Christian Theology* (Oxford: Oxford University Press, 1998, 2002).

science McGrath champions.[14] While many in popular culture may be puzzled and even put off by various scientific proposals, generally the findings of science are welcomed with enthusiasm. Indeed, science has become such an idol in our culture that one is branded an outcast and heretic if one does not commit wholeheartedly to its fruits.

McGrath could well assent to much of this, but the differences between science and theology play next to no role in his vision of the relation between theology and science. He can assent, because he is committed to the possibility of genuine differences between dissimilar academic disciplines. However, I suspect that he suppresses these differences because, following Torrance, he thinks there is a single rationality governing our intellectual endeavours; there is only one divine rationality present in creation and redemption. Working from above, we then expect to find this exemplified in both science and theology. However, this prediction is not borne out by what we actually find in science and theology. To be sure, we can find all sorts of interesting parallels, analogies, resonances, correlations, convergence, conciliances and the like.[15] And we can look to theological assumptions to make sense of the emergence of science in Western culture; or we can provide theological explanations for the intellectual capacities and foibles of scientists as made in the image of God or marred by sin. What is most striking, however, are the crucial differences between science and theology. Once these differences are enumerated, then the claim that there is one divine rationality embedded in the universe has next to no cash value. The characteristic form of argument deployed, the type of explanation invoked, the crucial dispositions cultivated, the kind of commitment fostered, the sort of mystery and anomaly tolerated, the place given or not given to mathematics and experiment, when taken together these make manifest radically different kinds of rationality. Or, to express it another way, it is strained in the extreme to claim that they exemplify one divine rationality at work in the universe.

It is even more strained to claim that they exemplify one single epistemology. The only serious epistemological platitude on offer is in fact terribly thin. To say that the object known should be allowed to determine our discourse about the known, while it rightly has a place within epistemology, tells us nothing about the epistemic status of any particular theology or science. In each case we need substantial and independent proposals about why we think this or that form or science or theology

---

[14] I have sought to delineate the crucial contours of that offence in 'The Offense of Divine Revelation', *Harvard Theological Review* 95:3 (2002), pp. 251–64.

[15] These are the terms deployed again and again by McGrath.

brings us into contact with reality. This is not to say that the arguments and proposals should take the form of classical foundationalism, appealing to absolutely certain, infallible foundations and the like. The objections to this enterprise are now well known and require no rehearsal here. What we need is detailed and careful epistemological work that avoids this dead end and that provides a genuinely realist vision of both science and theology. Moreover, we must work our way toward that realism and simply not assume it at the outset by front-loading the proposed realism with the truth claims that are at issue.

Working toward realism is precisely what is at stake in all forms of natural theology A and most forms of natural theology B. The use of the term 'natural theology' here is purely conventional, and its continued deployment has nothing to do with whether or not we can properly explicate the concept of 'the natural' or 'nature'. What is at stake for both enterprises is the goal of providing epistemological visions of any and all versions of theism that does not cook the books by assuming at the outset that which is at issue. It is precisely for this reason that Alston describes the kind of natural theology B that he develops as an 'enterprise of support for religious beliefs' that starts 'from premises that neither are nor presuppose any religious beliefs'.[16] This could equally apply to natural theology A.

We need to walk warily at this point. Recent work in general episte-mology has made us all too aware that much epistemology in the modern period has been captive to forms of internalism and methodism that suppress other ways of thinking about justification, warrant, ratio-nality, truth and knowledge.[17] Epistemologies developed in terms of reliable belief-producing mechanisms, proper functioning of our cogni-tive capacities, virtue theory, and the like, are now once again in vogue. Moreover, particularism has called into question how far we can hope to provide any single theory of justification or knowledge that fits all the relevant cases we need to secure. Once that new diversity within epistemology has been acknowledged, there may well be options in the epistemology of theology that are radically fresh and that have deep

---

[16] McGrath, *A Scientific Theology Volume 1*, p. 241.

[17] The term 'methodism' applies here to those who insist that we must have the right method of inquiry in place before we can know whether particu-lar propositions are true or false, justified or unjustified, rational or irrational, knowledge or opinion. Roderick Chisholm coined it in his seminal essay 'The Problem of the Criterion', which can be found in his *The Foundations of Knowledge* (Minneapolis: University of Minnesota Press, 1982), pp. 61–75.

affinities with some of the great theologians of the pre-Enlightenment period.[18] Furthermore, within some of these options we may well find ourselves landed with networks of argument that are circular in character, but not viciously so. From the philosophical side, Alvin Plantinga has recently displayed how epistemological proposals about warrant that supply a deep undergirding for Christian faith can be located in a robustly theistic worldview. Equally, from the theological side of the debate, Bruce Marshall has produced a brilliant *tour de force* in which the conception of truth is lodged in a richly Trinitarian vision of theology.[19] Both are robustly realist in their theological commitments.[20] So there may be a host of ways of developing a hearty realism in the epistemology of theology.

We should also be wary in claiming that natural theology A and natural theology B involve some kind of autonomous, rebellious spirit that is at odds with the Christian commitment to continuous creation or to justification by grace through faith. Engaging in natural theology, as I have described it, is simply a serious attempt to answer entirely appropriate epistemological questions that cannot be suppressed by a Barthian or Reformed theological veto at this point. We want to know if our theological proposals are warranted, justified, rationally defensible and the like. We desire to ascertain whether we can genuinely lay claim to knowledge in the public square. In doing so, our primary concern, as already indicated, is to evaluate the validity and soundness of various arguments. It is to examine critically various epistemological proposals, including those of Barth, Torrance and McGrath. Within this we can explore how far our epistemological theories are or are not compatible with the life of faith as undergirded from start to finish by divine grace. To put the matter plainly and sharply: it is a category mistake to confuse theological proposals, developed to resolve the soteriological crisis of the Reformation and crystallized in debates about justification by faith, with philosophical proposals that seek to evaluate arguments about the existence of God or to examine critically theories of proper function, perception of the divine, and the

---

[18] Even then we must be careful in our historical generalizations for Thomas Reid, clearly a crucial figure in the Scottish Enlightenment, was an externalist in epistemology.

[19] Bruce D. Marshall, *Trinity and Truth* (Cambridge: Cambridge University Press, 2000).

[20] I am referring here not to technical visions of philosophical realism but simply to the claim that theology successfully makes claims that are true, rather than simply expressing emotions, or projecting our wishes on to the universe.

like.[21] While theological and epistemological proposals cannot and should not be kept in airtight compartments, they do need to be carefully distinguished, so that each can be explored and examined in its own right.

However we proceed, we should heed two insights that lie buried within natural theology C. The first is that Christian theology depends crucially on both general and special divine revelation. This stems from the platitude that agents are made known through their actions. Thus the attempt to know God apart from Jesus Christ is thoroughly illegitimate, if it is in fact the case that God was incarnate in Jesus Christ. Such special revelation is at the core of Christian theology, though not at the expense of appropriate appeal to reason and experience. Much work remains to be done in fully explicating precisely how this appeal to special divine revelation is to be incorporated into a full vision of the epistemology of theology.[22] Moreover, and this is the second insight, a place must be found for a peculiar feature of the concept of revelation, namely, that revelation is a threshold concept. Thus, once one accepts special divine revelation, the divine revelation embraced may have significant implications for the way we think about everything, including the way we think about our cognitive failures and successes. One of the features of special revelation is that it is unlikely to leave a single square inch of the universe unbaptized or untransfigured. There is a kind of loop-back effect that may throw light on the very doxastic practices that brought us to faith in the first place and that may also throw light on those doxastic practices that are at the core of natural science. McGrath's work is clearly a valiant effort to preserve both these hard-won insights. It is hard to see, however, how well these insights can be retained if we reject the kind of reasoning that is constitutive of natural theology A and natural theology B.

---

[21] My own response to Barth's standard arguments against natural theology can be found in my *An Introduction to the Philosophy of Religion* (Englewoods Cliff, NJ: Prentice Hall, 1985), pp. 76–86.

[22] I have used this term throughout in order to call for the creation of a new field within theological studies that would systematically and self-critically examine the host of proposals that are currently hosted within philosophy of religion and deal with the epistemology of religious belief and appear within Protestant systematic theology within prolegomenae. Roman Catholic theologians often tackle the relevant issues in Fundamental Theology. Aside from the intrinsic need for this development, I think such a division of labour would free up systematic theologians to pursue their work along lines that are currently suppressed or sidelined.

In an interesting way McGrath's work also acts as a bridge between recent epistemological work within Barthian circles and within Anglo-American analytical philosophy. By formulating his central proposal in terms of a natural theology he has, wittingly or unwittingly, put a foot into the analytic camp, all the while keeping his other foot solidly placed within the world of Barth and Torrance. For too long these two great traditions have glared sullenly and polemically at each other across the divide that separates them. McGrath is well aware of how fragile the bridge can be. He has added fresh reinforcement by exploring the resources of the history and epistemology of science. My argument is that the ensuing bridge is in danger of buckling under the strains he has introduced. However, having sought to cross the bridge he has built for himself, such buckling should encourage us to add other and better reinforcement in the future.

12

Postmodern Evangelical Theology: A Nonfoundationalist Approach to the Christian Faith

John R. Franke

All human knowledge is situated. All human knowledge is influenced and shaped by the social, cultural and historical situation in which it emerges. As a human endeavour bound up with the task of interpretation, the discipline of Christian theology, like all other intellectual pursuits, bears the marks of the particular settings in which it is produced. That is to say, quite simply, that theology is a thoroughly contextual discipline. In one sense such an observation is so commonplace as to make its assertion at the opening of an essay seem banal. However, it is my conviction that an understanding of the thoroughly contextual nature of theology, while often acknowledged, has yet to take hold of the discipline as it is practised in North American evangelical Protestantism. It is my belief that a large part of the reason for this is the enduring propensity of conservative evangelical thinkers to embrace the characteristics and tendencies of modernity in the task of theological formulation, particularly those of foundationalism. This essay will suggest an alternative model for the theological task that takes seriously the contextual nature of all human knowledge while remaining faithful to core Christian commitments by drawing on the insights of postmodern theory from the perspective of evangelical and ecumenical orthodoxy.

1. Evangelical Theology and Theological Method

Before launching into a discussion of the shape and ethos of a nonfoundationalist theology, it will be helpful to consider briefly the status of methodological questions in evangelical thought. While theologians in the mainline have tended to fixate on questions of theological method to the neglect of actually putting methodological constructions to work in the task of doing theology, the situation in evangelical Protestantism has been, until recently, nearly the reverse. Evangelical theologians have produced numerous works concerned with the content and exposition of theology. Yet they have given little attention to methodological concerns. Nor have they applied themselves to the careful examination of philosophical presuppositions and theological hermeneutics. Evangelicals have tended to bypass questions raised by theological method and moved directly to the task of making theological assertions and constructing theological systems, as though the process of moving from ancient texts to the contemporary affirmation of doctrine and theology was largely self-evident. Such an approach has led evangelical theologian Richard Lints to comment that the evangelical theological tradition 'has not been nurtured to think methodologically'.[1]

A recent example of this long-standing tendency can be found in the best-selling work of Wayne Grudem, who defines systematic theology simply as any study that attempts to explain what the whole Bible teaches us today about any given topic. He goes on to explain that this definition suggests that an appropriate procedure in the task of doing theology 'involves collecting and understanding all the relevant passages in the Bible on various topics and then summarizing their teachings clearly so that we know what to believe about each topic'.[2] Earlier, Carl F.H. Henry asserted that the task of theology is simply 'to exhibit the content of biblical revelation as an orderly whole'.[3] This approach is based on the presupposition that the Bible, as the entirely truthful self-disclosure of God presented in propositional form, is the sole foundation for theology.[4]

This approach has typified evangelical theology and is characterized by a commitment to the Bible as the source book of information for systematic theology. As such, it is viewed as a rather loose and relatively disorganized collection of factual, propositional statements. The task of theology in turn becomes that of collecting and arranging these varied statements in such a way as to bring their underlying unity into relief and reveal the eternal system of timeless truths to which they point. This

---

[1] Richard Lints, *The Fabric of Theology: A Prolegomenon to Evangelical Theology* (Grand Rapids: Eerdmans, 1993), p. 259.

[2] Wayne Grudem, *Systematic Theology: An Introduction to Biblical Doctrine* (Grand Rapids: Zondervan, 1994), p. 21.

[3] Carl F.H. Henry, *God, Revelation and Authority* (Waco: Word, 1976), vol. 1, p. 244.

[4] For Henry's exposition of this thesis, see ibid., pp. 181–409.

'concordance' conception of theology looks back to Charles Hodge, arguably the most influential American theologian for evangelicals, and his view that the task of theology 'is to systematize the facts of the Bible, and ascertain the principles or general truths which those facts involve'.[5] Hodge's own understanding of theology is generally derived from the scholasticism characteristic of post-Reformation Protestant orthodoxy.[6] Evangelicals in the twentieth century, buoyed by the assumptions of modernity, have continued, with some modifications, to follow the theological paradigm of scholasticism as exemplified in the work of Charles Hodge and others from the 'old' Princeton tradition, such as B.B. Warfield and J. Gresham Machen.[7]

By limiting the scope of theological reflection to the exposition of the biblical text, evangelicals have been able to avoid the thorny issues surrounding the roles of tradition and culture in theology. Without sensing the need to deal with these concerns, due to their exclusive focus on the text of Scripture, evangelicals have generally seen little reason to participate in the contemporary methodological discussion that has so captivated the rest of the theological community. It is worth noting that this lack of reflection on, and engagement with, contemporary methodological/theological issues has not been because of the lack of an approach to method, but due to the particular understanding of method that evangelicals have generally followed.

Although this approach to theology is clearly still the dominant paradigm in traditional evangelical circles, there are signs that the situation is beginning to change. Recently, a number of theologians from within evangelicalism have called this paradigm into question. John Jefferson Davis, for example, critiques the concordance model of theology with the observation that it:

> does not take adequate account of the social context of the theological task and the historicity of all theological reflection. The method tends to promote a repetition of traditional formulations of biblical doctrine, rather than

[5] Charles Hodge, *Systematic Theology* (New York: Scribner, Armstrong, 1872), vol. 1, p. 18.

[6] For a detailed discussion of theological method in the Reformed scholastic tradition, see Richard A. Muller, *Post-Reformation Reformed Dogmatics* vol. 1: *Prolegomena to Theology* (Grand Rapids: Baker, 1987).

[7] For an assessment of the influence of the Princeton tradition on American evangelicalism, see George Marsden, *Fundamentalism and American Culture: The Shaping of Twentieth-Century Evangelicalism, 1870–1925* (New York: Oxford University Press, 1980).

appropriate recontextualizations of the doctrines in response to changing cultural and historical conditions.[8]

Similarly, Stanley Gundry raises the question as to whether or not evangelicals 'really recognize that all theology represents a contextualization', including evangelical theology.[9] Both Davis and Gundry urge evangelicals to adopt a contextual approach to theology that takes seriously the role of culture in theological formulation.

This concern is evident in the work of leading evangelical theologian Millard Erickson, who defines theology as 'that discipline which strives to give a coherent statement of the doctrines of the Christian faith, based primarily upon the Scriptures, placed in the context of culture in general, worded in contemporary idiom, and related to issues of life'.[10] Although this concern for contextualization is welcome, the traditional evangelical commitment to objectivism and propositionalism has worked against an adequate understanding of the relationship between theology and culture even among those who have called for contextualization as a part of the theological process. One of the significant results of this failure has been the relatively uncritical acceptance of modernist assumptions by evangelical theologians. If this is true, then the challenge of postmodern theory to the presuppositions of modernity also becomes a potential critique of standard forms of evangelical theology to the degree that those forms are indebted to modernity. What is important to note is that such critiques do not necessarily lead to the end of theology, only to particular conceptions of it.

2. Theology and the Postmodern Situation

The introduction of postmodern theory at this stage raises the question as to the proper conception of the postmodern situation. It is important to realize that a precise understanding of postmodernity is notoriously difficult to pin down. Despite the fact that there is no consensus concerning the meaning of the term, it has become almost a commonplace to refer to the contemporary cultural situation as postmodern. The lack of

---

[8] John Jefferson Davis, *Foundations of Evangelical Theology* (Grand Rapids: Baker, 1984), p. 67.

[9] Stanley N. Gundry, 'Evangelical Theology: Where Should We Be Going?', *Journal of the Evangelical Theological Society* 22 (1979), p. 11.

[10] Millard Erickson, *Christian Theology* (Grand Rapids: Baker, 1983), vol. 1, p. 21.

clarity about the term has been magnified by the vast array of interpreters who have attempted to comprehend and appropriate postmodern thought. Paul Lakeland observes that there are 'probably a thousand different self-appointed commentators on the postmodern phenomenon and bewildering discrepancies between the ways many of these authors understand the term *postmodern* and its cognates'.[11] In the context of this lack of clarity about the postmodern phenomenon, the term has come to signify widely divergent hopes and concerns among those who are attempting to address the emerging cultural and intellectual shift implied by the term.

One common to the emergence of postmodern thought has been of the negative variety. Many Christian theologians and thinkers have come to view postmodernity primarily as a threat to Christian faith. Catholic theologian Richard John Neuhaus summed up the reaction of many to postmodern thought by connecting it with relativism and subjectivism and calling it the enemy of basic thinking about moral truth.[12] This sort of response has been characteristic of thinkers across the theological spectrum. At the heart of this critique is the consistent identification of postmodern thought with relativism and nihilism. In this conception postmodernism is viewed as fundamentally antithetical to Christian faith. Merold Westphal comments that at 'varying degrees along a spectrum that runs from mildly allergic to wildly apoplectic' many Christian thinkers 'are inclined to see postmodernism as nothing but warmed-over Nietzschean atheism, frequently on the short list of the most dangerous anti-Christian currents of thought as an epistemological relativism that leads ineluctably to moral nihilism. Anything goes.'[13] This view has been particularly characteristic among evangelicals who, according to Mark McLeod, 'tend to think that postmodernism opposes the truth, and in particular, the absolute truth of the gospel'.[14]

However, the wholesale identification of postmodern thought as nothing other than a radical brand of relativism is simply too narrow to do justice to the actual breadth of the phenomenon and fails to account for the many postmodern thinkers who distance themselves from the

---

[11] Paul Lakeland, *Postmodernity: Christian Identity in a Fragmented Age* (Minneapolis: Fortress Press, 1997), pp. ix–x.

[12] Richard John Neuhaus, 'A Voice in the Relativistic Wilderness', *Christianity Today* (7 February 1994), p. 34.

[13] Merold Westphal, *Overcoming Onto-theology: Toward a Postmodern Christian Faith* (New York: Fordham University Press, 2001), p. ix.

[14] Mark McLeod, 'Making God Dance: Postmodern Theorizing and the Christian College', *Christian Scholar's Review* 21.3 (March 1992), p. 281.

more radical implications of poststructural and deconstructive thought. For instance, Nancey Murphy draws a sharp distinction between Continental forms of postmodernism and the more constructive concerns of Anglo-American postmodern thinkers and employs the term postmodern to describe emerging patterns of thought in the Anglo-American context and to 'indicate their radical break from the thought patterns of Enlightened modernity'.[15] The Reformed epistemology of Alvin Plantinga and Nicholas Wolterstorff offers a vigorous defence and affirmation of truth as well as a telling critique of modernity.[16] Moreover, postanalytical philosophers such as Cornel West, Jeffrey Stout and Hilary Putnam provide extensive critiques of modernity and move in postmodern directions.[17] In ethics, the constructive communitarian approach of Alasdair MacIntyre may be called postmodern.[18] Thomas Kuhn and Stephen Toulmin have sought to develop contextual, postmodern approaches to the philosophy of science.[19] In theology, the postliberalism associated with Hans Frei and George Lindbeck is indebted to postmodern theory and the later work of Wittgenstein.[20] Given the variety of intellectual endeavour that may be described as postmodern we must conclude that postmodern thought cannot be narrowly associated with only a few select interpreters. The breadth of postmodern thought suggested by the few examples offered here raises the question as to what, if anything, gives unity and cohesion to postmodern thought. Dan Stiver points out that we should not expect postmodernism to be

---

[15] Nancey Murphy, *Anglo-American Postmodernity: Philosophical Perspectives on Science, Religion, and Ethics* (Boulder: Westview Press, 1997), p. 1.

[16] Alvin Plantinga and Nicholas Wolterstorff (eds), *Faith and Rationality: Reason and Belief in God* (Notre Dame: University of Notre Dame Press, 1983).

[17] Cornel West, *Prophetic Thought in Postmodern Times* (Monroe, Minnesota: Common Courage, 1993); Jeffrey Stout, *Flight from Authority: Religion, Morality, and the Quest for Autonomy* (Notre Dame: University of Notre Dame Press, 1981); and Hilary Putnam, *Reason, Truth, and History* (Cambridge: Cambridge University Press, 1981).

[18] Alasdair MacIntyre, *Whose Justice? Which Rationality?* (Notre Dame: University of Notre Dame Press, 1988).

[19] Thomas Kuhn, *The Structure of Scientific Revolutions* (Chicago: University of Chicago Press, 1970); and Stephen Toulmin, *Cosmopolis: The Hidden Agenda of Modernity* (Chicago: University of Chicago Press, 1990).

[20] Hans Frei, *The Eclipse of Biblical Narrative: A Study in Eighteenth and Nineteenth Century Hermeneutics* (New Haven, Connecticut: Yale University Press, 1974); and George Lindbeck, *The Nature of Doctrine: Religion and Theology in a Postliberal Age* (Philadelphia: Westminster, 1984).

characterized by a tight conformity to particular categories and patterns of thought. He reminds us that we:

> use terms like analytic philosophy, existentialism, phenomenology, structuralism, process philosophy, and pragmatism with meaning but also with awareness that it is notoriously difficult to come up with demarcation criteria that will tell us in any and every case who is and is not in the pertinent group. Postmodernism is that kind of term.[21]

This situation presses the question as to whether any similarity can be found within the diversity of postmodern thought so as to make sense of the movement, while moving beyond the narrow understanding that only sees it as a synonym for radically deconstructive relativism. To address this circumstance it will be helpful to see postmodernism as a label that identifies an ongoing paradigm shift in Western culture. Stiver observes that when we survey 'the panorama of contemporary thought it is evident in field after field, in discipline after discipline, that a significant critique of modernity has arisen along with a discussion of a paradigm change. The upshot is that the kind of change under discussion is not incremental or piecemeal, but structural and thoroughgoing.'[22] Almost without exception, those who are engaged in the pursuit of this paradigm shift use the term postmodern. Stiver suggests that this engagement generally involves three dimensions: first, the stringent criticism of modernity; secondly, the belief that 'radical surgery' is required to address the ailments of modernity and that 'a massive reconfiguration' or major paradigm shift is unavoidable; and thirdly, the presentation of some basic sketch as to the possible shape of an alternative paradigm.[23] From this description it is clear that the unity of the movement lies not in any tentative sketch of the details of a new paradigm but rather in the rejection of the programme of modernity.

This insight enables us to suggest a basic, minimalist understanding of postmodernism. The term is best understood as referring primarily to the rejection of the central features of modernity. As Diogenes Allen puts it, postmodern thought is discourse in the aftermath of modernity.[24] At

---

[21] Dan R. Stiver, 'The Uneasy Alliance between Evangelicalism and Postmodernism: A Reply to Anthony Thiselton' in David Dockery (ed.), *The Challenge of Postmodernism: An Evangelical Engagement* (Wheaton: Bridge Point, 1995), p. 242.

[22] Ibid., p. 243.

[23] Ibid., p. 243.

[24] Diogenes Allen, 'The End of the Modern World', *Christian Scholar's Review* 22.4 (June 1993), p. 341.

this level we find a remarkable congruence among those who adopt the label postmodern as a description of their work, a congruence that extends from Derrida to postliberals and postconservative evangelicals. Broadly speaking the term postmodern implies the rejection of certain central features of the modern project, such as its quest for certain, objective and universal knowledge, along with its dualism and its assumption of the inherent goodness of knowledge. It is this critical agenda, rather than any proposed constructive paradigm to replace the modern vision, that unites postmodern thinkers. This postmodern quest for new paradigms has significantly shaped the discipline of theology in the past twenty years, as theologians from various contexts and traditions have sought to 'fill the void' left by the rejection of modernity. Terrence Tilley cites ten alternative postmodern theologies that he divides into four categories: constructive postmodernisms, postmodern dissolutions, postliberal theology and theologies of communal praxis.[25] Kevin Vanhoozer identifies eight types of postmodern theology: radical orthodoxy, postliberal theology, postconservative theology, deconstructive a/theology, reconstructive theology, postmetaphysical theology, feminist theology and Anglo-American postmodernity: a theology of communal praxis.[26] Each of these typologies indicates the presence today of a number of constructive postmodern theological programmes.

Clearly, postmodernism cannot be dismissed as nothing more than a deconstructive agenda that stands in stark opposition to Christian faith and thought. Instead, there is much evidence that suggests that the postmodern context has actually been responsible for the renewal of theology as an intellectual discipline after a period of stagnation under the weight of modernist demands concerning the acquisition of knowledge. Freed from the constraints of modernity, postmodern concerns have spawned numerous new theological programmes. This broad construal of postmodern thought as a critique and rejection of modernity leads to one central dimension of postmodern theory that is especially important for theology and theological method. At the heart of the postmodern ethos is the attempt to rethink the nature of rationality in the wake of the modern project. This rethinking has resulted not in irrationality, as is often claimed by less informed opponents of postmodern thought, but rather in numerous redescriptions and proposals concerning appropriate construal of rationality and knowledge

---

[25] Terrence W. Tilley, *Postmodern Theologies: The Challenge of Religious Diversity* (Maryknoll: Orbis, 1995).

[26] Kevin J. Vanhoozer (ed.), *The Cambridge Companion to Postmodern Theology* (Cambridge: Cambridge University Press, forthcoming).

in the aftermath of the modern project. In spite of their variety, these attempts can be broadly classified as producing a chastened rationality that is more inherently self-critical than the constructions of rationality common in the thought-forms of modernity.[27]

Several common features serve to distinguish this chastened rationality from the modernist conceptions it seeks to replace. Chastened rationality is marked by the transition from a realist to a constructionist view of truth and the world.[28] Postmodern thinkers maintain that humans do not view the world from an objective vantage point, but structure their world through the concepts they bring to it, such as language. Human languages function as social conventions that describe the world in a variety of ways depending on the context of the speaker. No simple, one-to-one relationship exists between language and the world and thus no single linguistic description can serve to provide an objective conception of the 'real' world. Chastened rationality is also manifest in the 'loss of the metanarrative' and the advent of 'local' stories. Postmodern thinkers assert that the all-encompassing narratives of scientific progress that shaped and legitimated modern society have lost their credibility and power. Further, they maintain that the very idea of the metanarrative is no longer credible.[29] This is not to suggest that narratives no longer function in the postmodern context. However, the narratives that give shape to the postmodern ethos are local rather than universal. Postmodernity embraces the narratives of particular peoples and celebrates the diversity and plurality of the world without attempting to discover a 'grand scheme' into which all of these particular stories must fit. Above all, however, the chastened rationality of postmodernity entails the rejection of epistemological foundationalism and the adoption of a nonfoundationalist and contextual approach to the theological enterprise. The centrality of this approach to the concerns of postmodern theory gives rise to the assertion that postmodern theology is nonfoundationalist theology. With this in mind we will now turn our

---

[27] For a helpful discussion of this rethinking of rationality, see J. Wentzel van Huyssteen, *The Shaping of Rationality: Toward Interdisciplinarity in Theology and Science* (Grand Rapids: Eerdmans, 1999).

[28] See, for example, Walter Truett Anderson, *Reality Isn't What It Used To Be: Theatrical Politics, Ready-to-Wear Religion, Global Myths, Primitive Chic, and Other Wonders of the Postmodern World* (San Francisco: Harper & Row, 1990).

[29] Jean-François Lyotard, *The Postmodern Condition: A Report on Knowledge*, Geoff Bennington and Brian Massumi (trs) (Minneapolis: University of Minnesota Press, 1984), p. xxiv.

attention to the case for such an approach to theology before offering a proposed construal of its formal principles.

3. The Case for a Nonfoundationalist Theology

In the modern era, the pursuit of knowledge was deeply influenced by the thought forms of the Enlightenment, with foundationalism lying at its heart. The goal of the foundationalist agenda is the discovery of an approach to knowledge that will provide rational human beings with absolute, incontestable certainty regarding the truthfulness of their beliefs. According to foundationalists, the acquisition of knowledge ought to proceed in a manner somewhat similar to the construction of a building. Knowledge must be built upon a sure foundation. The Enlightenment epistemological foundation consists of a set of incontestable beliefs or of unassailable first principles on the basis of which the pursuit of knowledge can proceed. These basic beliefs or first principles must be universal, objective and discernable to any rational person apart from the particulars of varied situations, experiences and contexts.[30]

This foundationalist conception of knowledge came to dominate the discipline of theology as theologians reshaped their construals of the Christian faith in accordance with its dictates. In the nineteenth and twentieth centuries, the foundationalist impulse produced a theological division in the Anglo-American context between the 'left' and the 'right'. Liberals constructed theology upon the foundation of an unassailable religious experience, whereas conservatives looked to an error-free Bible as the incontrovertible foundation of their theology.[31] What is particularly significant, and often overlooked, is the similarity between these two groups concerning the basic structure of theology. For all the differences between 'liberals' and 'conservatives' on the proper foundations for theology and, as a consequence, their (often) mutually exclusive conceptions of theological issues, both groups were drawing from commonly held foundationalist conceptions of knowledge. In other words, liberal and conservative theologians can often be viewed as

---

[30] For a more detailed description of foundationalism, see W. Jay Wood, *Epistemology: Becoming Intellectually Virtuous* (Downers Grove: InterVarsity, 1998), pp. 77–104.

[31] On this liberal-conservative debate concerning the proper foundation for theology, see Nancey Murphy, *Beyond Liberalism and Fundamentalism: How Modern and Postmodern Philosophy Set the Theological Agenda* (Valley Forge: Trinity Press, 1996), pp. 11–35.

working out the theological details of the two sides of the same modernist, foundationalist coin.

In the postmodern context, however, foundationalism is in dramatic retreat, as its assertions about the objectivity, certainty and universality of knowledge have come under withering critique.[32] Merold Westphal observes: 'That it is philosophically indefensible is so widely agreed that its demise is the closest thing to a philosophical consensus in decades.'[33] J. Wentzel van Huyssteen agrees: 'Whatever notion of postmodernity we eventually opt for, all postmodern thinkers see the modernist quest for certainty, and the accompanying programme of laying foundations for our knowledge, as a dream for the impossible, a contemporary version of the quest for the Holy Grail.'[34] And Nicholas Wolterstorff offers this stark conclusion: 'On all fronts foundationalism is in bad shape. It seems to me there is nothing to do but give it up for mortally ill and learn to live in its absence.'[35] The heart of the postmodern quest for a chastened rationality lies in the rejection of the foundationalist approach to knowledge.

Postmodern thought raises two related but distinct questions to the modern foundationalist enterprise. First, is such an approach to knowledge *possible*? And secondly, is it *desirable*? These questions are connected with what may be viewed as the two major branches of postmodern hermeneutical philosophy: the hermeneutics of finitude and the hermeneutics of suspicion. However, the challenges to foundationalism are not only philosophical, but also emerge from the context of Christian theology. Westphal suggests that postmodern theory, with respect to hermeneutical philosophy, may be properly appropriated for the task of explicitly Christian thought on theological grounds: 'The hermeneutics of finitude is a meditation on the meaning of human createdness, and the hermeneutics of suspicion is a meditation on the meaning of human fallenness.'[36] In other words, many of the concerns of postmodern theory can be appropriated and fruitfully developed in the context of the Christian doctrines of creation and sin. Viewed from this perspective, the questions that are raised by postmodern thought

---

[32] John E. Thiel, *Nonfoundationalism* (Minneapolis: Fortress Press, 1994), p. 37.

[33] Merold Westphal, 'A Reader's Guide to "Reformed Epistemology" ', *Perspectives* 7.9 (November 1992), pp. 10–11.

[34] J. Wentzel van Huyssteen, 'Tradition and the Task of Theology', *Theology Today* 55.2 (July 1998), p. 216.

[35] Nicholas Wolterstorff, *Reason Within the Bounds of Religion* (Grand Rapids: Eerdmans, 1976), p. 52.

[36] Westphal, *Overcoming Onto-theology*, p. xx.

concerning the possibility and desirability of foundationalism are also questions that emerge from the context of Christian theology.

The foundationalism of the Enlightenment, with its emphasis on the objectivity, universality and absolute certainty of knowledge, is an impossible dream for finite human beings whose outlooks are always limited and shaped by the particular circumstances in which they take shape. Further, the modern foundationalist emphasis on the inherent goodness of knowledge is shattered by the fallen and sinful nature of human beings who desire to seize control of the epistemic process in order to empower themselves and further their own ends at the expense of others. The limitations of finitude and the flawed condition of human nature mean that epistemic foundationalism is neither possible nor desirable for created and sinful persons. This double critique of foundationalism, emerging as it does from the perspectives of both postmodern philosophy and Christian theology, suggests the appropriateness and suitability, given the current intellectual situation, of the language of nonfoundationalism as descriptive of an approach to the task of theology that is both postmodern and faithful to the Christian tradition.

According to William Stacy Johnson, nonfoundationalist approaches to theology 'share a common goal of putting aside all appeals to presumed self-evident, non-inferential, or incorrigible grounds for their intellectual claims'.[37] They reject the notion that among the many beliefs that make up a particular theology there must be a single irrefutable foundation that is immune to criticism and provides the certain basis upon which all other assertions are founded. In nonfoundationalist theology all beliefs are open to criticism and reconstruction. This does not mean, as is sometimes alleged, that nonfoundationalists cannot make assertions or maintain strong convictions that may be vigorously defended. As Francis Schüssler Fiorenza says, to engage in nonfoundationalist theology is to accept that 'it is a self-correcting enterprise that examines all claims, all relevant background theories' without demanding that these be completely abandoned all at once.[38] Nonfoundationalist theology does not eschew convictions, it simply maintains that such convictions, even the most long-standing and dear, are subject to critical scrutiny and therefore potentially to revision, reconstruction, or even rejection.

---

[37] William Stacy Johnson, *The Mystery of God: Karl Barth and the Postmodern Foundations of Theology* (Louisville: Westminster John Knox, 1997), p. 3.

[38] Francis Schüssler Fiorenza, *Foundational Theology: Jesus and the Church* (New York: Crossroad, 1986), p. 287.

The adoption of a nonfoundationalist approach to theological method has raised concerns for many in the evangelical community who see the abandonment of foundationalism as little more than a potential (or actual) slide down the proverbial 'slippery slope' into nihilistic relativism.[39] We will return to this concern at the end of this essay. At this point let us note one of the potentially significant benefits of the nonfoundationalist strategy. A nonfoundationalist theology contains an inherent commitment to the contextual nature of theology and demands the opening of theological conversation to the voices of persons and communities who have generally been excluded from the discourse of the North American evangelical community. It maintains without reservation that no single human perspective, be it that of an individual or a particular community or theological tradition, is adequate to do full justice to the truth of God's revelation in Christ. Richard Mouw points to this issue as one of his own motivations for reflecting seriously about postmodern themes:

> As many Christians from other parts of the world challenge our 'North Atlantic' theologies, they too ask us to think critically about our own cultural location, as well as about how we have sometimes blurred the boundaries between what is essential to the Christian message and the doctrine and frameworks we have borrowed from various Western philosophical traditions.[40]

The adoption of a nonfoundationalist approach to theology accents an awareness of the contextual nature of human knowledge and mandates a critical awareness of the role of culture and social location in the process of theological interpretation and construction. However, the lingering presence of foundationalism and its intellectual tendencies has hindered the evangelical community from fully embracing the contextual nature of theology and its entailments, such as the legitimacy and integrity of genitive theologies. From the perspective of the ecumenically orthodox Christian tradition, nonfoundationalist theology seeks to nurture an open and flexible theology that is in keeping with the local and contextual character of human knowledge while remaining thoroughly and distinctly Christian.

---

[39] See, for example, Douglas Groothuis, *Truth Decay: Defending Christianity Against the Challenges of Postmodernism* (Downers Grove: InterVarsity Press, 2000).

[40] Richard Mouw, 'Delete the "Post" from "Postconservative" ', *Books & Culture* 7.3 (May/June 2001), p. 22.

A theology that seeks to take seriously postmodern sensitivities views itself as conversation. The task of theological construction may be characterized as an ongoing conversation we share as participants in the faith community as to the meaning of the symbols through which we express our understanding of the world we inhabit. This constructive theological conversation involves the interplay of three sources to which we will now turn our attention. We will begin with a consideration of the role of culture in theological construction in order to accent the social and historical contextuality of all human thought before turning our attention to the more traditional sources of Scripture and tradition. In addition, we will focus on the work of the Spirit with respect to each of these sources and in so doing seek to develop a nonfoundationalist and contextual approach to theology by means of a thoroughly pneumatological theological method.[41]

4. Nonfoundationalist Theology and Culture

The expression of Christian thought has taken shape and has been revised in the context of numerous social and historical settings. It has also developed in the process of navigating a number of significant cultural transitions: from an initially Hebraic setting to the Hellenistic world; from the thought-forms of Greco-Roman culture to those of Franco-Germanic; from the world of medieval feudalism to the Renaissance; from the Renaissance to the Enlightenment; and from the developed world to the Third World. Currently, theology is grappling with the challenges raised by the transition from a modern to a postmodern cultural milieu. Throughout this ongoing history Christian theology has been shaped by the thought forms and conceptual tools of numerous cultural settings and has shown itself to be remarkably adaptable in its task of assisting the church in extending and establishing the message of the gospel in a wide variety of contexts. At the same time, theological history also provides numerous examples of the inappropriate accommodation of Christian faith to various ideologies and cultural norms. This chequered past confirms the vitality of Christian theology while warning of the dangers of too closely associating it with any particular form of cultural expression. It also raises the question of the proper conception of the role of culture in the task of constructing theology.

---

[41] For a more detailed discussion of the approach summarized here, see Stanley J. Grenz and John R. Franke, *Beyond Foundationalism: Shaping Theology in a Postmodern Context* (Louisville: Westminster John Knox, 2001), pp. 57–166.

Apart from a few notable exceptions, a near consensus has emerged among theologians today, which says that theology must take culture seriously. Colin Gunton states the point succinctly: 'we must acknowledge the fact that all theologies belong in a particular context, and so are, to a degree, limited by the constraints of that context. To that extent, the context is one of the authorities to which the theologian must listen.'[42] Many evangelical theologians have been suspicious of such claims about the role of culture in theology fearing that they, at least implicitly, dilute the authority of Scripture and give rise to a cultural relativity in theology that they believe to be inappropriate for the discipline. This raises the question as to the form the 'listening' to context should take. To address this we must first be clear on our understanding of the nature of culture itself.

In recent years the notion of culture as traditionally conceived has come under such strident and thoroughgoing criticism that some thinkers came to believe that the term was so compromised that it should be discarded. While a few favoured this radical surgery, most anthropologists agree with James Clifford's grudging acknowledgment that culture 'is a deeply compromised idea I cannot yet do without'.[43] Thus, rather than eliminating the concept entirely, the criticisms of the term have led to a postmodern understanding of culture that takes the historical contingencies of human life and society more seriously.

Postmodern anthropologists have discarded the older assumption that culture is a pre-existing social-ordering force that is transmitted externally to members of a cultural group who in turn passively internalize it. They maintain that this view is mistaken in that it isolates culture from the ongoing social processes that produce and continually alter it.[44] Culture is not an entity standing above or beyond human products and learned mental structures. In short, culture is not a 'thing'.[45] The older understanding also focused on the idea of culture as that which integrates the various institutional expressions of social life and binds the individual to society. This focus on the integrative role of culture is now facing serious challenges. According to Anthony Cohen, it has become

---

[42] Colin Gunton, 'Using and Being Used: Scripture and Systematic Theology', *Theology Today* 47.3 (October 1990), p. 253.

[43] James Clifford, *The Predicament of Culture: Twentieth Century Ethnography, Literature, and Art* (Cambridge, MA: Harvard University Press, 1988), p. 10.

[44] Kathryn Tanner, *Theories of Culture: A New Agenda for Theology* (Minneapolis: Augsburg Fortress, 1997), p. 50.

[45] Roy G. D'Andrade, *The Development of Cognitive Anthropology* (Cambridge: Cambridge University Press, 1995), p. 250.

one of the casualties of the demise of 'modernistic grand theories and the advent of 'the interpretive turn' in its various guises'.[46] Rather than viewing cultures as monolithic entities, postmodern anthropologists tend to view cultures as being internally fissured.[47] The elevation of difference that typifies postmodern thinking has triggered a height-ened awareness of the role of persons in culture formation. Rather than exercising determinative power over people, culture is conceived as the outcome and product of social interaction. Consequently, rather than being viewed as passive receivers, human beings are seen as the active creators of culture.[48]

Clifford Geertz provided the impetus for this direction through his description of cultures as comprising 'webs of significance' that people spin and in which they are then suspended.[49] Geertz defines culture as 'an historically transmitted pattern of meanings embodied in symbols, a system of inherited conceptions expressed in symbolic forms by means of which people communicate, perpetuate, and develop their knowledge about and attitudes toward life'.[50] According to Cohen, Geertz was responsible for 'shifting the anthropological view of culture from its supposedly objective manifestations in social structures, towards its subjective realisation by members who compose those structures'.[51] Culture resides in a set of meaningful forms and symbols that, from the point of view of any particular individual, appear as largely given.[52] Yet these forms are only meaningful because human minds have the ability to interpret them.[53] This has led contemporary anthropologists to look at the interplay of cultural artefacts and human interpretation in the formation of meaning. They suggest that, contrary to the belief that meaning lies in signs or in the relations between them, meanings are bestowed by the users of signs.[54] However, this does not mean that individuals simply discover or make up cultural meanings on their own.

---

[46] Anthony P. Cohen, *Self Consciousness: An Alternative Anthropology of Identity* (London: Routledge, 1994), p. 118.

[47] Tanner, *Theories of Culture*, p. 56.

[48] Cohen, *Self Consciousness*, pp. 118–19.

[49] Clifford Geertz, *The Interpretation of Cultures* (New York: Basic, 1973), p. 5.

[50] Ibid., p. 89.

[51] Cohen, *Self Consciousness*, p. 135.

[52] Geertz, *The Interpretation of Cultures*, p. 45.

[53] Ulf Hannerz, *Cultural Complexity: Studies in the Social Organization of Meaning* (New York: Columbia University Press, 1992), pp. 3–4.

[54] Claudia Strauss and Naomi Quinn, *A Cognitive Theory of Cultural Meaning* (Cambridge: Cambridge University Press, 1997), p. 253.

Even the mental structures by which they interpret the world are developed through explicit teaching and implicit observation of others. Consequently, cultural meanings are both psychological states and social constructions.[55]

The thrust of contemporary cultural anthropology leads to the conclusion that its primary concern lies in understanding the creation of cultural meaning as connected to world construction and identity formation. This approach leads to an understanding of culture as socially constructed. The thesis of social constructionists such as Peter Berger is that rather than inhabiting a prefabricated, given world, we live in a social-cultural world of our own creation.[56] At the heart of the process whereby we construct our world is the imposition of some semblance of a meaningful order upon our variegated experiences. For the interpretive framework we employ in this task, we are dependent on the society in which we participate.[57] In this manner, society mediates to us the cultural tools necessary for constructing our world. Although this constructed world gives the semblance of being a given, universal and objective reality, it is actually, in the words of David Morgan, 'an unstable edifice that generations constantly labor to build, raze, rebuild, and redesign'.[58] We inhabit socially constructed worlds to which our personal identities are intricately bound. The construction of these worlds, as well as the formation of personal identity, is an ongoing, dynamic and fluid process, in which the forming and reforming of shared cultural meanings play a crucial role. Culture includes the symbols that provide the shared meanings by means of which we understand ourselves, pinpoint our deepest aspirations and longings and construct the worlds we inhabit. And through the symbols of our culture we express and communicate these central aspects of life to each other, while struggling together to determine the meaning of the very symbols we employ in this process.

To be human is to be embedded in culture and to participate in the process of interpretation and the creation of meaning as we reflect on and internalize the cultural symbols that we share with others in numerous

---

[55] Ibid., p. 16.

[56] Peter L. Berger, *The Sacred Canopy: Elements of a Sociological Theory of Religion* (Garden City, New York: Anchor/Doubleday, 1969), pp. 3–13.

[57] Ibid., p. 20. See also Peter L. Berger and Thomas Luckmann, 'Sociology of Religion and Sociology of Knowledge', *Sociology and Social Research* 47 (1963), pp. 417–27.

[58] David Morgan, *Visual Piety: A History and Theory of Popular Images* (Berkeley: University of California Press, 1998), p. 9.

conversations that shape our ever-shifting contexts. The question of the relationship between culture and theology has been implicit throughout the history of Christian theology. However, in the twentieth century the issue has moved to the forefront of theological concerns as the challenges of globalization and pluralism have infused the question with a new sense of urgency. Two approaches that have gained widespread attention are those of correlation and contextualization. The chief difficulty with both of these methods is their indebtedness to foundationalism. Rather than acknowledging the particularity of every human culture, correlationists are prone to prioritize culture through the identification of some universal experience and fit theology into a set of generalized assumptions. Contextualists, in contrast, often overlook the particularity of every understanding of the Christian message and too readily assume a Christian universal that then functions as the foundation for the construction of the theology, even though that will need to be articulated in the language of a particular culture. This is especially evident in models of contextualization that are based on a distinction between the trans-cultural gospel and its expression through neutral cultural forms.[59] Yet with few exceptions, most approaches to contextual theology move in the direction of some form of foundationalism that assumes the existence of a pure, transcendent gospel.[60]

Despite debilitating difficulties these approaches share as a result of their foundationalist assumptions, taken together correlation and contextualization point the way forward. The two models suggest that an appropriate theological method must employ an interactive process that is both correlative and contextual while resisting the tendencies of foundationalism. Theology emerges through an ongoing conversation involving both gospel and culture. While such an interactive model draws from both methods, it stands apart from both in one crucial way. Unlike correlation or contextualization, an interactionist model presupposes neither gospel nor culture as given, preexisting realities that subsequently enter into conversation. Rather, in the interactive process both the gospel and culture are viewed as particularized, dynamic realities that inform and are informed by the conversation itself. Understanding gospel and culture in this way allows us to realize that both our understanding of the gospel and the meaning structures through which

---

[59] For an extended development of this model by an evangelical missiologist, see Charles H. Kraft, *Christianity in Culture: A Study in Dynamic Biblical Theologizing in Cross-Cultural Perspective* (Maryknoll: Orbis, 1979).

[60] On the variety of approaches to contextual theology, see Stephen B. Bevans, *Models of Contextual Theology* (Maryknoll: Orbis, 1992).

people in our society make sense of their lives are dynamic. In such a model, the conversation between gospel and culture should be one of mutual enrichment in which the exchange benefits the church in its ability to address its context as well as the process of theological critique and construction.

5. Nonfoundationalist Theology and Scripture

While the socially and historically embedded nature of all interpretations and construals of Christian theology demands that culture be taken seriously as one of the sources for theological construction, culture does not function as the primary norm in that task. The Christian tradition has been characterized by its commitment to the authority of the Bible. Our communal identity is bound up with a set of literary texts that together form canonical Scripture. According to David Kelsey, acknowledging the Bible as Scripture lies at the heart of participating in the community of Christ and the decision to adopt the texts of Christian Scripture as 'canon' is not 'a separate decision over and above a decision to become a Christian'.[61] To be Christian is to participate in a community that acknowledges the authority of Scripture for life and thought. The question that arises is how this authority ought to be construed. This question leads us to consider how the Bible ought to function in theology by pursuing the traditional assertion that Scripture is theology's norming norm. The point of departure for this affirmation of Scripture as the norming norm for theology lies in the Protestant principle of authority articulated in confessions such as the Westminster Confession of Faith, which states: 'The Supreme Judge by which all controversies of religion are to be determined, and all decrees of counsels, opinions of ancient writers, doctrines of men, and private spirits, are to be examined, and in whose sentence we are to rest, can be no other than the Holy Spirit speaking in the Scripture.'[62] This statement reflects the concern of the Protestant Reformation to bind Word and Spirit together as a means of providing the conceptual framework for authority in the Christian faith and brings into focus the sense in which the Bible is conceived of as the norming norm for theology.

---

[61] David H. Kelsey, *Proving Doctrine: The Uses of Scripture in Modern Theology* (Harrisburg: Trinity Press International, 1999), p. 165.

[62] The Westminster Confession of Faith 1.10, in John H. Leith (ed.), *The Creeds of the Churches* (Atlanta: John Knox, 1982), p. 196.

The assertion that our final authority is the Spirit speaking through Scripture means that Christian belief and practice cannot be determined merely by appeal to either the exegesis of Scripture carried out apart from the life of the believer and the believing community or to any 'word from the Spirit' that stands in contradiction to biblical exegesis. The reading and interpretation of the text is for the purpose of listening to the voice of the Spirit who speaks in and through Scripture to the church in the present. This implies that the Bible is authoritative in that it is the vehicle through which the Spirit speaks. In other words, the authority of the Bible, as the instrument through which the Spirit speaks, is ultimately bound up with the authority of the Spirit. Christians acknowledge the Bible as Scripture because the Spirit has spoken, now speaks, and will continue to speak with authority through the canonical texts of Scripture. The Christian community came to confess the authority of Scripture because it experienced the power and truth of the Spirit of God through writings that were, according to their testimony and confession, 'animated with the Spirit of Christ'.[63] Following the testimony of the church of all ages, we too look to the biblical texts to hear the Spirit's voice.

In declaring the biblical canon to be closed at the end of the fourth century the church implicitly asserted that the work of the Spirit in inspiration had ceased. However, this did not mark the end of the Spirit's activity in connection with Scripture. On the contrary, the Spirit continues to speak to succeeding generations of Christians through the text in the ongoing work of illumination. On the basis of biblical texts that speak of the continuing guidance of the Spirit to the earliest believers, subsequent generations of Christians have anticipated that the Spirit would guide them as well. The Puritan pastor John Robinson proclaimed his famous and frequently quoted belief that God had yet more truth and light to break forth from his holy Word. This Puritan notion of further light has been expressed in the language of literary theory by Northrop Frye who notes that to an extent unparalleled in any other literature the biblical texts seem to invite the readers to bring their own experiences into a conversation with them resulting in an ongoing interpretation of each in the light of the other.[64] For this reason, Frye suggests that readers properly approach the text with an attitude of expectation,

---

[63] Thomas A. Hoffman, 'Inspiration, Normativeness, Canonicity, and the Unique Sacred Character of the Bible', *Catholic Biblical Quarterly* 44 (1982), p. 457.

[64] Northrop Frye, *The Great Code: The Bible and Literature* (New York: Harcourt Brace Jovanovich, 1982), p. 225.

anticipating that there is always more to be received from the Bible.[65] Through Scripture, the Spirit continually instructs the church as the historically extended community of Christ's followers in the midst of the opportunities and challenges of life in the contemporary world.

The Bible is the instrumentality of the Spirit in that the Spirit appropriates the biblical text for the purpose of speaking to us today. This act of appropriation does not come independently of what traditional interpretation has called 'the original meaning of the text'. Careful exegesis is required in an effort to understand the 'original' intention of the authors by determining what they said. However, the speaking of the Spirit is not bound up solely with the supposed 'original intention' of the author. Contemporary proponents of 'textual intentionality' such as Paul Ricoeur explain that although an author creates a literary text, once it has been written, it takes on a life of its own. While the ways in which the text is structured shape the 'meanings' the reader discerns in the text, the author's intentions come to be 'distanced' from the 'meanings' of the work. In this sense, a text can be viewed metaphorically as 'having its own intention'. This 'textual intention' has its genesis in the author's intention but is not exhausted by it. Therefore, we must not conclude that exegesis alone can exhaust the Spirit's speaking to us through the text. While the Spirit appropriates the text in its internal meaning, the goal of this appropriation is to guide the church in the variegated circumstances of particular contemporary settings. Hence, we realize that the Spirit's speaking does not come through the text in isolation, but rather in the context of specific historical-cultural situations and as part of an extended interpretive tradition.

The assertion that the Spirit appropriates the text of Scripture and speaks in and through it to those in the contemporary setting leads to the question of the goal or effect of the Spirit's speaking. What does the Spirit seek to accomplish in the act of speaking through the appropriated text of Scripture? An appropriate response to this inquiry suggests that through the process of addressing readers in various contemporary settings the Spirit creates 'world'. Sociologists point out that religion plays a significant role in world construction through a set of beliefs and practices that provide a particular way of looking at 'reality'. Wesley Kort suggests that certain specific types of beliefs are essential for the development of an 'adequate' and 'workable' world, such as those about temporality, other people, borders, norms and values. He maintains that these types of beliefs are closely connected to languages and texts and

---

[65] Ibid., p. 220.

'can be textually identified because they and their relations to one another are borne by language'. This observation leads to the importance of 'scriptures' in that such texts function by articulating 'the beliefs that go into the construction of a world'.[66] For this reason, Paul Ricoeur asserts that the meaning of a text always points beyond itself in that the meaning is 'not behind the text, but in front of it'. Texts project a way of being in the world, a mode of existence, a pattern of life, and point toward 'a possible world'.[67]

In the Christian tradition, the Bible stands in a central position in the practice of the faith in that the Christian community reads the biblical texts as Scripture and looks to it as the focal point for shaping the narrative world it inhabits. As Walter Brueggemann maintains, the biblical text 'has generative power to summon and evoke new life' and holds out an eschatological vision that 'anticipates and summons realities that live beyond the conventions of our day-to-day, take-for-granted world'.[68] This points to the capacity of the text to speak beyond the context in which it was originally composed. In short, as John Goldingay declares, the text 'calls a new world into being'.[69] However, the point that needs to be stressed here is that this capacity for world construction, while bound closely to the text, does not lie in the text itself. Instead, this result is ultimately the work of the Spirit speaking through the text as the instrumentality of world creation. Further, the world the Spirit creates is not simply the world surrounding the ancient text nor the contemporary world, but rather the eschatological world God intends for creation as disclosed, displayed and anticipated by the text.

We are now in a position to tie together the way in which Scripture and culture function together in the task of theology. Scripture functions as theology's norming norm because it is the instrumentality of the Spirit who speaks in and through the text for the purpose of creating a world that is concretely and particularly centred on the present and future Lordship of Jesus Christ. However, this speaking is always contextual in that it always comes to its hearers within a specific

---

[66] Wesley A. Kort, *Take, Read: Scripture, Textuality, and Cultural Practice* (University Park, Pennsylvania: Pennsylvania State University Press, 1996), pp. 10–14.

[67] Paul Ricoeur, *Interpretation Theory: Discourse and the Surplus of Meaning* (Fort Worth: Texas Christian University Press, 1976), p. 87.

[68] Walter Brueggemann, *Finally Comes the Poet* (Minneapolis: Fortress, 1989), pp. 4–5.

[69] John Goldingay, *Models for Scripture* (Grand Rapids/Carlisle: Eerdmans/Paternoster Press, 1994), p. 256.

social-historical setting. The ongoing guidance of the Spirit always comes as a specific community of believers, in a specific setting, listens for and hears the voice of the Spirit speaking in and to the particularity of its social-historical context. The specificity of the Spirit's speaking means that the conversation with culture and cultural context is crucial to the theological task. We seek to hear the voice of the Spirit through Scripture that comes to us in the particularity of the social-historical context in which we live. Consequently, because theology must be in touch with life in the midst of present circumstances, the questions, concerns and challenges it brings to the Scriptures are not necessarily identical with those of contemporary exegetes or even the ancient writers themselves. Douglas John Hall states that what theology seeks 'from its ongoing discourse with the biblical text is determined in large measure by its worldly context', in order that it might address that setting from 'the perspective of faith in the God of Abraham, Isaac, and Jacob'.[70]

In addition to listening for the voice of the Spirit speaking through Scripture, theology must also be attentive to the voice of the Spirit speaking through culture. While Western theology has tended to focus on the church as the sole repository of all truth and the only location in which the Spirit is operative, Scripture appears to suggest a much broader understanding of the Spirit's presence, a presence connected to the Spirit's role as the life-giver. The biblical writers speak of the Spirit's role in creating and sustaining life as well as enabling it to flourish. Because the life-giving Creator Spirit is present in the flourishing of life, the Spirit's voice resounds through many media, including the media of human culture. Because Spirit-induced human flourishing evokes cultural expression, we can anticipate in such expressions traces of the Spirit's creative and sustaining presence. Consequently, theology should be alert to the voice of the Spirit manifest in the artefacts and symbols of human culture. However, it should be added that the speaking of the Spirit through the various media of culture never comes as a speaking against the text. Setting the Spirit's voice in culture against the text is to follow the foundationalist agenda and elevate some dimension of contemporary experience or thought as a criterion for accepting or rejecting aspects of the biblical witness. Darrell Jodock notes this danger:

> The problem here is not that one's world view or experience influences one's reading of the text, because that is inescapable. The problem is instead that the

---

[70] Douglas John Hall, *Thinking the Faith: Christian Theology in a North American Context* (Minneapolis: Fortress, 1991), p. 263.

text is made to conform to the world view or codified experience and thereby loses its integrity and its ability to challenge and confront our present priorities, including even our most noble aspirations.[71]

Therefore, while being ready to acknowledge the Spirit's voice wherever it may be found, we must still uphold the primacy of the text as theology's norming norm. While we cannot hear the Spirit speaking through the text except by listening within a particular social-historical setting, the Spirit speaking through Scripture provides the normative context for hearing the Spirit in culture. Having said this, it must be affirmed that the speaking of the Spirit through Scripture and culture do not constitute two different communicative acts, but rather one unified speaking. Consequently, theology must listen for the voice of the Spirit who speaks normatively through Scripture, but also particularly in the variegated circumstances of diverse human cultures.[72]

6. Nonfoundationalist Theology and the Christian Tradition

Thus far we have suggested Scripture is authoritative because it is the vehicle through which the Spirit speaks and the instrumentality of the Spirit in the process of world creation. Further, we have maintained that the Spirit's speaking through Scripture is always a contextual speaking that is addressed to particular social contexts and historical situations. Hence, Scripture, which functions as theology's norming norm, is always in conversation with culture, which functions as theology's embedding context. In this way the Spirit continually speaks to the believing community in its present situation through the witness of Scripture to the paradigmatic events of God's revelation in Jesus Christ as a means of providing ongoing guidance for the church as it grapples with constantly changing circumstances. This raises implicitly the question of the role of the Christian tradition, as the historical witness to the speaking of the Spirit, in the task of contemporary theological construction.

---

[71] Darrell Jodock, 'The Reciprocity between Scripture and Theology: The Role of Scripture in Contemporary Theological Reflection', *Interpretation* 44.4 (October 1990), p. 377.

[72] For an example of the interpretive plurality that such a model seeks to authorize theologically, see John R. Levison and Priscilla Pope-Levison (eds), *Return to Babel: Global Perspectives on the Bible* (Louisville: Westminster John Knox, 1999).

Addressing this question leads us to the centuries-old debate between Roman Catholics and Protestants concerning the relationship between Scripture and tradition. While recent conversations between Catholics and Protestants about the relationship between Scripture and tradition have started to close the breach of the sixteenth century, significant differences still remain.[73] At the heart of the discussion lies the question of primacy: which has priority – Scripture, or the church and its tradition? This fundamental difference still animates contemporary dialogues between Catholics and Protestants. However, posing the question in this manner is ultimately unhelpful in that it rests on foundationalist understandings of the derivation of knowledge. Shifting to a nonfoundationalist conception can assist in moving the discussion beyond this impasse.

As I have already indicated, the close connection that the Reformers sought to maintain between Word and Spirit means that the authority of Scripture is ultimately derived from the authority of the Spirit who speaks in and through the text. This Reformation understanding of the relationship between Word and Spirit suggests the possibility of a parallel connection between the Spirit and tradition. The pathway to such an understanding, however, proceeds indirectly, through ecclesiology. The same Spirit whose work accounts for the formation of the Christian community also guides that community in the production and authorization of the biblical texts. This characterization of the role of the Spirit points toward an appropriate pneumatological-ecclesiological understanding of tradition. Crucial in the development of such an understanding is the observation of Catholic theologian Avery Dulles, who speaks about the process of 'traditioning', which began before the composition of the inspired books and continues without interruption through the ages.[74] This stands as a reminder that the community precedes the production of the scriptural texts. In a certain sense, the faith community was responsible for both the content of the biblical books and for the identification of particular texts for inclusion in an authoritative canon to which the community has chosen to make itself accountable. Apart from the Christian community, the texts would not have taken their particular and distinctive shape. Apart from the authority of the Christian community, there would be no canon of authorized texts. In

---

[73] For a helpful summary of these conversations and developments, see Avery Dulles, 'Scripture: Recent Protestant and Catholic Views' in Donald McKim (ed.), *The Authoritative Word* (Grand Rapids: Eerdmans, 1983), p. 250.

[74] Avery Dulles, *The Craft of Theology: From Symbol to System* (New York: Crossroad, 1992), p. 96.

short, apart from the Christian community the Christian Bible would not exist.

Viewed from the historical perspective, the Bible is the product of the community of faith that produced it. The compilation of Scripture occurred within the context of the faith community, and the biblical documents represent the self-understanding of the community in which they were developed. As Paul Achtemeier notes, the 'major significance of the Bible is not that it is a book, but rather that it reflects the life of the community of Israel and the primitive church, as those communities sought to come to terms with the central reality that God was present with them in ways that regularly outran their ability to understand or cope'.[75] The Scriptures witness to the claim that they are the final written deposit of a trajectory or a traditioning that incorporates a number of varied elements in their composition, including oral tradition and other source documents. The community of faith recognized these writings as authoritative materials, and these materials in turn were interpreted and reapplied to the various contemporary situations. Under the guidance of the Spirit, the community engaged in the task of preserving the canonical documents for the sake of the community's continuity. These writings contain the literary witness to the events that had given shape to the community, the prophetic interpretation of those events, and the various context-sensitive instructions regarding the implications of these events to the community's ongoing life.

That same faith community has corporately confessed the Spirit-inspired character of the canonical texts as a distinctive collection of documents to which it makes itself accountable.[76] Awareness of the role of the community in the production of the writings of Scripture, that is, to the process of traditioning present already within the biblical era, leads to a broader concept of inspiration. While inspiration includes the composition of particular writings produced by individuals, it also incorporates the work of the triune God in leading the people of the Hebrew and early Christian communities to participate in the process of bringing Scripture into being. By extension, the direction of the Spirit permeated the entire process that climaxed in the coming together of the canon as the book of the Christian community. Thus, although the church precedes Scripture chronologically and is responsible for its formation, it has nevertheless, by its own corporate affirmation in the

---

[75] Paul J. Achtemeier, *The Inspiration of Scripture* (Philadelphia: Westminster, 1980), p. 92.

[76] Gabriel Fackre, *The Christian Story: A Narrative Interpretation of Basic Christian Doctrine* (Grand Rapids: Eerdmans, 1996), p. 19.

establishment of the canon, made itself accountable to Scripture as the norming norm for its life, faith and practice. In this sense, the text produces the community.

What unifies this relationship between Scripture and communal tradition of the church is the work of the Spirit. It is the Spirit who stands behind both the development and formation of the community as well as the production of the biblical documents and the coming together of the Bible into a single canon as that community's authoritative texts. The community found these texts to be the vehicle through which the Spirit of God addressed them. The illuminating work of the Spirit brought forth these writings from the context of the community in accordance with the witness of that community. This work of illumination has not ceased with the closing of the canon. Rather, it continues as the Spirit attunes the contemporary community of faith to understand Scripture and apply it afresh to its own context in accordance with the intentions of the Spirit.

The contemporary process of illumination parallels that experienced by the ancient faith communities in so far as the Bible contains materials that represent the appropriation by the community of the writings and traditions of their heritage, some of which are rejected as being contrary to the established trajectory of the community. Hence, the Scriptures contain sharp critique and condemnation of some of the attitudes and actions of the ancient faith communities. At the same time, however, there is also a significant difference between the experience of the ancient faith communities and our relationship to Scripture. The people of Israel and the early Christian communities engaged in the interpretive task within the process of the formation of the canon. After the closure of the canon, the Christian community receives the illumination of the Spirit speaking through canonical Scripture. Thus, in terms of the basic character of the relationship between Scripture and the tradition of the church, canonical Scripture is on the one hand constitutive of the church, providing the primary narratives around which the life and faith of the Christian community is shaped and formed, and on the other hand is itself derived from that community and its authority. In the divine economy Scripture and tradition are in this manner inseparably bound together through the work of the Spirit.

For this reason, to suggest that the Protestant slogan *sola scriptura* implies an authority apart from the tradition of the church, its creeds, teachings and liturgy is to transform the formula into an oxymoron.[77]

---

[77] Robert Jenson, *Systematic Theology Volume 1: The Triune God* (New York: Oxford University Press, 1997), p. 28.

Separating Scripture and church in such a manner was certainly not the intention of the Reformers.[78] Indeed, historian Heiko Oberman contends that the issue of the Reformation was not Scripture or tradition but rather the struggle between two differing concepts of tradition.[79] Commenting on the role of the community in the process that led to the production and identification of Scripture, Achtemeier notes:

> If it is true, therefore, that the church, by its production of Scripture, created materials which stood over it in judgement and admonition, it is also true that scripture would not have existed save for the community and its faith out of which scripture grew. That means that church and scripture are joint effects of the working out of the event of Christ.[80]

This 'working out' is carried on under the guidance and illumination of the Spirit. In this conception, Scripture and tradition function together as distinguishable but inseparable aspects of the Spirit's work in guiding and directing the church in its mission to serve the world as the people of God in the contemporary setting.

7. Conclusion: Nonfoundationalist Theology and 'Foundations'

This nonfoundationalist conception envisions theology as an ongoing conversation between Scripture, tradition and culture in which all three are vehicles of the one Spirit through which the Spirit speaks in order to create a distinctively Christian 'world' centred on Jesus Christ in a variety of local settings. In this way, theology is both one, in that all truly Christian theology seeks to hear and respond to the speaking of the one Spirit, and many, in that all theology emerges from particular social and historical situations. Such a theology is the product of the reflection of the Christian community in its local expressions. Despite its local character, such a theology is still in a certain sense global in that it seeks to explicate the Christian faith in accordance with the ecumenical

---

[78] On the relationship between Scripture and tradition in the Reformation, see D.H. Williams, *Retrieving the Tradition and Renewing Evangelicalism: A Primer for Suspicious Protestants* (Grand Rapids: Eerdmans, 1999), pp. 173–204.

[79] Heiko A. Oberman, 'Quo Vadis? Tradition from Irenaeus to Humani Generis', *Scottish Journal of Theology* 16 (1963), pp. 225–55.

[80] Achtemeier, *The Inspiration of Scripture*, p. 116.

tradition of the church throughout its history and on behalf of the church throughout the world.

Further, despite its particularity as specifically Christian theology, such a theology is also public and carries an implicit claim to be articulating a set of beliefs and practices that are 'universal' in the only way that any claim to universality can be made, as the faith of a particular believing community. In this way, such a theology calls for a response beyond the confines of the particular community from which it emerges, and is set forth as a contribution to the wider public conversation about the nature of ultimate reality, meaning and truth. As Kathryn Tanner explains, there is no reason to think that a specifically Christian context rules out theological claims that are universal in scope or that a Christian context means that theologians are discussing matters that only concern Christians. Instead, theologians seek to:

> proclaim truths with profound ramifications for the whole of human existence; that they do so from within a Christian cultural context simply means that the claims they make are shaped by that context and are put forward from a Christian point of view. Indeed, if, as an anthropologist would insist, assertions always show the influence of some cultural context or other, following a procedure like that is the only way that universal claims are ever made.[81]

We now conclude with an issue we raised briefly earlier in the essay. Does not such an approach really amount to a theological relativism that allows for anything? We might first respond that no theological method can secure truth and that all are subject to distortion in the hands of finite and fallen human beings. A nonfoundationalist approach to theology seeks to respond positively and appropriately to the situatedness of all human thought and therefore to embrace a principled theological pluralism. It also attempts to affirm that the ultimate authority in the church is not a particular source, be it Scripture, tradition or culture, but only the living God. Therefore, if we must speak of 'foundations' for the Christian faith and its theological enterprise, then we must speak only of the Triune God who is disclosed in polyphonic fashion through Scripture, the church and even the world, albeit always in accordance with the normative witness to divine self-disclosure contained in Scripture. Put another way, nonfoundationalist theology means the end of foundationalism but not foundations. However, these 'foundations' are not 'given' to human beings. As Bruce McCormack notes, they 'always elude the grasp of the human attempt

---

[81] Tanner, *Theories of Culture*, p. 69.

to know and to establish them from the human side', and they cannot be demonstrated or secured 'philosophically or in any other way'.[82] Hence, human beings are always in a position of dependence and in need of grace with respect to epistemic relations with God. Attempts on the part of humans to seize control of these relations are all too common throughout the history of the church and, no matter how well intentioned, inevitably lead to forms of oppression and conceptual idolatry. Nonfoundationalist theology seeks to oppose such seizure through the promotion of a form of theology and a theological ethos that humbly acknowledges the human condition of finitude and fallenness and that, by grace if at all, does not belie the subject of theology to which it seeks to bear faithful witness.

---

[82] Bruce L. McCormack, 'What has Basel to do with Berlin? The Return of "Church Dogmatics" in the Schleiermacherian Tradition', *The Princeton Seminary Bulletin* 23/2 (2002), p. 172.

13

Postmodern Evangelical Apologetics?

David K. Clark

I'll call him George. He's a forty-something lawyer with a lovely wife, three kids and some intense in-laws. He grew up in a churched home. The rest of his family attends church, but he is agnostic. Ironically, he also has an interest in spiritual things. About eight years ago he turned up at a student ministry meeting at a university where I gave a talk. He came at the invitation of my friend Rob, the campus worker, who told him that I would discuss faith and epistemology. (Rob is friends with George. They go fishing together. That's something people do in Minnesota.)

As I said, George practises law. His specialty is suing companies that make defective products. So when XYZ, Inc. tries to defend itself against lawsuits by proving that its products are indeed safe, George earns his paycheck by assuming that all their reasoning is faulty.

George very much enjoys talking about religious matters. But just as he expresses suspicion toward corporate executives in court, he shows instinctive scepticism toward religious institutions and theological claims. As a matter of integrity, he dropped church attendance long ago. This creates tension at home. His wife and his in-laws really want the whole family to attend church together. George loves his family. It pains him to cause turmoil about church attendance. A lot of things would go more smoothly for him if he'd just go to church.

In my talk on faith and epistemology, I mentioned what I think is an important indicator of a transcendent Creator. I argued that the existence of a personal Creator accounts for the deep, undeniable sense of moral duty with which every human being is endowed. I believe the Christian worldview does this far better than does naturalism.

After my talk, Rob introduced me to George. I asked about his work and learned that he approaches court cases from a stance of extreme scepticism. I asked about his family and discovered that he takes a naïve realist account of all manner of everyday things, including his family's real metaphysical existence and the fact of their genuine love for him.

Then I asked George, 'What do you think of my suggestion that a transcendent Creator accounts for the profound moral sense that all humans experience?'

George said it was 'interesting'. As I pressed the question a little further, I sensed his lawyering habits and practices playing out in our conversation. At several points he dismissed my points rather offhandedly. He waved off what seem to me like good – not absolutely conclusive, but good – reasons to think a transcendent Creator explains our sense of moral obligation.

I decided to take a different tack: 'George, tell me. Do you think it's immoral for companies to build and sell products they know are dangerous?'

'Of course,' he replied.

'You know what I think. But what about you? What is your ground for saying that it's immoral for companies to sell products that injure people?'

'Well,' he said, 'no one likes to feel pain. The universal desire to avoid pain is the ground for human morality. We don't like pain, so we create rules against it. Gradually, all humans have come to experience a sense of moral duty. When companies make defective products, they inflict pain. We don't like that. So it's wrong.'

'But wait a second,' I said. 'It seems to me the simple fact that people feel pain they don't like isn't sufficient to ground moral obligation. If God doesn't exist and we're all simply the products of unplanned and natural evolutionary processes, then pain just is. It's simply part of the physiology that humans happened to develop. Without God, all we have is a physical response to a physical stimulus. That's not morality.'

'I would expect you to say that,' he said.

'The fact that we don't like pain may account for our moral beliefs, moral feelings or moral practices,' I argued. 'But our distaste for pain doesn't account for moral duties. Antelopes don't like the painful experience of being eaten by cheetahs, but that doesn't place cheetahs under any moral restraint whatever. The fact that creatures feel pain and want to avoid it doesn't create moral obligation. A sense of obligation requires a moral law, which in turn demands a moral authority, a transcendent Creator whom we should seek.'

George replied, 'Yes, I see that's your perspective, and it's a good one. It makes a lot of sense to you. But I prefer to take a more moderate, agnostic position.'

George displayed sensibilities typical of postmodern people: spiritual interest, distrust of institutions, a valuing of relationships and a relativist streak. He never pointed to a specific logical flaw in my argument. And he never let on that he sensed the force of what I was arguing. (He's a good lawyer.) I feel his position lacks merit. George's stance is flawed at the core, and I told him so (kindly). But he maintained his stance: 'I can see how your view would make sense to you,' he would say. We parted ways amiably. But I was frustrated.

1. On the Very Idea of Postmodern Evangelical Apologetics

What would good evangelical apologetic practice amount to in a conversation with someone with postmodern sensibilities like George? Indeed, is postmodern evangelical apologetics even possible? Many will think the very idea, the very concept, of 'postmodern evangelical apologetics' is incoherent. Postmodern evangelicalism? Yes. Evangelical apologetics? Yes. But genuinely postmodern, truly evangelical apologetics? No.

It's not immediately clear how to justify attaching a charge of incoherence to the very idea of postmodern evangelical apologetics. The charge rests, in part, on what freight we load on the ideas of apologetics and postmodernity. Some people think apologetics involves the attempt to provide deductively certain and universally compelling rationalist argumentation on behalf of the Christian faith. Some (not all) of these people support this kind of apologetics. Those who place their bets on this kind of apologetic have missed the memo on the demise of modernism, however. And they fail to understand contemporary culture. Only if we understand apologetics in a broader and more holistic sense is the very idea of postmodern evangelical apologetics coherent. (Of course, some will agree that evangelical apologetics is incurably modern, but they will infer from this that apologetics is passé, precisely because modernism is dead.)

Other people think postmodernity entails not just a rejection of various themes, values, emphases and sensibilities of modernism, but a robust commitment to strong forms of deconstruction, various kinds of relativism and certain sorts of non-realism. Some (but not many) evangelicals will defend these commitments. But this sort of postmodernism seems to undermine the evangelical commitment to an ultimate truth and a universal gospel. And it certainly sabotages any attempt to show the reasonableness of faith. (Again, some will agree that postmodernism is inherently deconstructive, and they will infer therefore that post-modernism is defective because relativism and non-realism are false.)

The incoherence arises when the words 'postmodern' and 'apologetics' are given certain strong connotations or taken in particularly narrow ways. An apologetic that is *both* (deconstructively) postmodern *and* (modernistically) evangelical is incoherent indeed. If this is the best we could do in developing a postmodern evangelical apologetic, then we do face a forced choice between 'postmodern faith' and 'evangelical apologetics'. If (and only if) we can articulate more modest and nuanced understandings of postmodernity and apologetics, however, we might render the idea of postmodern evangelical apologetics coherent. I think this goal would produce virtues that commend it. So my purposes in this essay are to plead for conceptual clarity and semantic consistency as we speak of postmodernity and apologetics, and to call for modesty and caution in our reflections on the viability of postmodern evangelical apologetics. I hope this straightforward exercise in philosophical analysis will help move us as evangelicals into full-bodied dialogue in the postmodern milieu. I envision us entering this sort of dialogue from a stance that avoids extreme versions of both modernism and postmodernism, even as it incorporates the wisdom of the historic biblical faith and preserves the substantial insights and practices of the rational tradition of evangelical apologetics in a dialogical context.

2. Postmodernism and the Destabilization of Evangelical Apologetics

Much evangelical theology in the last half century exhibits modernist sensibilities.[1] In that evangelical theological climate, leading evangelical apologists in the decades after the Second World War imbibed the modernist spirit. Evangelical apologists assumed that rational arguments are rhetorically persuasive, that philosophical syllogisms are more powerful than the gospel story, that logical certitude beginning with completely neutral premises is achievable and that rational knowledge is more trustworthy than, and preferable to, knowledge by experience, even experience of the Holy Spirit. One work in apologetics presents an appendix that explains to readers how to prove the Christian worldview by

---

[1] See Alister McGrath, *A Passion for Truth: The Intellectual Coherence of Evangelicalism* (Downers Grove: InterVarsity Press, 1996), pp. 166–79.

'Reasoning to Christianity from Ground Zero'.[2] In this case, the phrase 'Ground Zero' doesn't refer to the site of the World Trade Center, but to the allegedly neutral, supposedly assumptionless starting point of this argument for faith. Another book on classical apologetics suggests that the theistic arguments 'are compelling certainties and not merely suggestive possibilities'.[3] These kinds of evangelical apologetics emphasize objective truth, universal reason, neutral criteria, deductive proof and rational certitude.

Given this, it's not surprising that the dominant response of evangelical thinkers to postmodernism is largely critical, even if occasionally modestly appreciative. Douglas Groothuis states: 'Postmodernism, broadly understood, has dispensed with Truth and has replaced it with truths. Some take this as liberating, even for Christian endeavours. I take it to be very bad news – philosophically, ethically, apologetically and theologically.'[4] Though he clearly knows the weaknesses of modernity, William Lane Craig complains that we give 'this faddish movement [called postmodernism] far more credit than it deserves' for it's 'obviously self-referentially incoherent'. Postmodern themes, he continues, devastate evangelical theology:

> The abandonment of objective standards of truth and rationality could only undermine the Christian faith in the long run by making its call to repentance and faith in Christ but one more voice in the cacaphony [sic] of subjectively satisfying but objectively vacuous religious interpretations of the world.[5]

Clearly, the greatest concern lies with those themes in postmodernity that lead to the anarchy of metaphysical non-realism, epistemic relativism and social constructivism. Other evangelicals offer analyses that aren't utterly negative, but are still highly cautionary.[6]

---

[2] Norman Geisler and Ron Brooks, *When Skeptics Ask: A Handbook on Christian Evidences* (Wheaton: Victor, 1990), p. 291.

[3] R.C. Sproul, John Gerstner and Arthur Lindsley, *Classical Apologetics* (Grand Rapids: Academie, Zondervan, 1984), pp. 126, 136.

[4] Douglas Groothuis, *Truth Decay: Defending Christianity against the Challenges of Postmodernism* (Downers Grove: InterVarsity Press, 2000), p. 11.

[5] William Lane Craig, 'A Classical Apologist's Response' in Steven B. Cowan (ed.), *Five Views on Apologetics* (Grand Rapids: Zondervan, 2000), pp. 181–3.

[6] Gene Edward Veith, *Postmodern Times: A Christian Guide to Contemporary Thought and Culture* (Wheaton: Crossway, 1994), p. xiii, Millard Erickson, *Postmodernizing the Faith: Evangelical Responses to the Challenge of Postmodernism* (Grand Rapids: Baker, 1998), p. 20, Roger Lundin,

The fabric of the evangelical world is quite diverse, however. Among its strands are several historic voices that counterbalance overly rationalist and assertively objectivist approaches to faith. One such voice is pietism. At its best, pietism leads to a spiritually vital faith. In reacting to intellectualized or ritualized forms of faith and practice, pietism stressed genuine spiritual connection with God, personal transformation of the human spirit and a life of virtue that pleases God. The downside of pietism, at least on the American scene, is its tendency to encourage anti-intellectual sentiments. Many evangelical believers influenced by pietism have a love-hate relationship to doctrine. They believe certain doctrines with deep conviction, but also feel vaguely negative about rationalistic theology and subtly suspicious of apologetics. Some, like Stanley Grenz, who self-consciously tries to write robust, evangelical, pietistic theology, are (not surprisingly) more open to postmodern emphases than most evangelical theologians.

Another voice (or cluster of voices) is the Dutch Reformed heritage. This theological tradition emphasizes the uniqueness of Christian thinking. It spawned the presuppositional apologetic method of Cornelius Van Til and his followers, including John Frame. It also produced the Reformed epistemology movement that includes William Alston, Alvin Plantinga and Nicholas Wolterstorff. This movement has powerfully influenced not just Christian thinking, but the whole world of philosophy of religion. Those who live and think in the categories of this heritage react quite strongly against modernism's tendency to seek supposedly neutral categories of thought. They challenge any modernist apologetic strategy that appeals to supposedly impartial canons of rationality or allegedly neutral ranges of evidence.

Yet another voice is the cluster of evangelicals who embrace and promote postmodernity directly. Some of these are evangelical academics. In *Ancient-Future Faith*, Robert Webber focuses on re-presenting classical Christian thought and experience for the postmodern world.[7] Stanley Grenz reveals his sympathies with 'Star Trek' culture in *A Primer on Postmodernism*.[8] Leonard Sweet, in books like *Aquachurch* and *Soul Tsunami*, offers racy enticements to induce theologians and church leaders to embrace the waves of social change they see around

---

[6] (*continued*) *The Culture of Interpretation: Christian Faith and the Postmodern World* (Grand Rapids: Eerdmans, 1993), p. 5.

[7] Robert Webber, *Ancient-Future Faith: Rethinking Evangelicalism for a Postmodern World* (Grand Rapids: Baker, 1999), p. 30.

[8] Stanley Grenz, *A Primer on Postmodernism* (Grand Rapids: Eerdmans, 1996).

them.[9] (*Aquachurch* has its own website.) Many others are church leaders. Andrew Jones offers regular forums on a postmodern church website, 'The Ooze'.[10] Pastor Brian McLaren wrote a balanced assessment of postmodern ministry in *The Church on the Other Side: Doing Ministry in the Postmodern Matrix*.[11] His article entitled 'Honey, I Woke Up in a Different Universe' includes the subtitle 'Confessions of a Postmodern Pastor'.[12] These individuals clearly see the flaws, not only intellectually, but also practically, of sterile modernity.

Postmodernity obviously hasn't evoked a consistent response from evangelicals. Nevertheless, the *dominant* postwar tradition in evangelical apologetics generally mirrors the modernist sensibilities found in the mainstream theological trajectory of the evangelical movement. Since this is so, one could easily think that evangelicals' typically negative stance toward postmodernism is at heart an unjustified, knee-jerk reaction rooted in uncritical allegiance to an inherited modernism. On the contrary, the evangelical critique of postmodernism raises several important points. On a variety of specific themes, the alternatives offered by strong versions of the postmodern perspective are sometimes no better than, and sometimes a lot worse than, modernism. Many postmodern theories, especially in their more robust forms, are in fact destructive of core evangelical commitments. So if the semantic field of the word 'postmodernism' denotes a modest version of postmodernity, then there's much to learn. But in response to the anarchic themes that some radical thinkers promote, the negative critique of postmodernity proffered by evangelicals is amply justified.

As examples, consider three postmodern themes in epistemology that destabilize evangelical commitments. First, postmoderns often deny the correspondence view of truth. The correspondence view of truth means that utterances are true, either individually or in patterns, if they adequately depict aspects of a mind-independent world. Put simply, true affirmations are statements that correlate to reality. To say that truth corresponds to reality is to say, for example, that the statement 'I'm

---

[9] Leonard Sweet, *Soul Tsunami: Sink or Swim in New Millennium Culture* (Grand Rapids: Zondervan, 1999) and *Aquachurch: Essential Leadership Arts for Piloting Your Church in Today's Fluid Culture* (Loveland, Colorado: Group, 1999).

[10] < www.theooze.com >.

[11] Brian McLaren, *The Church on the Other Side: Doing Ministry in the Postmodern Matrix* (Grand Rapids: Zondervan, 2000).

[12] Brian McLaren, 'Honey, I Woke up in a Different Universe!: Confessions of a Postmodern Pastor', *Mars Hill Review* 15 (1999), pp. 35–46.

looking at a dragonfly' is very simply about that fact that I'm actually looking at a dragonfly. This means that reality itself is the ontological ground for the truth of true affirmations. So the word 'correspondence' denotes a proper connection or correlation between reality and language. 'Truth is always *about* something', wrote C.S. Lewis, and 're-ality is that *about which* truth is.'[13]

Since virtually all people, including especially those who haven't ever studied epistemology, typically assume something like this notion of truth, this is a *pretheoretic* intuition regarding truth. I'm not talking here about a complete *theory* of correspondence. A well-articulated theory about correspondence is yet to come. I'm talking about a basic intuition that humans share about the nature of their true beliefs. To say this intuition is *pretheoretic* is to say that it doesn't *result from* complex theory building about the nature of truth. Rather, it's a belief people *bring to* their theorizing about truth. It's a basic assumption, rooted in experience. It's something people philosophize *with*, not something they philosophize *to*.

Correspondence isn't a popular notion in some circles. Philip Kenneson encourages his readers to abandon the correspondence theory of truth. He argues that by leaving behind the Enlightenment epistemo-logical project – and that includes abandoning the correspondence theory of truth – we can avoid the dilemmas of modern philosophy. We can avoid, for example, the forced option of absolute certainty or com-plete scepticism. 'In short, this old paradigm of knowledge and truth is a dead-end street down which we need not continue to travel.'[14]

Giving up correspondence as a core intuition is a risky business, how-ever. Opponents of correspondence will say that we are still waiting for a full theory of correspondence, and they're right. The question is whether we can assume and use a basic intuition of correspondence as the core of a concept of truth prior to producing a full theory about that. I think the answer is obvious. Many people rightly use language even though they cannot give anything like a full theory about the status of language. So I don't claim that we must adopt a modernist *theory* of correspondence. But I do contend that we should retain two minimalist insights: language refers to reality and true statements are true because

---

[13] C.S. Lewis, 'Myth became Fact' in *God in the Dock* (Grand Rapids: Eerdmans, 1970), p. 66.

[14] Philip D. Kenneson, 'There's No Such Thing as Objective Truth, and it's a Good Thing, Too' in Timothy R. Phillips and Dennis L. Okholm (eds), *Christian Apologetics in the Postmodern World* (Downers Grove: InterVarsity Press, 1995), p. 158.

they reflect (to a contextually appropriate degree) the way things are. Hanging on to this intuition is especially important given that the alternative theories of truth that philosophers offer as replacements run into severe difficulties.

Secondly, related to this is the denigration of propositional truth. In the post-Second World War era, evangelicals stressed propositional revelation in contrast to the Barthian emphasis on personal revelation. The point of emphasizing propositions is *not* to say that *only* declarative statements count as revelation. No. The entire Bible, in all its genres, is revelatory. The idea of propositional revelation emphasizes that *written* biblical expressions, whatever their genre, are genuinely divine revelation. It denies that revelation is limited to personal revelation, the personal encounter with the Living Word, Jesus Christ. Propositional revelation denies Karl Barth's famous view that the Bible is not revelation, but *witnesses* to revelatory experiences of spiritual encounter. A proper commitment to the idea of propositional revelation means only that Scripture *itself* is revelation. Scripture, of course, isn't God's only mode of revelation, for other kinds of revelation are possible. The point is that these experiences do not exhaust revelation. A proper commitment to proposition revelation *does not entail* that revelation is limited to *statements* (that is, to declarative sentences) or to *propositions* in the philosophical sense (that is, to the conceptual dimension of declarative statements) in Scripture.

Evangelical sympathizers of neo-orthodoxy wrongly place the person-oriented understanding of truth in strong opposition to an informational or contentful notion of truth. They persist in placing the personal and the propositional concepts of truth in a disjunctive, either/or relation. Donald Bloesch, for example, says:

> Truth in the Bible means conformity to the will and purpose of God. Truth in today's empirical, scientific milieu means an exact correspondence between one's ideas or perceptions and the phenomena of nature and history ... The difference between the rational-empirical and the biblical understanding of truth is the difference between transparency to Eternity and literal facticity.[15]

I see this as a mistake. Evangelical theology should interpret the personal and descriptive uses of the word 'truth' as distinct, yet positively related. To get at this, we may ask: Which is ontologically prior – *Jesus'* actually

---

[15] Donald G. Bloesch, *The Future of Evangelical Christianity: A Call for Unity Amid Diversity* (Colorado Springs: Helmers & Howard, 1988), p. 120.

being the Truth or a *proposition* describing and corresponding to his actually being that Truth? Ontological priority surely goes to the reality of who Jesus is. The *ground* of a proposition's being true is the determinate nature of whatever actually is real. The truth value of the cognitive language that describes Jesus' status depends on what Jesus' status actually is. The statement is true only if it adequately corresponds to the inherently reliable, trustworthy, genuine reality of Jesus' own person. The statement 'Jesus is the way to God' is true if and only if Jesus *is* the Truth – if, in other words, Jesus is *not* a counterfeit and is actually the genuine path to God.[16] Conversely, commitment to a correspondence notion of truth is completely consistent with saying 'Ian is a true-blue friend.'[17] The personal sense of 'truth' stands in intrinsic relation to its propositional sense.[18]

This clarification is important, for the view that revelation is *only* personal, and *not* propositional, is attracting attention among some evangelicals. They say things like 'Jesus *is* truth. In John 14:6, Jesus himself says, "I am the way, the truth and the life."' Truth, these theologians stress, is an attribute of persons, not of propositions. Persons, not propositions, are bearers of truth. Jesus did not come to tell us true information, they say. He embodied the truth. One defender of this view wrote, 'Jesus did not arrive among us enunciating a set of propositions that we are to affirm ... Jesus never asks us to agree; he asks us to join up, to *follow*. He did not call for cognitive assent; he asked for a life of discipleship involving the whole self, not just the mind.'[19] Christ offers something much better than objectively true propositions we are supposed to grasp with our minds. Christ offers himself.

---

[16] See Arthur F. Holmes, *All Truth is God's Truth* (Downers Grove: InterVarsity Press, 1977), pp. 37–8.

[17] D.A. Carson, 'Recent Developments in the Doctrine of Scripture' in D.A. Carson and John D. Woodbridge (eds), *Hermeneutics, Authority, and Canon* (Grand Rapids: Academie, Zondervan, 1986), p. 26.

[18] '*The full Bible concept of truth involves factuality, faithfulness, and completeness.* Those who have stressed one of these features in order to downgrade either or both of the others are falling short of the biblical pattern. Notably those who have stressed faithfulness, as if conformity to fact did not matter, are failing grievously to give proper attention to what constitutes probably a majority of the passages in which the word *truth* is used.' Roger Nicole, 'The Biblical Concept of Truth' in D.A. Carson and John D. Woodbridge (eds), *Scripture and Truth* (Grand Rapids: Zondervan, 1983), p. 296.

[19] William H. Willimon, 'Jesus' Peculiar Truth', *Christianity Today*, 4 March 1996, p. 21.

Jesus 'did not call for cognitive assent; he asked for a life of discipleship involving the whole self, not just the mind'.[20] True enough. But surely the correct point here is that Jesus does not ask for *merely* cognitive assent. He asks for more than cognitive assent, but he *does not ask for less*. It *is* the case that Jesus' call to discipleship does not involve cognitive assent *alone*. It's *not* the case that Jesus' call to discipleship involves no cognitive assent *at all*. Those who adopt a neo-orthodox, postliberal and narrative theological method in an extreme way can easily confuse these two claims. There's all the difference in the world between them. And it isn't an illicit commitment to modernism that drives this clarification.

Thirdly, connected with this is a denial of the objectivity of truth. So Kenneson again writes, 'I don't believe in objective truth or relativism. Moreover, I don't want you to believe in objective truth or relativism either, because the first concept is corrupting the church and its witness to the world, while tilting at the second is wasting the precious time and energy of a lot of Christians.'[21] Kenneson believes apparently that fleeing from objective truth doesn't lead him to run to the open arms of a waiting relativism. Rather, he claims to avoid both by rejecting the entire modernistic mentality upon which the forced dilemma – objectivity versus relativism – depends. This relieves the pressure and reduces the need to fight tooth and claw against relativity.

Because everything that exists, including both God and God's creation, in some sense possesses a definite character (even when the creation involves a changing process), true descriptions of reality (if they are indexed for a particular time and place) don't change. Clustered and properly related together, these true descriptions are the whole of truth. This truth is ultimately unified because of the unity of reality that it describes. All that exists – and all truth that describes it – is known within God's unified purview. In this sense, all truth is God's truth, as Arthur Holmes said. We should not shy away from saying that the content of God's truth amounts to 'absolute truth'. Using the word 'absolute' to modify 'truth' means that what God knows as true is not a function of, contingent upon or limited to any finite perspective. God's knowledge of truth isn't imprisoned within a particular viewpoint that is somehow on a par with many other viewpoints. Absolute truth is co-extensive with God's comprehensive knowledge of reality.[22] It

---

[20] Ibid.
[21] Kenneson, 'There's No Such Thing as Objective Truth', p. 156.
[22] Richard Bernstein rejects absolutism because he believes all knowledge is criticizable, that is, he adopts fallibilism. *Beyond Objectivism and Relativism*

makes a huge difference, of course, what the phrase 'objective know-ledge' connotes.

Without a realist view of reality and truth, the evangelical biblical worldview is, in my view, severely undermined. St Paul stated that if Christ didn't rise from the dead, then Christian faith is in vain. I take that in a straightforward way. The proposition 'Jesus arose from the dead' is true because, and only because, Jesus actually arose from the dead. If the truth of theological statements about the world does not correspond to reality, if such theological claims are true *only* in some non-realist (pragmatic?) way, and if they are true only for those in the Christian form of life, then an evangelical stance toward faith and life fumbles badly. In that case, wisdom dictates abandoning evangelical faith. To the degree that 'postmodernity' entails a denial of correspondence and a rejection of objectivity, postmodernity destabilizes evangelical faith and with it, evangelical apologetics. In order to build a postmodern evangelical apologetic, we must part ways with the fashionably chaotic versions of postmodernism.

There's another track worth exploring. Some evangelicals who advocate for a postmodern stance do recognize the need for caution in embracing postmodernity. It's possible (and desirable!) to embrace the correctives of postmodernity and still to acknowledge properly limited understandings of the correspondence view of truth, prepositional truth and the objectivity of truth. McLaren writes: 'I am not recommending anything less than objectivity; I'm recommending something more. I am not against objectivity, absolute truth, propositions, or anything of the sort. Remember: my definition of post modernity is not less than moder-nity, and not against modernity.'[23] McLaren asserts that postmodernism is modernism *plus something*. He speaks wisely.

Postmodernism is not monolithic. Different thinkers don't necessar-ily endorse the themes of postmodernism in just the same way. It's possible to hold the insights of postmodernity in a modest form. Clarity on this point is often overlooked, but essential. We can think of hard postmodernity as distinct from a softer form of postmodernity such as

---

[22] (*continued*) (Philadelphia: University of Pennsylvania Press, 1983), p. 12. The word 'absolute' scares contemporary writers. The problem is that many think a commitment to 'absolutism' implies not merely the claim that God possesses a transcendent perspective, but the contention that ordinary Chris-tian theologians can fully capture the absolute divine perspective. The idea that we understand God's mind with anything beyond minimal adequacy is false and arrogant.

[23] McLaren, 'Honey, I Woke up in a Different Universe', p. 44.

McLaren defends.[24] One way to speak of this is the distinction between deconstructive postmodernity and reconstructive postmodernity. Deconstructive postmodernity isn't deconstruction specifically. It's a broader concept used to denote all chaotic and anarchic forms of postmodernity that make sweeping, negative, universalizing (and therefore self-referentially incoherent) statements about the impossibility of hermeneutics and the failure of epistemology. Reconstructive postmodernity is a position that recognizes the failures of modernism, but offers instead modest yet positive accounts of interpretation and knowledge.[25] The sort of postmodernism I have in mind is positive and constructive.

An instance of the more deconstructive form of postmodernity is attempts to disconnect the meaning of language from its author. Advocates of this theme say, in various ways, that texts convey meanings that go beyond what authors could have intended. They also imply that texts fail to capture fully what authors want to say. So on both sides texts misrepresent authors: they say what authors don't want to say, and they can't say what authors do want to say. Now what can we take from these claims? Stated carefully, this amounts to the observation that language is inexact. It teaches us to pay extra attention in our efforts at communication, for success is not guaranteed. Epistemic humility says we should affirm these points. But in strong form the claims regarding inexactitude of language lead to the conclusion that contrary readings of a particular text are equally satisfactory or – it amounts to the same thing – equally unacceptable. Epistemic courage dictates that we not concede that point. In no way does recognizing the imprecision of all language entail the complete indeterminacy of textual meaning. This is a *non sequitur* of apocalyptic proportions. There is all the difference in the world between saying that language communicates truly, but never perfectly, and saying that texts mean what readers take them to mean.[26]

Now the subtle contrast between exaggerated versions of these insights and properly qualified expressions of such ideas seems rather obvious. But remembering to apply that distinction is absolutely critical to apologetics. I have been on the receiving end of blistering critiques

---

[24] Erickson, *Postmodernizing the Faith*, p. 19.

[25] David Ray Griffin, 'Series Introduction' in David Ray Griffin et al., *Founders of Constructive Postmodern Philosophy*, SUNY Series in Constructive Postmodern Thought (New York: SUNY Press, 1993), pp. viii–x.

[26] See Christopher Norris, 'Kant Disfigured: Ethics, Deconstruction and the Text Sublime' in *The Truth about Postmodernism* (Oxford: Blackwell, 1993), pp. 182–256.

that dismiss traditional Christian affirmations that (I think) are grounded in what the Bible rather straightforwardly seems to mean. The criticism goes essentially like this: 'Because texts do not have determinate meanings, the Bible can't mean what you think it means.' The obvious problem is that these strong forms of epistemic anarchy annihilate themselves in the act of demolishing their opponent. In this case, either the critic admits that his or her critique cuts against and negates his or her own interpretation every bit as much as it cuts against mine, or else he or she exhibits in the end a kind of inconsistency and arbitrariness by disallowing my interpretation and allowing his or hers. I'm not suggesting that the great thinkers of deconstruction commit this sort of error. I doubt they do. Indeed, evidence from the writings of Jacques Derrida suggests that he defends a rather modest thesis regarding the ambiguity of texts.[27] My point isn't to claim that Derrida or any other particular thinker is culpable for sliding back and forth from harder to softer versions of their theses. Rather, my point is this: experience suggests that some of Derrida's admirers are guilty of this epistemic sin. And apologists shouldn't let people get away with this.

Several years ago, I defended a hermeneutic of authorial intention at a regional meeting of the American Academy of Religion. The other members on the panel that morning fell all over themselves to say that an authorial intention hermeneutic is impossible in our postmodern era. I failed then (and still fail today) to see why. I happen to think that we have a very basic intuition that any act of communication means what its utterer meant it to mean.[28] And further, this basic intuition comes into play every time we hold a conversation or read a book. I made reference to a particular philosopher who rejected authorial intention. But a defender of that philosopher took me to task. I was on the receiving end of a ten-minute tirade at several decibels above the pain threshold. Authorial intended meaning is *not* the right way to interpret texts, I was told. That is modernistic and passé. Furthermore, I had grossly misunderstood what the favourite philosopher had said on the point. He did *not* mean what I said he meant. He meant something quite different. And his loyal follower then went on to explain that meaning to me. When he was finished, I thanked the man for making my point: what the

---

[27] See Jacques Derrida, *Margins of Philosophy*, Alan Bass (tr.) (Chicago: University of Chicago Press, 1982).

[28] I think the best way to account for this is to see communicative acts as possessing illocutionary force. This is an aspect of speech act theory that develops a positive rationale behind the practice of author-based interpretation.

philosopher's written text means is integrally connected to what he
meant it to mean.

All this is to say that whenever we appropriate the thought forms
of some pattern of thought that comes from a source outside the Bible
we must do so knowingly and critically, not naïvely. And this critical
appropriation must play out – this is essential – *both for themes typical
of modernity and for theses common to postmodernity.* Developing a
postmodern evangelical apologetic will require rejecting the acidic claims
of modernity that corrupt Christian theology. (Part of the argument
would involve showing how the acids of modernity are cannibalistic,
eating away at modernist claims as well.) But a postmodern evangelical
apologetic shouldn't give up on the core insights that lie behind certain
modern claims. Although modernism was wrong to privilege an artificial
and absolute objectivity in epistemology, it just doesn't follow that we
must reject chastened objectivity. Rather, we must value objectivity even
as we work humbly toward a more reasonable and holistic account of
objectivity. Similarly, a postmodern evangelical apologetic shouldn't
grasp the latest versions of chaotic postmodernity. Postmodern insights
on how power interests corrupt knowledge claims are deeply perceptive.
(See Mt. 23:1–33, for example.) But that insight doesn't even hint at, let
alone justify, the exaggerated claims for relativity of truth, indeterminacy
of texts and universality of power agendas. A postmodern evangelical
apologetic will move beyond modernism by preserving modernism's
valid insights in ways that allow us to incorporate certain positive
postmodern notions as well. If, through intellectual virtue, we discipline
ourselves not to exaggerate the import of our insights, this kind of
holistic stance is reasonable and achievable.

3. Building Postmodern Evangelical Apologetic Practice

The next time I saw Rob, I asked what he thought about the conversation
I'd had with George. George had found the discussion stimulating, Rob
reported. Rob said he continues to interact with George every now and
then. Every spring they spend a day fishing together. They find it relax-
ing. I told Rob how much I respected that commitment to friendship.

I mentioned to Rob that I find it ironic that George is so sceptical
about experiences and reasons relating to the existence of God, but so
trusting about experiences relating to the actual existence of other minds
– for instance, of his wife and children. I had in mind the arguments
made famous by Alvin Plantinga, who claimed that if evidentialism (and
classical foundationalism) were true, then we couldn't know that other

minds exist. On the other hand, if we do directly know that other human minds exist (as we obviously do), then we can know in much the same way that God exists.[29] So given modern epistemic theories, George couldn't rationally or justifiably believe that his wife actually exists as a person. Yet George does accept the actual existence of his wife's mind or soul without a second thought. His wife isn't just a body whom he detects by taking the stance of detached, empirical observer. His wife is a person who connects with him in passionate love relationship, a real spiritual being whom he knows and loves in return. By analogy, I said to Rob, George shouldn't apply to God the sceptical orientation and arguments he employs in the courtroom any more than he should apply them to his wife. He's right to accept the reality of his wife as a spiritual person. He'd be right to do that with God as well.

Could these points fit within an apologetic that coheres with postmodern sensibilities? I believed these rational appeals would carry weight with George, in spite of his tendency to retreat to 'That's a good interpretation from your point of view.' So I tried (both directly and indirectly, by coaching Rob) to practise a postmodern evangelical apologetic. I sought to appropriate two traditions. I approached both the heritage of modernity and the tradition of chaotic postmodernity with a sharply critical spirit. I adopted a reconstructive postmodernity by recognizing that both hard-line modernity and anarchic postmodernity have tapped into some basic and correct insights. I remained critical in that these two patterns of thought have both left a legacy where they overstate their insights so dramatically that they destroy themselves. Postmodern evangelical apologetic practice requires a middle way, balancing values and insights from both modernity and postmodernity. This is an apologetic that seeks to help people experience transformation by connection to God. There is *true connection* to God, as opposed to the detached neutrality fostered by overblown modernism. There is true connection *to God*, in contrast to the nebulous spirituality encouraged by excessive postmodernism.

This middle way requires certain conceptual commitments, interpretative skills and personal sensibilities.

3.1. *Conceptual commitments*

First, postmodern evangelical apologetic practice must value truth, beauty and goodness. And it must regard them equally and in relationship

---

[29] Alvin Plantinga, *God and Other Minds: A Study of the Rational Justification of Belief in God* (Ithaca, New York: Cornell University Press, 1967).

to each other. Modernist evangelical apologists place rationalistic truth at the summit. They ignore (at best) or disparage (at worst) the other two values, beauty and goodness. Philosophers, said William Lycan, 'like language to be literal'.[30] Like Aristotle, some philosophers and apologists see figurative dimensions of metaphorical or symbolic language as unnecessary ornamentation. Non-literal language might be emotionally satisfying or aesthetically enriching, they will say, but getting down to the serious work of thinking requires cutting away the frilly ornamentation. Metaphor reduces clarity and produces confusion. On the other hand, in contrast to this prejudice among philosophers, many non-evangelical theologians view all religious language as metaphor. This is panmetaphoricism.[31] Neither of these stances is wise.

I say we defend truth and place it in relationship with beauty and goodness. We can't live humane lives if all we have is large blocks of intellectual truth. God is a Creator of creaturely beauty and finite goodness. As his creatures, we are innately beautiful and good. (Of course, just as we suffer the noetic effects of the fall, so we experience the aesthetic and moral effects of sin as well.) Just as God gave us belief-forming capacities to know what is true, he created us with aptitude for delighting in beauty and treasuring goodness. Just as we tend to act according to what we believe is truth (unless swayed by evil), so we are moved by beauty and inspired by goodness. So a full-bodied apologetics won't see the aesthetic and moral dimensions as frilly and expendable ornaments. These dimensions of the human spirit exist because of the Creator. Indeed, a worldview should account for these humane experiences. The human thirst for beauty and goodness (despite terrible maiming due to sin and evil) is something that needs explaining. 'There is the music of Johann Sebastian Bach. Therefore there must be a God,' write Peter Kreeft and Ronald Tacelli. They add, 'You either see this one or you don't.'[32] And we do! (Or, if we don't, we see a culturally appropriate style of music.) Whatever the specific style, humans see beauty at a deep level. It adds to a richly satisfying life. A truly postmodern evangelical apologist won't give an inch on truth, but will apply him or herself to

---

[30] William G. Lycan, *Philosophy of Language: A Contemporary Introduction* (New York: Routledge, 2000), p. 209.

[31] William P. Alston, 'Irreducible Metaphors in Theology' in *Divine Nature and Human Language* (Ithaca, New York: Cornell University Press, 1989), 17–38.

[32] Peter Kreeft and Ronald K. Tacelli, *Handbook of Christian Apologetics: Hundreds of Answers to Crucial Questions* (Downers Grove: InterVarsity, 1994), p. 81.

point to God as the Creator of the good and the beautiful – as well as the Creator of human passion for them.

Secondly, a postmodern evangelical apologetic practice must humbly recognize the fallibility of human attempts to gain knowledge. According to a survey among American college students in 2002, 97 per cent of a random sample of seniors agreed that their college studies had prepared them to behave ethically in their chosen profession. But when asked whether their professors taught them that right and wrong depend on individual and cultural differences, 73 per cent agreed. Only 25 per cent agreed that all persons should be judged by uniform standards of right and wrong.[33] This seems to coincide with my experience that many adults in Western countries – or at least in North America – harbour deeply relativistic intuitions regarding morality. And they harbour similar feelings regarding truth claims.

The fallibility of human knowledge should not lead us to desert either universal morality or objective truth, however. Many epistemic practices allow us to work through differences of opinion. These epistemic practices permit those who will use them to overcome biases. Those who are content to lounge in their intellectual easy chairs may not exert effort or open their minds to the kind of sharpening of thought that these practices can bring. But those who are properly epistemically virtuous can seek out contrary points of view, falsifying information and rational critiques to test their views. Still, though we can seek successive approximation of the truth, we as humans do not achieve a God's-eye perspective. So we can seek knowledge virtuously, feel confidence in what we have explored, and yet let others see our humility and openness to correction. This humility is not only intellectually virtuous, but personally persuasive as well. For it is just the response needed to overcome the postmodern obsession with avoiding being taken in.

Thirdly, a postmodern evangelical apologetic will defend rationality, but without caving in to untenable, modernistic versions of rationalism such as modernist classical foundationalism, evidentialism and positivism. Modernist rationalism defended a narrowly defined epistemic stance. It was obsessed with propositions and evidence and deduction as necessary to the highest and best form of truth. It privileged detached, objective, empirical, quantitative knowledge. It denigrated other forms of knowing, like knowledge by acquaintance, for example. Postmoderns rightly reject these constricted, monochromatic forms of rationalism.

---

[33] < www.nas.org/reports/zogethics_poll/zogby_ethics_report.htm >. This web page is supported by the National Association of Scholars, 221 Witherspoon St, 2nd Floor, Princeton, NJ 08542-3215. The margin of error is ± 5%.

And evangelicals should join hands with postmoderns in recognizing these modernist prejudices for what they are.[34]

A clear understanding of the demise of modernist rationalism, on the other hand, doesn't begin to justify a move to the opposite extreme where subjective knowledge is promoted at the expense of objectivity in knowledge. The failure of modernism doesn't prove that every appeal to evidence is a covert power play. Indeed, after abandoning modernist rationalism, we must still promote rationality. Rationality is part of God's image in the human spirit. Humans are much more than rational, but not less. So loving God with the mind includes developing epistemic virtues such as love of truth over error, readiness to consider evidence even when it contests a favoured position, discipline to follow reasoning where it leads and humility to hear another's perspective even when it challenges the majority view. Postmodern evangelical apologetics should decry modernist rationalism, but endorse a properly qualified, broadly construed, but rigorously applied human rationality as a gift of God and as one of the tools by which to arrive at genuine knowledge about God and his ways.

3.2. Interpretative skills

First, our postmodern evangelical apologetic practice should develop skill in preserving core insights and pretheoretic intuitions that emerge in sometimes contrary patterns of thought. This may include abandoning *specific theories* about these insights or intuitions. But core insights – for example, the alethic realist claim that truth is about a world that possesses a definite character – are expressed both articulately and confusedly. When some thinker expresses a correct intuition confusedly, the best response isn't abandoning the intuition. The best response is developing chaste accounts of the intuition. Obviously, I've tried to use this strategy throughout this essay. I've tried to develop a reconstructive postmodern account of apologetics that retains what is right about modern emphases without making the standard modern mistakes. I commend this attention to detail and precision in the current chaos of the intellectual world. Without it, we shall lose too many tiny but valuable flecks of gold in our haste to throw out the ore.

---

[34] Indeed, William Lane Craig, despite very harsh words about postmodernism, clearly understands the bankruptcy of modernist epistemology. He defends the idea that Christians may know about God in a properly basic way through personal experience. Obviously, therefore, this critique of postmodernism is directed to its deconstructing forms.

Secondly, given that the purpose of apologetics is personal transformation, we must develop skill in combining abstract and concrete modes of expression. Abstractions that emerge in building theories and clarifying propositions serve a valid purpose. But they aren't sufficient to accomplish what concrete modes of expression – story, symbol, narrative, analogy and metaphor – can accomplish. If apologetics is about persuading and forming both mind and heart, it's obvious that something in addition to abstract propositions is called for. 'Modern evangelicalism reads like an IRS 1040 form: It's true, all the data is [*sic*] there, but it doesn't take your breath away.'[35] Story is the language of the heart. Good apologetic practice incorporates it. None of that takes away from the value of hard-headed effort at clear, well-grounded accounts of the Christian faith. The heart can be seduced by error that packages itself in attractive stories. We need both powerful stories and precise analyses. G.K. Chesterton once wrote, 'Christianity got over the difficulty of combining furious opposites by keeping them both and keeping them both furious.'[36] This is true here.

Thirdly, as I already suggested, we must cultivate epistemic humility and balance it with epistemic courage. If modernist thinkers became too arrogant, postmoderns can become too docile. (I note, however, that this isn't always so, as postmodern individuals can sometimes become arrogant about their privileged awareness of the fact that knowledge is always conditioned by time and place.) Still, in spite of modernity's claims, humility is a proper intellectual virtue. Despite postmodernity's emphases, so are honesty and courage. Being humble intellectually requires retaining an open spirit of correction. Being honest means making a fair appraisal of the evidence at hand, dedicating effort to reaching all conclusions, admitting personal biases that affect beliefs and seeking to override or reduce those biases. In an intellectual context, courage involves, among other things, being willing to take minority positions when the evidence points in that direction. All these virtues are important, not just in finding knowledge – that is good in itself – but also in commending to others what knowledge is found. A virtue-oriented approach to building knowledge is all the more critical in a postmodern context where the prevailing expectation is that people hold their beliefs because it is useful to do so or because it gives them more power. Postmodern evangelical apologetics must operate with keen awareness

---

[35] Brent Curtis and John Eldredge, *The Sacred Romance: Drawing Closer to the Heart of God* (Nashville: Nelson, 1997), p. 45.

[36] Quoted in Philip Yancey, 'Living with Furious Opposites', *Christianity Today*, 4 September 2000, p. 74.

that cynicism exists all about and with deep commitment to show that the suspicions are unfounded, at least regarding faith.

3.3. Personal sensibilities

First, we should recognize – even feel empathy with – one of the deepest common threads of postmodernity: its cynicism toward powerful, self-serving interests. In the philosophical forms of postmodernity, deconstructive strategies undermine all metanarratives in order to ensure that no allegedly absolute truth can ever oppress the weak and marginalized person. In the popular culture, postmodern sensibilities are distrusting of institutions like big government, multinational corporations and megachurches. (Note, ironically, that people who fancy themselves postmodern – and have the tattoos to prove it – routinely pay good money to sit in darkened theatres and to gulp down the anti-establishment messages embedded in movies produced by huge, multinational firms, the movie studios. But I digress.) Postmodernism involves a deeply rooted allergic reaction against power. At its worst, this translates into an inability or unwillingness to trust.

This cat-like skittishness regarding trust is deeply regrettable. Relationships of love require trust. God created us for relationship, first with him, and then with other humans. If the postmodern distrust of institutions, truth claims and powerful persons is allowed to grow unchecked, those influenced by this trait will be cut off from the very source of life. That, obviously, would defeat the purposes of apologetic practice. The solution here is not pounding the pulpit about how trust-worthy we postmodern apologists are. There's just no substitute for actually being trustworthy. I urge apologists to do their work only in the context of deeply authentic relationship and respectful dialogue.[37]

Finally, as postmodern evangelical apologists, we should point people to the eternity in their hearts. This directs our gaze through mystery to transcendence. A powerful example of this is the dialogue between apologist Greg Boyd and his agnostic father. At the end of one in the series of letters, Boyd writes, 'Doesn't the proclamation confirm the longings of the heart in the same fashion it answers the questions of the mind?' On another occasion he says, 'But isn't there something in the depth of your heart which refuses to accept this ["life is a bitch, then you die"] as the whole truth?' As the letters continue, Boyd becomes more

---

[37] This is the most important point I make in *Dialogical Apologetics: A Person-Centered Approach to Christian Defense* (Grand Rapids: Baker, 1993).

forceful concerning his father's relationship with God. At the end of the sixteenth letter, he pleads:

> I encourage you, Dad – I implore you – don't cut yourself off from Jesus Christ. Don't reject Him. All that you were meant to be, all the longings of your heart, your need for love, for hope, for significance, for happiness, all are fulfilled in a relationship with God through Christ. You were made for this.[38]

Of course, this is right. Mere cognitivity does not appeal to the deepest dimensions of the human heart. But if God created us for eternity, it should come as no surprise to think that God created us with a belief-producing capacity to feel his eternal presence. Just as the Creator formed the human eye to detect colour, so he attuned the human heart to its eternal destiny. Apologetic rationality must in the end – and maybe in the beginning – make connection to that.

So the very idea – postmodern evangelical apologetics – is indeed coherent. More than that, it's exactly what we should promote and practise. In saying this, I'm not at all giving away our pretheoretic insights on such things as a correspondence notion of truth, an alethic realism regarding theological propositions or a reasoned objectivity in knowledge despite our fallibility. It doesn't follow from the fact that modernism has imploded – from the fact that *modernist theories* of correspondence, propositional truth and objectivity in knowledge are obviously false – that we should leap toward undisciplined versions of postmodernism. It is in fact all the more important for evangelical apologetics that we develop properly qualified theories about such things. If we don't, we shall not be able to commend the gospel of Jesus Christ as a true message for all peoples.

On the flip side, I'm not giving anything away regarding the centrality of spiritual experience, the value of personal relationships, the importance of authenticity in dialogue with non-Christians, the power of concrete stories and symbols or the need for a churchly apologetic. These modes of life, experience and communication are essential to moving through information toward transformation. And spiritual transformation is the ultimate point of theology and apologetics. Now it doesn't begin to follow from the fact that personal transformation is a central goal of apologetics that we should propound incoherent theses regarding properly chastened appeals to reason and evidence. It is

---

[38] Gregory A. Boyd, *Letters from a Skeptic* (Wheaton: Victor, 1994), pp. 28, 98, 109.

indeed all the more crucial for postmodern evangelical apologetics that we both practise Christian virtues and pursue apologetic clarity in our interactions with others. If we don't, we may offer them a set of abstract ideas that will completely lack the power of God.

So postmodern evangelical apologetics must resist the forced either/or dilemmas: either perfect objectivity or utter ambiguity. Those who defend modernism and those who promote deconstructive postmodernism are both tempted to cast the issues in such stark terms. The fact is that both/and – both a chastened version of the objectivity that modernism sought to promote and the modest recognition of the ambiguity that postmodernism emphasizes – is right. In fact, we can often defend a carefully crafted both/and. But not always. Sometimes we need the either/or. Either Jesus Christ is the Saviour of the world, or he is not. Evangelicalism is true in the first instance, but false in the second. So postmodern evangelical apologetics is *both* both/and in its thinking and practice *and also* either/or – as appropriate. It's holistic, systemic, spiritual, reasoned, churchly and dialogical. This sort of apologetics is the best means to fulfil in the postmodern context the high calling of offering a reason for the hope that lies within us.

4. Conclusion

By the way, I should mention that a fortnight ago I ran into Rob. He told me that George started coming to church with him six months ago. Then, after several months of attending worship, George committed his life to Jesus Christ. This happened about eight years after I first met George. What made the difference? Not my conversation with him, I'm sure. Nor any other one thing, I suspect. I'd say the Holy Spirit used a loving wife, a couple of philosophical insights, a long-term friendship, the experience of the worshipping church, some precision on evangelical theological claims and the eternity tucked inside George's heart. Both philosophy and friendship. Both worship and wisdom. Both experience and eternity. Furious opposites. Together, using these various threads, the Spirit gradually knit between George and Christ a tapestry of love relationship. This is the fabric of postmodern evangelical apologetics.

14

Contributors: An Appreciation and Response

Alister E. McGrath

Dr Sung Wook Chung has put together a remarkable collection of essays, which is itself a fine tribute to the growing confidence and sophistication of evangelical theology.[1] While he has very generously chosen to focus on my own small contribution to this development, evangelical theology as a whole is a corporate effort, in which the evangelical community seeks to express and extend its grasp of the living God. While I count myself honoured to be part of such a venture, its true greatness lies in its collegiality. I suspect that I have learned far more from others than I can ever hope to pass on.[2]

I am more than a little overwhelmed that my colleagues should have so graciously contributed to this volume when I am a mere fifty years old. I am delighted that they have done so, because I will be able to make use of their comments, criticisms and counterproposals in the years of reflection and writing which I hope remain to me, and in which I plan to publish some substantial works of both historical and systematic theology.

But first, I feel I owe my readers an account of my overall vision of my agenda, to allow them to judge how this has shaped my theological development thus far, and understand what is yet to come. The first thirteen years of my life were spent in Downpatrick, a market town of about 3000 people in County Down, Northern Ireland. Its chief claim to fame was that it was the site of the grave of Patrick, the patron saint of Ireland. I never had the slightest interest in religion as a young boy,

---

[1] For comment, see Carl E. Braaten, 'A Harvest of Evangelical Theology', *First Things* 61 (March 1996), pp. 45–8.

[2] For example, I am indebted to J.I. Packer for many aspects of my thought, not least his emphasis on evangelical theologizing within the 'great tradition': see Alister E. McGrath, *J.I. Packer: A Biography* (Grand Rapids: Baker, 1997).

initially regarding it as a waste of time. When I left the local high school to attend the Methodist College in Belfast in 1965, I found my attitudes hardening. A growing interest in Marxism led me to the view that Christianity was oppressive and outdated. Like many young people in those heady days of the late 1960s, I believed that a new world lay around the corner. It would be a world without war, conflict or religion. The student revolts in Paris and other events were harbingers of the new age that was to dawn. Few could fail to be excited by such a vision. Like many others, I found myself entranced by the ideas set out by writers such as Theodore Adorno.

At this stage, I was deeply immersed in the study of the natural sciences. My initial inclination had been to follow the family tradition and enter the medical profession. However, I found the appeal of pure science to be far more exciting, and ended up specializing in mathematics, chemistry and physics. Having obtained top grades in these subjects at A level, I stayed on at the Methodist College for an additional year, in order to sit the Oxford entrance examinations. Oxford University offered what was indisputably the finest chemistry course in Britain, and I was determined to study there. I was drawn to Wadham College by its outstanding chemistry dons at the time – R.J.P. Williams and Jeremy R. Knowles – and also by the college's reputation for left-wing politics. I still have the letter from Stuart Hampshire, Warden of Wadham College, informing me that I had been awarded a scholarship at the college.

Studying chemistry at Oxford was an intellectually invigorating exercise, and I shall remain indebted to those who taught me for the rest of my life. Yet my life was in turmoil. I had discovered that Christianity was rather more exciting and intellectually resilient than I could ever have imagined. I was converted to Christianity in November 1971, and found myself having to rethink countless questions, not least that of what I should do with the rest of my life. I was now determined to bring my Christian faith into direct contact with the working methods and assumptions of the natural sciences. Though tempted to change course to theology immediately, I was strongly advised to complete my studies in chemistry before moving on.

In 1976, I was awarded a Senior Scholarship at Merton College to continue my research work in molecular biophysics. This award was unusual, in that it allowed both the funding of a research or a second first degree. Merton College gave me permission to continue my scientific research while simultaneously studying theology at Oxford at undergraduate level. Taking advantage of the flexibility of Oxford's degree in theology, I was able to take special optional papers in medieval thought and the relation of Christianity to the sciences. The result was that in 1978 I was awarded my doctorate in molecular biology, while at the same time gaining first-class honours in theology, and winning the Denyer and Johnson Prize in theology for the best performance that year. As a result, I was invited to lunch shortly afterwards by a senior editor at Oxford University Press, who asked me to consider writing a book on the theme of Christianity and the natural sciences, in particular to respond to Richard Dawkin's book *The Selfish Gene*. I gave this proposal very serious consideration. However, I came to the conclusion that I would need to immerse myself in the further study of religion, and especially the history of Christian theology, before I could make a positive and informed contribution to this field.

I then moved to Cambridge, having been awarded the Naden Research Studentship in Theology at St John's College for a period of two years to study sixteenth-century religious thought under the supervision of the late Professor E. Gordon Rupp, while training for the ministry of the Church of England at Westcott House. My initial intention had been to pursue research in theology and the natural sciences. However, it became clear that I would need to drink deeply of the Christian theological tradition if that research were to avoid being amateurish, superficial and simplistic. I therefore opted for the model of theological research I found in German theological writers who I admired, such as Gerhard Ebeling, Wolfhart Pannenberg and Jürgen Moltmann, all of whom had cut their theological teeth through major research in historical theology, and whose subsequent writings in systematic theology were characterized by an informed and serious engagement with the Christian tradition. Inspired by this, I chose to study one thinker (Martin Luther), one doctrine (justification) and one historical period (the Reformation, set against its later medieval context) in detail, and found this an invaluable preparation for serious theological reflection.[3]

Meanwhile, I moved to work as an ordained minister of the Church of England in a parish in Nottingham. This was an invaluable experience, not least in that it raised questions in my mind concerning the spiritual relevance and intellectual viability of the dominant thought forms within Anglicanism at this time. Having been converted through

---

[3] For the resulting books, see Alister E. McGrath, *Luther's Theology of the Cross: Martin Luther's Theological Breakthrough* (Oxford: Blackwell, 1985); Alister E. McGrath, *Iustitia Dei: A History of the Christian Doctrine of Justification* (Cambridge: Cambridge University Press, 1998[2]); Alister E. McGrath, *The Intellectual Origins of the European Reformation* (Oxford: Blackwell, 1987).

evangelical ministries in Oxford in late 1971, I found myself regaining confidence in the intellectual and spiritual vitality of evangelicalism as a result of my pastoral and preaching ministries.[4] Preaching regularly to a suburban congregation, week by week, convinced me of the need to be able to interpret the Christian theological tradition in terms that ordinary people could understand, and in ways that conveyed its relevance to their lives. Like many others, I began to grow impatient with academic theology, which seemed at times to dismiss the questions and concerns of ordinary Christians, and speak a language that nobody could understand. My natural home is the world of the Christian community of faith, rather than the dwindling ranks of academic theologians, and I have to confess my concerns over the viability of the latter.[5]

Oxford, however, is my spiritual and intellectual home. A landmark in the shaping of my theological mind therefore took place in 1983, when I returned to Oxford as a lecturer at Wycliffe Hall, an evangelical theological college of the Church of England with close links with Oxford University. As a member of Oxford's Faculty of Theology, I was able to lecture on topics that excited me, such as the development of Luther's theology. I became the Principal of Wycliffe Hall in 1995, and as my first major project secured its full integration within Oxford University as a 'Permanent Private Hall'. In addition to this institutional development and its implications for my role within the university, my personal commitment to Oxford continued to deepen. In 1999 I was elected to a personal chair of theology by the University; in 2001 I was awarded the degree of Doctor of Divinity. Like many who have settled in Oxford, I cannot really see myself as being at home – physically, psychologically and intellectually – anywhere else. It is an outstanding platform from which an evangelical can address the academy and the church, and I hope to be able to continue to do so for many years.

I now turn to the distinguished contributions, which are the real meat of this volume, offering an appreciative response to each author.

* * * * *

---

[4] For my reflections on my renewed confidence in evangelicalism, which has defined my writing and speaking ministries since then, see Alister E. McGrath, 'Confessions of a Disillusioned Liberal' in Gordon Kuhrt (ed.), *Doctrine Matters* (London: Hodder & Stoughton, 1993), pp. 1–18.
[5] For my later reflections on the relation of academic theology and the life and witness of the churches, see Alister E. McGrath, *The Future of Christianity* (Oxford: Blackwell, 2002), pp. 120–55.

Dr Graham Tomlin examines the role that the cross plays in my thinking. He is well qualified to write on this topic, having distinguished himself as a scholar of the 'theology of the cross' in Paul, Luther and Pascal.[6] I have no doubt that we will be hearing much more of Tomlin as a writer in the future, and believe that he will be an important catalyst to our thinking on the full impact of the cross, and its importance to the mission of the church.[7] Tomlin offers an accurate and insightful account of the central-ity of the cross to my thinking. Revelation and salvation are both made possible and made known through the cross. He rightly notes that I insist upon an 'objectivist' approach to the cross; I am quite convinced of the theological deficiencies of subjectivist approaches, and regularly critique these in lectures and publications. He further observes – again, absolutely correctly – that I am reluctant to sloganize the cross, reducing it to a slick phrase or neat aphorism. Tomlin is therefore probably right when he suggests that my sympathies lie with pietistic, rather than more explicitly theological, approaches to the cross. Although I value systematic theology immensely, I am occasionally driven to despair by those who insist that we must use exactly the right form of words to describe the cross, and refuse to countenance that those who decline to use them are 'unsound'. I used to think that myself. However, reading J.I. Packer's later works challenged me to rethink my views. His charge that many evangelicals had fallen victim to what was virtually a 'cultic heresy' of 'justification by right words' pulled me up short, and forced me to rethink.[8]

It is the way of fundamentalists to follow the path of contentious orthodoxism, as if the mercy of God in Christ automatically rests on persons who are notionally correct and is just as automatically withheld from those who fall short of notional correctness on any point of sub-stance. But this concept of, in effect, justification, not by works, but by words – words, that is, of notional soundness and precision – is near to being a cultic heresy in its own right.

I am sure that there is much that is lacking with a pietistic approach to the cross. Yet it seems to touch on something that is too easily missed, and obscured by an obsession with words. The cross, as Luther stressed, is shrouded in mystery, and we delude ourselves if we think we can adequately package it in the neat terms of systematic theology.

---

[6] Graham Tomlin, *The Power of the Cross: Theology and the Death of Christ in Paul, Luther and Pascal* (Carlisle: Paternoster, 1999).

[7] For his excellent exploration of the ecclesiological aspects of mission, see Graham Tomlin, *The Provocative Church* (London: SPCK, 2002).

[8] J.I. Packer, 'On from Orr: The Cultural Crisis, Rational Realism, and Incarnational Ontology', *Crux* 32 (1996), pp. 12–26.

As my writings make abundantly clear, I regard the cross as the foundation and criterion of true Christian thinking and living. Perhaps this helps explain why I value some of the great artistic depictions of the crucifixion – such as Matthias Grünewald's Isenheim altarpiece – in that they enable me to focus on the cross in personal meditation or theological reflection. I am aware that I have not addressed the spiritual dimensions of the cross with anything like the attention and care that it demands. However, in some of my more popular writings on spirituality, I try to convey something of my own deep love of the cross, and my sense of amazement that our Creator God should have redeemed us in this way.[9] I particularly admire Luther's reflections on the topic, as summarized in his *Greater Catechism* (1529):

> But all the points which follow in order in this article serve no other purpose than to explain and express this redemption, how and whereby it was accomplished, that is, how much it cost Christ, and what he spent and risked in order that he might win us and bring us under his dominion, namely, that he became a human being, was conceived and born without sin of the Holy Ghost and of the Virgin Mary, that he might overcome sin; moreover, that he suffered, died and was buried, so that he might make satisfaction for me and pay what I owe, not with silver nor gold, but with his own precious blood. And all this, in order to become my Lord; for he did none of these for himself, nor had he any need for it.[10]

*   *   *   *   *

Dr Gerald Bray engages with my attempt to make sense of the long and complex development of the doctrine of justification, and raises some very helpful points of discussion. He is well qualified to raise these concerns, as his own publications show him to be a competent historical theologian, with a genuine concern to relate the riches of the Christian theological tradition to the tasks and challenges of today.[11] In

---

[9] See Alister E. McGrath, *The Journey: A Pilgrim in the Lands of the Spirit* (New York: Doubleday, 2000); Alister McGrath, *Knowing Christ* (New York: Doubleday, 2002).

[10] *Die Bekenntnisschriften der evangelisch-lutherischen Kirche* (Göttingen: Vandenhoeck & Ruprecht, 1952), p. 652.

[11] See, for example, his work on the great debates of the patristic period, and more recently his admirable introduction to the doctrine of God: Gerald Bray, *Creeds, Councils and Christ* (Leicester: Inter-Varsity Press, 1984); Gerald Bray, *The Doctrine of God* (Leicester: Inter-Varsity Press, 1993).

his assessment of my work, he raises two legitimate concerns: that I do not adequately link Luther's pioneering insights on justification *per solam fidem* to the Reformation as a whole; and that I fail to deal with the question of what the Pauline corpus really teaches concerning justification.

There is, in my mind, no doubt that Luther's doctrine of justification was of decisive importance to his own theological breakthrough, and that it played a critically important role in the Wittenberg Reformation. Those around Luther – especially Melanchthon and Karlstadt – stood alongside him at this point throughout the 1520s. There is no doubt that Luther's distinctive ideas concerning the doctrine found their way into the great Reformational currents sweeping Europe in the 1530s and 1540s. The Osiandrist controversy clearly heightened the importance of the notion of *iustitia imputata*. Yet my own researches into the theological origins of the Reformation suggested to me that the reception of Luther's distinctive ideas was a little more variegated and nuanced than the standard accounts of the Reformation allow. From about 1542, the ecclesiological issue seems to become more important, as the evangelical communities come under pressure to justify their existence as churches – that is, as distinct ecclesiological entities, having no institutional links with the medieval church, yet still claiming to be *Christian* churches.

Dr Bray's second point is especially important. Why do I not deal directly with Paul? My colleague N.T. Wright made a similar criticism some years ago, when he remarked that *Iustitia Dei* told you just about everything about justification – except what it actually *is*. Let me begin by saying that I have spent many years pondering this difficulty, and am still not sure that my approach to this issue is right. My concerns over this began when working through the three volumes of Albrecht Benjamin Ritschl's work *Die christliche Lehre von der Rechtfertigung und Versöhnung*. The first volume contained his analysis of the dogmatic development of the doctrine from the eleventh to the nineteenth century; the second his understanding of the biblical basis of the doctrine; and the third set out his own understanding of the doctrine. In effect, the three volumes are best understood as works of historical, biblical and systematic theology respectively. Of those volumes, the second was the least successful, and was never translated into English. Far from being a definitive interpretative account of the biblical material on justification, it was soon seen as a minor curiosity, merely reflecting the assumptions of its day and age. It was read, not to find out what Paul believed, but to find out what liberal Protestant writers of the 1870s believed Paul believed.

My concerns over this issue were reinforced as I worked through countless Pauline commentaries, from the patristic period to the present day. A persistent pattern of scholarly provisionality emerged. What was once regarded as a state-of-the-art account of Paul's doctrine of justification was subject to rapid historical erosion, eventually becoming 'what used to be thought about Paul'. Inevitably, any chapter that I produced on 'Paul's doctrine of justification' would be subject to this same process of erosion. As *Iustitia Dei* was in one sense an historical account of what people have taken Paul to mean by 'justification', I felt that it would be immodest and inappropriate to add my own views on the matter. And if I were to summarize what scholars of the year 2000 believed, would not those reading the work in 2050 read this to find out what was believed about Paul fifty years earlier, rather than to find out what Paul believed? However, Dr Bray's helpful comments will be invaluable as I continue to review this matter. There seems no easy answer to the problem.

The second edition of *Iustitia Dei* appeared in 1998. For economic reasons – the publisher did not want to reset the work – it was basically the original two volumes merged into one, with two additional chapters concerning justification in recent ecumenical discussions, and in recent New Testament scholarship. Cambridge University Press have now agreed to a third edition, and have given me the freedom to completely rewrite the work. This will allow me to revise every aspect of the work, and thus to incorporate much recent scholarly work in the field. This may allow me to include a chapter on Paul, as Dr Bray suggests.

*   *   *   *   *

I have worked with Dr John Roche on a number of projects, including establishing and running the Oxford Templeton Seminars on Science and Christianity. Dr Roche offers a long and exceptionally thorough examination of the first two volumes of my 'Scientific Theology' trilogy from his own perspective of a physicist and an historian of science.[12] His perception that I write with a 'sense of controlled urgency' is a rather nice way of expressing the relentless urge I often feel to put a difficult idea into words, approaching it from many angles, and often experiencing frustration at not quite being able to get it right.

In view of the importance of the 'Scientific Theology' trilogy to my vision of theology, I feel I ought to say a little more about it. The project aims to set out an approach to theology that draws upon the working

---

[12] John Roche, *Physicists Look Back: Studies in the History of Physics* (Bristol: Hilger, 1990).

assumptions and methods of the natural sciences. The three constituent volumes of my 'Scientific Theology' set out to plot a trajectory for Christian theology which maintains its academic and spiritual integrity – above all, its biblical roots and foundations – while encouraging a direct and positive engagement with a scientific culture, understood as both scientific theory *and* practice. The work is marked throughout by a sustained and critical engagement with the history and philosophy of the natural sciences, and a passionate commitment to the legitimacy of Christian theology as an academic discipline in its own right. The work argues for a direct engagement between Christian theology and the natural sciences without the need for surrogates or intermediaries, such as the 'process thought' favoured by many American writers in this field.

My role model here was Thomas F. Torrance, unquestionably the greatest British theologian of the twentieth century. A happy by-product of my engagement with his ideas was a growing interest in Torrance as a person. Theologians sometimes treat theology as a disembodied intellectual pursuit, and I found it important to affirm that Torrance (like other theologians) was actually a living human being, who connected his theology with his life and work. Researching his biography was one of the more personally fulfilling research projects of recent years.[13] Although I diverge from Torrance at points, there is little doubt that he has provided a decisive stimulus to those wishing to take the interaction of theology and the natural sciences seriously, rather than just play around with vague notions of human religiosity.

The structure of the three volumes of *A Scientific Theology* makes it clear that this work is primarily concerned with theological method, rather than with specific theological topics. It is a systematic work of theology, rather than a work of systematic theology. The work crystallizes around three specific topics, each of which demanded a full volume to be dealt with properly.

Nature
This opening volume clarifies the general position to be adopted, before moving on to a detailed engagement with the concept of 'nature', which is of such decisive importance in any discussion of the relation of the natural sciences and theology. 'Nature' is often treated as a fundamental resource for theology, on the basis of the assumption that it is an unmediated and uninterpreted concept. Yet there is a growing and settled view that the concept of 'nature' actually represents a socially mediated

---

[13] Alister E. McGrath, *T.F. Torrance: An Intellectual Biography* (Edinburgh: T. & T. Clark, 1999).

construct. Nature is thus to be viewed as an interpreted notion, which is unusually vulnerable to the challenge of deconstruction. The implications of this for a 'theology of nature' are explored, with especial reference to the Christian understanding of nature as creation.

Reality

The second volume in the series deals with the issue of realism in science and theology, and sets out both a critique of anti- and non-realism, and a positive statement of a realist position. In light of this, the nature of a scientific theology is explored, with particular emphasis being placed upon theology as an a posteriori discipline which offers an account of reality. This volume develops the theological potential of the programme of 'critical realism' developed in the writings of Roy Bhaskar, which has considerable potential for Christian theology in general, and for the interaction of that theology and the natural sciences in particular.

Theory

The third and final volume in the series, which should be published in October 2003, deals with the manner in which reality is represented, paying especial attention to the parallels between theological doctrines and scientific theories. This volume considers the origin, development and reception of such doctrines and theories, and notes the important parallels between the scientific and theological communities in these important matters.

And where do I go next? The three volumes of *A Scientific Theology* explore the issue of theological method and demonstrate the viability of this general approach. Yet the method remains to be applied. It is my intention to follow this up with an original work of systematic theology, entitled *A Scientific Dogmatics*. I anticipate that it will take me ten years to research and develop this major project, which I expect to take the form of three major volumes of systematic theology. But we will see if this ever comes to pass.

*   *   *   *   *

Denis Okholm of Wheaton College offers a most interesting account of my views on postliberalism. Okholm was involved, along with the late Timothy Phillips, in convening the highly important dialogue between evangelicals and postliberals at Wheaton back in 1995, and he must be given much praise both for that specific consultation and the annual Wheaton theology conferences that he has been instrumental in convening. I am critical of postliberalism in my writings, and continue to be so – perhaps most notably in the second volume of my *Scientific Theology*, where I suggest that Lindbeck's account of postliberalism is inherently coherentist in its approach to its own justification, and is not adequately grounded in the history of the Christian tradition.

Yet I must stress that I regard postliberalism as deficient, rather than wrong, and have great respect for the intentions and perceptions of its leading figures. My ongoing concerns relate to its historically dislocated understanding of the Christian tradition, and its apparent inability to offer an account of how any given doctrinal statement or trend may be evaluated. Since I do not equate anti-foundationalism with anti-realism, as the second volume of my *Scientific Theology* makes clear, I do not have any particular problems with Okholm's approach on this specific point. However, I am puzzled by Lindbeck's attitude to 'correspondence', mirrored in Okholm's article.

Okholm rightly raises the issue of realism as being of importance to any evaluation of postliberalism, and correctly points out that postliberalism is not actually anti-realist. This is true, but I'm not sure where it takes us. If Lindbeck is sympathetic to any form of realism, he disguises the fact with remarkable skill, placing a Wittgensteinian veil between himself and whatever might be real. On Lindbeck's reading of the nature of doctrine, theology can only be 'talk about talk about God'. What really interests Lindbeck is language; what that language is about, and where it came from, tends to be treated as a side issue. Sure, it might refer to something (Lindbeck never *explicitly* denies the notion of reference). Then again, it might not.

Lindbeck seems to me to dismiss any correspondence theory of truth with almost indecent haste, perhaps failing to point out that there are several such approaches, and that his 'one size fits all' approach is inadequate to meet the points at issue. Correspondence theories of truth adopt a number of approaches to the nature of the referential relation, including causal accounts (such as those found in the writings of F.I. Dretske, Hilary Putnam and Saul Kripke)[14] and more recently teleofunctional accounts (Ruth Millikan).[15] I don't see Lindbeck paying much attention to these. It is indeed the case that what we might term 'naïve' correspondence theories of truth are treated with something approaching amusement within the professional theological community. Yet there is no shortage of philosophers prepared to defend more

---

[14] See Saul A. Kripke, *Naming and Necessity* (Oxford: Blackwell, 1980); Hilary Putnam, *Representation and Reality* (Cambridge, MA: MIT Press, 1991).

[15] Ruth G. Millikan, *Language, Thought and other Biological Categories: New Foundations for Realism* (Cambridge, Massachusetts: MIT Press, 1984).

sophisticated correspondence theories of truth. An excellent example of this may be found in the writings of Laurence Bonjour, where we find a correspondence theory of truth is held in tandem with a coherentist theory of justification.[16] Perhaps more worryingly, Lindbeck's tantalizingly brief references to correspondence theories of truth raise the question of whether he has confused these with the much-criticized *identity* theory of truth.[17]

Okholm ends his excellent essay with the plea that evangelicalism might 'defend a nonfoundationalist realism that seems most faithful to the theology of pre-modern evangelicals like Luther and Calvin'. I fully concur. Lindbeck has challenged evangelicals, not to imitate him, but to transcend him. I have tried to rise to this challenge, but do not for one moment believe that I have resolved it. We have much to do in reclaiming the theological heritage of the past, while extricating it from the morass of foundationalism.

We shall see where the dialogue with postliberalism takes evangelicalism. I continue to be somewhat pessimistic about the prospects, largely because new theological trends have emerged which have displaced it – for example, the 'Radical Orthodoxy' movement, associated with people like John Milbank of the University of Virginia.[18] While I have many concerns about this new style of theology – as do others[19] – it does seem to be rather more interesting and productive than Lindbeck's postliberalism. Maybe evangelicals will want to move on, and engage with this new programme, and others? Postliberalism has slipped into the slow lane, and I am not sure it is worth following it there.

*   *   *   *   *

---

[16] Laurence Bonjour, *The Structure of Empirical Knowledge* (Cambridge, Massachusetts: Harvard University Press, 1985).

[17] On which see Thomas Baldwin, 'The Identity Theory of Truth', *Mind* 100 (2001), pp. 35–52; Julian Dodd, *An Identity Theory of Truth* (New York: St Martin's Press, 2000).

[18] See John Milbank, *Theology and Social Theory: Beyond Secular Reason* (Oxford: Blackwell, 1993); John Milbank, Catherine Pickstock and Graham Ward (eds), *Radical Orthodoxy: A New Theology*. London: Routledge, 1999).

[19] See, for example, Frederick Christian Bauerschmidt, 'The Word made Speculative? John Milbank's Christological Poetics', *Modern Theology* 15 (1999), pp. 417–32; Douglas Hedley, 'Should Divinity Overcome Metaphysics? Reflections on John Milbank's *Theology beyond Secular Reason* and *Confessions of a Cambridge Platonist*', *Journal of Religion* 80 (2000), pp. 271–98.

John Frame has gained an impressive reputation as an apologist, most notably in developing the approach of the noted apologist Cornelius Van Til.[20] Yet his competencies extend far beyond this, as his study of controversies within twentieth-century evangelicalism makes clear. In his stimulating and important essay on 'Machen's children', Frame traces the development of the new denomination founded by J. Gresham Machen following the Presbyterian controversies which rumbled on throughout the 1920s and beyond.[21] The Orthodox Presbyterian Church subsequently itself proved vulnerable to further controversies, almost as if its members, having previously directed their energies against their liberal opponents, now turned them against themselves. A spirit of contentiousness, once developed, seems difficult to neutralize, and direct in more positive manners.

With admirable concision and immense care, Frame sets out the main controversies to have split Reformed evangelicalism in the last few decades. Some of these resonate throughout the global evangelical community – most notably, debates over the role of the Holy Spirit in Christian life and thought, and the place of women in Christian leadership and ministry. Yet it is significant to note that many of these debates are largely unknown outside the United States. Frame has done us a service both by introducing us to them, and also alerting us to the ease with which evangelicalism can fragment over what are proposed as fundamental doctrinal issues, yet are in fact exploratory thoughts, divergent emphases or personality issues. For example, 'theonomy' is a word that has yet to register on British evangelical radar screens, or become an issue in church life over here.

Nor have British evangelicals ever been entirely persuaded of the merits of heated eschatological debate, tending to see these questions as *adiaphora* on which evangelicals can (more or less) happily disagree. From a British perspective, it is often difficult to understand why, for example, John Murray and his Bible Presbyterian Church regarded it as so important to revise the Westminster Catechism in a premillennial manner, when the original seemed to be possessed of a generous degree of tolerance on this issue. The 'eschatological liberty' that gradually

---

[20] John M. Frame, *Cornelius Van Til: An Analysis of his Thought* (Phillipsburg, New Jersey: Presbyterian & Reformed, 1995). He has also been involved in the 'open theism' controversy: see John M. Frame, *No Other God: A Response to Open Theism* (Phillipsburg, New Jersey: Presbyterian & Reformed, 2001).

[21] Bradley J. Longfield, *The Presbyterian Controversy: Fundamentalists, Modernists and Moderates* (New York: Oxford University Press, 1991).

developed within American Reformed evangelicalism has always been a feature of British evangelicalism from the eighteenth century, despite the attempts of one or two firebrands to heat things up.

Frame's conclusion is a plea for graciousness, understanding, wisdom and patience in dealing with controversies within evangelicalism. My heart warmed to his wise words. There has never been a shortage of evangelicals who equate 'heresy' with 'disagreeing with me', or who define 'biblical' as 'my reading of the Bible', subtly devaluing a serious debate over theological provenance into a more sinister bid for power and influence within the evangelical community. Frame's approach, if widely adopted, would lead to an evangelicalism characterized by a culture of civility and a spirit of graciousness, genuinely concerned to understand where others are coming from (after all, they might be God's means of correcting others!), and only registering concerns about orthodoxy where these are clearly merited, and all other modes of theological diplomacy have been exhausted. I shall try to follow his wise advice.

*   *   *   *   *

Clark Pinnock has made distinguished contributions to evangelical reflection, not least in the field of apologetics. His early works, which focused on issues of biblical authority and Christian apologetics, were well received within the evangelical community.[22] When researching the early history of Regent College, Vancouver, in connection with my biography of J.I. Packer, I was intrigued to learn that Pinnock was associated with the first years of this immensely important evangelical institution, serving as its professor of theology before moving on to serve at McMaster Divinity School.

In recent years, Clark Pinnock has championed the movement that has come to be known as 'open theism'. His contribution to this present volume is an eloquent affirmation of some of the leading themes of this movement, as well as a helpful source for its distinctive ideas, representatives and critics. There is no doubt that many evangelicals have become engaged in this discussion, which has generated both heat and light, and made John Frame's advice to theological disputants acutely relevant.

Reading Pinnock's more recent writings suggests that he has become deeply frustrated with the movement which is often referred to as

---

[22] See, for example, Clark H. Pinnock, *Biblical Revelation – The Foundation of Christian Theology* (Chicago: Moody Press, 1971); Clark H. Pinnock, *Reason Enough: A Case for the Christian Faith* (Downers Grove: InterVarsity Press, 1980).

'classical theism', and which he links particularly with Augustine and Aquinas.[23] I share many of Pinnock's misgivings concerning classical theism but differ fundamentally from him concerning how they are to be resolved. 'Classical theism', as I understand the term, is essentially an a priori conception of God, which is somewhat loosely accommodated to the biblical revelation of God.[24] It does not designate the evangelical enterprise of construing God biblically. As an historical theologian, I have often noted the tensions which exist on account of this imperfect adjustment between Scripture and a philosophically preconceived God who is defined as perfect and omnipotent – to mention just two attributes – in terms which are ultimately derived from a priori philosophical reflection.

Open theism has a tendency to picture the God of classical Christian theism as a distant, despotic sovereign and insensitive to the pain and suffering of the world. I have no doubt that such a view can be found in the writings of some classical writers. Philo, a Hellenistic Jew whose writings were much admired by early Christian writers, wrote a treatise entitled *Quod Deus immutabilis sit* ('That God is Unchangeable'), which vigorously defended the impassibility of God. Biblical passages that seemed to speak of God suffering were, he argued, to be treated as metaphors, and not to be allowed their full literal weight. To allow that God changes was to deny the divine perfection. 'What greater impiety could there be than to suppose that the Unchangeable changes?' asked Philo. It seemed to be an unanswerable question. Yet Martin Luther's celebrated 'theology of the cross' can be seen as a powerful challenge to such a philosophically preconceived notion of God, along with a demand to rediscover a more biblical understanding of 'the crucified and hidden God'.[25] Perfection is not to be defined philosophically, but theologically.

---

[23] The works I have in mind include Clark H. Pinnock, *A Wideness in God's Mercy: The Finality of Jesus Christ in a World of Religions* (Grand Rapids: Zondervan, 1992), which expresses dissatisfaction with Augustine's soteriology, and Clark H. Pinnock, *Most Moved Mover: A Theology of God's Openness* (Carlisle/Grand Rapids: Paternoster/Baker, 2001), which offers a critique of the 'classical' view of God.

[24] For some of the issues, see J.G. McLelland, *God the Anonymous: A Study in Alexandrian Philosophical Theology* (Cambridge, Massachusetts: Harvard University Press, 1976). For a critique of the metaphysical presuppositions of classical theism, see Eberhard Jüngel, *Gott als Geheimnis der Welt: Zur Begründung der Theologie des Gekreuzigten im Streit zwischen Theismus und Atheismus* (Tübingen: Mohr, 1982).

[25] I explored this theme in some detail in my first book, *Luther's Theology of the Cross* (Oxford: Blackwell, 1985).

Similarly, some classical theists (unwisely) define divine omnipotence in terms of 'God's ability to do anything'. This may well be a perfectly logical way of looking at things, but it is seriously deficient theologically, as has been pointed out by theologians for the last thousand years.[26] God's actions are consonant with his nature; therefore God cannot do certain things, not because they are too hard for him, but because they contradict his revealed will. For example, consider the following question: Can God break a promise? At one level, the answer seems simple: of course he can – even human beings, who are less powerful, can do this. Surely God can as well!

Yet a moment's reflection soon counterbalances this intuition. The whole of the biblical witness revolts against it. The very idea of a covenant, on which the history of Israel and the church depends, is grounded in God's *faithfulness* – that is to say, God's principled decision to act in certain ways, and not others, which he has disclosed to us. This is not a denial of God's *power*; it is an affirmation of God's *faithfulness*. Having promised to forgive those who repent, God abides by that promise. The whole Christian gospel stands on the faithfulness of God. This is no new idea; it is deeply embedded in the Christian theological tradition of the last thousand years.[27]

Like Pinnock, I reject classical theism – by which I mean a philosophically predetermined understanding of the nature of God. As an evangelical, I affirm the supremacy of the biblical revelation of God over and against human preconceptions of what God ought to be like. But as a Reformed writer, I also affirm the slogan *ecclesia reformata, ecclesia simper reformanda* – that is, that the process of 'being reformed' has not been concluded, but is *ongoing*, representing a constant demand that we check out all our ideas against Scripture to make sure that we have not got locked into unbiblical ways of thinking. The risk of misreading Scripture demands constant vigilance and a willingness to check things out. For this reason, I hold that Pinnock and his colleagues are right to wish to reopen some questions, even if I disagree with the answers that they provide.

---

[26] For the idea in the medieval and Reformation periods, see Berndt Hamm, *Promissio, Pactum, Ordinatio: Freiheit und Selbstbindung Gottes in derscholastischen Gnadenlehre* (Tübingen: Mohr, 1977).

[27] Similarly, the question of God's knowledge of the future was debated endlessly in the Middle Ages, with outcomes that we might learn from: see, for example, William J. Courtenay, 'John of Mirecourt and Gregory of Rimini on whether God can undo the Past', *Recherches de Théologie Ancienne et Médievale* 39 (1972), pp. 224–56; 40 (1973), pp. 147–74.

*   *   *   *   *

Elmer Colyer is a young theologian who clearly has much to offer the church. We share a common interest in the writings of Thomas F. Torrance, whom we both regard as offering some very important perspectives and insights for the contemporary theological task.[28] Torrance's Trinitarian vision of Christian theology is compelling, and it is no surprise that Colyer has sought to develop this concern in this essay. I welcomed the insights which saturate this essay, and hope that it may serve as a model for the recovery of the Trinitarian dimensions of the thought of past evangelical giants – as with John Wesley, in this piece.

Colyer's conclusion is that his own American Methodist tradition has not been sufficiently attentive to its Trinitarian foundations, and has consequently been impoverished, theologically and spiritually. Having read his paper, I find myself in agreement with him, and applaud him for his insight and discernment. However, I would like to offer some reflections on the role that Trinitarianism plays within evangelicalism, which suggest that the nature and extent of this shortcoming may not be quite as straightforward, and its remedy a little more elusive.

In February 1998 I was invited to give a lecture at Harvard Divinity School on 'Trinitarian theology' within evangelicalism. I duly researched the matter fairly thoroughly, focusing on the Trinity in the writings of John Stott, an evangelical writer for whom I have high regard. Positively, Stott regards the doctrine of the Trinity as the basis of an evangelical understanding of the Bible: 'the Bible is the witness of the Father to the Son through the Holy Spirit'.[29] Negatively, he treats it as a difficulty that requires to be overcome in discussions with Judaism and Islam, in that it can be misunderstood as compromising the unity of God.[30] In general, Stott, while affirming the Trinity, tends to stress that the Christian faith is Christ-centred, and cites the relative weighting of the clauses in the Apostles' Creed as an illustration of this point.[31]

---

[28] For his approach, see Elmer M. Colyer, *How to read T.F. Torrance: Understanding his Trinitarian and Scientific Theology* (Downers Grove: Inter-Varsity Press, 2001); for mine, see McGrath, *T.F. Torrance*.

[29] John Stott, *The Bible: Book for Today* (London: Inter-Varsity Press, 1982), p. 36.

[30] John Stott, *The Lausanne Covenant: An Exposition and Commentary* (Minneapolis: World Wide, 1975), p. 5.

[31] John Stott, *The Authentic Jesus* (Downers Grove: InterVarsity Press, 1985), p. 9.

On the basis of a close reading of many of Stott's leading works, I came to the conclusion that his thought was explicitly Christ-focused, and only implicitly Trinitarian. Let me make it clear that this is not to be understood as a criticism of Stott; it is merely an observation. Such a concern for the person and work of Christ is characteristic of evangelicalism, and is unquestionably one of its greatest strengths.

Some years earlier, I had found a similar emphasis in the writings of John Calvin, which seem to me to be admirably focused on Christ.[32] I was interested to see that I was subsequently criticized by another Calvin scholar, who argued that I had failed to do justice to the Trinitarian dimensions of Calvin's thought.[33] I naturally went back to Calvin, and studied the passages I was alleged to have misread. I came away from that engagement still convinced that Calvin's explicit focus was fundamentally Christ-centred. My critic had indeed, I believe, shown that an *implicit* Trinitarian framework undergirded Calvin's writings. Yet Calvin did not choose to make such a framework *explicit* to anything like the extent that was being suggested. It generally required to be read into, rather than read out of, the passages in question.

Now, what is the relevance of this digression? Simply this: I have formed the impression that it is not *instinctive* for evangelicals to speak, write, or think in explicitly Trinitarian terms. Colyer has unquestionably shown that Wesley's thought presupposes and ultimately rests upon Trinitarian foundations; yet I sense that Randy Maddox is right in not identifying the Trinity as being a central concern for Wesley, in that Wesley himself does not appear to make explicit and extensive use of the motif in his writings.[34] What Colyer has done, and done very well, is to demonstrate how this doctrine underlies and undergirds Wesley's affirmations.

So the question I want to pose – even if I do not get round to answering it – is whether evangelicals ought to be *explicitly* Trinitarian? Colyer clearly believes that we should, and has set out some excellent reasons for doing so. As a Trinitarian theologian, I am entirely in sympathy with him at this point. But I wonder. Evangelicalism has always liked to stay close to the language of Scripture, and thus prefers a Christological to a

---

[32] See my attempt to explore his development and significance in Alister E. McGrath, *A Life of John Calvin* (Oxford: Blackwell, 1993).

[33] Philip Walker Butin, *Revelation, Redemption, and Response: Calvin's Trinitarian Understanding of the Divine–Human Relationship* (New York: Oxford University Press, 1995).

[34] Randy L. Maddox, *Responsible Grace: John Wesley's Practical Theology* (Nashville: Kingswood, 1994).

Trinitarian idiom. More generally, evangelical populism – which must never be underestimated as a shaping influence upon its preaching and writing – finds the Trinitarian vocabulary a little alienating, and prefers such simple affirmations as 'Jesus saves!' or 'Jesus is Lord'. While there is unquestionably a Trinitarian substructure to such affirmations, it is implicit rather than explicit. It will be interesting to see if the evangelical homiletic and devotional works of the twentieth century recover and develop a more *explicitly* Trinitarian mode of speaking and thinking.

✳   ✳   ✳   ✳   ✳

Sung Wook Chung's excellent paper on evangelical approaches to Karl Barth opens up a highly important discussion. Chung is ideally placed to advance this. His doctoral thesis at Oxford University focused on Karl Barth's interaction and use of the writings of John Calvin, identifying some important trends in Barth's writings which reopen the question of how evangelicals – who in many ways share something of Calvin's heritage – may draw on Barth as a fellow-disciple of the Genevan Reformer.[35] As Chung himself notes – and here both Elmer Colyer and I would agree – T.F. Torrance is becoming an increasingly important dialogue partner for evangelicals. Torrance can be regarded as mediating a particular interpretation of Barth,[36] which many evangelicals are finding to be fruitful and productive in their own theological enterprises.

Chung rightly points out many positive features of Barth's thought, not least his absolute determination to reaffirm and develop the theological heritage of the Reformation. So why have evangelicals been reluctant to embrace Barth? Chung hints at part of the answer in the final paragraph of his essay. There is no doubt that the North American evangelical community formed a negative impression of Barth from his early evangelical interpreters, especially Cornelius Van Til.[37] In his review of Cornelius Van Til's *The New Modernism*, Torrance complained of an inept analysis of the theology of Barth and Brunner.[38] On Torrance's reading of this work, Van Til expounded and excoriated

---

[35] This thesis has now been published, and merits close study: see Sung Wook Chung, *Admiration and Challenge: Karl Barth's Theological Relationship with John Calvin* (New York: Peter Lang, 2002).

[36] See McGrath, *T.F. Torrance*, pp. 118–45.

[37] Cornelius Van Til, *The New Modernism* (Phillipsburg: Presbyterian & Reformed, 1946).

[38] T.F. Torrance, 'The New Modernism', *Evangelical Quarterly* 19 (1947), pp. 144–9.

the views of 'modernism', prior to linking – on the basis of what Torrance regarded as highly suspect grounds – both Barth and Brunner to the modernist project.

Now let me concede immediately that there may be reasons for linking Barth and the Enlightenment, especially in relation to his understanding of the nature of salvation.[39] This is not, however, what Van Til argues. As he later explains: 'I tried to point out to a considerable extent with the help of Dooyeweerd, that the Greek form-matter scheme and the Kantian freedom-nature scheme are together the one scheme of apostate human thought.' If your only tool is a hammer, everything looks like a nail. It was natural for Van Til to link Barth and Brunner to these forms of 'apostate human thought'; it now seems to many, however, to have been quite unreasonable to do so, especially given the formidable challenge that Barth issues, on the basis of any reasonable reading of his writings, to the quest for human autonomy, whether epistemic or soteriological.[40]

One of the most welcome features of evangelical theological scholarship in recent years has been its willingness to revisit old controversies, reconsider old evaluations and reappropriate approaches which a previous generation had rejected, often for reasons specific to their time and culture. As James I. Packer has stressed, engaging with the 'great tradition' has much to offer evangelicalism today.[41] An important part of that process of review and reassessment concerns the extent to which the writings of Karl Barth may serve evangelicals as they seek to affirm the truth of the gospel, defend its coherence and proclaim its relevance to the world. While I am quite clear that there are points at which evangelicals will wish to critique or distance themselves from Barth – such as his concept of revelation (see David Clark's comments in this volume) – there are others at which he can be both a challenge and resource.

---

[39] See Alister E. McGrath, 'Karl Barth als Aufklärer? Der Zusammenhang seiner Lehre vom Werke Christi mit der Erwählungslehre', *Kerygma und Dogma* 30 (1984), pp. 273–83.

[40] See, for example, John Macken, *The Autonomy Theme in the Church Dogmatics of Karl Barth and His Critics* (Cambridge: Cambridge University Press, 1990).

[41] J.I. Packer, 'The Comfort of Conservatism' in M. Horton (ed.), *Power Religion* (Chicago: Moody, 1992), pp. 283–99; J.I. Packer, 'On from Orr: The Cultural Crisis, Rational Realism, and Incarnational Ontology', *Crux* 32.3 (1996), pp. 12–26. For my own reflections, see Alister E. McGrath, 'Engaging the Great Tradition: Evangelical Theology and the Role of Tradition' in John G. Stackhouse (ed.), *Evangelical Futures: A Conversation on Theological Method* (Grand Rapids: Baker, 2000), pp. 139–58.

Sung Wook Chung entitled his excellent study of Barth's ambivalent relationship with Calvin *Admiration and Challenge*, thus drawing his readers' attention to the fact that Barth genuinely admired and respected Calvin, adopting and appropriating many of his ideas, while at the same time dissenting from him on others.[42] Perhaps evangelicals can adopt a similar attitude as they engage with Barth – putting everything to the test, and retaining what is good.

* * * * *

Gabriel Fackre has a long and distinguished career as an academic theologian at Andover Newton Theological School, and has been an important and influential voice for orthodoxy within his own denomination, the United Church of Christ. I have long valued his works for their intelligent exploration of the role of narratives in an evangelical theology.[43] His contribution to this volume is exemplary, showing how narrative approaches to the theological enterprise avoid the pitfalls of a long discredited Enlightenment foundationalism on the one hand, and a postmodern relativism on the other. Fackre argues that the postmodern critique of *les grands récits* is itself a *grand récit*. The point he scores is telling, and demonstrates how widely postmodernism has fallen victim to the self-referential fallacy – the notion that individuals are somehow exempt from the criteria of judgement that they apply to others.

Fackre's excellent article will encourage others to explore further this highly significant approach to theology. It is, however, important to recall that 'narrative theology' was once regarded with intense suspicion by evangelicals, who saw it as undermining the prepositional truth of revelation. Such concerns must be respected, even when they arguably rest on misunderstandings of what a narrative theology proposes. Scripture does not primarily take the form of credal and doctrinal statements, although these are unquestionably interwoven within its structure. Its primary – although by no means its *exclusive* – concern is with narrating what happened at moments held to be of particular importance to the self-definition of the community of faith – moments such as the exodus from Egypt or the resurrection of Jesus of Nazareth. Scripture presents us with a narrative, which purports to tell of God's dealings with humanity, culminating in – but not ending with – the history of Jesus of Nazareth. There is, as can easily be shown, a firm and

---

[42] Chung, *Admiration and Challenge*, pp. 221–5.
[43] See his earlier work: Gabriel Fackre, 'Narrative Theology: An Overview', *Interpretation* 37 (1983), pp. 340–52.

robust link between narrative and doctrine; the two genres, however, are different, and it is important to allow the biblical witness to speak to us in its own form and its own manner, rather than trying to reduce everything to one genre.[44]

Earlier evangelicalism was fully aware of the importance of narrative. Martin Luther is an excellent example of an earlier evangelical approach to this matter. He neither (to anticipate the Enlightenment) regarded narrative as something to be eliminated, in order to get at the 'points' it was making; nor (to anticipate Romanticism) did he regard 'story' as the unique vehicle of truth.[45] Yet despite all its criticisms of the theological and exegetical programmes of the Enlightenment, evangelicalism seems to have chosen to follow it in this respect. The narrative character of Scripture has been subtly marginalized, in order to facilitate its analysis purely as a repository of propositional statements, capable of withstanding the epistemological criteria of the Enlightenment. As Frei points out, the theme of 'narrative' remained present within evangelicalism, but was transferred from Scripture to the believer's personal spiritual journey.[46] It was seen as proper for evangelicals to speak of 'their story' (meaning 'the account of how they came to faith, and are progressing in the Christian life').

While all such judgements are prone to distortion through the situation and personal concerns of the observer, I would judge that evangelicalism began to lose its suspicions of narrative theology around the year 1990. Fackre himself has made a very significant contribution to this process,[47] and must be given much credit for this development. It is, however, helpful to ask why evangelical theology has gradually come round to accepting the validity and utility of narrative approaches. I discern three considerations which are of importance in this respect: (1) A growing realization of the need to remain faithful to the literary genres of Scripture, not simply the ideas that it mediates. (2) An increasing awareness of the theological resilience of narratives in the face of

---

[44] See Alister E. McGrath, *The Genesis of Doctrine* (Oxford: Blackwell, 1990), pp. 52–66.

[45] See R. Lischer, 'Luther and Contemporary Preaching', *Scottish Journal of Theology* 36 (1983), pp. 487–504. See also his subsequent article 'The Limits of Story', *Interpretation* 38 (1984), pp. 26–38.

[46] Hans Frei, *The Eclipse of Biblical Narrative: A Study in Eighteenth and Nineteenth Century Biblical Hermeneutics* (New Haven, Connecticut: Yale University Press, 1977), pp. 141–2.

[47] See especially Gabriel J. Fackre, *The Doctrine of Revelation: A Narrative Interpretation* (Edinburgh: Edinburgh University Press, 1997).

postmodern rejection of 'metanarratives' (*les grands récits*).[48] (3) A growing realization, especially within North American evangelicalism, that some of the key ideas of the Enlightenment might actually be wrong, leading to a new interest in exploring alternatives.

In all three respects, Gabriel Fackre has encouraged evangelicalism to rediscover and critically reappropriate the distinctive features of an older, more biblical approach to theology, which stresses the importance of attentiveness to God's actions in history, recounted and interpreted in Scripture.

*   *   *   *   *

Andrew Goddard is a rising star in the field of evangelical social ethics. He began his academic career with an impressive Oxford doctoral dissertation on the ethics of Jacques Ellul, the noted French Protestant sociologist and theologian.[49] In his essay, Goddard explores the delicate interaction of tradition and innovation in Christian ethics – the question of how we remain faithful to the past, while addressing new situations. How can one remain faithful to Scripture, while maintaining an ability to engage with the new challenges that a rapidly changing world daily throws our way?

Goddard navigates a course between an unthinking conservatism ('we've always done it this way') and an irresponsible liberalism ('we will do precisely what we like'). Evangelicals have often been prone to confuse the content of tradition with any one given moment of tradition – for example, by insisting that we must agree with the Reformers at all points (thus freezing this moment in evangelical history, and declaring it to be binding for all time – and overlooking its diversity and disagreements), or similarly fossilizing some evangelical writers of the eighteenth, nineteenth or twentieth century. In doing so, we disregard the fact that each of these writers faced precisely the challenge that we face – namely, how to relate the gospel to a given moment, to a specific situation.

A case study always helps illustrate a complex point, and Goddard's choice is as judicious as it is illuminating – Calvin's views on usury. Goddard's analysis partly concerns the identification and evaluation of

---

[48] For a stimulating example of some possibilities, see Henry H. Knight, *A Future for Truth: Evangelical Theology in a Postmodern World* (Nashville: Abingdon Press, 1997).

[49] Andrew Goddard, *Living the Word, Resisting the World: The Life and Thought of Jacques Ellul* (Carlisle: Paternoster, 2002).

the general principles employed by Calvin in moving from the (apparent) biblical prohibition of usury to the judgement that, in early modern Europe, the practice was legitimate. Theological continuity can lead to ethical change – not because of a changed divine will, but partly on account of dispensational and societal shifts. In exploring the nature and grounds of this development, Goddard is acutely aware of its relevance to two major debates within contemporary evangelicalism – namely, the social status and ministerial functions of women and homosexuals – where the same issues apply. Goddard's wise and careful exploration of the issues will be read with despair by those who believe that the task of the Christian ethicist is merely to affirm the Old Testament prohibitions, and as a breath of fresh air by those who, like Calvin, realize that such an approach rests upon a seriously deficient theology, which abuses both text and context.

Goddard has no easy answers, but his article has the immense merit of highlighting the issues we must face in being faithful to Scripture in engaging our culture. He gently chides both those who believe that evangelicalism is best served through a wooden repetition of the social and sexual norms of Calvin's Geneva, and those rather more presumptive voices which suggest that we should abandon any quest for social ethics altogether as unworkable. There is a viable alternative; but it is one that demands patience and prayer, and above all a faithful and coherent engagement with Scripture and the situations we face. We can do far worse than look attentively to people like Andrew Goddard to guide and stimulate our quest for authenticity.

*   *   *   *   *

William Abraham has taught for many years at the Perkins School of Theology at Southern Methodist University, Dallas, Texas. He and I share a common background in Belfast, Northern Ireland. Abraham was studying at the Queen's University of Belfast at the same time that I was completing my studies at the Methodist College – just over the road from Queen's – prior to going to Oxford. His distinguished record of publications shows him to be a theologian with strong interests in issues of theological method[50] – an issue that concerns me throughout the three volumes of *A Scientific Theology*. In his essay, Abraham offers a major

---

[50] See, for example, William J. Abraham, *The Divine Inspiration of Holy Scripture* (Oxford: Oxford University Press, 1981); William J. Abraham, *Canon and Criterion in Christian Theology from the Fathers to Feminism* (Oxford: Clarendon Press, 1998).

evaluation of my approach in the first volume of this work, which is both sensitive to my aspirations for that project and alert to its potential weaknesses. In focusing on my understanding of the purpose and place of natural theology, Abraham raises questions that demand answers. In what follows, I shall sketch my responses to the important points that he raises.

Let me begin by affirming that Abraham has generally understood me correctly. He states that I advance 'a bold epistemological thesis about the relation between theology and science on the grounds that both disciplines share the same subject matter, namely, the created order made *ex nihilo* by the God and Father of our Lord Jesus Christ'. This is a core element of my thinking about a scientific theology. He also recognizes that, following on from this, natural theology plays a critical role in my thought. Abraham then moves on to suggest that there are three possible ways of approaching natural theology, as follows:

Conception A: natural theology designates the intellectual attempt to provide support for any form of theism by means of deductive or inductive appeal to premises that do not presume the truth of the theism in question.

Conception B: natural theology designates the attempt to argue for the justification of theistic belief on the grounds of apparent awareness of the divine in nature and in personal experience.

Conception C: natural theology designates the appeal to various features of the universe as confirmation of a prior appeal to special divine revelation.

In broad terms, he suggests that I would fit within Category C of this tripartite approach. Abraham locates writers such as Richard Swinburne in Category A; William Alston and Alvin Plantinga in Category B; and presumably includes Karl Barth in Category C.

Now, while both Abraham and I are Trinitarian in our outlooks, I do not hold that such a framework demands either three-point sermons or three-category analyses of complex situations. On Abraham's reading of the available styles of natural theology, there are only three approaches, and, since I must be included somewhere, it must be in the third category. But there is a fourth, and I belong there.

So what is this fourth? In his elegant and immensely rewarding paper, Abraham does not engage with the question which follows the demise of the Enlightenment project – namely, how can one do natural theology (or, indeed, any kind of theology or philosophy) in the absence of a universally acknowledged conception of rationality? William Alston defined natural theology as 'the enterprise of providing support for religious beliefs by starting from premises that neither are nor presuppose any religious beliefs'.[51] I regard the following definition as more appropriate: natural theology is *'the enterprise of seeing nature as creation, which both presupposes and reinforces fundamental Christian theological affirmations'*. And these affirmations are mediated through a tradition.

Where Abraham and I differ is that I hold that rationality is mediated and constituted by traditions. In taking this position, I have been influenced both by the general collapse of the Enlightenment project, by a reading of modern Western philosophy which stresses its failure to achieve its own goals, and by the writings of Alasdair MacIntyre, which offer both a demonstration of these failures and an alternative approach.[52] In the second volume of my *Scientific Theology*, entitled 'Reality', I set out the reasons for adopting MacIntyre's approach, and then proceed to consider the place that a natural theology has within it.

The notion of tradition-constituted rationality means that it is impossible for one tradition to judge another in terms that would command universal assent, in that each party to this debate 'succeeds by the standards internal to its own tradition of inquiry, but fails by the standards internal to the tradition of its opponents'. This being the case, how can competing traditions be evaluated? MacIntyre offers two answers. First, each tradition is to be analysed on its own internal terms, to establish whether it is internally coherent, and whether it is able to address the questions that the tradition itself generates. We have already noted the importance of intrasystemic coherence, and will return to this point again later.

It is MacIntyre's second criterion that is of especial interest. Can questions that cannot be answered by tradition A be answered by tradition B? In other words, can tradition A recognize that tradition B is able to answer a question that tradition A has been unable to answer satisfactorily in its own history? The Christian doctrine of creation is thus of metatraditional significance. The scientific tradition, for example, finds

---

[51] William P. Alston, *Perceiving God: The Epistemology of Religious Experience* (Ithaca, New York: Cornell University Press, 1991), p. 289.

[52] See, for example, Alasdair MacIntyre, *Whose Justice? Which Rationality?* (London: Duckworth, 1988). For comment, see L. Gregory Jones, 'Alasdair MacIntyre on Narrative, Community and the Moral Life', *Modern Theology* 4 (1987), pp. 53–69; Mark Achtemeier, 'The Truth of Tradition: Critical Realism in the Thought of Alasdair MacIntyre and T.F. Torrance', *Scottish Journal of Theology* 47 (1994), pp. 355–74.

itself having to presuppose the uniformity and ordering of creation; Christian theology offers an account of this. The scientific tradition recognizes that the natural world has a rationality which human rationality can discern and systematize; Christian theology, however, offers an explanation of why this is the case.[53] On both MacIntyre's criteria, the Christian tradition is able to set forth a plausible claim to represent a robust and resilient account of reality. The important point about a natural theology is that it offers us an interpretative grid by which other traditions may be addressed on the common issues of existence, enabling the coherence and attractiveness of the Christian vision to be affirmed.

In the second volume of my work, I thus explore the ways in which a natural theology corroborates, to the extent that this is possible, the specific rationality mediated by the Christian tradition. Under the broad heading of 'The Role of a Natural Theology in Transcending Traditions', I consider five broad areas in which a natural theology can be seen as a trans-traditional device. These are:

1. Mathematics and Trans-Traditional Rationality
2. Incarnation and Trans-Traditional Rationality
3. Natural Theology and the Trans-Traditional Religious Quest
4. Natural Theology and the Trans-Traditional Sense of Wonder
5. Natural Law and the Trans-Traditional Quest for Goodness

In that Abraham did not have access to this second volume at the time of writing, it would be completely unfair to criticize his categorization of my approach. Nevertheless, I believe both that his categories require expansion, and that my location within those categories equally requires revision.

The debate over natural theology within evangelicalism is set to continue, and Abraham's analysis makes it clear that he is a highly significant voice in that discussion, deserving to be listened to attentively. The approach I offer, however, does not really fit his analysis. In a nutshell, my approach is particularist with universal extensions; in other words, I hold that the Christian tradition is determined and defined by a set of particularities, but that it nevertheless possesses universal explanatory potential and salvific efficacy. A Christian natural theology, speaking from within the Christian tradition and from a Christian – not universal – perspective offers a specific vantage point from which the intellectual landscape may be charted and explained. Though tradition-

---

[53] See my extended discussion in *A Scientific Theology Volume 1: Nature* (Edinburgh: T. & T. Clark, 2001), pp. 196–218.

specific, it has aspirations to universality precisely because the story that it relates offers an ultimate and coherent organizing logic that accounts for its own existence, as well as that of its rivals. In short: natural theology offers and accounts for a trans-traditional rationality, which is grounded in the particularities of the Christian tradition alone.

* * * * *

I first met John Franke in 1990, while I was Ezra Squire Tipple Visiting Professor of Historical Theology at the Theological School, Drew University, Madison, New Jersey. It was clear that Franke was a very able young scholar, and I counted it a privilege to be able to supervise his research at Oxford University the following academic year. The final outcome in 1996 was a fine study of John Hooper, an Elizabethan bishop who disliked wearing clerical robes, and consequently provoked a fascinating ecclesiastical disputation. Although an able church historian, Franke has shown himself to be far more than that. His book on how Christian theology can relate to postmodernity, co-authored with Stanley Grenz, is highly regarded, and rightly so.[54] In his contribution to the present volume, Franke summarizes the main arguments of this important work, and explores their implications.

Franke – in common with many other younger evangelical writers – insists that a foundationalist approach to theology is no longer viable. I agree with him, and find his exposition of the weaknesses of the approach commendable, although I did miss any attempt to explore the coherentist aspects of the matter. It is, however, something that requires to be explained to evangelicalism as a whole. The systemic metaphor of a 'foundation' implies that knowledge is based upon something – that is to say, that it is not arbitrary, irrational or simply wrong. Many evangelicals perceive the rejection of foundationalism to entail the idea that there is no basis to the Christian faith – and hence that it lacks reliable content. While it is easy to assert that this is not so, much more is required. The ideas need to be explained. Much evangelical resistance to nonfoundationalism in theology rests on the belief that to reject *foundationalism* is to reject the idea of *warranted knowledge of God* – something that is simply unacceptable to evangelicals.

So how do we go about reassuring the evangelical constituency that postfoundationalism is not about abandoning a quest for truth? Or reliability in theological judgements? Or about abandoning any idea

---

[54] Stanley Grenz and John R. Franke, *Beyond Foundationalism: Shaping Theology in a Postmodern Context* (Louisville: Westminster John Knox, 2001).

that theology tries to address and explain something that is real, not something that we have arbitrarily created out of the fabric of our minds? One means of doing this is to revert to the language of 'reference' or 'correspondence', being careful to concede certain weaknesses in advance.

Millard Erickson, in defining theology as 'that discipline which strives to give a coherent statement of the doctrines of the Christian faith, based primarily upon the Scriptures, placed in the context of culture in general, worded in contemporary idiom, and related to issues of life',[55] manages to include two general criteria of justification – correspondence to reality and internal coherence. Similarly, Alfred North Whitehead argued that metaphysical views should satisfy both *empirical* and *logical* criteria before gaining acceptance. The empirical criterion is that philosophical theses should apply adequately to experience; the logical criterion is that they should be consistent and coherent with each other. In effect, Whitehead comes close to fusing correspondence and coherentist approaches to knowledge, insisting upon both intra-systemic and extra-systemic criteria in theory choice. Adequacy of scientific theories could thus be tested *formally* by a consistency analysis via mathematical proofs and *empirically* by experimental procedures. To be taken seriously, a theory must resonate with what may be observed, and be internally consistent.

This kind of approach finds widespread acceptance within the natural sciences, presumably because it combines an insistence upon the empirical foundations of scientific knowledge with the belief that the scientific theories developed on the basis of the analysis of experience should be internally consistent. It also finds much support among theologians. Thus Wolfhart Pannenberg's theological programme could be stated in terms of demonstrating on the one hand the internal coherence of Christian doctrines, and on the other the external coherence or consistency of those doctrines with the world of reality and other intellectual disciplines.[56] While some philosophers have insisted that we are obligated to accept either a correspondence or a coherentist approach to justified belief, there are excellent reasons for suggesting that both can be seen as intrinsic elements of a robust view of reality.

Latent within Whitehead's brief statement are two criteria, whose interplay has been the subject of considerable debate within the philo-

---

[55] Millard Erickson, *Christian Theology* (Grand Rapids: Baker, 1983), vol. 1, p. 21.

[56] Wolfhart Pannenberg, *Systematic Theology* (Grand Rapids: Eerdmans, 1991–98), vol. 1, pp. 21–2.

sophical community. The two criteria are (1) being appropriately grounded in the real world and (2) being possessed of an appropriate degree of internal consistency. How those criteria are to be defined, and whether they are complementary or contradictory, remains a matter of considerable debate. For example, W.F. Sellars' philosophy can be argued to be a complex meld of foundationalist and coherentist elements, based on the perception that neither is adequate on its own.

Sellars points this out in his oft-cited study 'Empiricism and the Study of Mind', in which he explores the interplay of an image of foundationalism (an elephant standing on a tortoise) and an image of coherentism (a serpent whose tail is in its mouth). The former, Sellars argues, is a mythical representation of the need for a foundation for knowledge; the elephant has to stand on *something*. The latter is to be seen as representing the unbroken circle which is characteristic of the ideas of a coherent philosophy. As Arthur Kenyon Rogers pointed out, the justification of a belief on this approach rests on its 'inclusion within a coherent system'.[57] Yet each of these approaches, Sellars insists, is deficient.[58]

One seems forced to choose between the picture of an elephant which rests on a tortoise (what supports the tortoise?) and the picture of a great Hegelian serpent of knowledge with its tail in its mouth (where does it begin?). Neither will do.

Although Sellars is sometimes taken to be an anti-foundationalist, the situation is not quite that simple. As William Alson points out, Sellars seems to advocate a 'sort of synthesis of foundationalism and coherentism'.[59] The synthesis seems perfectly viable, not least on account of the well-known weaknesses of both accounts of justified beliefs.

I suspect that evangelicals such as myself and Franke, who are dissuaded of the viability of the Cartesian foundationalist project, have a communication problem on our hands, and need to work hard at explaining what we mean. Nonfoundationalism does not entail anti-realism – but that is to anticipate another theme I develop at length in the

---

[57] Arthur Kenyon Rogers, *What is Truth? An Essay in the Theory of Knowledge* (New Haven, Connecticut: Yale University Press, 1923), p. 12.

[58] Wilfrid Sellars, *Science, Perception and Reality* (New York: Humanities Press, 1962), p. 170.

[59] William P. Alston, 'What's Wrong with Immediate Knowledge?', *Synthese* 55 (1983), pp. 73–96. See also James Cornman, 'Foundational versus Nonfoundational Theories of Empirical Justification', *American Philosophical Quarterly* 14 (1977), pp. 287–97, who notes that Sellars can be taken as a foundationalist in certain respects.

second volume of my *Scientific Theology*. The approach I have sketched out above allows evangelical theology to maintain that it offers an account of things which aims to represent the way things are in a consistent manner – a brief statement of purpose which urgently needs philosophical extension, but nevertheless reassures our constituency that we have no attempt of abandoning any notion that evangelical theology believes it is representing the way things really are.

*   *   *   *   *

Finally, I turn to the excellent essay by David Clark on the possibility of a postmodern evangelical apologetics. I have spent many hours wrestling with the question of how we can faithfully yet effectively engage with our postmodern world, and found Clarke's essay immensely stimulating and encouraging. It's nice to know that others are struggling with the same questions. Clarke resolutely – and rightly – wants to hold on to the notion of an objective truth, and I'm with him on this all the way. The question we have to face is how we communicate this to our culture, especially when that culture thinks that claiming to tell the truth is just a camouflaged attempt to dominate or oppress people. I am sure that all readers of this article will want to thank Clarke for his lucid account of the issues, and his own way of dealing with them.

Many evangelical writers have treated postmodernity as self-evidently wrong, and been more than a little rude about those foolish enough to buy into it, and especially those evangelicals who have tried to take it seriously. The real problem is that the category of the 'obvious' is contested. What is obvious to an American evangelical, brought up within an intellectual framework heavily influenced by only slightly baptized modernist presuppositions, is certainly not obvious to a young college kid from the University College of Los Angeles. If anything is 'obvious' to this kid, it is our right to pick and choose, constructing worldviews that we happen to like in a kind of theological counterpart to fusion cuisine. The big challenge to the evangelical apologist is to step inside the worldview of postmodernity, and *understand* why so many find it attractive. Clarke's engaging essay encourages its readers to do precisely this.

I have tried to do this myself. Back in 1997, I gave the Griffith-Thomas Lectures at Dallas Theological Seminary, taking as my theme the apologetic strategies we can identify in the Acts of the Apostles. I noted that Acts seems to presuppose three main audiences for the gospel proclamation – Jews, Greeks and Romans – and examined addresses to each group, to see how the proclamation was particularized to meet each group's specific situation. Like many, I was especially drawn to the Areopagus Sermon (Acts 17),[60] with its powerful appeal to the ambiguities of human experience as pointers to God, and especially Paul's subtle use of the doctrine of creation as an apologetic device.[61] I wondered if I could do the same.

So I wrote two books, each aimed at trying to engage a postmodern reader with a sense of intrigue or wonder at the natural world,[62] or human longings for transcendence.[63] In each case, the strategy was the same: arguing from an aspect of God's creation to its origins and source in God. I don't think the works are especially sophisticated theologically, and they certainly aren't in the least literary. But they seem to have scratched where a lot of postmodern people itch. Others will respond to Clarke's challenge in different ways. But the really important thing is to take his challenge seriously, and see where this leads us.

* * * * *

Let me close as I began, by thanking those who have contributed to this volume, but more importantly, for their wider contributions to the nourishing and stimulating of the evangelical theological vision. If these contributors are in any way representative of evangelicalism, it has a distinguished and productive future ahead of it. I pray that we may all live up to the challenges that lie ahead of us. The essays in this volume have touched on many great themes that will continue to occupy us as a theological community – how we handle our differences, centre our theology, cope with the collapse of the Enlightenment project, and effectively and faithfully connect up with our culture. These are indeed great challenges. Yet I believe that we may rise to them, and that this collection of essays shows both a competence and determination to do so. Under God's grace, evangelical theology has come a long way in recent years; I believe these contributions show it can go still further.

---

[60] See Hans Conzelmann, 'The Address of Paul on the Areopagus' in L.E. Keck and J.L. Martyn (eds), *Studies in Luke-Acts: Essays in Honor of Paul Schubert* (Nashville: Abingdon Press, 1966), pp. 217–30; Dean Zweck, 'The *Exordium* of the Areopagus Speech, Acts 17.22, 23', *New Testament Studies* 35 (1989), pp. 94–103.

[61] Bertil Gartner, *The Areopagus Speech and Natural Revelation* (Uppsala: Gleerup, 1955).

[62] Alister E. McGrath, *Glimpsing the Face of God: The Search for Meaning in the Universe* (Oxford: Lion, 2001). US edition published by Eerdmans.

[63] Alister E. McGrath, *The Unknown God: Searching for Spiritual Fulfilment* (Oxford: Lion, 1999). US edition published by Eerdmans.